South of Appomattox

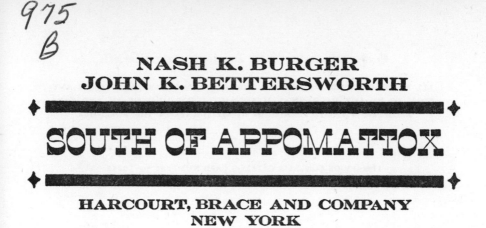

NASH K. BURGER
JOHN K. BETTERSWORTH

SOUTH OF APPOMATTOX

HARCOURT, BRACE AND COMPANY
NEW YORK

Contents

v

17997

Illustrations

vii

South of Appomattox

Introduction

Little did it matter when or where it ended, for it was a war that was already over months before April 9 and Appomattox. Lee and Grant met at the Virginia courthouse village of Appomattox in the home of a man named McLean, who had another home at Manassas, used by General Beauregard as headquarters when the War's first battle was fought four years before. There at Appomattox in 1865 began the chain reaction of surrenders, and in the weeks to come army after army laid down its arms: in Carolina, in Alabama, and across the Mississippi. There was a somber dignity to it all; quite in contrast was the indignity of the headlong flight of Jefferson Davis' crumbling government through the Carolinas and Georgia only to be tracked down by the pursuing Union army.

Generals have not always cut much of a figure as statesmen. But there was statesmanship at Appomattox, a statesmanship that should have set a pattern for the peacetime years to follow. Grant and Lee, men of battle, contrived a peace that was not Yankee or Confederate, Republican or Democratic, but simply American. The politicians, who had exercised themselves in the talking war, not in the fighting one, were not as sick at heart as these generals were. In fact, the talking war would go on long after the fighting one had ended; but the generals—even Sherman and Forrest, the fiercest of the fierce—had had enough of it all. Indeed, the peace that Sherman tried to give Joe Johnston in North Carolina was even more generous than that Grant gave Lee—though Re-

3

publican politicians in Washington kicked Sherman back in line.

For a moment, while the smoke drifted from the battlefield, the generals were making peace. Hungry Confederate soldiers would be fed. Confederate cavalrymen would take their horses home to plow with, not fight. Confederate officers would even retain their sidearms. All that the makers of surrender required was that the Confederates "observe their paroles and the laws in force where they may reside." That was all.

The statesmanship of generals could make a peace. Could the postwar generalship of self-styled statesmen keep it? This was to be determined in the years to come by the men who in point of time and by accident of geography lived north or south of Appomattox.

The grateful public, North and South, insisted upon elevating generals to office after the war. Indeed, Confederate officers were destined to become key figures in the Reconstruction and the redemption of the South. Perhaps foreseeing this, the Radical Republicans at first shrewdly excluded these warriors from officeholding. When amnesties gave the Confederates back their full rights as citizens, they promptly took over state political leadership so completely that men came to speak of the post-Reconstruction era as the "rule of the Brigadier Generals."

Surprisingly enough, it was these old soldiers—the men who were jestingly dubbed "Brigadiers," no matter whether they had been generals or lieutenants—who were to teach the South the calmer ways of reconciliation, to the confounding of the vengeful hotheads of both North and South. "It is remarkable," wrote the Richmond editor Edward A. Pollard in 1867, "that in proportion as the military men of the Confederacy were active and brilliant fighters in the war, they have given pacific and conservative councils since its close. Those soldiers and officers who did most to uphold the Southern cause in arms, appear to be foremost to recommend prompt and cheerful acquiescence in the results of the issues which were decided on the field of battle."

Their Southern constituents knew only that these Brigadiers had redeemed the South from the hated "carpetbagger" in the late seventies; hence the name "Redeemers." The Brigadiers liked to call themselves that. But the redemption by the Redeemers did not come when the last Yankee soldiers marched out of Southern capitals in 1877. It came when these Redeemers, as governors of Southern states and members of Congress, effected through their steadying conservatism a policy of peace and reconciliation between North and South that effectively silenced the Radicals of the North and—at least for a time—held in rein the Southern radical, the embattled dirt farmer, who was soon to prove as much a menace to sectional peace as the Northern hothead of Reconstruction had been.

The generals of the North had won the war. It was the defeated generals of the South that in the end had to win the peace.

Not all the leaders of the postwar South were veterans of the battlefield, but most of them were. Only a handful were career soldiers—men like Lee and Joe Johnston and Longstreet. Most of them were planters and businessmen who had also seen military service before, as had Davis and Forrest. A few, like the naval scientist Matthew Fontaine Maury, were military men only by courtesy, though Maury loved to maintain the fiction that he was on "active" duty.

In the heyday of the Brigadiers, a man had to have a military record, however tenuous might be his claim to it. Every last one of them, too, had to have been an officer. In Mississippi "Private" John Allen achieved unique distinction in Congress by his humorous assertion that he had been no more than a humble private— the only one, perhaps, in the whole Confederacy! Suffice it to say that whatever their rank in wartime happened to be, these elected leaders of peacetime, chosen in a manner not unlike the wartime habit of Southern troops who insisted upon electing their own officers, were regarded by their Southern constituents as generals commanding the armies of Southern redemption. So if they had their military title from no other source, the public conferred it upon them.

This book is an attempt to have a few of these Southern leaders sit for portraits—not for the first time, for each has been sketched before by biographers, who have either done them to death as with Lee and Davis or underdone them almost to the point of semioblivion, as with Johnston and Breckinridge. The purpose of this volume is to select ten from various sections of the South and various walks of life and to put them in matching frames, to show both the variety and the unity of Southern life. No one will wonder why Lee and Davis are included. For some of the others there will be rivals for attention who were actually greater and more influential in postwar life than the ones included here. The authors have in such cases sought not superlativeness or uniqueness so much as representativeness. Each represents a constituency much like himself. In these ten may be seen not only the Reconstruction South, but something of the Confederate South and of that older South that made the Confederacy.

That older South was basically conservative, predicated upon the conviction that certain traditional values were true and should be preserved. That older South, its agricultural prosperity year by year dependent on the bounty of nature, was aware of a power outside itself that had created man and the world around him. In urban society man seems master of all things; in rural society, nature and nature's God are everywhere seen as larger than man. It was no accident that when the United States Constitution was adapted for use by the Confederacy, the words "invoking the favor and guidance of Almighty God" were added to the Preamble. Your Southerner, then as now (as Francis Simkins reminds us in *The Lasting South*), "can scarcely conceive of a person who is decent in dress, manners, and morals who has no church inclinations."

That older South emphasized the right relation of man to nature and to other men. This involved a loyalty to and a love of place, an attachment to family. It called for good manners and consideration for others in all human relations. That older South was a settled rather than a restless society, a society that considered the pleasures of life's journey as well as the destination. It believed with Jefferson that the best governed people were the least governed, and it believed in state rights and opposed centralization because a government close to the people was better subject to control by the people. It did not believe that the world and human nature need be reshaped each morning, or that they could be.

For thirty years before the Civil War, the accidents of geography, climate, and history had combined with the divergent convictions and attitudes of North and South to intensify Southern apartness. Because its economy was based on the land, its population not gathered into towns and cities and little altered by immigration, the South's viewpoint tended to remain in the mold of an earlier America, the conservative, classical, eighteenth-century liberalism that is enshrined in the Constitution and Bill of Rights.

That the Southern system had also found the peculiar institution of slavery economically feasible beyond the time it had been found so in the North served further to distinguish the section. It is hardly likely, however, that the Southerners who owned slaves (a minority) were any less moral or humanitarian than the Yankee traders and shipowners who had sold them. But the increasing cries from the North, compounded of sincere Abolitionist indignation, of economic self-serving and political expediency, had the effect of destroying emancipation sentiment in the South (Virginia had almost abolished slavery in the 1830's) and strengthening the Southern philosophic defense not only of slavery, but of all its traditions and institutions.

If, as the rest of the country rapidly reshaped itself to an urban, industrialized pattern, that older South came to seem more and more provincial, it was a provincialism that existed only in regard to the rest of the nation. The South continued to be aware of and to nurture its spiritual and cultural kinship with the civilization of Europe and the British Isles. If the ante-bellum South, for example, was little given to reading such newfangled writers as Longfellow, Emerson, and Whittier, it did read Scott, Addison, Shakespeare, and the Greek and Roman classics. Many of the Southern objections, then and now, to Yankee manners and Yankee ways are the same as those made now by Europeans when criticizing American culture. As a result of Civil War and Reconstruction, the Yankee image became the American image, and Southerners resisting the Yankeefication of their region and Europeans resisting Americanization have been fighting the same devil. But that is to get ahead of our story. . . .

The ten Confederate leaders assembled here were products of that older South, and shapers of the new. They are but a few trees in a forest. They have been singled out for close-ups; but as the viewer turns away from the book, we who have done these sketches would like to hope that all the portraits will in the end merge and that the reader will see not so much the individual trees but the forest from which they were singled out. For this book is not only the story of ten men but a single South—the South that presented itself to the view of the world that looked down the years, lying south of Appomattox.

In the Reconstruction South, as in the South today, there was one South, a "solid South"—but there were varying degrees of reconstructibility. The attitude of the leaders toward Reconstruction ranged from that of Jefferson Davis, a stubborn idealist who refused to alter in any degree his views on the Constitution and state rights or to make any compromise with the victorious North, to that of pragmatic General Longstreet, who was willing to make the best of a bad situation by accepting (and even seeking) political jobs from President Grant.

Between these extremes were men like General Lee, who lost a war but still possessed his soul; Confederate Vice President Alexander Stephens, a peace-loving aristocrat who had no patience with extremists; General Nathan Bedford Forrest, with whom men rode as cavalrymen in war or Klansmen in peacetime; L. Q. C. Lamar, the Confederate officer who became a postwar Congressman and had a vital part in winning the peace of 1877 and a subsequent niche on the United States Supreme Court; General Joseph E. Johnston, who had an amazing facility for landing right side up—he never lost a battle, even if he hardly ever won a victory, either in war or Reconstruction; General John C. Breckinridge, who could reconcile himself to any *status quo,* for before he was a Confederate General and Cabinet member, he had been a United States Vice President and a candidate for President; General Wade Hampton, a past master at the fighting of bloodless battles, whether in war or in peace; and oceanographer Matthew Maury, who fled his homeland to set up a short-lived Confederate colony in Mexico, only to return to repossess his soul in Virginia.

In their backgrounds, these men reveal a great deal about the pattern of Southern life. They range from Hampton, the wealthy South Carolina patrician, to Forrest, the self-made son of a Tennessee blacksmith. Geographically, they encompass Virginia's Lee and Johnston, Georgia's Stephens, and Mississippi's Davis. Lamar was a lawyer and teacher; Maury was a scientist. Of widely different origins and achievement, each was as individual as the South that made him.

These men illustrate also the basic unity undergirding the diverse Southern society. There was considerable disagreement among them after the war. Longstreet went the whole way in accepting the Northern victory and endured for a time considerable ill feeling. Yet even Longstreet was typical of a definite, if small, group of reconstructible former Confederates. In time, the memory of the four-years' struggle to create a Southern nation merged with the unifying forces of Southern tradition and post-bellum experience to restore Longstreet, and those who believed as he did, to Southern esteem. After all, they had fought on the "right" side in the war; and whatever else may have become tarnished, their swords had not.

The difference between the extremes represented by Davis and Longstreet was more over the question of means than ends. Longstreet, no less than Davis, was dedicated to the preservation of the Southern way of life within a restored Union. Longstreet thought that this could best be done by working with the dominant Republican party, but the Republican party was too closely identified with what the South considered a Northern "war of aggression" and a vindictive postwar Reconstruction for his view to prevail. The conviction died hard in the South that the ultimate treason was alliance with the party that subjected the South to invasion and ruin. Even today many Southerners who might prefer the more conservative social and economic policies of the Republican party cannot bring themselves to admit it. A slight movement in that direction died aborning when another Republican President sent Federal troops once again into the South at Little Rock, in 1958.

Just as the Abolitionist agitation of the slavery question solidified Southern opinion on that issue, so did the Northern victory on the battlefield strengthen the Southern determination to remain itself. The War did not create a new Southern heritage. It sustained an old one, now called Confederate, and gave it renewed life. Ironically, the Northern determination to fight and win a war, if necessary, to enforce its views on the South had the effect of guaranteeing that its views did not prevail. The North won a war and prolonged and intensified a conflict. Even then, had the North denied itself the heady pleasures of social engineering, a military occupation, and a carpetbag Reconstruction, the South would have re-entered the Union more readily and more fully.

The influence of the Confederate leaders in the South was, if anything, greater in the postwar era than during the War. It was these leaders who beat their swords into plowshares and led their region back to its proper role in a new and united nation. Their impress on the political, economic, cultural, and social pattern of the South may be traced down to our own day. It was they who, heedless of the "rednecks" who suspected "Big Business," went about heading insurance companies, promoting factories, and building railroads so that there would be a "New" South for the Georgia editor Henry Grady to talk about.

It was they who preserved the ancient social order amid the changes and chances of partisan politics and public law. As a result, the legal and political aspects of Southern race relations today are deeply rooted in the experience of these Reconstruction patriarchs. Actually, it is the South that these Confederate leaders shaped and reshaped and to an amazing degree were able to preserve that still lives and asserts itself in the region's concern for its past and the traditional values, its attachment to the land, its opposition to outside interference, and its insistence upon a caste system that manifests itself in racial apartness.

Not only have these Confederate leaders of the Reconstruction era influenced the South, they have also left their mark upon the American nation. No matter how firmly and consciously Southern they may have been, all of these men were also national figures, sitting in the seats of the educational, governmental, or commercial mighty. They are remembered today not only because they fought four years to destroy a Union, but because they devoted the rest of their lifetimes to learning to live with a new concept of that Union. After all, every last one of them—even the supposedly irreconcilable Jefferson Davis—died not as a Confederate but as an American.

The events in the South of the third of a century following the losing of its cause are as much American history as they are Southern history. Even the problems that beset the South were of national concern; and they became everybody's business, at least that of the crusading Radicals of the North. The South did not have time to devote to other people's problems; it was too busy with its own. It was part of the Southern tradition, then as now, that good manners as well as good sense preclude gratuitous, absentee meddling in other people's problems.

The surrender of Lee at Appomattox on April 9, 1865, was the beginning of the end of Confederate military collapse, which reached its conclusion with the capitulation of the Trans-Mississippi Army on May 28. The Confederate government had collapsed sometime between April 2, when Richmond was evacuated, and May 11, when Jefferson Davis was captured in flight in Georgia. To all intents and purposes, the civil authority of the Confederacy ceased at Abbeville, South Carolina, on May 2, where Davis had held his last council of war and been forced to acknowledge defeat. The rest was the flight of a man, not of a government.

But the Confederacy had been dying by inches for a long time: Vicksburg and Gettysburg in 1863; Atlanta in 1864; and Petersburg in 1865. Talk of peace had begun with the first occupation of Southern cities along the Gulf of Mexico in 1862. It had grown to a vigorous crescendo by February, 1865, when Davis sent the peace-seeking Vice President, Alexander Stephens, to meet Lincoln at Hampton Roads. Now Confederate commanders were laying down their arms and watching their men set out homeward on parole.

Lincoln was prepared for the end. Whatever he was—and Southerners, looking for a devil to curse, had already made of him just such a monster as the Northerners had made of Davis— Lincoln could forget his politics. Yet his Republican bedfellows in Congress were determined to make the South suffer for the folly of secession. They would also seek to build up their party by enfranchising every freed slave and decimate the Democratic party by withholding the suffrage from many who had taken up arms against the Union.

In order to justify their deeds, these "Radicals" in Congress would insist with Charles Sumner that the Southern states had committed suicide or with Thaddeus Stevens that they were a conquered province, and therefore, in either case, in the status of territories completely subject to Congressional rule. Lincoln could see them only as states returning to the Union; so he would be generous with the prodigals. Insofar as he was concerned, a state might qualify for "reconstruction" if ten per cent of those who voted in 1860 should take the oath of allegiance to the Union; then a loyal government could be set up and the Thirteenth Amendment ratified in recognition of the acceptance of emancipation.

Congress would demand that at least half of the white voters take the oath and would require the new government to give the vote to the freedmen. Lincoln had no objection to allowing some Negroes to vote; he would not, however, enfranchise them wholesale. After all, it was Lincoln who had said, "I am not, nor ever have been in favor of bringing about in any way the social and political equality of the white and black races. I am not nor ever have been in favor of making voters or jurors of Negroes, nor of qualifying them to hold office, nor to intermarry with white people. And I will say in addition to this that there is a physical difference between the white and black races which I believe will forever forbid the two races living together on terms of social and political equality."

As a matter of fact, it was also Lincoln who had said, "Any people anywhere, being inclined and having the power, have the *right* to rise up and shake off the existing government and form a new one that suits them better. This is a most valuable right— a most sacred right"—but that was Congressman Lincoln speaking about the Texas war for independence from Mexico, not about the Southern war for independence from the United States.

Before a showdown could occur with Congress, the assassin's bullet on April 14, 1865, had killed Lincoln. The Congressional Radicals now wept, privately for joy and publicly for grief, over their lost President, and set out to blame the deed on every Southerner from Davis on down. It was a remarkable stroke of good political fortune. In the name of the benevolent President, the Radicals set out to persecute the bewildered South.

In the White House now was Andrew Johnson, prewar Senator from the mountains of Tennessee, who had not seceded when his state did and was paired with Lincoln on a coalition ticket in 1864 in order to win support from the Northern Democrats— though Johnson had voted for Breckinridge and against Lincoln in 1860. Johnson hated the Southern aristocrats, and accordingly the Congressional Radicals hoped he would join with them in their designs against the South. All might have been well had not the Radicals wanted to enfranchise the Negro. But Johnson, in true mountaineer fashion, hated Negroes as much as he did planters. He was willing to disfranchise the upper-class Southerner —every man worth $20,000 or better. All he would allow the freedmen was freedom, by virtue of a requisite ratification of the

Thirteenth Amendment; he would not hear of enfranchisement, except to a very limited degree. It was on this point that Johnson and Congress parted company.

Johnson, ignoring Congress, appointed provisional governors in the former Confederate states, and the process of "Presidential reconstruction" moved full speed ahead. Johnson depended, ironically enough, upon the old well-to-do Whiggish leaders to carry out his plan in the South. They obliged. By autumn 1865, the Southern states were completing the final steps for their restoration to the Union. Elections were held, and, to Johnson's embarrassment, the South almost to a man turned not to Unionists but to Confederate leaders, civil and military, for leadership. In Mississippi a Brigadier, B. G. Humphreys, had to be hastily pardoned by the President so he could assume office as the new governor. Some of the Brigadiers, as did Lee, wisely chose to decline to be considered for office; but many of those who did not "order" their supporters to desist, ended up in office.

The Radical reaction to all this was immediate. The South was still rebellious; there was no doubt about it. Then, to make matters worse, the new Brigadier-controlled legislatures, though they went through the form of abolishing slavery, were soon adopting "black codes" designed to restrain the freedmen. Negroes had been placed under the tutelage of the Freedmen's Bureau but the Bureau had given the Negro a false sense of the benevolence of his new "massa" at Washington—a mythical grant of "forty acres and a mule," and all that. At the same time, the Republicans were preparing to organize the Negro into "Loyal Leagues," which would serve as training grounds for colored voters.

The freedman was often loath to settle down to work again. Crops were imperiled in the South, and by the autumn of 1865 the desperate legislators were resorting to vagrancy laws designed to force the freedmen to go back to work. The infamous "black codes," harmless on their face, were copied from Northern lawbooks, just to be on the safe side. Northerners feared that this was only an excuse for a subtle revival of slavery. The Negro could not vote in many parts of the North, but the Radicals determined he should vote everywhere in the South.

It must be said that, considering the circumstances, race relations in the South remained, on the whole, remarkably good. John R. Lynch, a Negro Congressman from Mississippi, bore testimony to the "bond of sympathy between the two races at the South—a bond that the institution of slavery with all its horrors could not destroy, the Rebellion could not wipe out, Reconstruction could not efface, and subsequent events have been unable to change."

The reply of the Radicals in Congress to the "black codes" was the rejection of the Congressional delegations of the offending states (even of Kentucky, which had never seceded—though many Kentuckians had), thus leaving the South half in and half out of the Union. Johnson was furious, but except for the veto power, he was almost helpless. His verbal blasts against the Radicals were passed over with the glib remark that the President was drunk again. Actually, the Tennessean had been drunk at his inauguration back in 1865—from overdoing a piece of medical advice to reinforce his stamina after a battle with typhoid fever. Lincoln had passed it all off with the remark that he knew Andrew "ain't a drunkard." So had Congress, then, but it revived the memory for a new occasion.

By 1866, Congress had the upper hand in its battle with Johnson. The Southern states that had been reorganized under Johnson were still operating under the Presidential plan at home but were unrepresented in Washington. Now Congress set up its own scheme, overriding Presidential vetoes and ordering the Southern states to ratify the Fourteenth Amendment if they wished reinstatement in the Union. The Fourteenth Amendment provided for Negro suffrage and at the same time excluded most of the leadership of the Confederacy from voting unless permitted by Congressional action.

Only Tennessee acquiesced; so in March 1867, Congress instituted "military reconstruction," placing the Southern states under army rule. Registration of voters—black as well as white—

now took place. New conventions and new constitutions resulted; Negroes were allowed to vote for their own enfranchisement.

It was now that the era of carpetbag and Negro rule flourished unabated in the South. When carpetbaggers arrived from the North to control the Negro, Southern "scalawags" emerged to cooperate in the profitable undertaking, while the Negro's inexperience led him often to excess and fraud as legislator and officeholder. In a few years, state debts in the South had reached astronomical heights and high tax levies had brought many landowners to bankruptcy. The social and economic system of the South had received a wound more lethal than any it had suffered during the war.

Meanwhile, in 1868 Andrew Johnson had come within one vote of being unseated from the Presidency, thanks to impeachment proceedings initiated by the Radicals. His enemies, who made a number of poorly substantiated charges, correctly argued that he had been playing Democratic politics; but such antics have never been considered in the realm of the "high crimes and misdemeanors" requisite for impeachment. Actually his term was nearly over, anyway; so he was spared. In 1868 the Democrats were unable to defeat the burgeoning Radicals, who sent the reluctant Democrat, Horatio Seymour, down to defeat at the hands of General U. S. Grant, who wanted very much to be President.

The year 1868 delivered the Southern states to the Radical Republicans; it also delivered the whole country to the same party— a party which had spearheaded the Northern conquest of the South's "cotton barons," only to be conquered itself by the "robber barons" of Big Business, who now controlled the Republican party. The corruption that soon pervaded the Southern carpetbag governments was, as historians like C. Vann Woodward have shown, paralleled in the North, not only in Washington but also in nearly every state capital of the North. The state of New York enjoyed the ambiguous honor of maintaining Republican corruption at Albany and Democratic corruption at New York City, compared to which the picayune thievery in any

Southern state capital was as undistinguished as a cold piece of corn bread.

The Southern whites lost no time in devising ways and means of thwarting the carpetbag regimes. Little could be accomplished except by going underground. The result was the appearance of a number of secret terrorist organizations, the chief of which was the Ku Klux Klan. More will be said of the Klan in the chapters to follow, particularly as it figured in the Reconstruction career of Nathan Bedford Forrest, who was for a time its Grand Wizard. The Klan, too secret for its own good, soon harbored irresponsible elements, and men like Forrest washed their hands of it; but it persisted longer than the age of violence which had begot it.

In the North, the Klan had its counterparts. The bloody "Molly Maguires" in the Pennsylvania coal mines and the gentler "Knights of Labor" were battling their oppressors. And whether Klan or Molly or Knight, the agencies of secret action were placed under interdict, and efforts were made by Congressional act and court decree to destroy them.

Finally, it was the triumph of conservative elements that brought to an end this age of corruption and violence. In the South, it was the Brigadiers who gradually insinuated themselves into the leadership. Their cause was aided by the ever enlarging white electorate, as more and more Confederate veterans received amnesty. Helpful, too, was a subtle exercise of persuasion and intimidation in reestablishing Southern white control over the Negro. The final overthrow of the carpetbaggers came in the wake of a taxpayers' revolt, in which conservatives of all colors and parties joined when taxes had got out of hand, proving that what morality and politics could not do to restore governmental honesty, economics could do.

There had been an ill-fated attempt at national "redemption" in 1872, but it lacked the substantial conservative base needed for success. The Liberal Republicans, disgusted at the corruption of Grant's Administration and tired of the senseless Radical persecution of the South, bolted their party and with Democratic co-operation presented a united front for reform. With Horace

Greeley as their joint candidate, the coalition attempted to bring to an end the abuses from which the country suffered. Greeley went down in defeat and Grant was re-elected. Quite a number of Southern leaders had refused to support Greeley, and Northern moderates had their doubts about a man who in the past had been a bit too ardently dedicated to reform for reform's sake.

It was the conservatives, North and South, who finally brought the evils of Reconstruction to an end. Using circumspect methods and playing heavily for the vote of responsible Negroes, the Southern "Redeemers" set about taking over their state governments. In 1876 a Democratic conservative from New York, Samuel J. Tilden, seemed to have defeated a Republican conservative, Rutherford B. Hayes from Ohio; seemed, until the Republicans marshaled in their favor the electoral votes of South Carolina, which they had apparently won; Louisiana, which they had apparently lost; and Florida, which they had plainly lost. The vote of all these states combined would give Hayes an electoral majority of one. Both sides had cause to blush, for each had been guilty of frauds in this close election; it remained to be seen which could outsmart the other in the showdown that followed.

As for the three states in question, the Republicans controlled the official election boards; so there was little question as to the outcome. All three states were given to Hayes. The Democrats contested these decisions, and the controversy was tossed into the lap of Congress, which attempted to effect a compromise by setting up an electoral commission to decide the contest. When the commission by a strict party vote ruled in favor of Hayes, the Democrats, who controlled the House of Representatives, were determined to resist, either by filibustering to prevent the customary joint resolution whereby both houses had to declare the winner, or by causing Democratic states to hold back the certification of returns beyond the date of the inauguration. In either case, the Democratic tactics would leave the country without a President on March 4, 1877, throwing the decision to the Democratic House. Ironically enough, these extreme measures were dreamed up by the Northern Democrats, not by the South. Southerners were still too few, too new in Congress, and too cautious to be so militantly inclined.

The Democratic South, moreover, had a goal even more important to achieve than the election of a Democratic President—the removal of Federal troops. Such a step would cause the carpet-bag regimes to collapse immediately, bringing to an end the oppressions of Reconstruction. Out of the bitter conflict emerged at last a compromise, the first one since Henry Clay's patched-up Compromise of 1850. It was the "Bargain of '77," drafted by Republicans and Democrats who knew that the alternative to compromise might well be civil war, as had been the case in 1861. The chief Southern architect of this compromise was Senator L. Q. C. Lamar of Mississippi. Other leaders were involved—Hampton of South Carolina and Ben Hill and John Gordon of Georgia—but Lamar was by now the South's recognized spokesman in Congress. The Compromise gave the Presidency to the Republicans, the group in the best position to seize it anyway if forced to do so. It guaranteed to the South the removal of Federal troops. Almost overnight the Radical governments of the South collapsed, and Reconstruction was over.

A study of the bargain of 1877 suggests that while Northern Democrats did most of the shouting and gun-toting, Southern Democrats did the bargaining. In fact, there appeared here for the first time since the Civil War evidences of a now familiar predilection for coalition between conservative Southern Democrats and conservative Northern Republicans.

Southern Democrats cared not a fig for Tilden. He had been almost afraid to acknowledge their support, for their state tickets were loaded too heavily with Brigadiers, all liabilities to the party in the North. Hayes, on the other hand, realized that the Republican party must sooner or later cease being a sectional party. Knowing that stripped of the ephemeralities that divided them, Northern and Southern conservatives had more in common than most of them would admit, Hayes set out to build a respectable Republican machine in the South to replace the moribund carpet-bag element, which was now all but out of a job. Hayes was, therefore, willing to make peace with these Southern conservatives, who were really Whigs reluctantly camping with the new "Solid" South's only party, the Democrats. In the bargain of 1877, Hayes gave to the Southern states—to the conservatives who ran them, that is—their cherished home rule. They, in turn, offered up Tilden.

However consciously or not these political exchanges were made, they indubitably occurred; and for a moment it even appeared that another two-party division was imminent in the South. It did not come, largely because the conservative Democrats, instead of becoming Hayes Republicans, took over the Democratic party and fixed upon it a conservative façade that was not to be changed until the Nineties, when the dirt farmers would take the Democratic machines away from the Brigadiers and join with Northern liberals to champion reform.

For nearly two decades, though, the South was run by the Brigadiers. Little did they do that was not in the best tradition of the old Whigs and of most conservative Republicans. They fought cheap money. They clamored for internal improvements. They even had their own favorite railroad, the Texas and Pacific, for which they sought Congressional bounties, hoping to make of it a transcontinental outlet for the South. In their own states they were in the forefront of railway building and industrialization. They were on the side of the financiers, many of whom were Yankee capitalists who had come South. After Reconstruction, when at last they had political power, they eagerly cast their lot with the same forces that had been causing the North to grow.

The Southern Brigadiers welcomed the Yankee entrepreneurs with open arms. Railroads were built. Factories were brought in, often encouraged with tax exemptions. The Brigadiers soon had the South well on the way to becoming what Jefferson Davis prophetically said it would be, another New England. For their efforts the Southern leaders were to be branded as "Bourbons." It was just the old wine—or Old Bourbon—of privilege in new bottles. Suddenly, the dirt farmer concluded that the Northern investors and their Brigadier friends had become the carpetbaggers and scalawags of the "Redemption," and must be overthrown.

In this atmosphere arose the Southern Demagogue. He was the spiritual descendant of the embattled farmers who had belonged to the Patrons of Husbandry (Grange) and the Farmers' Alliance, which became the Populist Party. The Demagogues, or "leaders of the people," as they styled themselves, were men like "Pitchfork Ben" Tillman in South Carolina, Tom Watson in Georgia, and James K. Vardaman in Mississippi. Each state had at least one. It was the "Demagogue" who brought about the virtual disfranchisement of the Negro by constitutional revisions that set up restraints upon suffrage—notably educational qualifications. In the end, most of the Brigadiers acquiesced, for they were dubious about enfranchising the Negro indiscriminately—even when they could control him.

There had been a time when the Brigadier would have turned the South economically into another North. Indeed, the industrial age did establish itself in the seaboard states, where textile and tobacco factories had come to stay. Elsewhere—Mississippi, for example—agrarianism stifled industrial enterprise. The Democratic party of the North had been captured by the liberal reformers. The Democratic party of the South now surrendered to the Demagogues.

The Brigadier began to pass from the scene. Had he accomplished anything at all? Had his postwar leadership of the Southern people simply been a waste of time? The Brigadier provided a leavening savor of conservatism that served to promote domestic peace in a troubled age. Perhaps, after all, it was he who saved the Union, not the Radicals who had claimed the honor only to strive for a decade to keep the South out of the Union.

Ironically enough, it became the penance of the Southern Brigadiers to lead the pilgrimage toward reunion. They had accepted the severing of the Union back in '61, when they had put their guns to shoulder. Defeated in '65, they had patiently set about the task of submission and in the fullness of time had led the South back to its old place in the Union.

The Brigadier had the power to make as well as break the Union. No President, no Congress, no court, no occupying army could really have brought the South back—only he. And he fulfilled his appointed mission. The Demagogues, however, undid a lot of the work. Yet one thing could not be undone—the "more perfect Union," which the Founding Fathers had bravely talked about in 1787, the Yankee soldiers had fought for in 1861, and Southern Brigadiers had achieved in 1877.

Some of these Redeemers—Lee, for example, and Breckinridge—did not live to see what happened in 1877. Yet, living or dead, these men provided the spiritual leadership for reunion. They were, indeed, the veritable prophets and forerunners of the event. Lee knew it would come, for he knew that the South would attend his orders, whether he gave them as a wartime general or a peacetime college president. Longstreet knew it—and proved a Southerner could even become a Republican and survive. Johnston, Stephens, and Hampton knew it and proved it in the Congress of the United States. Forrest knew it, just as surely as he knew when to join and when to disband the Klan. Maury, the "Pathfinder of the Seas," knew it—just as if he had also carefully charted the winds and currents of American politics. Lamar knew it and, as much as anyone, set the time and prepared the terms of reunion.

Someone else knew it, too, one who saw it happen, though he was loath to admit it until the very last. He was Jefferson Davis— still unrepentant, unforgetting, unforgiving and unforgiven, but bowing as always, when he could no longer resist the inevitable. He who had been a prisoner of war and then his own prisoner became a prisoner of peace. He had been the first to turn southward from Appomattox; he was the last to come back. But he came.

1

Quiet Gentleman
ROBERT E. LEE

"There is nothing left for me to do." Thus did General Robert E. Lee explain the decision he had made on that Sunday morning of April 9, 1865, at Appomattox. There was, indeed, nothing left for the general to do. Tomorrow, however, there would be much for "Marse Robert" to do; for perhaps, as the general was the first to lose the War, so it would become Marse Robert's task to be the first to win the peace. But today he was still commander of the Army of Northern Virginia, which had been moving westward from fallen Richmond and now found itself blocked near Appomattox by a force of Federal cavalry and infantry. The main body of Federal troops, strong and overpowering, was close on the Confederate rear, and Lee's soldiers, worn out, short of food and ammunition and reduced to fewer than 15,000 effective troops, were in no condition to win a major battle.

Two days before, General Ulysses S. Grant, the Union Commander, had written Lee: "The results of the last week must convince you of the hopelessness of further resistance on the part of the Army of Northern Virginia in this struggle. I feel that it is so, and regard it as my duty to shift from myself the responsibility of any further effusion of blood, by asking of you the surrender of that portion of the C. S. Army known as the Army of Northern Virginia." Lee showed the letter to his "Old War Horse," General James A. Longstreet. "Not yet," said Longstreet. But there had been a further exchange of notes, and now Lee's army was hemmed in, outnumbered ten or more to one.

So he had nothing left to do but "go and see General Grant, and I would rather die a thousand deaths." To one officer who spoke of the humiliation of surrender, Lee replied, "That is not the question, Colonel: The question is, is it right to surrender this army. If it is right, then I will take all the responsibility."

To another of his staff, who suggested that small groups of Confederates break through the surrounding Federal troops, return to their states, and continue the fight, Lee said: "You and I as Christian men have no right to consider only how this would affect us. We must consider its effect on the Country as a whole. Already it is demoralized by four years of war. If I took your advice, the men would be without rations and under no control of officers. They would be compelled to rob and steal in order to live. They would become mere bands of marauders. . . . We would bring on a state of affairs it would take the country years to recover from."

It is even clearer today than it was on April 9, 1865, that only the genius of Lee and the soldiers' devotion to him kept the Army of Northern Virginia in the field those last months. "You are the country to these men," one of Lee's staff told him. "They have fought for you. They have shivered through a long winter for you. Without pay or clothes or care of any sort their devotion to you and faith in you have been the only things that have held this army together. If you demand the sacrifice, there are still left thousands of us who will die for you."

Such a sacrifice Lee was not disposed to ask. Putting on his finest uniform, he rode off on his horse Traveller, that had carried him through so many historic and victorious battles, to surrender himself and his army to General Grant. At that surrender, both Grant and Lee were revealed in their finest hour. Had the spirit of Grant at Appomattox been shared by Congress and the officials at Washington, the nation would have been spared the turmoil and bitterness of the tragic Reconstruction years.

Lee in the postwar years, in seeking to temper as best he could the evils of Reconstruction, to rebuild the physical and spiritual resources of the South and to restore a unified nation, demonstrated, no less than in his wartime career, his wisdom and great-ness. Lee survived Appomattox by only five years, but he was able in that time to show the South, as no one else could have done, the way to reconciliation and reunion.

Lee remained in camp at Appomattox three days after the surrender, not wishing to leave the field until his men had been paroled and had set out for their homes. Then, mounting Traveller, and accompanied by a few fellow officers, he rode to the house in Richmond that had been home for Mrs. Lee and their family during the War.

At the War's end Lee was fifty-eight years old. His influence in the South and the esteem in which he was held had been well earned by his courage, devotion to duty, military genius, con-sideration for his men, and unfailing gentlemanly conduct to friend and foe alike. Lee was a handsome man, sturdily built, just under six feet in height. The black hair and moustache of prewar days had changed during the war to the white hair and beard of most of the familiar portraits. Sam Watkins, a private from Tennessee, said Lee "looked like some good boy's grandpa. I felt like going up to him and saying, 'Good evening, Uncle Bob.' I am not certain that I did not do so. . . . His whole make-up of form and person, looks and manner, had a gentle and soothing magnetism about it. I fell in love with the old gentleman. . . ."

Southerners, and those outside the South, too, for that matter, were mindful of the Lee family's role in the American Revolution and in the founding of the nation. Two signers of the Declaration of Independence—Lee's grandfather Richard Henry Lee and Francis Lightfoot Lee, the latter's brother—had been born in the Lees' Virginia mansion, Stratford, where Robert E. Lee himself was born, in 1807. Lee's father was the famous Revolutionary general and friend of Washington, Henry ("Light-Horse Harry") Lee. Lee's wife, Mary Custis, whom he married in 1831, was a great-granddaughter of Martha Washington, and her father's residence, Arlington House, across the Potomac from Washing-ton, had been their home until the Civil War.

Unlike the man to whom he had surrendered at Appomattox, Robert Edward Lee could look back upon a distinguished career as a cadet at West Point. Both Lee and Grant had served in the Mexican War. Grant's part in this conflict was minor, though he was twice promoted for gallantry, and though his instinct for artillery maneuvering moved him to plant a howitzer in a church steeple outside Mexico City. Lee served as chief of staff to General Winfield Scott, who described him as "the very best soldier he ever saw in the field." Difficulties with the bottle caused Grant to be separated from the service in the fifties. Lee, on the other hand, went back in 1852 to West Point, where he stayed as superintendent until 1855. In 1859, it was Lee who led the Marines in the capture of John Brown at Harpers Ferry.

Although Lee was a major participant in that bloody business, he was no Southern hothead. In any crisis that faced the South, however, he felt he had only one choice of loyalty. He wrote from Texas in January 1861: "The South in my opinion has been aggrieved by the North. I feel the aggression and I am willing to take every proper step for redress. It is the principle I contend for, not individual or private interest. As an American citizen I take great pride in my country, her prosperity and institutions. I can anticipate no greater calamity for this country than a dissolution of the Union. . . . Still a union that can only be maintained by swords and bayonets, and in which strife and civil war are to take the place of brotherly love and kindness, has no charm for me. . . . If the Union is dissolved and the government disrupted, I shall return to my native State and share the miseries of my people, and, save in defence, will draw my sword no more."

A month before, South Carolina had seceded from the Union. Following in quick succession came Mississippi, Florida, Alabama, Georgia, Louisiana, and Texas. On April 12, 1861, Fort Sumter, in Charleston harbor, was fired upon by Confederate cannon. Three days later Lincoln asked the remaining states—including Virginia—for 75,000 troops to maintain the Union by force. Virginia, which had been in doubt about secession, entertained no doubt about a state's right to secede; moreover, it would have no part in coercing a state to remain in the Union. So Virginia itself seceded on April 17.

Lincoln's call for troops precipitated the withdrawal from the Union of three other states: Arkansas, North Carolina, and Tennessee. The reluctance of the Founding Fathers to define precisely the relationship of the state and the Federal governments had now borne bitter fruit. Of course, the Fathers had their reason: any attempt to grant unlimited power to the Federal government would certainly have meant that the Constitution would not have been ratified. Few of the original states would have accepted a constitution which dared to assert that in adopting union the states were thereby surrendering their right to leave the union if they so desired.

Three days after Virginia seceded, Lee resigned his commission in the United States Army. Though owning no slaves and dubious about secession, he felt Virginia's action carried him with it. To General Scott's plea that he not resign from the Army, Lee replied: "I am compelled to; I cannot act otherwise." To his sister he wrote: "With all my devotion to the Union, and the feeling of loyalty and duty of an American citizen, I have not been able to make up my mind to raise my hand against my relatives, my children, my home."

Offered the command of the Union Army if he would side with the North, Lee declined. On April 23, 1861, he accepted command of the Virginia troops, which he organized quickly and efficiently before they were incorporated into Confederate service. Then, as commander of the Army of Northern Virginia, he led his men in a series of battles and campaigns that still serve as models of military strategy and won for him and his Army undying fame, even though they could not win a war. For in the end, it was not the genius of warriors but the sinews of war, which the North had and the South did not, that settled the issue.

On April 15, 1865, Lee, defeated, returned to Richmond, a city disorganized and partly in ruins. Now he was a mere paroled prisoner of war; he had not yet taken an oath of loyalty to the

Union. The war was not yet ended. In Washington, President Lincoln lay dead, and it was inevitable that the South he had defeated and then befriended would be blamed for the assassination. Meanwhile, General Joseph E. Johnston fought on in North Carolina, and elsewhere in the South desperate commanders held out against Federal forces; but in a matter of weeks it would all be over. Lee's surrender meant the end of the Confederacy.

For several weeks, Lee remained quietly at his home on Franklin Street. With him were Mrs. Lee, long an invalid from arthritis; three daughters, Mary, Agnes, and Mildred (a fourth daughter, Annie, had died during the War), and three sons, Custis, William H. Fitzhugh ("Rooney") and Robert Jr. All the boys had served with their father in the Army of Northern Virginia. There was a steady stream of visitors at the house—old friends and strangers, officers and soldiers of North and South.

One of the callers was a member of Lee's old prewar Federal Second Cavalry who brought a basket of provisions, having heard, erroneously, that the Lees were in want. "God bless ye," said the soldier. "If I could have got over in time, I would have been with ye!" There was a member of Hood's Texas brigade who wanted to shake Lee's hand before setting out to walk to Texas. Another was the photographer Mathew Brady, who made the now familiar portrait of Lee with his son Rooney and Colonel Walter H. Taylor. But the strangest of all was the delegation of farmers from the Blue Ridge Mountains who offered to establish Lee on their land, to work it for him and to beat off any Yankees seeking vengeance, if need be.

On a night visit to the home of a friend, Lee encountered one of Mosby's Rangers who had slipped into the city. Mosby was still fighting, and wanted advice whether to surrender or fight on. Lee argued that since he was on parole he felt it improper to give military advice. But Lee did give the Ranger personal counsel, and it was typical of that which he consistently gave, by word and example, in the years ahead: "Go home, all of you boys who fought with me, and help build up the shattered fortunes of our old state."

Among the Yankees who called on Lee was General George G. Meade, who had been Lee's opponent at Gettysburg and had also been present at Appomattox. A friend from prewar days, Meade urged Lee to take the oath of allegiance to the Federal government, both for his own sake and for that of the South. Lee answered that while he recognized the decision of the War and the authority of the United States, he preferred to wait and see what policy toward the South was to be followed at Washington. He made it clear, however, that he would remain in Virginia and do what he could to rebuild both the state and the nation.

Other Confederates, including such prominent ones as Secretary of War John C. Breckinridge, Secretary of State Judah P. Benjamin, General Jubal A. Early, and Captain Matthew Fontaine Maury of the Confederate Navy were already in exile; Lee not only declined to do so but encouraged others to remain in the South.

On May 29, 1865, President Andrew Johnson issued a proclamation offering amnesty and pardon to former Confederates who would take an oath of loyalty to the United States. Certain Confederate leaders were excepted from the privileges of the proclamation. Lee was one of them; but he and the others were to be allowed to make individual applications for pardon, each application to be acted on "as may be consistent with the facts of the case and the peace and dignity of the United States." The proclamation seemed to Lee to indicate that Johnson and the Congressional leaders were inclined to accept Lincoln's moderate Reconstruction policy, one that Lee felt would most speedily and effectively alleviate the bitterness and hostility between the sections of the country and revive national unity. He could support such a policy, and decided to make his individual application for pardon and the restoration of citizenship.

Before he could do this, a Federal grand jury in Norfolk, on June 7, indicted him and other Confederates for treason against the United States, in violation of the terms of the parole given Lee at Appomattox and a process that might well be extended to all soldiers of the Confederacy. Under the circumstances, Lee thought his application for a pardon at this time might be construed an attempt to escape trial for a course of action he considered, and was always to consider, eminently proper and constitutional. He communicated indirectly with General Grant about the relationship of his parole to the indictment and Grant replied that he would insist the terms of the parole be respected by Washington leaders. Grant himself would endorse the request for pardon he hoped Lee would now make.

Grant's assurance was sufficient. Lee wrote out a two-sentence application for pardon addressed to the President and enclosed it in a letter to General Grant. Lee reiterated that the appeal had been made only with the understanding that the treason indictment was not to be pressed. "I am ready to meet any charges that may be preferred against me and do not wish to avoid trial," he wrote Grant, "but if I am correct as to the protection granted by my parole, and am not to be prosecuted, I desire to comply with the provisions of the President's proclamation." The letters to Johnson and Grant were copied by Lee's son, Custis, who later wrote: "When General Lee requested me to make a copy of this letter to President Johnson, he remarked: It was but right for him to set an example of making formal submission to the Civil Authorities; and that he thought, by so doing, he might possibly be in a better position to be of use to the Confederates, who were not protected by military paroles—especially Mr. Davis."

Grant was as good as his word. He endorsed and forwarded Lee's letter of application for pardon to the President. At the same time, Grant urged that all indictments against paroled prisoners of war be quashed, and he earnestly recommended favorable action on Lee's application. Lee was not optimistic. He wrote his son Fitzhugh on July 29: "As to the indictment, I hope you, at least, may not be prosecuted. I see no other reason for it than for prosecuting *all* who were ever engaged in the war. I think, however, we may expect procrastination in measures of relief, denunciatory threats, etc. . . . We must be patient and let them take their course. As soon as I can ascertain their intention toward me, if not prevented, I shall endeavor to procure some humble, but quiet abode for your mother and sisters where I hope they can be happy." The indictment against Lee was not quashed; the pardon was never granted.

A few die-hard Confederates thought Lee had made a great mistake in deigning to ask for Federal pardon; but most of his fellow Southerners admired his courage and were quite willing, in peace as in war, to follow where Lee led. To his friends Lee expressed his views more precisely. He wrote to Colonel Walter H. Taylor, a former member of his staff: "I am sorry to hear that our returned soldiers cannot obtain employment. Tell them they must all set to work, and if they cannot do what they prefer, do what they can. Virginia wants all their aid, all their support, and the presence of all her sons to sustain and recuperate her. They must, therefore, put themselves in a position to take part in her government, and not be deterred by obstacles in their way. There is much to be done which they only can do."

Lee practiced what he preached, and began himself to look around for work. He had lost most of his money and property in the war, though he had, in fact, never been wealthy. The Arlington estate inherited by Mrs. Lee from her father, George Washington Custis, had been seized by the Federal government. Much of the rest of her rather extensive holdings in land and property seemed likely to be lost. At the best, there would be little income for the foreseeable future. Fortunately, the house the family had been occupying in Richmond was owned by a well-to-do and generous Scotsman, John Stewart, who insisted that if the Lees continued to pay rent at all it must be in Confederate money (now worthless, of course), just as the lease originally stipulated.

But Lee wanted to get out of the city and away from the unending crowd of friends and curious people who called at the house on Franklin Street. He thought, too, that a country home would be better for Mrs. Lee, as well as advisable for financial reasons. Finding no suitable place to purchase immediately and unsure where in the state he wanted to settle, Lee accepted Mrs. Elizabeth Randolph Cocke's offer of a vacant farmhouse on her James River estate, fifty-five miles above Richmond. He could use the adjoining land as long as his family desired. Lee's sons Fitzhugh and Robert moved to the country also, working farms left them by Mrs. Lee's father.

In late June, Lee, Mrs. Lee, and their daughters went to Mrs. Cocke's plantation. In August, John W. Brockenbrough, rector of tiny Washington College at Lexington, in the Shenandoah Valley, appeared with an unexpected announcement. The trustees of the college had, on August 4, unanimously elected Lee president. The salary would be $1,500 per year, with a house and garden, and one-fifth of the $75 tuition fee charged each student. The president was expected to administer the college and to teach philosophy.

Lee agreed to consider it. He wrote to his old friend W. N. Pendleton, a former Confederate Brigadier General and Lee's chief of artillery, now rector of Grace Church, Lexington, and discussed the offer with another Episcopal clergyman living nearby, the Reverend J. P. B. Wilmer, later Bishop of Louisiana. Bishop Wilmer recalled that he at first discouraged Lee by pointing out that Washington College was only "of local interest and comparatively unknown" and that many more famous institutions would be glad to have him at their head:

But, I soon discovered that his mind towered above these earthly distinctions; that, in his judgment, the *cause* gave dignity to the institution, and not the wealth of its endowment or the renown of its scholars; that this door and not another was opened to him by Providence, and he only wished to be assured of his competency to fulfill his trust and thus to make his few remaining years a comfort and blessing to his suffering country. I had spoken to his human feelings; he had now revealed himself to me as one "whose life was hid with Christ in God". . . . I congratulated him that his heart was inclined to this great cause, and that he was spared to give to the world this august testimony to the importance of Christian education. . . . How his whole countenance glowed with animation as I spoke of the Holy Ghost as the great Teacher, whose presence was required to make education a blessing, which otherwise might be the curse of mankind; how feelingly he responded, how *eloquently* as I never heard him speak before.

Following this, Lee wrote a letter, on August 24, conditionally accepting the offer of the trustees. "The proper education of youth," he observed, "requires not only great ability, but I fear more strength than I now possess, for I do not feel able to undergo the labor of conducting classes in regular courses of instruction. I could not, therefore, undertake more than the general administration and supervision of the institution." He pointed out to the trustees his embarrassing status with respect to Federal amnesty, from which he was still excluded by Presidential order. Since he continued to be "an object of censure to a portion of the Country," he feared lest his "occupation of the position of President might draw upon the College a feeling of hostility. . . . I think," he wrote, "it the duty of every citizen, in the present condition of the Country, to do all in his power to aid in the restoration of peace and harmony, and in no way to oppose the policy of the State or General Government directed to that object. It is particularly incumbent on those charged with the instruction of the young to set them an example of submission to authority, and I could not consent to be the cause of animadversion upon the College."

The trustees replied with a unanimous vote to sustain their original choice. They also promised to relieve him of teaching duties. Lee accepted, and on September 1, 1865, the appointment was publicly announced. The trustees said:

In dedicating his future life to the holy work of educating the youth of his country, General Lee presents a new and interesting phase of his grand and heroic character—a character than which no more perfect model exists among living men. . . . Let the young men of the country, North as well as South, be wise, and profit not less by his precepts than by his great example.

Washington College dated from 1749. First located at Greenville in Augusta County, it had taken the name Augusta Academy. In the Revolution, it appropriately changed its name to Liberty Hall. When, in 1796, George Washington turned over to it a hundred shares of stock given him by the state of Virginia in the James River Company, the trustees obligingly changed the name to Washington Academy. The school moved to Lexington in 1802 and was chartered as Washington College in 1813. During the Civil War, it shared with its neighbor, the Virginia Military Institute, considerable damage from Federal troops. Books, equipment, and some buildings were destroyed. Since its student body had enlisted as a unit in the Confederate Army in 1861, the school's academic fortunes had suffered also. By the end of the war, there were only four professors and some forty-five students. In the summer of 1865, the trustees borrowed $5,000 so the college could open in the fall.

On September 15, Lee set off alone on Traveller from the farmhouse where he had spent the summer toward Lexington, more than a hundred miles away across the Blue Ridge. His deliberate pace was symbolic, indeed, for the general had taken his good time in making his decision. Something of his frame of mind at this point is revealed in a letter he wrote to former Governor John Letcher only two weeks before departing for Lexington:

The questions which for years were in dispute between the State and General Government, and which unhappily were not decided by the dictates of reason, but referred to the decision of war, having been decided against us, it is part of wisdom to acquiesce in the result, and of candor to recognize the fact.

The interests of the State are therefore the same as those of the United States. Its prosperity will rise or fall with the welfare of the country. The duty of its citizens, then, appears to me too plain to admit of doubt. All should unite in honest efforts to obliterate the effects of war, and to restore the blessings of peace. They should remain, if possible, in the country; promote harmony and good feeling; qualify themselves to vote; and elect to the State and general Legislatures wise and patriotic men, who will devote their abilities to the interests of the country, and the healing of all dissensions. I have invariably recommended this course since the cessation of hostilities, and have endeavored to practice it myself.

Lee was now ready to preach what he practiced. He set to work in his new role as educator with the same thoroughness and wholehearted attention to detail he had employed in battle. He began his day invariably at seven-forty-five at the chapel service led by the local ministers in turn. Then he set to work, not only at the administrative and financial duties of a college president, but also at rebuilding his small and almost moribund institution.

With the constant and energetic support of the trustees, who were wholly conscious of the sacrifice Lee had made in taking up the work at Lexington, Lee undertook an ambitious program of expansion. This involved not only the raising of funds and the enlargement of the physical plant, but also an expansion of the curriculum designed to serve the needs of students in the postwar era. Agents of the college solicited contributions in all parts of the country. Donations came from North as well as South. Some Northern extremists were indignant that Lee, so recently leader of the armies of the Confederacy, should now lead a college, but most Northern comment was favorable. Although many Southerners were hard pressed financially, they gave funds generously. The South also gave its young men; a steady stream of students, among them bearded veterans, began to arrive, many on foot. All over the South there was enthusiasm and admiration for "General Lee's college," and by the end of the new president's first year enrollment reached nearly one hundred and fifty students.

It was December before Lee's wife and daughters joined him. His son Custis was also at Lexington, teaching at V.M.I. The family took up residence at the president's home, where, only a few years before, had lived an earnest young professor from the Institute, Thomas Jonathan Jackson—not yet a "Stonewall"— whose wife was daughter of the then president of Washington College.

Lee's chief interests in the college were two: the courses of study and the students, always "my boys." He knew the boys all by name. On occasion, though somewhat reluctantly, like the Southern gentleman that he was, Lee also deigned to bother with finances. He appeared at Richmond before the Assembly on behalf of the college claim for interest on bonds guaranteed by the state. Lee's solicitation for funds was quite effective. His letter to Cyrus H. McCormick, inventor of the reaper and a native of Rockbridge

County where the college was located, produced a donation of $10,000, followed later by other large gifts. Another $10,000 in this early and critical time came from Warren Newcomb of New York. At the end of the first year, however, the trustees were still forced to borrow. Lee at one time made a loan of $6,000 to the college, probably for the building program.

If hope and progress reigned at the little college in the Valley during the 1865-66 session, the same could not be said elsewhere. The cause of harmony and reconciliation to which Lee had dedicated himself was threatened by political developments in Washington. From April to November Congress was not in session, and President Johnson had been free to follow his own temperate plan for restoring the Southern states. By the end of the year, all of these states but Texas had fulfilled the Presidential requirements for restoration of civil government, including repealing the ordinances of secession, abolishing slavery, and repudiating Confederate debts. But now Northern extremists and Johnson's political opponents, led by Charles Sumner of Massachusetts in the Senate and Thaddeus Stevens of Pennsylvania in the House, were determined to force a sterner policy on the South. Ostensibly, the chief issue was the status of the freed Negroes, a vital factor in continued Republican control of the government.

In December, Congress created a joint committee to "inquire into the condition of the States which formed the so-called Confederate States of America, and report whether they, or any of them, are entitled to be represented in either house of Congress." Between January and April, the Committee summoned and interrogated a great number of witnesses, Northern and Southern. In February, Lee was called to testify. It was his first visit to Washington since he declined the command of Federal troops and resigned from the United States Army in April 1861. He was questioned exhaustively about Southern attitudes before and since the war, about secession, the War, the Negro, and Southern conditions generally, but he never lost his temper or his dignity. His answers, while forthright and sincere, avoided the carefully set traps. When he was questioned about conditions in wartime

Southern prison camps, he criticized the Federal reluctance to exchange these prisoners, and his inquisitors hastily shifted the subject.

Whenever possible, Lee attempted to promote an understanding of the Southern viewpoint. Thus, in regard to Reconstruction policy:

> QUESTION: You do not feel down there that while you accept the result, that we are as generous as we ought to be?
> ANSWER: They think the North can afford to be generous.
> QUESTION: That is the feeling down there?
> ANSWER: Yes, and they think it is the best policy.
> QUESTION: It is your opinion that generosity and liberality toward the entire South would be the surest means of regaining their good opinion?
> ANSWER: Yes, and the speediest.

Later, Lee observed prophetically: "My own opinion is that, at this time, they [the former slaves] cannot vote intelligently, and that giving them the right of suffrage would open the door to a great deal of demagogism, and lead to embarrassments in various ways. What the future may prove, how intelligent they may become, I cannot say any more than you can."

Lee seems to have sensed that the Committee, or at least the Radical Republican leadership in Congress, was not so much interested in the facts as in justifying preconceived and vengeful plans for Reconstruction. He doubted that public discussion or investigation could help either the South or the nation. Certainly, as far as the Joint Committee on Reconstruction was concerned, Lee was proved right. It concluded that the former Confederate States were not entitled to representation in Congress and that Reconstruction was a Congressional, not an Executive, function.

Wrangling between Congress and the President was already well under way. Shortly after his testimony, Lee wrote General Early: "We shall have to be patient, and suffer for a while at least; and all controversy, I think, will only serve to prolong the angry and bitter feelings, and postpone the period when reason and

charity may resume their sway. At present the public mind is not
prepared to receive the truth."

Like many Southerners, Lee was disturbed by the severe
Northern treatment of Jefferson Davis, held prisoner, in irons,
at Fortress Monroe. "Mr. Davis," argued Lee, "has done nothing
more than all the citizens of the Southern States, and should not
be held accountable for acts performed by them in the exercise
of what had been considered by them unquestionable rights."

Lee expressed his concern over the former President in a letter
to Mrs. Davis a few days after his appearance before the committee
in Washington:

I have thought, from the time of the cessation of hostilities, that
silence and patience on the part of the South was the true course; and I
think so still. Controversy of all kinds will, in my opinion, only serve to
continue excitement and passion, and will prevent the public mind from
acknowledgment and acceptance of the truth. These considerations have
kept me from replying to accusations made against myself, and induced
me to recommend the same to others. . . . I have felt most keenly the
sufferings and imprisonments of your husband, and have earnestly consulted with friends as to any possible mode of affording him relief and
consolation. He enjoys the sympathy and respect of all good men; and
if, as you state, his trial is now near, the exhibition of the whole truth
of his case will, I trust, prove his defense and justification.

Neither Davis nor Lee was ever tried. Davis was released from
prison, on bond, May 13, 1867. The former Confederate President and Lee were summoned several times to Richmond on one
legal pretext or another, but Chief Justice Salmon P. Chase and
other authorities seemed reluctant to risk having the North's
victory, gained by force of arms, diminished on constitutional
grounds in a court of law. President Johnson's General Amnesty
Proclamation of December 25, 1868, relieved Lee of prisoner-of-
war status and put an end to the possibility of treason proceedings
against any other former Confederates. The Fourteenth Amendment, however, had excluded Lee from holding state or Federal
office, unless excused by a two-thirds vote of Congress. Lee, in any
case, had no desire for such office.

Lee's increasing alarm at the course of Radical Republican policy was made clear in May 1866, during an interview with the Marquess of Lorne, later Duke of Argyll. To the Marquess, who called on him in Lexington, Lee said:

The Radical party are likely to do a great deal of harm, for we wish now for good feeling to grow up between North and South, and the President, Mr. Johnson, has been doing much to strengthen the feeling in favor of the Union among us. The relations between the Negroes and the whites were friendly formerly, and would remain so if legislation be not passed in favor of the blacks, in a way that will only do them harm. [The Radicals] are working as though they wished to keep alive by their proposals in Congress the bad blood in the South against the North. If left alone the hostility which must be felt after such a war would rapidly decrease, but it may be continued by incessant provocation.

In December of the same year, the distinguished Englishman Sir John Acton, later Lord Acton, sought Lee's views on "the current policies of America" in a letter revealing great admiration for Lee and obvious sympathy for the Southern cause. Lee's reply reaffirmed his acceptance of the verdict of the war "that the union of the states is inviolable and perpetual under the Constitution." But it naturally followed, he said, that the government had no more competence to impair its integrity by the exclusion of a state from the Union, as the Radical Republicans seemed bent on doing, than the states had to impair the Union by secession. At the same time Lee argued that although he had "considered the preservation of the constitutional power of the General Government to be the foundation of our peace and safety at home and abroad," he believed that, "the maintenance of the rights and authority reserved in the states and the people [is] not only essential to the adjustment and balance of the general system, but the safeguard to the continuance of a free government."

In March 1867 the Radicals pushed through the first Reconstruction Act over President Johnson's veto. The result of this and subsequent legislation was to abolish existing civil governments in ten Southern states, including Virginia, and to substitute military rule. Virginia became a part of Military District No. 1,

commanded by Major General John M. Schofield. The new laws
provided for state conventions to draw up a new constitution for
adoption by the people. A *sine qua non* of the new Reconstruction
process was the ratification by each state of the Fourteenth Amendment, which was presumed to guarantee suffrage to the former
slaves, "many of whom," wrote Mrs. Lee, "do not even compre-
hend what a vote means." At the same time, many ex-Confederates,
who were trained leaders, were disenfranchised. This could result
only in chaos and intensification of sectional and racial bitterness.

Under the Johnson Reconstruction plan, the state government
of Virginia had been operating moderately well, though there
were, of course, Federal garrisons in the towns and cities, and
there were substantial evidences of recovery from the ruin and
devastation of war. Lee had been urged to become a candidate for
governor, not only by leaders in Virginia but by Union General
Meade and others who were aware of the need for the best possible
leadership in this critical time. But he declined on the ground that
his election would be the signal for an outcry in the North "and
thereby increase the evils under which the State at present labors."

There was much bitterness in Virginia over the Congressional
plan of Reconstruction. Many persons urged a boycott of the
elections prescribed in Congress; others threatened violence. It
was in May 1867 that, as a reaction to Reconstruction excesses,
the Ku Klux Klan held its first convention, in Nashville,
Tennessee. Klan members heard that Lee had received a Klan
delegation, that he had encouraged the Klan as a "protective
organization," and that he had described the Klan as an "invisible
empire." All of this, however, is only legend.

What is certain is that Lee, as was his wont, let it be known
by private conversation and correspondence to his friends that
patience and conformity to the law, however unjust, was the wisest
course. He advised all his friends to vote who could, though he
himself was disenfranchised. He urged them to take part in the
elections, rather than turn the control of the state over to the
Negroes and "carpetbaggers." To his son Rooney he wrote:
"Although the future is still dark and the prospects gloomy, I am

confident that, if we all unite in doing our duty, and earnestly work to extract what good we can out of the evil that now hangs over our dear land, the time is not distant when the angry cloud will be lifted."

The increasing tensions of Reconstruction naturally affected the students at Washington College. The presence of a Federal garrison at Lexington during most of Lee's presidency was a constant reminder of the lost War. During the month the first Reconstruction Act was passed, five students set out for Lexington to attend a nighttime meeting of Negroes. One of the students was armed, and in the disturbance that followed a Negro was beaten. Lee called in the students, expelled the ringleader, and reprimanded the rest.

A more serious incident occurred in February 1868, involving a former Union soldier, E. C. Johnston, who had come to Lexington in 1865 as a teacher of the Negroes but had soon left teaching to run a store. Skating on the river one day, Johnston was jeered by a group of students and boys of the town. He lost his temper and drew a gun, but the crowd drove him away. Lee again asked the students involved to withdraw from college. There was an investigation by the U.S. Army, a general from Lynchburg arrived on the scene in full panoply; and the episode, much distorted, was reported in the New York press. It threatened to impair the college's reputation and fund-raising activities in the North at a time when even the Abolitionist Henry Ward Beecher had contributed $1,000 to Washington College. To the Army's credit, the investigation concluded that Lee and the college had acted promptly and correctly.

Another time, Lee, by his presence and a few quiet words, prevented the lynching of a horse thief who was being held in the Lexington jail. A mob was about to overpower the jailer, when Lee arrived on the scene. Moving among the crowd he asked the people to leave and let the law take its course. If Lee wanted them to leave, that was enough. They might ignore the law; they would not ignore a request from Marse Robert. The mob was no longer a mob.

Under Lee's watchful eye, the college continued to grow. By the session of 1867-68, there were four hundred students from twenty states, and twenty-two faculty members. By June 1868 the endowment had been increased by $88,848. In 1866, the trustees had doubled Lee's salary to $3,000. There were additions to the physical plant, including a new chapel, in the building of which Lee took a close interest. New courses were added to the curriculum.

The spirit of college life, even more than the physical plant and curriculum, best showed Lee's influence. "We have no printed rules," he told a new student. "We have but one rule here, and that is that every student must be a gentleman."

Being a gentleman involved a great deal more in Lee's code than good manners—though it included that, too. An "honor system" placed much of the responsibility for student conduct, in and out of the classroom, on the students themselves. They were expected to work hard and attend classes regularly. Lee made it a point to know personally how each of his "boys" was doing. Those who shirked or were not doing well were summoned to Lee's study.

His remarks to erring students were firm but kindly—and usually effective. Times were hard; a student could attend college only at a real sacrifice to his family; the South needed trained leaders if it were ever to regain its former happiness and prosperity —these were Lee's words of wisdom for the youthful scapegrace. By precept and example Lee sought to instill moral and religious ideals. Though he had proudly built the new chapel, he abolished compulsory attendance at its services. He was always present, encouraging student conformity by his own conduct. "He had the power to bring out, and did bring out, the very best that there was in every student," one Washington College alumnus wrote years afterward.

In the summers, after the school year was over, it was the custom of the Lees to go to one or another of the famed watering places of the vicinity—nearby Rockbridge Baths, or Warm Springs, Hot Springs, and White Sulphur Springs. The waters were supposed to relieve Mrs. Lee's arthritis, and a change of scene proved good for all the family. Their daughters enjoyed the social life, their sons came for visits, and often relatives and friends arrived from other parts of the South. Northern visitors, too, began to reappear at the Virginia and West Virginia spas, and Lee took the leadership in breaking down hostility and preventing acts of discourtesy. When he chided one young Southern belle for her bitterness toward the Yankees, she asked, "But General Lee, did you never feel resentment toward the North?" His answer would have seemed rank hypocrisy in anyone other than Lee: "I believe I may say, looking into my own heart, and speaking as in the presence of God, that I have never known one moment of bitterness or resentment."

In August 1868, White Sulphur was abuzz with excitement over the first postwar Presidential election. The Republicans had resorted to the "man on horseback," General Grant. The Democrats found an available governor, Horatio Seymour of New York, whose opposition to Lincoln's Emancipation Proclamation as unconstitutional was sufficient to endear him to the South. The election was full of portent: a Democratic victory would most certainly mean an easing of the rigorous Radical Republican Reconstruction policy.

Aware that many important Southern leaders were at White Sulphur, Union General William S. Rosecrans, who was active in the national Democratic campaign, came down from New York, hoping to obtain for the party's cause a statement from the Southerners affirming that the South desired peace and that its citizens were reconciled to the outcome of the War. This move was intended to counter Radical Republican charges that the South was unrepentant and on the verge of a new rebellion, an eventuality which, indeed, Radical policy seemed calculated to effect.

Such Confederate worthies as General P. G. T. Beauregard and Vice President Alexander Stephens were there. Rosecrans asked Lee, who was also at White Sulphur, to call a meeting of the Southerners. Lee had avoided political discussion, but he was willing to bring together the Union general and the former Confederates to create harmony. From the meeting came a letter drawn by H. H. Stuart, a Virginian who had served as Secretary of the Interior under President Millard Fillmore. The letter, which was widely published, carried the signatures of Lee and thirty-one others from nine Southern states. It said what Lee had been saying ever since the War's end—that the South accepted the verdict of the War, that the Negro would be fairly treated, that if the South's efforts to resume its role in national life "had been met in a spirit of frankness and cordiality, we believe that, ere this, old irritations would have passed away, and the wounds inflicted by the war would have been, in a large measure, healed." It went on to say:

The great want of the South is peace. The people earnestly desire tranquility and restoration of the union. They deplore disorder and excitement as the most serious obstacle to their prosperity. They ask a restoration of their rights under the Constitution. They desire relief from oppressive misrule. Above all, they would appeal to their countrymen for the re-establishment, in the Southern States, of that which has been justly regarded as the birthright of every American, the right of self-government.

Rosecrans' later efforts to bring Lee actively into the 1868 Presidential campaign were unsuccessful. "When I united with the gentlemen at White Sulphur Springs," Lee insisted, "I went as far as I thought it was proper for me to do under the circumstances of the case, and did not intend to connect myself with the political questions of the Country, or to depart from the course I had adopted on entering upon my present vocation." Strangely enough, during this same summer the New York *Herald* suggested Lee as a democratic Presidential candidate to oppose Grant. Lee, said the *Herald*, "is a better soldier . . . and a greater man" than any American military leader, North or South. "It is certain," the paper added, "that with half as many men as Grant he would have beaten him from the field in Virginia, and he affords the best promise of any soldier for beating him again."

Under the terms of the First Reconstruction Act, a State Constitutional Convention met at Richmond in December 1867.

Negroes had been allowed to vote on the delegates, and the Radicals and Negroes controlled the Convention. The proposed constitution that emerged, while supposedly granting universal suffrage to white and Negro alike, also contained provisions that would have disfranchised all Virginians connected in any way with the Confederacy. This would have meant, as it was intended to mean, continued domination of Virginia's white majority by a Radical-Negro minority for a generation at least.

The national and state political situation was so confused, that the constitution was not submitted to a state-wide referendum until July 1869. Many Virginians saw no reason to take any part in the balloting, since the choice seemed only to be either continued military rule or rule by the Radical-Negro coalition.

Lee's influence as usual was on the side of moderation, and he urged his friends to participate in the election, to vote for the new constitution, but against the discriminatory clauses. His advice was delivered quietly and to individuals only, for he took no public part in the excited and critical election campaign. His views were widely known nonetheless, and they certainly contributed to the result. In the end, the constitution was approved, and an acceptable slate of state officials elected. In January 1870, President Grant, who had defeated Seymour, signed a bill readmitting Virginia to the Union—five years after the end of a war the North had fought, and won, on the premise that the Southern states had never left the Union.

During the political excitement of 1868-69, Lee remained quietly at Lexington. Nothing could divert him from the task he had set for himself of helping to prepare a new generation—of which there were now representatives at Washington College from every state of the former Confederacy—for its task of rebuilding the South. "Work is what we now require," he had written a friend. "Labor and economy will carry us through. . . . By this course the good old times of former days which you speak of will return again. We may not see them but our children will, and we will live over again in them." To another friend he had said, "You can work for Virginia, to build her up again, to make

her great again. You can teach your children to love and cherish
her." These were the ideals that animated Lee in these years; set
forth in countless letters and conversations, they heartened and
guided many others in the South during the grim Reconstruction
years.

Lee had received several flattering and remunerative business
offers, but he preferred to continue at his small salary the work he
had begun. To aid the development of the still somewhat isolated
area around the college, he accompanied a delegation of citizens
to Baltimore in April 1868 to promote a railroad through the
Shenandoah Valley as part of a new North-South transportation
route. Large crowds, white and Negro, came to see and welcome
Lee. Later, in the summer of 1870, at the insistence of his friends,
who stressed the importance of the project to the college and
Lexington, Lee accepted the presidency of the Valley Railroad.

On the way back from Baltimore in April 1869, Lee stopped at
Washington at the invitation of President Grant, who asked him
to call at the White House. This was their first and the last meeting
after Appomattox. It seems to have been brief and purely social.
There is a legend that Grant said to Lee that they had both had
more to do with destroying railroads than with building them,
and Lee was not amused. Certainly, Lee would not have relished
Grant's quip, for the war and its devastation were still too real
in the South for jesting. One is inclined to doubt that the President
had the tactlessness to make such a remark. In fact, that the meeting took place at all shows Grant's sober respect for Lee and the
course Lee was following. Already Grant had said of him, "All
the people except a few political leaders in the South will accept
whatever he does as right and will be guided to a great extent by
his example."

The college session of 1868-69 was the last to which Lee was
able to give his usual intense and careful attention. By this time,
however, he had solidly established the college finances. He had
attracted a student body that in size and quality compared favorably with any college in the nation, and he had expanded the
curriculum to add the scientific and practical training sorely needed

in the South to balance the literary and classical courses of the traditional liberal arts college.

Especially advanced for the time were Lee's plans for a school of commerce to include practical skills like bookkeeping, stenography, and penmanship; a school of agriculture; and the beginnings of one of the nation's first schools of journalism, offering scholarships to aspiring printers and newspaper men, with practical instruction in a Lexington printing plant. The New York *Sun* published a detailed report of the journalism experiment by a correspondent sent to observe the college, and the New York *Herald* was convinced that Lee's innovations were "likely to make as great an impression upon our old fogy schools and colleges as Lee himself did in military tactics upon our old fogy commanders in the palmy days of the rebellion."

Yet undergirding the budget, the buildings, the curriculum at Lee's college was an even stronger emphasis, the real reason for Lee's presence at the school—religion, morality, and gentlemanly conduct. His honor system was basic to the life of the school, and religion and morality though not taught—they are, after all, better caught than taught—were implicit in the curriculum and every phase of college life. "If I could only know," said Lee, "that all the young men in the college were good Christians, I should have nothing more to desire."

Lee was only sixty-three years old in 1870, but the arduous years of war and postwar strain had weakened his resources. He spoke often of weariness and fatigue and complained of pains in the chest, difficulty in breathing and other symptoms that have been diagnosed as a heart condition, probably angina pectoris. In response to the urgings of his doctors, the faculty, and others, Lee agreed, in March, to take a two-months leave of absence. He wrote his daughter Mildred, who was away from Lexington:

The doctors and others think I had better go to the South. . . . I think I should do better here, and am very reluctant to leave home in my present condition; but they seem so interested in my recovery and so persuasive in their uneasiness that I should appear obstinate, if not perverse, if I resisted longer.

It was his plan to visit the grave of his daughter Annie near Warrenton, in North Carolina, and spend several weeks in the Carolinas and Georgia. It was too much of a trip for Mrs. Lee, but his daughter Agnes went with him. For a heart patient, it was also, as we now know, too much of a trip for Lee; what had been envisaged as a quiet and leisurely excursion, became, in spite of Lee's own wishes, a triumphal tour almost without precedent in American history.

This was Lee's first venture outside Virginia since the war, except for his appearance in Washington before the Congressional Committee and the journey to Baltimore in connection with the Valley Railroad. Both of those trips also created great excitement, convincing evidence of his popularity. This time he went first to Richmond, where the Virginia Senate, then in session, hoped to hold a formal reception, but he demurred. There was a steady stream of visitors, including several of his former subordinates: Colonel John S. Mosby, General George E. Pickett and Colonel J. L. Corley, Lee's chief quartermaster. Colonel Corley, concerned over Lee's condition and the possible difficulties of the trip, tactfully arranged to meet Lee in North Carolina and help look after him.

After a quiet visit to his daughter's grave in Warrenton, not far from the Virginia line, Lee set out by train for Georgia. Word of his trip had become widely known. At all the towns along the way—Raleigh, Salisbury, and Charlotte in North Carolina, Columbia in South Carolina, Augusta and Savannah in Georgia—there were demonstrations. Stores closed, crowds gathered at the stations (they stood waiting in the rain at Columbia), military formations of ex-Confederates marched, bands played, food and flowers were passed into the train. "Lee! Lee!" the crowds shouted, and once again the Rebel yell echoed in the streets.

Agnes wrote her mother about the crowds of "wounded soldiers, servants, and working men." Dozens of Lee's namesakes "of all sizes" appeared along the way. "The sweetest little children" they were, "dressed to their eyes, with bouquets of japonica—or tiny cards in their little, fat hands—with their names." Old ladies popped their heads into the car windows to see him. Small boys squirmed through the crowds to get near Lee, to touch him. One boy at Augusta, who was to tell of it long after, had also been born in Virginia and, like Lee, was to make his mark on history. His name was Woodrow Wilson.

Lee spent several days in Savannah where he tried to rest, but the bands continued to play, the crowds stubbornly gathered at the home where he stayed, and a steady stream of visitors called. Here he saw again his old friend and fellow Confederate general, Joseph E. Johnston. From Savannah, Lee and Agnes went by boat to Cumberland Island, where "Light-Horse Harry" Lee was buried. They even ventured as far as Palatka and Jacksonville in Florida. Returning by way of Charleston and Wilmington to Norfolk, all along the way they met crowds, bands, receptions, and speeches. Lee politely listened to the speeches but made none.

Lee's progress through the South, where memories of war and the presence of Reconstruction still kept tensions high, was fully reported in the North; the ovations he received were carefully noted. The New York *World* observed:

It will be seen that the "Southern heart" is still fired by emotions that kindled the late civil strife, and it is pleasant to witness the dignified and temperate course of General Lee. . . . The name of Lee is identified with the most heroic deeds of the war for independence, and it is pleasant in these latter days to find it connected with words and acts of fraternal reconciliation and pacification.

This was not the vacation Lee had planned. It by no means offered the relaxation he needed; but he suffered the public meetings and social functions in good grace, with his usual patience and courtesy. Indeed, his presence gave support to the policy of hard work and reconciliation he had urged on the South. If a public appearance could help his South, he did not care if his own life was shortened. No victorious leader returning grandly from a foreign war ever received a more tumultuous or heartfelt ovation than that accorded in the Carolinas and Georgia to the aged, ailing military chieftain of the South's Lost Cause.

As he came up from Norfolk, Lee visited with friends and relatives in Tidewater Virginia. He spent a few days at his son Fitzhugh's place, the White House, where he met Mrs. Lee, who had come down from Lexington. He also visited Robert's nearby farm. Lee was back at the college in time for commencement and the last few weeks of the college year.

The trip had benefited the South—but not Lee. His physical condition had deteriorated. Probably he had not expected his health to improve; indeed, he had taken the tour primarily to satisfy his insistent friends and family, to visit the graves of his daughter and father, and to enjoy a last sight of some of his old comrades. His work would encourage them and their families to persevere in the task of rebuilding the South and of reunifying the nation. In the summer of 1870, he took a shorter and quieter trip to Baltimore, for medical examination and treatment, and saw for the last time his friends and relatives there and at Alexandria. He spent the rest of that summer at the Hot Springs, near Lexington.

When Washington College opened in September, Lee was at his usual post. It was his custom to work in his office from early in the morning straight through until two o'clock, when he went home for dinner. After a brief nap, he might return to the college or attend to some other matter of business. Often, if the day was good, he went for a ride on Traveller. In previous years, he ventured perhaps as far as the Rockbridge Baths, ten miles away; such rides were rare now.

On September 28, Lee finished his work at the college and was ready to start home. As he left his office, he met a student carrying a picture of Lee which a girl had asked to be autographed. The student offered to come back some other time. Lee smiled and said, "No, I will go right back and do it now." It was the last time he signed his name.

That afternoon after his dinner and a nap, he went through the rain to preside at a vestry meeting in Grace Church, where he sat for three hours in the damp, unheated building discussing parish finances. There was the question of the salary of the rector, Lee's old artillery chief, W. N. Pendleton. Funds were insufficient; so Lee offered to increase his own already generous contribution by the amount needed. His companions noted that he seemed tired, but he made no complaint.

At seven o'clock, Lee walked home through the chill night and the rain to find his family waiting to serve "tea," as the light night meal was called. He took off his wet hat and cape and went into the dining room, where he stood at his chair as usual to say grace—but the words did not come. After a moment of silence, he sank into his chair.

He remained alive but weak and listless for two weeks, taking some nourishment and medicine, able to speak but saying little. On the morning of October 10, he announced to the doctor, "I feel better."

"You must make haste and get well," the doctor replied. "Traveller has been standing so long in the stable that he needs exercise."

Lee shook his head and closed his eyes.

Later that day and the next, Lee grew weaker, and half asleep or in delirium, he muttered words and names, sometimes understandable, sometimes not. Once, reliving some battlefield incident, he spoke clearly and distinctly, "Tell Hill he *must* come up!"

Then, finally, about nine-thirty on the morning of October 12, came the words, "Strike the tent." And the order was obeyed.

At the bedside during some of these last hours was one of Lee's professors, W. P. Johnston, son of an old friend of the West Point and Mexican War days, Albert Sidney Johnston, who had died at Shiloh. "Never," wrote Johnston, "was more beautifully displayed how a long and severe education of mind and character enables the soul to pass with equal step through this supreme ordeal. . . . As the old hero lay in the darkened room, or with the lamp and hearth fire casting shadows upon his calm, noble front, all the massive grandeur of his form, and face, and brow remained; and death seemed to lose its terrors, and to borrow a grace and dignity in sublime keeping with the life that was ebbing away."

Already up and down the great Valley, in the hills and lowlands of the Blue Ridge and all over the South, the legend of Lee—of his living and dying—was being shaped. Already he was to many in the South simply the greatest man who ever lived, the greatest general, the greatest gentleman. Others, more cautious, or perhaps more possessive, were content to consider him (though the distinction is, perhaps, a minor one) the greatest Virginian. They recounted the marvels of his passing: the flickering lights in the sky before he died, a sure sign in many an old Scotch-Irish and English tale of a great chieftain's death, the unprecedented heavy rains and flooding streams, as though all nature mourned; the coffin for his burial miraculously appearing on the waters of the river at Lexington. (The coffin used was, indeed, recovered from the flood waters.)

Outside the Valley and the South, the world, too, knew that it was no ordinary man who had died. Even in the North, tribute was paid. The New York *Herald* said:

Here in the North, forgetting that the time was when the sword of Robert Edward Lee was drawn against us—forgetting and forgiving all the years of bloodshed and agony—we have long since ceased to look upon him as the Confederate leader, but have claimed him as one of ourselves; have cherished and felt proud of his military genius as belonging to us; have recounted and recorded his triumphs as our own: have extolled his virtue as reflecting upon us—for Robert Edward Lee was an American. . . . From the hour that he surrendered his sword at Appomattox to the fatal autumn morning, he passed among men, noble in his quiet, simple dignity, displaying neither bitterness nor regret over the irrevocable past. He conquered us in misfortune by the grand manner in which he sustained himself, even as he dazzled us by his genius when the tramp of his soldiers resounded through the valleys of Virginia.

Years later a British biographer, Sir Frederick Maurice, observed that though Lee's conduct while an officer of the United States Army was indeed distinguished, as was his conduct upon the field of his embattled South, "nothing in his life became him more than its end." Despite the temptation "to take part in . . .

the controversies which the war evoked," Lee chose to give himself to his college, where he sought to train the "young men of the South to forget the quarrels of the past and to be good Americans."

Douglas Southall Freeman, Lee's biographer, who managed to say just about all that could be said about his fellow Virginian, wrote:

Because he was calm when others were frenzied, loving when they hated, and silent when they spoke with bitter tongue, they shook their heads and said he was a superman or a mysterious man. Beneath that untroubled exterior, they said, deep storms must rage: his dignity, his reserve, and his few words concealed sombre thoughts, repressed ambitions, livid resentments. They were mistaken. Robert Lee was one of the small company of great men in whom there is no inconsistency to be explained, no enigma to be solved. What he seemed, he was—a wholly human gentleman, the essential elements of whose positive character were two and only two, simplicity and spirituality.

Lee is buried in the chapel of the college he had raised from postwar ruin to an eminent place in American education, a college that is now a university, bearing the name of Lee linked with that of Washington. Lee may not have restored the Union to life; but he helped by restoring his own South to life. The miracle of the New South was incontestably the work of Robert E. Lee, who taught Southerners to accept the verdict of Appomattox with courage and discipline and yet cling to those things that were finest in the Southern—and the American—heritage, those principles of religion, morality, honor, and devotion to duty that can roll away any gravestone, even that of Appomattox.

2

The Man Who Ran Away
MATTHEW FONTAINE MAURY

On the day Lee's men laid down their arms at Appomattox—
April 9, 1865—Matthew Fontaine Maury, like Joe Johnston,
John Cabell Breckinridge, Wade Hampton, and Nathan Bedford
Forrest, was still fighting the War, but on the other side of the
Atlantic. Maury, famed as a scientist and oceanographer, was in
England where he had been since 1862 on a mission for the Con-
federate government. Tidings of the disaster in Virginia had come
to him before he left England on May 6, but not until he reached
St. Thomas in the Virgin Islands did he learn the worst. He wrote
a letter of surrender dated "At sea, May 25th, 1865," and ad-
dressed to "the Officer commanding the United States Naval
Forces in the Gulf of Mexico."

Maury began: "In peace as in war, I follow the fortunes of my
old native state, Virginia." He now considered himself technically
a prisoner of war, but he carefully avoided running the risk of
capture and imprisonment. Instead, he chose the life of an exile.

The exile's life was nothing strange to this seafarer, who had
never been home much anyway—not since that day in 1825 when
he set out on a borrowed mare to become a midshipman in the
United States Navy. Henceforth he was a citizen of the world—
whether at sea or in foreign lands. Absence would seem to have
made his heart grow fonder of Virginia, where he was born, and
of his adopted home of Tennessee, which he loved as much as
any native Virginian was capable. Though a man of the sea,
blood was thicker than water. When Virginia left the Union, so

54

did he; when Virginia "laid down her arms," he felt that "in that act, mine are grounded also."

Maury dared not set foot on Virginia or Tennessee soil. During the next ten years he would become a Confederate exile, wandering into Mexico, then back to England, before he returned home to become, like Lee, a distinguished postwar educator, casting his lot at last with the landlubbers of Virginia.

What befell Maury once the war was over was a fate many Southerners contemplated—escape. There were only a handful of wandering Confederates. Most chose to stay home. Perhaps even at home one could escape—from reality, if not from the country. Thus was conjured up a dreamland of the past: old soldiers dreamed of battles; old civilians dreamed of an antebellum utopia. And for a time the South was too busy with dreams of the past to see visions of the future. Perhaps there should have been more expatriates like Maury. Perhaps the South gave up too easily.

Maury was the epitome of the Southern intellectual. The Southerner with brains never felt it necessary to make a show of them. Such ostentation was too vulgar. Instead, a Southern intellectual would ride and shoot as well as read books and contemplate the mysteries of nature. A Southern intellectual would no more have wanted to be thought learned than drunk; in the South a gentleman was expected to hold both his liquor and his learning but never seem to be intoxicated with either. It was an ideal reminiscent of the *uomo universale* of the Renaissance. Old Thomas Jefferson had set the pattern for the Southern man of parts. And Matthew Fontaine Maury was to the pattern born.

Matthew's father, Richard, was a Virginian of French Huguenot descent. Matthew's mother, Diana Minor, belonged to a Virginia family founded by a Dutch sea captain who had settled in the colony in the days of Charles II. Matthew Fontaine was born near Fredericksburg in Spottsylvania County on January 14, 1806. Some five years later the Maurys ventured forth to become Tennessee pioneers, settling at Franklin, near Nashville. In the frontier wilderness the family set about making a new home. Matthew soon learned to do his stint. In fact his schooling was somewhat haphazard during the early Tennessee years. Not until he was nearly killed in a fall from a tree at the age of twelve did he ever have time to do much with books. No longer able to do hard work, he was sent to near-by Harpeth Academy to get some book-learning. He did well, particularly in mathematics and Latin, and soon became an assistant teacher. Actually, his inspiration in mathematics had been a village shoemaker who was wont to cover shoe soles with algebraic computations.

Matthew early decided on a military career. He toyed with the idea of West Point; then, unbeknownst to his father, talked Congressman Sam Houston of Tennessee into getting him an appointment as a midshipman in the United States Navy. Early in 1825 young Maury set out toward Washington to begin his naval career. His father was so furious that he would not even bid his son farewell. One other Maury son had already joined the Navy, the eldest brother, John. All that the father could remember was that John, despite a brilliant naval career which led him to the rank of captain, had died of yellow fever in the service. Matthew, however, recalled the wondrous tales of a brother's adventures on the high seas and in the exciting years of the War of 1812.

Matthew's trip to Washington was undertaken on a mare bought on credit, and the only money he could command was thirty dollars earned from teaching. When he reached his kinsmen in Virginia, he sold the horse to the man who was eventually to be his father-in-law, securing enough money to repay his credit. Then, after casting an amorous eye at Ann Herndon, he proceeded on to Washington, where he received the munificent travel reimbursement of fifteen cents a mile.

Since there was no naval academy at that time, young Maury was precipitated at once into sea duty. Shipping on the U.S.S. *Brandywine,* he studiously set about learning his sea craft. Even when he walked the deck on watch, he would chalk problems in spherical geometry on the cannon balls in the racks. In five years he had served on three ships and was ready to take his examinations for an officer's commission, out of which he emerged an undistinguished twenty-seventh in a class of forty and an Ensign, U.S.N. Already, however, he had begun to achieve distinction as a practical navigator; he managed to draw up for publication a set of lunar tables.

In 1831 Maury became sailing master of the U.S.S. *Falmouth* and set out for the Pacific. These were the days when the long journey around Cape Horn had moved New England shipbuilders to develop the streamlined China "clipper" ship and New England captains to vie with one another as speed demons, while sturdy New England landlubbers sat at home resolutely betting on the speeds of these phenomenal craft.

Maury possessed an urge for speed himself. Finding that exact information on winds and currents was nonexistent, he set about compiling data on his cruise. Here was the beginning of a life's work in oceanography. In 1833, Maury published a paper on the navigation of Cape Horn. Now in rapid succession he began to turn out the papers, charts, and books on which his fame as "Pathfinder of the Seas" was to rest. By the mid-thirties, he had married his first love, Ann Herndon, had reclaimed Virginia as his home, and was busily seeking a publisher for a textbook on navigation that was to achieve world acclaim.

By now Maury had decided that the Navy was in as great need of reform as was its navigational data. In the year 1838, he began to write articles for the Richmond papers and the Richmond *Southern Literary Messenger* under the pseudonyms "Harry Bluff" and "Will Watch." He was highly critical of navy inefficiency. These articles became more frequent after 1839 when he was permanently lamed after an accident in which he was thrown from the top of an overturning stagecoach (he had given his seat inside to a Negro woman). For the next few years he was confined to shore duty.

Meanwhile, the identity of the writer of the articles had become known, and Maury's obvious ability, together with his forthright campaigns for a naval academy and the employment of steam motive power and world-wide telegraphic communication, had given him wide notoriety. In fact, he was even being talked of as a prospect for the post of Secretary of the Navy. But the crippled Maury would be satisfied with nothing short of a return to the sea. Instead, he was in 1842 assigned to shore duty in the Depot of Charts and Instruments. Here he made ample use of the naval observatory and the neglected archives of ships' logs to further his research in oceanography. This work was the beginning of the Navy's present-day Hydrographic Office.

Maury set about systematically charting the seas. He ordered the careful logging by sea captains of temperatures of air and water, wind directions, current set, and barometric pressure. Bottles were set afloat to determine the direction of currents. By the late 1840's, sufficient navigational data had been gathered to cut in half the time required for many voyages. So accurate were his charts that Maury successfully predicted the location of a shipwrecked troop ship lost in an Atlantic hurricane. Eventually Maury developed the "lane route" now followed by transatlantic steamships.

Meanwhile, he had developed a new system of deep-sea sounding, and his superior knowledge of the earth under the waters enabled him to discover the "Telegraphic Plateau," a level area stretching across the Atlantic which became the route for the first transatlantic cable.

Maury's multifarious interests did not stop with charts and soundings. He expanded his activities to the making of trade, trade wind, pilot, thermal, rain, storm, star, and whale charts. There was little in the science of oceanography that he did not develop. The old Depot of Charts and Instruments blossomed into the Hydrographic Office.

It was not surprising that Maury eventually argued for a system of meteorological observations on land. He solicited weather data from farmers just as he had done from sea captains. Congress, however, refused to give financial support and the project was dropped until after the Civil War.

Maury never forgot that he was a Virginian and a Southerner. Much of his activity centered around the development of the South. Early in his career he made a survey of Southern harbors. He wrote an article in the *Southern Literary Messenger*, which was as concerned with "message" as it was with literature, advocating direct foreign trade for the South to counteract the "hobnail" vassalage of South to North. He talked of connecting the Great Lakes and the Mississippi by canal, of establishing a shipyard at Memphis, of deepening the Mississippi below New Orleans, and of building a railroad or a canal across Panama. In 1849, he presided at a convention in Memphis which met to promote the construction of a railroad across the Rockies.

Maury's interests were not confined to the material progress of the South. He was among the active promoters of the Episcopal University of the South at Sewanee, and at Bishop James Hervey Otey's invitation he spoke at the laying of the cornerstone of that institution on the eve of the Civil War. There "the newly ordained science" of physical geography, to which Maury had contributed so much, would be taught to Southern sons.

Ironically this prophet with honor remained to all intents and purposes practically unrewarded for his great services to his country and to navigation. Not only did Congress fail to approve a committee recommendation in 1855 that a special reward of $25,000 be given Maury, but also in the same year he was retired from active duty by the Naval Retiring Board, which had been created at that time ostensibly "to promote the efficiency of the Navy." He was ordered to remain on duty at the Naval Observatory and Depot of Charts and Instruments but only on leave-of-absence pay. For Maury, who limping or not would readily have gone aboard ship for duty, this was a blow as much to his pride as to his pocketbook. There was also an embarrassing irony to it all. He who had so much to say barely a decade past about improving the efficiency of the Navy was humiliated, a victim apparently of his own preachments.

The board had met secretly, and there were strong intimations that its members, who were mostly high-ranking Navy men with records of considerable sea duty and no scientific attainment, were not a little jealous of the man whose brilliant achievements and international reputation had added more luster to the Navy than had any one of them, with the possible exception of Commodore

Perry. Perry had publicly belittled Maury's work. From another standpoint, there is a likelihood that the retirement had political origins. Maury was more of a Whig than anything else, and good Democrats like Jefferson Davis, who stood high enough in the Pierce administration to hold the post of Secretary of War, were openly hostile toward the distinguished naval scientist. It could well have been that President Pierce, who signed the retirement order, had listened to partisan voices.

The public reaction to the Board's move had been so violent that finally, in February 1858, Maury not only was restored to his active status by a special act of Congress but also was promoted from the rank of lieutenant to that of commander retroactively to the date of his previous retirement.

From the controversy over retirement Maury was now projected into another crisis—slavery and secession. Maury had little interest in slavery as a system or desire for its perpetuation. To him the institution was unquestionably a "curse." He would have liked to see it abolished, but he realized that this was more easily talked of than done.

Although it was a proposal of his in the *Southern Literary Messenger* that suggested to Lord Ashburton a scheme for patrolling the coast of Africa as a means of wiping out the slave trade, Maury was eminently practical about what could and could not be done. "We must take things as we find them," he observed, "and if we would be practical and do good, we must deal with mankind as they are, and not as we would have them."

There were some sensitive souls who professed to be shocked at Maury's proposal in the fifties that the South's excess slave population be shipped to Brazil, where there was a great demand for such labor in subduing the Amazon wilderness. Such a scheme, he asserted, would be "putting off indefinitely the horrors of that war of races which, without an escape, is surely to come upon us."

Above all else, Maury did not wish the slavery issue to lead to the sundering of the Union. As the election year of 1860 brought the crisis to a head, he became quite disconsolate. "As for the

Union," he wrote Bishop Otey, "I see that it will have to drift. The dissolution of it will, I fear, come before you or I would be willing to see it." Maury blamed the situation upon the "politicians." Yet he desperately sought intervention by political leaders to prevent the worsening of the crisis. Early in 1860 he wrote to the governors of Delaware, Pennsylvania, New Jersey, and Maryland asking their good offices in preserving the peace. To Governor Packer of Pennsylvania he wrote:

The most remarkable feature in the whole case is, it appears to me, this—that here we have a national family of States that have lived together in unity for nearly three-score years and ten, and that a portion of them are preparing to dissolve these family ties and break up the Union, because—because of what, sir? Ask legislators, ask governors, ask whom you will, and there are as many opinions as to the causes of discontent and the measures of redress as there are leaves in the forest. At no time have the people of any one of the discontented States, acting in their sovereign capacity, even authorized a remonstrance to be made to their sister States of the North against their course of action. We have heard a great deal of this from politicians, partisans and others, but if the people of any one of the Southern States, acting in their sovereign capacity, have ever remonstrated with the people of the Northern States as to the causes of dissatisfaction and complaint, and thus laid the matter formally before you of the North, I cannot call it to mind. Neither has any Northern State so much as inquired of the people of any Southern State, either as to the cause of their offence, or as to the terms and conditions upon which they would be willing to remain in the Union.

In October Maury left for England, and while he was gone, the crucial Presidential election took place, and there were wild rumors about imminent secession. On his return voyage Maury wrote to a Northern friend: "Do we belong to the same country yet? A queer question to ask. . . . Unless you good men of the North and South will bestir yourselves, and take matters into your own hands, and out of those of the politicians, I fear me—I fear me, we shall not be long of one country!"

Much as he abhorred the idea of secession, Maury had no doubt about his own course of action. "No military man can permit himself to accept service with a mental reservation . . . there-

fore, if we have a war between the sections, every man who con-
tinues in Uncle Sam's service is, in good faith, bound to fight his
own, if his own be on the other side. The line of duty, therefore,
is to me clear—each one to follow his own state, if his own state
goes to war. . . ."

Maury continued his "quiet physical researches" in Washington
as long as possible. Already the urge to flee was upon him. On
April 10, 1861, he was trying to "get up an expedition to the
South Pole." When Fort Sumter fell on April 13 and Virginia
chose secession rather than the taking up of arms against the
South, Maury resigned from the Navy. This action he knew "was
the death-warrant to his scientific life—the cup of hemlock that
would paralyze and kill him in his pursuit after the knowledge
of nature and of nature's laws." Lincoln perversely refused to
recognize Maury's resignation, and he was branded a deserter.

Although he was offered refuge in Russia and France, Maury
chose to return to Virginia and moved his family to Fredericksburg on April 20, 1861. He was promptly made a commodore in
the Virginia navy and the Confederacy placed him in charge of
its harbor and river defenses.

The Confederate government proved dilatory in listening to
Maury's defense pleas, and he was once more driven to the pseudo-
nym and the press. As "Ben Blow" he urged the South to "get rid
of all the navy notions borrowed from the old navy at Washington as to what constitutes a navy." He felt that the Confederacy
must man its waters with a fleet of small floating batteries of guns
on small ships. Maury invented an electric torpedo for mining
harbors and rivers and helped equip the famed iron-clad *Merrimac,* renamed *Virginia.*

In 1862, Maury was sent to England, where he stayed for the
remainder of the War. He could not fail to see how futile the
War actually was. Back when the Union was falling apart he had
hoped, after peaceable secession, Union-lovers might "hoist the
flag of re-annexation" in the 1864 elections. When 1864 found
him far from home in England, he set about organizing a society
for the "Promotion of the Cessation of Hostilities in America."

A petition was drawn up addressed to the "People of the United States" arguing that it was "utterly impossible to subdue the South, or to restore the American Union, as it was in the past days of the Republic." Was it not time, asked the petitioners, to "take counsel together as to the best means of restoring peace?" The document was submitted for signatures all over the British Isles and apparently received widespread attention—except in the United States.

In 1865, the Confederacy approached its doom. Maury, convalescing from an operation, set out from England for the West Indies in the spring. Learning there of Lee's surrender, he chose to become an exile in Mexico. Maury, who regarded himself a prisoner of war, was unwilling to run the risk of being shot as a traitor. He had already been advised by his brother-in-law, Brodie Herndon, against return to the United States:

In view of the state of the public mind in the North at present, I think it would be decidedly unsafe for you to return to this country. Your absence abroad in a semi-diplomatic character, your prominence, and the earnest part taken by you in the cause, would make you a decided object of that "Vengeance against leaders" so openly proclaimed and so plainly visible. In time, I hope, these vindictive feelings will subside, and then, and only then, would it be safe and prudent for you to return. A good many of the young men of the South will go abroad, and this is one of the gloomy features of our future.

Herndon was doubtless right. In fact, no lesser person than the United States Ambassador to England, Charles Francis Adams, advised Maury's friends to discourage his return. "The feeling there is very bitter against him, and I believe the consequences of a step of that kind on his part at this time would be very unfortunate for him."

At that time, Emperor Maximilian of Mexico, formerly Archduke of Austria, attempting to maintain a French-dominated Mexico backed by the French emperor, Napoleon III, was seeking colonists. Maury had known Maximilian for some time. The Archduke, who had commanded the Austrian Navy in 1854, had been one of the recipients of the *Sailing Directions* and had awarded the American the Austrian gold medal of the arts and sciences. During the Civil War, Maury and Maximilian had corresponded, anticipating co-operation between the Mexican Empire and the Confederacy.

As the fortunes of the South waned, Napoleon III toyed with the colonization idea, and, in 1864, Maximilian, who had at first demurred for fear of United States protests and public opposition among the Mexicans, began to undertake immigration activities. By the time Maury decided to offer his services to Maximilian in 1865, Mexico's usefulness as a refuge for Southern exiles was apparent; now large numbers of defeated Confederates might easily be lured into the country. Maury wrote Maximilian of his desire to come, then set out without awaiting an answer. In June, 1865 Maury was in Mexico and the Confederate colonization boom was well under way.

Some of the expatriates went on to Brazil, where their descendants remain to this day. A few fled to British Honduras. But it was Mexico that offered the most enticing and most accessible prospects.

The earliest Confederate colonization scheme in Mexico actually dated from 1863, when Dr. William M. Gwin, just released from imprisonment by the Union forces in New York, secured the support of Napoleon III for a plan to colonize the Sonora district, in the northwest. The exploitation of metals there would furnish an appreciable return on Napoleon III's investment in Imperial Mexico, and the presence of a colony of Confederates near the Rio Grande would serve as a buffer against any action the United States might take against the French intervention. Although he appeared to be committing himself to the Confederate cause, Napoleon approved the Gwin plan and arranged through the Mexican Council of Regency that Sonora be placed under the "direct and sovereign protection" of France for a period of fifteen years; during that time all metal prospecting rights would be controlled by the French while the Mexican government would be rewarded with a ten per cent royalty.

Dr. Gwin arrived at Veracruz in 1864. He was joined later by Dr. Thomas C. Massey and Pierre Soulé, an incorrigible rebel who had suffered the wrath of General Butler at New Orleans and had gone to Mexico, where he worked to involve the French with the United States over the Monroe Doctrine. Gwin also found among the members of the American colony at Mexico City a small group of enthusiasts who favored his scheme. Maximilian, who opposed this project, did all he could to thwart it. Yet Gwin talked willingly and optimistically of his plans, alluding proudly to "my colony," "my policy," and "my Army" which Maximilian was to furnish for the venture. With supreme confidence he pursued his course, and even boldly invited his friends to Christmas dinner in Sonora. The dinner appointment was never kept. When Maximilian did decide to embark upon colonization, it was with a man of his own choosing—Matthew Fontaine Maury.

The close of the Civil War brought to Mexico a swarm of Confederate soldiers who came hoping either to revive their forces for a final offensive against the North or to enter the struggle between the Imperialists and the rebels of Juárez. Few expected to colonize. Soon plans of resuscitating their scattered forces were forgotten. The emphasis now was upon colonization.

Maury was unable to begin his plans at once because Maximilian hesitated for fear of appearing to violate Mexico's neutral status. Maury, in the meantime, could enjoy the safer perquisites of another title Maximilian had given him—Director of the Astronomical Observatory.

Not until September 5, 1865, did Maximilian finally issue a series of decrees directing the *Ministro de Fomento* to provide ways and means for encouraging colonization according to Maury's plans. A dozen rural estates in the district of Córdoba, in Veracruz state, were taken over to be divided into small lots for sale to settlers. Mexico was declared open to immigration from all nations. Each immigrant was to receive a title of landed estate and a certificate that his land was free from mortgage. For the first year, the government would exempt the property from taxes, and on the first sale, the tax on all property transfers would be suspended. Immigrants might be naturalized as soon as they had become established as settlers. All personal effects of the immigrant might be brought in duty-free, and transportation would be furnished within the country. Immigrants were exempt for five years from military service, though they had to form a stationary militia to protect themselves and their property. The government guaranteed freedom of worship. Since slavery was forbidden in Mexico and already hostile critics in the United States had branded the proposed peonage system as a return to slavery, Maximilian took special precautions to guarantee the integrity of immigrant laborers. His decree declared that all persons of color who entered Mexico were free. Each employer had to maintain his laborers, pay them regularly a set sum of money, and deposit in a government savings bank one-fourth of each laborer's wages at a five percent annual interest. The employer was required to support the children of his peons, and if their father should die, he would become the children's guardian. They would remain in his service until they were of age. Each laborer was to receive a book containing his description, a statement of his place of labor, and certification of his life and habits. If he deserted his master, the peon would be employed without pay, on public works, until reclaimed. If the worker should die without a will, his earnings were to be appropriated by the government. Injustice on the part of the master toward his laborers was to be brought before a magistrate and a special police commission created for the prosecution of violators.

Maury prepared a memorandum containing a set of forty-two "regulations" and some general remarks on the nature of the country to be colonized. He assured prospective immigrants that agencies would be established at once in the United States to afford "information to immigrants there as to the country, its lands, the best way of reaching them, and upon all other subjects appertaining thereto." Provision was made for two classes of immigrants: (1) Those who had lost everything in the recent War, for whom the Mexican government would provide free passage to Mexico and an allowance of one *real* per mile on transportation to the various "undeveloped" parts of the public domain to which this class was destined. A single man would receive 160 acres; a married man, 320 acres. In either case, settlers might preempt additional land in proportion to their original purchases. (2) Those who, not being in straitened circumstances, could afford to buy, through the government, lands on private haciendas which had previously been under cultivation.

To advertise the new colonization movement, Maximilian sponsored the establishment of an English language weekly known as the *Mexican Times,* edited by former Governor Henry W. Allen of Louisiana, and published in Mexico City.

The first issue of the *Times* printed a list of ninety-seven Confederates who had come to Mexico during the summer and invited renewed immigration from the South in an ecstatic editorial: "To those in the United States whose fortunes have been swept away by the terrible tempest that has long raged in that afflicted land—to those who have drunk the cup of bitterness to the very dregs—we say welcome to Mexico. *Here you can get homes without money and without price."*

The project had only moderate success, and in September 1865 Maury wrote gloomily to his wife, who had refused to go to Mexico, "I am by no means sanguine about my 'New Virginia.' " At that moment, he said, there were in Mexico about one hundred "first-rate men," from various parts of the South, but the government had no lands to offer them and many were leaving in disgust. "I am not yet in the harness," he complained. "I now almost despair of seeing it [the project] well in motion before this time next year."

The day after Maury's despondent letter was written, the Emperor authorized him to appoint agents of colonization in Virginia, South Carolina, North Carolina, Texas, Missouri, California, New Orleans, Louisiana, and Mobile, Alabama. These agents were to receive $100 a month and a yearly allowance of $300 additional for necessary expenses. Three days later, Maximilian, urged on by Empress Carlota, to whom Maury had gone the preceding day for assistance, appointed him Commissioner of

Immigration and Colonization and provided $150 for furnishing his office, $500 for a year's running expenses, $1,200 for a clerk, and $300 for a private messenger. On the same day, the Emperor issued a decree establishing in Mexico City, the capital, a Land Office of Colonization, headed by another Confederate, General John B. Magruder, at a $3,000 salary and directing the General to furnish the data on the number of engineers and surveyors to be engaged and the amount of money necessary for their salaries.

Maury and Magruder proceeded to secure and survey lands for settlement. On October 5, the Colonization Office issued a notice offering its services to landowners who wished to dispose of their estates. The office would provide a free survey of the lands, advertise them through its agents abroad, and arrange for direct negotiations between buyer and seller.

Interest in the United States, especially in the South, increased rapidly as favorable rumors of the progress of colonization were followed by the arrival of Maury's agents. Reports from New Orleans and Mobile indicate that throughout the autumn, immigrants were setting out from these and other ports along the Gulf and arriving at Veracruz, Tampico, and Campeche regularly. The *Mexican Times* of January 27, 1866, said 260 immigrants had landed in Campeche and Tampico during the months of November and December 1865. From prospects who had not yet come to Mexico numerous letters were received asking for descriptive circulars about Mexico and the way to reach it. Maury always replied realistically to their inquiries. He did not reveal the worst conditions but regularly advised prospective immigrants to be cautious. In a statement issued on November 18 and published in *La Sociedad,* December 7, 1865, Maury insisted that before taking a hasty step all persons of small means should organize in groups of twenty-five or more families and send advance agents to purchase a hacienda or some other lands and to prepare for the coming of the entire party.

As the conditions grew worse for those who had already come to Mexico under the delusion that land was free for the asking, many becoming burdens upon their friends and the government, the Colonization Office began bluntly to advise the poor not to immigrate. Landowners who were offering their lands for sale by the Office soon devised means by which these lands would be sold in large sections only, by subscription at rates that would discourage persons of small means.

The approach of spring in 1866 brought increased emigration activity in the South. The New York *Daily News,* lamenting the fact that hostility in the North had made many Southerners decide to leave the country, printed news of twenty-five families in Georgia, sixty in Tennessee and Kentucky, and fifty in West Virginia—all leaving for Mexico. In Tennessee, the Lebanon *Herald* reported twelve families from Smith County preparing to leave in the spring. "We have daily a great number of visits from persons who are going to Mexico, all asking for information about the country," said the Memphis *Appeal.* In Alabama, the Selma *Times* estimated that two hundred families were preparing to leave that state. Newspapers in South Carolina and Virginia brought similar tidings.

In New Orleans, which the *Daily Crescent* was about to envision as a major port among the commercial cities of the world as a result of trade with Mexico developed by immigrants from the South, General Philip Sheridan, the local military commander, made a futile attempt to prevent the departure of Southern emigrants for Veracruz. In January, two shiploads of prospective colonists left under pretense of sailing for Havana. The United States government arrested as many of Maury's agents as could be found and required them to give up their appointments, but emigration continued.

The Colonization Office received the new immigrants enthusiastically and ordered the preparation of a guidebook under the supervision of Maury's son, Richard, who had joined him in Mexico. The *Mexican Times* reported it was deluged by inquirers and dispatched to each two copies of an issue containing news about the Empire, lists of the various settlements made or projected, route directions to those who planned to come by boat, and a mild injunction to all indigent persons and professional men (except surveyors) to stay at home.

Unfortunately, the advice of the *Mexican Times* did not arrive early enough. Mexico was already fairly swarming with penniless immigrants from Louisiana, Kentucky, and Alabama. If the new throng of immigrants came unprepared, they were hardly as poorly prepared as Maury's Colonization Office. It found itself unable to obtain cheap land for the settlers and proved to be interminably slow in surveying what lands it did secure. It became almost entirely subordinate to the private land companies, which used it occasionally and patronizingly as intermediary.

Even the most favorable estimates of immigrants rarely passed 2,500. A correspondent for the New York *Herald* in Córdoba estimated that there were hardly more than 250 in the Córdoba Valley. In Córdoba itself and its environs there were about thirty American families, most of them from the South.

As the new wave of immigration began to spend itself, Maury's interest in the Mexican venture waned. He had been warned against expatriation by his friend Commodore Jansen, of the Netherlands Navy: "Don't emigrate! Stand by your country with stern courage. . . . I don't think that you can return now to Virginia, but, in three or four years, great changes will take place in opinions. . . . You ought to go back . . . as soon as you can do so safely. . . ." Both Jefferson Davis and General Lee also counseled against expatriation. In a letter to Maury, Lee was quite explicit:

We have certainly not found our form of government all that was anticipated by its original founders; but this may be partly our fault in expecting too much, and partly due to the absence of virtue in the people. As long as virtue was dominant in the Republic, so long was the happiness of the people secure. I cannot, however, despair of it yet; I look forward to better days, and trust that time and experience—the great teachers of men under the guidance of our ever-merciful God—may save us from destruction, and restore to us the bright hopes and prospects of the past. The thought of abandoning the country, and all that must be lost in it, is abhorrent of my feelings, and I prefer to struggle for its restoration, and share its fate, rather than to give up all as lost. I have a great admiration for Mexico; the salubrity of its climates, the fertility of its soil, and the magnificence of its scenery, possess for me great charms; but I still look with delight upon the mountains of my native state. To remove our people to a portion of Mexico which would be favourable to them would be a work of much difficulty. Did they possess the means, and could the system of apprenticeship you suggest be established, the United States Government would, I think, certainly interfere; and, under the circumstances, there would be difficulty in persuading the free men to emigrate. Those citizens who can leave the country, and others who may be compelled to do so, will reap the fruits of your considerate labours; but I shall be very sorry if your presence will be lost in Virginia. She has now sore need of all her sons, and can ill afford to lose you. I am very much obliged to you for all you have done for us, and hope your labours in the future may be as efficacious as in the past, and that your separation from us may not be permanent.

Maury had decided to return to England by the spring of 1866, leaving the administration of the Colonization Office to his son. The *Era,* a French paper published in Mexico City, was demanding that the government halt the work of Maury and his agents, who, said the *Era,* were attracting large numbers of credulous immigrants from the United States who became burdens upon Mexico or went home, carrying with them reports which would place Maximilian's entire immigration program in disrepute. Disgruntled settlers were writing home in haste to prevent their friends' emigrating. An Alabamian who had come to Veracruz attracted by a circular from the Colonization Office wrote to the New Orleans *Times* on April 7 that he had investigated the prospects and was coming home to save others from going to join the "poor unfortunates among the rocks and rattlesnakes of Orizaba." From Havana, former Confederate General Jubal A. Early, who had left Mexico disgusted after three months' experience, wrote the New York *Times* a letter condemning the colonization movement.

To make matters worse, the Southern agents for the Colonization Office had been arrested. The United States government, which had earlier appointed General John A. Logan as minister to the rebel Mexican leader Juarez in retaliation for Maximilian's favors to the Confederates, was winning its fight to stem emigration. Napoleon III, on the other hand, was preparing to remove his support of Maximilian, leaving the tottering Empire to its fate.

With Matthew Fontaine Maury safely out of the country, Maximilian yielded to pressure within Mexico and from the United States and abolished the Colonization Commission, adding the Commission's clerks, surveyors, and agents to the ranks of disgusted Confederates stranded in Mexico. With the increasing disorder after the withdrawal of the French army, many an unpopular American colonist fell prey to the guerillas. Immigrants fled to the larger towns, where they waited to return to the United States. An observer at Veracruz pictured restless exiles "running about" daily with petitions, seeking money to send themselves and their unfortunate countrymen "back to the arms of Uncle Sam."

Maury, however, was not yet ready to return to the arms of Uncle Sam; he chose further exile in England. Mrs. Maury, who had refused to come to Mexico, joined her husband in England in March, 1866, for the first family reunion since 1862.

Maury made one final contribution to his Mexican friends— packages of cinchona seed. These were planted successfully near the site of one of the ill-fated colonization projects at Córdoba, thus introducing quinine production into Mexico. Confederate settlers Maury could not produce; quinine he could. The adventure ended in August, 1866, when Maximilian honored him with the Grand Cross of the Order of Guadalupe.

For two years Maury remained in England. There he returned to the life of the scholar-scientist. In 1866 he was honored with a testimonial dinner sponsored by Sir John Pakington, the First Lord of the Admiralty, and attended by admirers from all over Europe. They gave Maury a silver casket with $15,000 in gold, a welcome gift, for his property in the United States was inaccessible.

Maury was never, however, in real want; his services were in constant demand. In July, 1866 he contracted to produce a series of five school geographies for an American publisher and wrote two volumes before he returned home. They were told in simple language, had the charm of a story, with maps by his young son "Brave." The Maury geographies set a new trend. They were a pioneering venture in relating geography to the lives of people. Soon Maury was to geographies what McGuffey was to readers.

Maury was both busy and solvent with his scientific activities. The electric torpedo, which he had invented during the war, was still an object of great curiosity. He gave several demonstrations of the torpedo and instructed military engineers in its handling. He was paid $5,000 for a demonstration in May, 1866, before Napoleon III on the Seine. In July, 1866, he conducted a school at London for experts from the Scandinavian countries and Holland. The completion of the third transatlantic cable was, like the first, also a monument to Maury's genius. Cyrus Field had said at the completion of the first cable in 1858 that others furnished the money and did the work; Maury "furnished the brains."

It was Maury's brains that brought to him in 1868 the honorary degree of LL.D. from Cambridge University. His citation described him as a man who "while serving in the American Navy did not permit the clear edge of his mind to be dulled, or his ardour for study to be dissipated. . . ." His work in nautical science was singled out; but so also were his "noble manners and good morals." As for his actions in war and peace:

When that cruel civil war in America was imminent, this man did not hesitate to leave home and friends, a place of high honour and an office singularly adapted to his genius—to throw away, in one word, all the goods and gifts of fortune—that he might defend and sustain the cause which seemed to him the just one. "The victorious cause pleased the gods," and now perhaps, as victorious causes will do, it pleases the majority of men, and yet no one can withhold his admiration from the man who, though numbered among the vanquished, held his faith pure and unblemished even at the price of poverty and exile.

Both poverty and exile came to an end in 1868 when Maury at last set out for the United States, taking advantage of a general amnesty act. He was returning to accept a professorship of meteorology at Virginia Military Institute in Lexington. This was but one of many positions offered. Napoleon III wanted him for the directorship of the Imperial Observatory, and other crowned heads of Europe would have employed him if they could. From the United States had come an opportunity to serve as vice chancellor of the University of the South, which, after failing to open on the eve of the Civil War, was at last in operation. Maury was also mentioned for a post at the University of Virginia.

He chose Virginia Military Institute, largely because his friend Robert E. Lee was president of Washington College, also at Lexington. Maury was not expected "to undertake a regular course of lectures as one of the faculty." He felt untrained for such duty and wanted to be allowed to pursue his scientific work, "a field of research in which I am not altogether a 'raw hand!' "—in particular, to conduct a physical survey of Virginia to aid the development of the agricultural, mineral, and hydraulic resources of the state.

The Maurys reached the United States in July. In September, he was inducted formally, with Robert E. Lee and the Washington College faculty in attendance. Wearing his numerous decorations for the occasion, he gave both an impressive appearance and an impressive address.

Maury was convinced that Virginia needed an agricultural school. The land-grant movement initiated by the Morrill Act of 1862 was still in its first decade, and Maury gave it his ardent support. He campaigned to promote a more thorough teaching of natural science in the public schools. Virginia's response came in 1872 with the founding of Virginia Polytechnic Institute at Blacksburg. However, Maury never forgot his sea, and among his new interests was a projected ship line between Flushing in Holland and Norfolk, Virginia.

Maury's prime interest was the rebuilding of his languishing South. With a scientist's ability to get down to basic things, he sought to tackle a serious health problem of the malaria-ridden South. He attempted to introduce cinchona trees, as he had in Mexico, so that quinine might be more plentiful.

At an address at the October, 1868, Staunton fair, Maury attacked the South's alleged psychological problem—its loss of energy and enterprise. He refused to admit that the South had given up the struggle. He was an apostle of the "New South," although the term was not yet coined. Like a number of other Southern leaders of the time, he called for new blood—that of the enterprising Dutch and German immigrants. He also challenged the South to realize its tremendous potential of water power and to build new roads to promote commerce and industry.

In the next few years, Maury rarely hesitated when called upon to speak. Mostly he talked of resources, railroad routes, roads, and the like. The burden of his last great crusade—a crusade he had undertaken in the fifties with no success—was the collection and dissemination of meteorological data for farmers. Taking a leaf from his oceanographic books, he felt that a "National Weather Bureau and Signal Service" was needed for the land just as much as a Naval Observatory and Hydrographic Office were needed for the sea.

Back in 1858, Maury had argued the possibility of using the Army's well-established meteorological observation service to bring weather information by telegraph to the people with unheard-of rapidity. After the Civil War, telegraphic weather forecasting was in operation; but Maury wanted to go further— to predict crops as well as the weather. In 1871, he estimated that because of "the lack of . . . accurate crop estimates," cotton planters for the previous six years had lost many millions of dollars. "The crops may be regarded in one sense," he said, "as a meteorological expression of the weather, from seed time to harvest." Were the weather recorded accurately, the crops could be predicted so that there would be no misinformation about their actual cash value at the time of sale.

Maury pointed out that the Signal Office, already transmitting weather forecasts as he had proposed before the War, could coordinate its work with the statistical services of the Agricultural Bureau, to do for agriculture what the wind and current charts had done for commerce and navigation. Maury went on to propose a *modus operandi* that has become standard procedure today:

Do you mean to say that amid all the mind, means, and appliances of the age, the relations between the weather and the crops are past finding out? If I could, with just such a system of researches for the sea, sit down in my office and tell the navigator how he would find the wind, at any season of the year, in any part of the ocean through which he wished to sail, am I promising too much when I tell you, that by the plan I now propose the relation between the weather and the crops is as capable of scientific development as were the relations between sea-voyages and the winds twenty-five years ago?

But let us suppose, for the sake of illustration and by way of showing the main feature of the plan, that the proper meteorological stations have been occupied, and that the observers and co-operators report upon the crops as well as upon the weather; and that, at first and in a tentative way, a special crop-reporter be assigned to every district of 10,000 square miles in the states, who should travel over his beat continually and keep the central office posted, by monthly reports at first, as to the state and promise of the staple crops of his district; at the same time the meteorological observers in this district would send in their observations in detail for the same period, also by mail, while by telegraph both observers keep up their daily reports, both as to the weather and crops.

Maury proposed an international conference on agricultural meteorology, similar to the Brussels meeting in 1853 for merchants and navigators. He did not live to attend the Vienna Congress held in 1873, but it was one of his great triumphs.

In one of his last public addresses, made at St. Louis before the National Agricultural Congress in October 1872, he pleaded his unselfish interest in the cause most eloquently. He pointed out that "I am under the ban of the nation and can hold no office in it, either State or Federal. The moment the government takes hold of it, my association with it ceases. I cannot share in the honour of helping to organize or of assisting to carry it out. I have no farm, neither do I cultivate a parcel of ground. . . . There is no one in the land who is less to be benefited by its success than I." All, indeed, that he could reap in the way of reward was the fame of the authorship of the plan.

Certainly fame had provided him with many laurels. Technically he could not hold office, but that was to him a meaningless deprivation. Despite his years of expatriation, he was every bit a citizen, highly respected in both North and South. In 1870, St. John's College at Annapolis approached him for its presidential office, but he refused to live any farther north—and be any colder —than he already was. In 1871, he was called to the presidency of the University of Alabama, whose attractive salary of $5,000 and milder climate moved him to accept. The pleas of his Virginia friends and his fear that Alabama could not put its money where its promises were changed his mind. He finally decided to remain at V.M.I. He was now much troubled by gout, and his lameness complicated his precarious state of health. In July 1872, he offered to resign, but the Board of Visitors would not agree.

On October 23, 1872, Maury returned from his trip to St. Louis so ill that he announced on arrival he had "come home to die." He cancelled a scheduled address in Norfolk on that date. The manuscript of the undelivered speech was a plea for his forecasting scheme, and for following such reform trends of the times as government regulation of the railroads, one of the pet projects of the postwar farm organization, the Grange.

For the next four months, Maury methodically set about the business of dying. He dictated the last revision of his *Physical Geography*. His final report on the survey of Virginia had been completed and would be published posthumously. He sent farewell messages to his friends. In his last week, he called in his children, speaking to each one individually and enjoining them to use a prayer he had written years ago. Toward the end, he asked his son-in-law, S. W. Corbin, to nurse him. A few days before the end, Maury dismissed his doctor.

Everything moved along as precisely as if it had been recorded on a wind and current chart. On the final evening, he listened to his favorite hymn, then extended his hands. "The peace of God," he intoned, "which passeth all understanding be with you all— all!" Next day, February 1, 1873, a few minutes before the end, the man of science who had kept his wits about him to the last, sent the women from the room so they might be spared the last agonizing moments. "Are my feet growing cold? Do I drag my anchors?" he asked his son Richard. "They are sure and steadfast," was the answer. Then came the last words: "All's well," and the bells tolled all over Lexington and the flags at V.M.I. went to half-mast; for all was not well. A great man was gone.

Maury lay in state in the library of the Virginia Military Institute—a fitting spot. The services were held there, too. In the procession were the staff and cadets of the Institute and the faculty and student body of Washington College (now Washington and Lee, for there had been another distinguished lying-in-state there two years before).

A citizen of the world was dead. Eulogies, resolutions, and letters of condolence came from all over the globe. No eulogist grasped the essence of Maury's greatness quite so succinctly as his biographer, John W. Wayland, who wrote in 1930:

> The thing above all others that made Maury a great man was his ability to see the invisible. He was a seer. He saw the cable before it was laid. He saw a railroad across the continent before it was built. He saw a ship canal from the Mississippi to the Great Lakes before it was dug. He saw the free navigation of the Amazon River before it was free. He saw a great training school for our naval officers, a weather bureau and weather reports for our farmers, long before either was a reality. He saw a ship canal across the Isthmus of Panama more than half a century before it was constructed. He was a seer and a pathfinder not only on the seas, but under the seas, across the lands, and among the stars.

Maury's body was eventually removed to Richmond. By 1929, when a monument was dedicated to the "Pathfinder of the Seas," the name of the great oceanographer was already a strange one even to the South and Virginia, which had once paid him lavish homage. Men asked why there were Maury Halls at V.M.I., Annapolis, and Virginia State Teachers College. Why had the Virginia Legislature decreed an annual Maury Day for the Virginia schools? Why was a U.S. destroyer christened in his honor? Somehow Maury's fame and Maury's name could not stand the ravages of mankind's forgetting. Perhaps only the sailors bothered to remember. They could not help it, for at the top of every pilot chart in the U.S. Navy are the words: "Founded upon the researches made in the early part of the nineteenth century by Matthew Fontaine Maury, while serving as lieutenant in the United States Navy."

So a great Southerner had passed into obscurity. Most of the other men whose stories are the burden of this volume are far better known to the present generation. Somehow the names of men of war and men of politics manage to survive; the scholar and the scientist more often go down into oblivion. Perhaps, though, the fame of a great name with its handful of sententious legends is more evanescent than the fame of a great idea, of a great scientific discovery—even though the man who thought and discovered is forgotten. It is perhaps a trifling thing after all to be a name remembered; there is something far more permanent in the fathering of an idea or an action that becomes a part of the life of the race. Perhaps some day there may be men who have even forgotten the great Lee himself. But even then there will still be sailing charts and hydrographic offices and weather bureaus. The world can learn to get on without its great men; it cannot survive without its great ideas.

Maury was the Confederate who ran away—the Confederate who already escapes the minds of the second and third generations. But in reality he could never run away. Wherever he was—in England, in Mexico, in Virginia, or in the grave—he was never really away. The real Maury was a chart at sea—any sea; a weather forecast—anywhere; a geography book in the hands of any lad—in Appomattox or in Hong Kong.

Maury never belonged to the biographers and historians—for he was not a part of the past—the past that in order to survive has to be remembered. Rather he belonged to the present, the future even—a present and a future that have to be experienced, not remembered. Perhaps, even forgotten, he would in the end prove to be the greatest Confederate of them all.

3

Militant Moderate
JOHN C. BRECKINRIDGE

On the day of Appomattox, April 9, 1865, John Cabell Breckinridge, Confederate Secretary of War, Major General in the Confederate Army, former Vice President of the United States, sometime Senator from Kentucky and candidate for the Presidency in 1860, arrived in the Danville area to join President Davis and the Confederate Cabinet members who had fled after the evacuation of Richmond. It was a message from Breckinridge, delivered to Davis in St. Paul's Church, on Sunday, April 2, that had informed the President the city could no longer be held.

Danville was 140 miles southwest of the Confederate capital. Breckinridge had set out from Richmond on April 3 with a small group of mounted officers and men, traveling through southern Virginia, after visiting Lee's headquarters near Appomattox on April 7. It had been a dangerous, exhausting trip, marked by frequent skirmishes with Federal troops, but Breckinridge and his companions had successfully eluded the vast Federal concentrations closing in on the Army of Northern Virginia. From Danville the fugitives would go on to North Carolina, where they would seek the protection of the forces of General Joseph E. Johnston.

Breckinridge had served ably in many of the War's campaigns, from Louisiana to Virginia. He was a born leader of men, skilled in the arts of persuasion and negotiation, adaptable, realistic, and intelligent. It was the esteem held for Breckinridge, both in the Army and among Confederate Congressmen and government officials, that had caused Davis in the final months of the conflict to bring him into the Cabinet as the sixth and last Confederate War Secretary.

Many in his own time and since have thought that this brilliant, well-born Kentuckian would have made a better choice for President of the Confederacy than the high-minded but unyielding and doctrinaire Mississippian, Jefferson Davis. Indeed, if the divided Democratic party had united behind Breckinridge in the national elections of 1860 and placed him in the White House, there might have been no secession and no war.

Breckinridge, forty-four years old in 1865, was already an old politician. He had been Vice President under Buchanan and had served as United States Senator. He had labored mightily to preserve the Union, and had continued in the Senate through the first five months of Lincoln's Administration, after the Confederacy was established and the Civil War was well underway. He had hoped to the last that war, at least, if not secession, could be averted. Though he was the darling of the slave states of the Deep South in the Presidential elections of 1860, he was really a moderate who had repeatedly affirmed his loyalty to the Union. In fact, he had expressed a willingness to withdraw from the Presidential race if the Democrats would agree on a single candidate. Stephen A. Douglas, nominee of the Northern Democrats, refused this offer. Breckinridge had wide national support, and was less of a sectional candidate than either Douglas or Lincoln. He received more electoral votes than Douglas and many more votes in the North than Lincoln did in the South.

Both by inheritance and training Breckinridge was well prepared for his role in the crisis of 1861-65. His father, Joseph, had achieved distinction in Kentucky as a lawyer in Lexington, a member of the Legislature, the Speaker of the Lower House and Secretary of State—all before he died at 34. John's grandfather, also John, was born in 1760 near Staunton, Virginia, attended William and Mary College, and was elected three times to the Virginia Assembly before he was permitted to take his seat—his constituents insisted on voting for him even though he was under age.

Grandfather John was later elected to the United States Congress from Virginia, but moved to Kentucky before taking office. There he settled near Lexington at a spot that came to be known as Cabell's Dale and was soon in state politics, as a legislator and Attorney General. He next went to the United States Senate; then, as Thomas Jefferson's Attorney General he encouraged the President in the bold step of purchasing the Louisiana Territory from France. He was only forty-six when he died.

John C. Breckinridge was born in the family's two-story log house at Cabell's Dale, January 15, 1821. A few years earlier, two other notable Americans, Abraham Lincoln and Jefferson Davis, first saw the light of day in even simpler Kentucky homes. Young Breckinridge received his first schooling at Pisgah Academy near Lexington. It was typical of many private Southern institutions of the time, giving a sound classical and moral education without frills and preparing its students as well for life as for college. He graduated in 1838 at the age of seventeen from Kentucky's Centre College and took courses at the College of New Jersey (later Princeton) and at Transylvania College in Lexington, where he studied law.

In the forties Breckinridge practiced law at Lexington and several other towns in Kentucky and in Iowa. But Iowa he found too far from his Kentucky home. In 1843, he returned, married Mary Cyrene Burch, and began to gain fame as an orator. In the summer of 1847, he delivered the memorial address in Lexington for Kentucky soldiers who had fallen in the still raging Mexican War. He spoke movingly and eloquently to a great throng gathered from all over the state. Indeed, he may have talked himself into the army, because in the fall he became major of the Third Regiment of Kentucky volunteers. He and his regiment reached Mexico too late to take part in much of the fighting, but as an officer he displayed those qualities of leadership, initiative, and self-denial that were later to serve him well. "On our march from Vera Cruz," wrote a fellow soldier, "I do not believe he rode a whole day during the march. On his war-breathing steed I noticed every day a worn down soldier unable to walk mounted and he himself on foot."

Two years later, at 28, Breckinridge ventured into politics and ran for the Legislature. Though a Democrat in a district that was normally Whig, he was elected. In that contest and in debates on the revision of Kentucky's state constitution, Breckinridge revealed himself as a moderate on the issues of slavery and state rights, yet a moderate who held his moderation fiercely and defended it effectively in public and private debate. Slavery existed; it was to be defended, but not necessarily extended to the new states. It was, he held, for the new states themselves to decide. Then, as ever, he insisted that the Federal government stay out of state affairs. This the Constitution decreed, and common sense approved.

Even the Whig of Whigs, Henry Clay, was moved to praise the talents of this obviously rising young Democrat. And the Legislature chose Breckinridge to deliver the address of welcome when Clay returned to the state after pushing through Congress the Compromise of 1850, which the moderates confidently expected would mean "peace in our time" in the struggle between the North and the South. So far this was a talking war, not a shooting war.

Breckinridge's remarks of 1850 and Clay's appreciative response brought many Whigs to support Breckinridge in his successful race for Congress in 1851. Breckinridge assumed more and more the role of Kentucky spokesman Clay had so long filled, and the old compromiser seemed content for his "eloquent young friend" to succeed him. When Clay died in 1852, Breckinridge was chosen by the Kentucky delegation to deliver a eulogy in the United States House of Representatives. A fellow Kentuckian, Cassius M. Clay, described the rising political leader as "tall, well-formed, with fair complexion, regular face of great mental power, large blue eyes, and auburn hair; intellectual, composed, and full of conscious genius and future prowess." He was a man to reckon with.

Breckinridge was re-elected to Congress in 1853 against the

formidable opposition of R. P. Letcher, an ex-Governor, former Congressman and Minister to Mexico. This victory, made possible by the great majority given him in Owen County, so delighted Breckinridge that he changed the name of his three-year-old son John to Owen.

A rough-and-tumble Congressional debate in 1854 almost led to a duel between Breckinridge, ordinarily calm in argument, and New York's Francis B. Cutting. But the two men and their seconds were unable to agree which was the challenged party and whether the weapons should be rifles at sixty paces (as Breckinridge demanded) or pistols at ten (as called for by Cutting). Friends eventually settled the quarrel peaceably.

Toward the end of his second term, Breckinridge decided not to run again for Congress but instead to resume his law practice in Lexington. He gave as his reason the need to increase his income for the support of a growing family. Perhaps he was a bit homesick for his home state as well as his home. He was fond of Kentucky social life, of Kentucky viands—juleps.

He was a leader in the councils of his state and party, and in 1856 headed the Kentucky delegation to the Democratic National Convention at Cincinnati, where he placed in nomination for Vice President the name of Linn Boyd, a Kentucky favorite son. He made such an impression on the Convention that he got the nomination himself.

Breckinridge campaigned in several Northern and Midwestern states, arguing as was his wont, not for slavery or sectional privilege but for constitutionalism and state rights. His influence gave the Democrats a comfortable majority in Kentucky. After a nationwide Democratic victory, he was inaugurated with James Buchanan in 1857 at the age of thirty-six—the youngest Vice President in the nation's history.

As presiding officer of the Senate, he worked for compromise and conciliation, one of many who thought that the establishment of Liberia as a haven for freed slaves would benefit the Negro and help ease sectional tension.

In January 1859, the Senate moved into the new Senate Chamber in the Capitol, and Breckinridge made one of his most memorable addresses, tracing the history of the Republic in a strong plea for national unity. He reminded his listeners that the nation was a "confederacy" of states, that it existed under an "admirable Constitution" which limited Federal power, and that "this double scheme of government, State and Federal, so peculiar and so little understood by other powers, protects the earnings of industry and makes the largest freedom compatible with public order."

On contested questions Breckinridge had always yielded to established law and court decisions. He accepted the Missouri Compromise of 1820, even though he did not approve of it since he felt Congress had thereby legislated on a question that should have been left to the states. He was delighted with the Dred Scott decision of 1857, for of this he did approve.

Of the Dred Scott decision he declared in an address before the Kentucky Legislature in 1859: "Gentlemen, I bow to the decision of the Supreme Court of the United States upon every question within its proper jurisdiction, whether it corresponds with my private opinion or not; only I bow a trifle lower when it happens to do so, as the decision in this Dred Scott case does. . . . I repose upon the decision of the Supreme Court of the United States, as to the point that neither Congress nor the territorial legislature has the right to obstruct or confiscate the property of any citizen, slaves included, pending the territorial condition." Of course, in the Dred Scott decision the Supreme Court was accused of playing politics in favor of the South, just as a century later it was accused of doing against the South.

Breckinridge voiced his hope that Kentucky would "cling to the Constitution while a shred of it remains, and if unhappily madness and folly and wicked counsels succeed to destroy the fairest fabric ever erected to liberty among men, she will conduct herself with so much wisdom, moderation, and firmness as to stand justified before the tribunal of history, and in the eye of Heaven, for the part she will play in the most disastrous drama ever enacted." The Kentucky Legislature showed its approval of these remarks by electing him to the United States Senate for the term beginning in 1861, over a year away.

The Legislature elected him to the United States Senate, and at the Charleston meeting of the Democratic National Convention in 1860, he was mentioned as a Presidential nominee. He asked that his name be withdrawn. A split between Northern and Southern Democrats brought adjournment without any nomination. Later, the Southern Democrats, meeting in Baltimore, nominated Breckinridge. He was reluctant to accept, still hoping that Northern and Southern Democrats could unite behind a single candidate. But when it became obvious the party breach would remain unhealed, Breckinridge campaigned vigorously. His basic political credo was simple and unchanged: "Our Union is a confederacy of equal sovereign States, for the purposes enumerated in the Federal Constitution. . . . The Constitution and the equality of the States! These are the symbols of everlasting Union. Let these be the rallying cries of the people." To the charge that Breckinridge favored secession, the *Kentucky Statesman* of Lexington replied, "His slanderers cannot find in all the speeches he has made, one word, one sentiment, which, by the most forced construction, can be made to militate against the Union. . . . The principles and measures he has advocated, the platform on which he stands, and the record of his life, have been scanned and searched in vain for a sentiment which is not one of loyalty and love for the Union."

"I am an American citizen, a Kentuckian," he said, "who never did an act or cherished a thought that was not full of devotion to the Constitution and the Union." And Jefferson Davis, who likewise hoped to avoid secession, said Breckinridge was "the best representative of the interests and avowed policy of the South, as well as the best hope of the preservation of our Constitutional Union."

It is certainly true that Breckinridge hoped and worked for the preservation of the Union, but it is also true that he never doubted secession was constitutional. Stephen A. Douglas, candidate of the Northern Democrats, wryly remarked: "Breckinridge may not be for disunion, but all the disunionists are for Breckinridge." Southerners who feared the secessionist bent of Breckinridge's supporters found more comfort in supporting John Bell of Tennessee, put forward by the Constitutional Union party, whose chief aim was to rally Southern support for the Union. The effect, however, was to make still more certain the election of a sectional President, Abraham Lincoln. Despite a strong campaign and the public support of President Buchanan and, incidentally, of Andrew Johnson of Tennessee, later Lincoln's Vice President, Breckinridge carried only the states of the Deep South. He had considerable nationwide support, nonetheless, and in New England alone he received more votes than Lincoln did in the entire South. In Kentucky, Breckinridge got 53,000 votes to Lincoln's 1,000.

On February 13, 1861, it was Breckinridge who, as presiding officer of the United States Senate, solemnly announced to a tense Congress assembled to certify the results of the election that "Abraham Lincoln, having received a majority of the whole number of electoral votes, is duly elected President of the United States for the four years beginning on the fourth of March, 1861." There had been rumors that Southern sympathizers, in the majority in Washington, would seize the capital and prevent the announcement of Lincoln's election. Three-fourths of the members of Congress were said to be armed.

Six Southern states had already left the Union, and had set up the Southern Confederacy with Jefferson Davis as its President. Between the election and the inauguration of Lincoln, Breckinridge, who had been a childhood friend of Lincoln's wife and had known Lincoln himself for many years, called on the President-elect several times and urged that he make known his willingness to have a national and representative administration rather than a partisan one. He hoped to allay the fears of the Deep South and perhaps forestall secession. Lincoln promised nothing.

In Mrs. Lincoln's presence Breckinridge told Elizabeth Todd Grimsley, a mutual relative of his and Mrs. Lincoln's, who was visiting at the White House: "Cousin Lizzie, I would not like you to be disappointed in your expected stay at the White House, so I will now invite you to remain here as guest, when the Confederation takes possession." A fiery dialogue ensued between him and the President's wife—"two bright, quick, embittered brains and tongues," Cousin Lizzie reported.

A teen-age nephew of Breckinridge who called on Lincoln in Washington during the War to ask a favor was asked by the President, "Do you ever hear from your Uncle John? I was fond of John, and I was sorry to see him take the course he did. I regret he sided with the South."

Many of Breckinridge's followers had looked to him for guidance in the tense and deteriorating situation of 1861. The Washington *Evening Star* urged him to lend his influence to discourage the "current revolutionary schemes" in the South. "It is well known," the paper declared, "that he utterly repudiates the propriety of revolution because of Lincoln's election"; some were saying Breckinridge wanted to be the President of a Southern Confederacy, which the paper rejected as "an unworthy motive, which no man would scorn more than John C. Breckinridge."

He did what he could to stem the tide. He was already on record as supporting the Crittenden Compromise, another attempt to solve the old problem of slavery in the territories and new states. Returning to Kentucky, he found his native state, on the border of North and South, a storm center of conflicting views. The controversies that had divided the nation were concentrated here. He made a strong speech before the Legislature in joint session, and he was selected as member of a group, made up of all parties, designated to chart a course for the state. The committee recommended that Kentucky take no part in any conflict between the Federal government and the Southern states and that she resist any invasion of her border by either side. Breckinridge did not think this course feasible or desirable, but he accepted it and defended it in the United States Senate.

In Washington, Breckinridge resisted all efforts to coerce the Southern states. When war broke out in April, he was outspoken against Lincoln's war measures. On July 16, 1861, he said, "I have cherished all my life an attachment to the Union of these States under the Constitution of the United States, and I have always revered that instrument as one of the wisest of human works, but now it is put aside by the Executive of the United States, and these acts are about to be approved by the Senate." In August, he declared in Congress, "Gentlemen talk about the Union as if it was an end instead of a means. They talk about it as if it was the Union of these States which alone had brought into life the principles of public and personal liberty. Sir, they existed before and they may survive it." He warned that if Kentucky gave up her neutrality and abandoned her policy of mediation by taking part in what he called "a war of subjugation and annihilation," his state would have to find another Senator.

In September, the Confederate and Union armies both invaded Kentucky, but Union forces were more numerous. Union supporters also had control of the Legislature, which affirmed its loyalty to the Union. Knowing that Kentucky was the key to the Ohio and Mississippi valleys, Lincoln wrote in September, 1861, "I think to lose Kentucky is nearly the same as to lose the whole game. Kentucky gone, we cannot hold Missouri, nor, as I think, Maryland."

Feeling was intense; families were divided, including Breckinridge's own. His uncle, Robert J. Breckinridge, for example, was an ardent Unionist, later chairman of the Republican National Convention that renominated Lincoln, and an adviser to Lincoln on Kentucky affairs. Two of Robert Breckinridge's sons fought with the Confederacy, two with the North.

Meanwhile Senator Breckinridge confessed to Jefferson Davis that he feared bodily harm in Washington. Returning to Kentucky, he narrowly escaped arrest in that part of the state controlled by Union sympathizers. It was now clear that the state could no more remain united than the nation; so Breckinridge helped to organize a Confederate provisional government for Kentucky. He warned his fellow Kentuckians that the Lincoln Administration was a "Federal despotism . . . a power which respects neither

Constitution nor laws." At Richmond, J. B. Jones, a Philadelphia editor turned War Department clerk, wrote happily in his diary, "No one doubts that Breckinridge is now with us and will do good service." One of the thirteen stars in the Confederate flag was for Kentucky, and she was represented in the Confederate Congress.

Meanwhile a United States District Court at Frankfort indicted Breckinridge and more than thirty other Kentuckians sympathetic with the Confederacy as traitors. The Union-dominated Legislature in October and the United States Senate in December declared Breckinridge expelled from the Senate. He had already, however, thrown in his lot with the Confederacy, and in a speech at Bowling Green on October 8, declared, "I exchange with proud satisfaction, a term of six years in the Senate of the United States for the musket of a soldier."

The Confederate government had no intention of letting a leader of Breckinridge's ability and influence carry a musket. He was appointed a brigadier general and ordered to report to General Albert Sidney Johnston, who was in command of forces in the mid-South. The remarkably long and drooping mustache so familiar in the Breckinridge portraits was a product of these army years. As leader of the Kentucky Brigade, he took part in the early fighting in Kentucky and Tennessee and in the crucial and bloody battle of Shiloh (Pittsburg Landing) in 1862, where he commanded a division that was hotly engaged. At Breckinridge's side in this and other battles was his teen-age son Cabell, whose horse was shot from under him at Shiloh. Later Cabell was taken prisoner at Missionary Ridge, but was exchanged and served again as his father's aide in Richmond during the final months of the war. Shiloh, where General Johnston was killed, had been Breckinridge's first real battle, but his courage and handling of his troops led to his promotion to major general soon thereafter. Later in that same year he performed well at Vicksburg, in an attack on Baton Rouge, and at Port Hudson.

Breckinridge and his fellow Kentuckians joined the ineffectual General Braxton Bragg in Tennessee in what they hoped would be a successful campaign to free their native state from Union control. In March 1863, the Kentucky Brigade was in the thick of the fighting and suffered many casualties at the battle of Murfreesboro, or Stone River, where Breckinridge commanded the Second Division of General William J. Hardee's Corps. Breckinridge had opposed Bragg's plans for the attack at Murfreesboro but, overruled, carried out his role energetically. His command suffered 1,700 casualties out of a force of 4,500. After the battle, a soldier's account reads, "contemplating this awful sacrifice as he rode by the dead and dying in the rear of our lines, General Breckinridge, with tears falling from his eyes, was heard to say, in tones of anguish, 'My poor Orphans! My poor Orphans!' " The casualties were great and Kentuckians in the Confederacy were men without a state. Henceforth, the Kentucky Brigade became the Orphan Brigade. When Bragg withdrew from Murfreesboro, the disappointed "Orphans" covered his retreat skillfully.

In June, 1863, the Brigade was back in Mississippi with General Joseph E. Johnston, and took part in the battle of Jackson during Grant's Vicksburg campaign. Returning to Tennessee, Breckinridge commanded a division of General D. H. Hill's Corps at Chickamauga and at Missionary Ridge. Something of the esteem in which Breckinridge was held not only by his own men but by the enemy was shown when, after the battle of Chickamauga, a Confederate victory, a group of Federal prisoners asked to see Breckinridge. It had been a grueling and exhausting battle, and Breckinridge said to the prisoners, "Well, gentlemen, this is what is left of me." One replied, "Yes, and a damn fine specimen of humanity you are too! There is not another such hunk of humanity in our land! I voted for you once, and I want this cussed war over with so I can vote for you again for President!"

In February 1864, Breckinridge was ordered to take command of the forces in southwest Virginia. This difficult assignment involved vigilance against Federal attack and the protection of important salt and lead mines, and the supply lines to Lee's army. In May, Union General Franz Sigel, in a surprise move that endangered the rear of Lee's army, was marching up the Shenandoah Valley toward Staunton. Breckinridge with 3,500 men, including

225 teen-age cadets of the Virginia Military Institute, hastened to meet him. Outnumbered two to one, Breckinridge's force attacked vigorously nevertheless and routed Sigel's troops at the battle of New Market.

"Tall, erect, and commanding in physique," wrote General John B. Gordon, "Breckinridge would have been selected in any martial group as a typical leader. In the campaign in the Valley of Virginia . . . he exhibited in a marked degree the characteristics of a great commander. He was fertile in resource, and enlisted and held the confidence of his men, while he inspired them with enthusiasm and ardor. Under fire and in extreme peril he was strikingly courageous, alert, and self poised."

Breckinridge commanded a division under Lee at the battle of Cold Harbor in June and was injured by an exploding shell that killed his horse. He accompanied General Jubal Early on the daring raid to the outskirts of Washington in July. The troops under his command won victories against great odds at Martinsburg and Monocacy. "I have never, I think," wrote an officer who served under him, "witnessed an indifference to danger so absolutely calm and imperturbable as I have seen him display under very extraordinary exposure to personal peril."

In the hard winter of 1864-65, Breckinridge was in southwest Virginia, where he and his men suffered severely from lack of food and supplies. There was constant fighting and maneuvering against vastly more numerous Union forces. General Basil Duke observed, "Although this unfortunate department was worse handled by the enemy after he commanded it than ever before, he came out of the ordeal, fatal to most other generals, with enhanced reputation. His great energy and indomitable resolution were fairly tried and fully proven. He could personally endure immense exertions and exposure."

Breckinridge was called to Richmond in February 1865 to become Secretary of War. At the same time Robert E. Lee was made commander of all the South's armies. Lee immediately restored President Davis' enemy, General Joseph E. Johnston, to command of the forces opposing General W. T. Sherman moving north from Georgia after the Union march to the sea. The combination of Breckinridge, Lee, and Johnston might have been effective earlier in the war; now it was too late. Breckinridge had been suggested for Secretary of War in 1861, but it was felt at the time that he might help hold Kentucky and the border states for the South by serving there with the Army. That, too, is what Breckinridge undoubtedly preferred.

In the War Department, he found its affairs effectively administered by the experienced Assistant Secretary, John A. Campbell, former United States Supreme Court Justice. Campbell knew the Confederacy could not hold out much longer. A negotiated peace recognizing Southern independence might still be possible, he thought.

From the time he took over the secretaryship, Breckinridge seems to have held similar views. He sent out a request to all bureau heads as soon as he took office, asking for a frank statement on resources available and of the outlook for the future. The reports were uniformly pessimistic. Food and materials were scarce. The troops were inadequately armed, and the South's armament centers almost completely destroyed. Breckinridge became convinced that the South's best hope was an early and orderly peace settlement. He said:

What I propose is that the Confederacy should not be captured in fragments, that we should not disband like banditti, but that we should surrender as a government, and we will thus maintain the dignity of our cause, and secure the respect of our enemies, and the best terms for our soldiers. As for myself, I may be, for reasons known to us all, more obnoxious to the North than many others, but I am willing to assume the risk, and to surrender as Secretary of War. . . . This has been a magnificent epic; in God's name let it not terminate in a farce.

Breckinridge spent much of February and March in conference with civilian leaders in Richmond and with military leaders on the battlefield. He told a group of Confederate Senators, "Our first duty, gentlemen, is to the soldiers who have been influenced by our arguments and example, and we should make every sacrifice to protect them." He was especially concerned about the soldiers from his native Kentucky and Missouri, the border states which had not joined the Confederacy. He wanted to be sure these men could return home safely at the war's end. He was in close touch, of course, with President Davis, whose will to continue the war never flagged, and he faithfully carried out the President's orders.

Breckinridge himself was determined to fight on as long as necessary to achieve the best possible peace terms. He suggested to Lee the possibility of sending troops from Virginia to Johnston in North Carolina and proposed that Lee himself should then lead the combined force in a blow against Sherman. Lee, facing the huge forces of Grant, did not feel strong enough to spare men to execute this plan, though when he evacuated Richmond in April he did hope to join with Johnston.

Breckinridge remained briefly in Richmond the first days of April 1865, when the city was evacuated by President Davis and the rest of the Cabinet, to supervise the destruction or removal of military supplies and other material that might be of value to the enemy. All day Saturday and Sunday, April 1 and 2, he was busy packing War Department records for shipment by train to Danville, near the North Carolina border. Captain William H. Parker, Superintendent of the Confederate States Naval Academy that had been training midshipmen on ships in the James River since 1863, was in charge of the Confederate treasure of about half a million dollars, which was likewise being shipped to Danville. He wrote, "While waiting in the depot I had an opportunity of seeing the President and his Cabinet as they went to the cars. Mr. Davis preserved his usual calm and dignified manner, and General Breckinridge (the Secretary of War), who had determined to go out on horseback, was as cool and gallant as ever—but the others, I thought, had the air (as the French say) of wishing to be off. General Breckinridge stayed with me sometime after the President's train had gone, and I had occasion to admire his bearing under the circumstances."

Early on the morning of April 3, while it was still dark, Breckinridge with a few officers and members of his staff, rode out of the city toward the rear of Lee's army. As they approached the hardpressed remnants of the Army of Northern Virginia, they saw long lines of Confederate army trains still burning from Federal cavalry raids.

From Amelia Springs, near Farmville, after a visit to Lee's headquarters, Breckinridge wired President Davis at the temporary capital in Danville that Lee's situation was critical. He informed Davis that Lee still hoped to lead his army to join Johnston in North Carolina. By the time Breckinridge and his little force had ridden and fought their way to Danville, Davis, his Cabinet and Government were preparing to move on to Greensboro, North Carolina.

When Davis and the Cabinet left for Greensboro, Breckinridge again stayed with his accompanying cavalry. It was typical of Breckinridge's activity as Secretary of War that in the final weeks of the Confederacy he chose to be with the Army in the field rather than with the civilian officials clustered about the President.

At Greensboro, Davis conferred with Generals Johnston, Bragg, and Beauregard. He hoped to move with as many men as possible to join Generals Richard Taylor in Alabama and Nathan Bedford Forrest in Mississippi and then continue on beyond the Mississippi to join the forces of General Edmund Kirby-Smith in Texas, where he thought the Confederacy could hold out for a long while. Yet Davis agreed Johnston should negotiate with Sherman, on the possibility that peace terms satisfactory to the South might be arranged.

Davis and his Cabinet moved on toward Charlotte on April 15. Breckinridge went along, not only as Secretary of War but as commander of the troops guarding the government party. Breckinridge, Secretary of the Navy Stephen Mallory, Postmaster General John H. Reagan and Davis rode horseback; Secretary of State Judah P. Benjamin, Attorney General George Davis, and other less active officials were in wagons, ambulances, or any conveyance available. The roads were in bad repair and muddy from spring rains. The Cabinet members, officers, and men often had to get out and push their wagons from a mudhole.

Near Lexington, North Carolina, Governor Zebulon B. Vance of North Carolina caught up with the party. Davis urged him to join them with as many soldiers as he could and continue the War in Texas. Others gave the same advice, but Breckinridge advised Vance to stay in his state and help to guide it through the difficult days ahead—an illustration of his realistic appraisal of the situation (he seems never to have thought it feasible to continue the War after Lee's surrender). Indeed, General Duke, the Confederate cavalry leader accompanying the Cabinet on its wandering course, later wrote that Breckinridge was the only one of the officials who "knew what was going on, what was going to be done, or what ought to be done."

Before the party reached Charlotte, a message from Johnston asked for help in the negotiations with Sherman. The obvious choice was Breckinridge, who was familiar with both the military and political situation, and he and Postmaster General Reagan, a rugged and intelligent Texan, set out for Johnston's headquarters near Durham. The two rode from 10 o'clock one night to noon the next day to reach their destination and arrived in time for the second day of negotiations. Sherman demurred, insisting that he could negotiate only with military leaders and on strictly military matters. He finally agreed that Breckinridge might participate in his capacity as major general, but not Reagan. It was from Sherman that the Confederates learned of Lincoln's assassination on April 14 and Breckinridge telegraphed the news to President Davis.

Breckinridge and Johnston, both skilled in history and military law and masterful in argument, presented the Confederate position so skillfully in the discussions with Sherman that at one point the Federal commander is reported to have risen to his feet and exclaimed, "Who's doing the surrendering here? At this rate, you'll soon have me sending an apology to Jeff Davis!" Indeed, the final terms agreed on by the generals did go far beyond a strict military settlement, even to the point of recognizing the existing Southern state governments. These terms were unacceptable at Washington.

The negotiations were not conducted in abstinence. As the meeting got underway, Sherman offered a bottle of whiskey to Johnston and Breckinridge, who was quite weary from his long night ride. Johnston described Breckinridge's expression at this invitation as "beatific." He tossed his quid of tobacco into the fire, rinsed his mouth the better to savor the whiskey, and poured himself a tremendous drink which he swallowed with great satisfaction. Thus fortified, he embarked on the negotiations which, from the Confederate viewpoint, were so brilliantly concluded. Sherman reached for his bottle and poured himself another drink. Breckinridge again tossed out his tobacco in pleasant anticipation. But Sherman, perhaps absent-mindedly, put the bottle away and took his drink alone, and Breckinridge, disappointed and indignant, later said to Johnston, "General Sherman is a hog. Yes, sir, a hog. Did you see him take that drink by himself? No Kentucky gentleman would ever have taken away that bottle!"

The terms eventually accepted by Johnston, on April 26, after Breckinridge had rejoined Davis and the Cabinet at Charlotte, were less favorable than the original ones. Strictly military and applying only to the forces under Johnston's command, the second "peace" did not include the civilian members of Breckinridge's party or the troops accompanying them. They pushed on from Charlotte toward South Carolina, moving slowly and over back-country roads where the chance of meeting large Federal detachments was less likely, pausing in Abbeville, South Carolina, on the banks of the Savannah River.

The Northern newspapers spurred on the Federal troops seeking their capture, and the Government offered large rewards. "We trust that the government will spare no efforts to catch Jeff. Davis and all his lieutenants in treason," cried the New York *Times.* Other papers called for summary execution of the Confederate officials.

At the home of Major Armistead Burt in the peaceful town of Abbeville, where the countryside was green and flowering with spring and little scarred by war, oblivious of the Northern hue and cry, the hunted men met on May 2 in what has been called "the last Confederate council of war." Davis presided and in the group were Breckinridge, General Braxton Bragg, and five brigade commanders: S. W. Ferguson of South Carolina, J. C. Vaughn and George G. Dibrell of Tennessee, and Basil Duke and W. C. P. Breckinridge (a cousin of the Secretary of War) of Kentucky. Davis seemed cheerful and confident, with no thought to surrender. He continued to urge a movement across country to Texas. The Secretary of War pointed out the many hazards and difficulties of such a course through country controlled by the Federal Army, and suggested instead that Davis disguise himself as a private soldier and make his way to Florida, thence by boat to Cuba and across the Gulf of Mexico to Texas. The Secretary of War and Reagan offered themselves to attempt the overland trip with any others who cared to go along.

Davis refused to leave Southern soil for Cuba while a single Confederate soldier continued the War. "I know him so well," Breckinridge said earlier, "that I am satisfied he would consent to no arrangement which would exclude him from the common peril." Captain Parker, who at Abbeville turned over the Confederate treasure, noted Davis' reluctance to escape and Breckinridge's "usual, bold cavalier manner."

Still the military leaders told Davis frankly that it would be useless to continue the War. Davis abruptly concluded the meeting. "When he arose to leave the room," wrote General Duke, "he had lost his erect bearing, his face was pale, and he faltered so much in his step that he was compelled to lean on General Breckinridge."

The President and Cabinet left Abbeville and moved toward Washington, Georgia. Breckinridge's troops were poorly mounted, inadequately armed, and worn from lack of rest and long weeks in the saddle. At Abbeville he had permitted those who wished— about half of them—to return to their homes. To confuse Federal pursuers, he divided the remainder of his force into several groups on different roads. Encounters with Federal patrols became more frequent; the only hope of eluding pursuit was for each Cabinet member to make his way alone. Judah P. Benjamin went alone to Washington, Georgia, and eventually reached Cuba and England. On the road to Irwinville, Davis, Reagan and others were seized by Federal troops on May 10. Clifton, one of Breckinridge's two sons in Confederate service, was also captured that day. He had been one of the midshipmen with Captain Parker charged with guarding the Confederate treasure.

Breckinridge, with a few officers and men near Washington, Georgia, met a large Federal detachment. His cousin parleyed with a Federal officer, while the Secretary of War, now perhaps the most prominent Confederate leader still at large, made his escape. He left orders for the officers and men with him to surrender and avoid further bloodshed. Unlike him, his soldiers were eligible for parole. He told an aide, "I will not have one of these young men to encounter one hazard more for my sake." He had advised the Kentucky troops in his command not to settle in Mexico but "go to your Kentucky homes and there make such citizens as you have made soldiers, and your future is assured."

A small boat was hidden in the Indian River in Florida and an officer had been sent ahead to make it ready to take Davis and several Cabinet members to Cuba. Breckinridge determined to join them.

Now began a game of hide-and-seek between Breckinridge and the Federal troops. He slipped by backroads through southeast Georgia and arrived safely in Florida around the middle of May, accompanied by his son Cabell; an aide, Colonel James Wilson of Kentucky; and his Negro servant, Thomas Ferguson, who had been with him all through the War. At Madison, Florida, he found Colonel John Taylor Wood of President Davis' staff, who had been captured with Davis but had escaped. Breckinridge insisted now that his son Cabell accept a parole and return to Kentucky. The little group passed from friend to friend, from plantation to plantation. The boat that had been hidden in the Indian River had in the meantime been destroyed, but a Confederate naval officer, Captain J. J. Dickison, offered a lifeboat he had seized when he captured the U.S.S. *Columbine.* Dickison agreed to deliver the boat to Fort Butler, on the St. Johns River.

Breckinridge, Wilson, Wood, and the Negro, Tom, set out on May 26 with two weeks' supply of grits and sweet-potato coffee, making their way through thirty miles of sand, scrub oak, and pine wilderness toward Fort Butler. They found the boat ready and manned by three Confederate soldiers. It was a four-oared craft, about seventeen feet long, with a small mast.

The seven men in the little vessel rowed south on the St. Johns River—one of the few rivers in the United States that flows north. They ate fish and figs, oranges and other fruit from near-by shores. Sometimes at night they slept anchored in midstream where the mosquitoes were less thick. When the St. Johns became too shallow they found a man with an ox team to haul the boat across country to the Indian River, which could lead them to the Atlantic.

"The road, if it could be called one," wrote Breckinridge, "was full of ruts which rocked everything badly and several times the front wheels ran away from the hind ones, bringing the end of the boat to the ground with a heavy thump." Men and oxen suffered from the heat, mosquitoes, and sand flies.

On May 31, they reached the Indian River, opposite Cape Canaveral, and resumed their journey southward by boat. They kept a close lookout for Union troops, and one night slipped down midstream past an encampment. They dug in the sand of the shore for fresh water to drink and turtle eggs to eat. The river was wide, with many twistings and turnings, and the group was sometimes lost. On June 3, about 150 miles down river, they pulled their boat across a sand spit into the ocean. It was dangerously small for ocean sailing but the risk of being picked up along the coast was great. But Colonel Wood was an experienced seaman, an Annapolis graduate, who had served aboard the C.S.S. *Virginia* (formerly *Merrimac*) in her fight with the *Monitor* and had commanded the Confederate raider *Tallahassee*. On June 4, Colonel Wood read prayers for the voyage and they set out on the sixty-mile passage to the Bahamas. Sighted by a Federal ship, they returned hastily to land, followed by a boat sent to investigate. Colonel Wood and the two soldiers (one had gone home earlier) convinced the Yankees that they were just a group of fishermen.

Down the coast toward Cuba the boat moved when the coast was clear. Near Lake Worth, they encountered three suspicious looking men, whom they took to be pirates or deserters, in a larger, more seaworthy boat. So they turned pirate themselves and forced the others at gun point to swap boats.

By night the new boat was pulled over the sand bars into Biscayne Bay; and as they sailed down the Bay, they had another narrow escape. They had come close to shore at Fort Dallas to buy food and water. The colony of wreckers and outlaws there was a villainous-looking group, heavily armed. Some started out in canoes to force the party ashore, but a few shots warned them off. Eventually supplies were obtained and paid for, and the Confederates hastened off southward again, moving down the Bay inside the Florida keys. A Federal launch sighted them and gave chase, but they escaped in water too shallow for the launch to follow.

Finally, the little boat with its bearded, piratical-looking crew, set out bravely into the Gulf Stream, running into rough weather, wind, rain, and heavy seas. Only the seamanship of Colonel Wood got them through and he himself was washed overboard, saving himself by a rope.

One day, with the sea calmer, they were able to get fresh water from an American merchant ship, the brig *Neptune* out of Bangor, Maine, whose captain had first threatened to shoot them as pirates. Colonel Wood hardly blamed him, "for a more piratical-looking party than we never sailed the Spanish Main." Breckinridge, "bronzed the color of mahogany, unshaven, with long mustache," wearing an old slouch hat and a "blue flannel shirt open at the neck, exposing his broad chest, veritably looked the buccaneer's part," Wood wrote later. "They stared very hard at us," said Breckinridge, "but no explanations were demanded or given."

On the afternoon of June 10, small islands were sighted off the coast of Cuba, and on the next morning they sailed into harbor at Cardenas, seventy-five miles east of Havana. It was more than two months since Breckinridge had left Richmond, and he was the first Confederate Cabinet member to reach safety. All the party were worn and exhausted from fatigue and hardships. "At my request," said Breckinridge, "Colonel Wood again read prayers, and I am sure we all felt profoundly grateful for our deliverance."

Breckinridge and his companions were warmly welcomed in Cardenas by the local inhabitants and Southerners who gave them new clothes and entertained them at a festive dinner. The Governor of Cuba sent an officer to escort them to Havana. Breckinridge was offered a home in Havana but decided to take passage to England. Colonel Wilson and Charles J. Helm, a Confederate agent in the West Indies, went along.

Breckinridge had reported by letter to Captain Dickison their safe arrival in Havana after "adventures which may be termed both singular and perilous." He wrote also to Charles O'Conor of New York, one of several Northerners interested in seeing that Davis received a fair trial when and if the Federal government attempted to try the Confederate President in the civil courts for treason. To aid in the defense of Davis, Breckinridge was to send O'Conor the funds remaining in the care of Colonel Helm, and in Canada in January 1866 he conferred with George Shea, a well-known New York lawyer, who was working with O'Conor and Horace Greeley on Davis' defense.

Breckinridge arrived in Southampton in July 1865. From England he took ship again, this time for Canada, where, at Toronto, he was joined by his wife, his son Owen, and his daughters, Mary and Frances. There for a few weeks he taught law to a few young Confederate officer refugees. He was probably informed that President Johnson and his Cabinet had ordered his arrest if he returned to the United States, and in August 1866 he returned to England with Mrs. Breckinridge, Owen and Frances, and spent the next two years there, on the Continent and in the Holy Land, Greece, and Egypt.

From his exile, the watchful and affectionate father sent a list of precepts to his daughter Mary, now with relatives in New York. This list she treasured all her life. He urged her to say her prayers morning and night; to obey her teacher and all in authority "promptly and cheerfully"; to consider the wishes and pleasures of others; to speak no evil of others; to avoid envy; to make, as becomes "a Christian or a lady . . . a full and cheerful acknowledgement if you do wrong"; to "try to be happy by being good and try to make others happy"; and finally, as an aid in all of these things, to "read the Ten Commandments and the teachings of Christ" as contained in the Bible. Breckinridge's relations with his family seem to have been singularly close and affectionate. "I never saw him come without being glad," Mrs. Breckinridge once said to Mary, "or leave without being sorry."

Like most Confederate leaders in exile, Breckinridge was short of funds, but he enjoyed the hospitality of more prosperous Southern exiles and English friends. A. J. B. Beresford-Hope, Member of Parliament from Cambridge University, who had aided the Confederacy during the war, wrote that "of the persons of distinction with whom, in the course of my life I have in various ways been thrown, General Breckinridge was among those who had most irresistibly struck me with a feeling of ability and ready power." He visited the Archbishop of Canterbury, attended Parliament, dined with Gladstone, and enjoyed the social life, including the races. On a visit to one stately home he was mistaken for a prospective butler. "Well, my man," he was asked, "what was your last position?" "Madam," he said, "my last position was Secretary of War of the Confederate States of America. Before that I was a major general in the Confederate Army. Prior to that I was Vice President of the United States." The lady's reply is not recorded.

England was not Kentucky, and Breckinridge was homesick. He was not content to be abroad while his state was undergoing the tribulations of Reconstruction. His fellow Kentuckians missed his spirited leadership. In the turbulence of Reconstruction politics, Kentucky, on the border of North and South, was, as in the pre-war years, a key state, violently contended for by Radicals as well as moderate Republicans, by the unreconstructible as well as by less intransigent Democrats. Horace Greeley, editor of the New York *Tribune,* wrote that he wished Breckinridge could come home and calm things down. There was even fear that a "little civil war" would break out in Kentucky, so intense was the feeling.

Kentucky had remained in the Union but had supplied nearly 40,000 troops to the Confederacy (and 65,000 to the Union), and Lincoln had put the state under martial law early in the war. At the end of the war the state was still under martial law and hopping mad.

It has often been said that Kentucky waited until after Appomattox to secede. In any event, as fast as elections rolled around, the voters chose Confederate veterans or sympathizers for office from Governor and Congressman on down. The Legislature persistently refused to approve the Thirteenth and Fourteenth Amendments. Instead, it appropriated funds to honor the Confederate dead. Confederate monument associations sprang up all over the state. Many voters demanded that Breckinridge be considered for Senator and also for Governor. Indeed, the mention of his name at a Democratic nominating convention brought tumultuous cheering.

In 1867, the United States Congress had refused to seat the nine Democrats elected from Kentucky. It argued that the voters "had been overawed and prevented from a true expression of their will by those who have sympathized with or actually participated in the late rebellion." "The Kentucky Legislature," said the Cincinnati *Gazette*, "was as disloyal in spirit as any that ever met in Richmond or South Carolina." Certainly the Legislature that had condemned Breckinridge in 1861 now longed for his return. General Clinton B. Fisk of the Freedmen's Bureau was convinced that Kentucky was made up of "the meanest unsubjugated and unreconstructed rascally rebellious revolutionists that curse the soil of the country."

In February 1866, seventy members of the Kentucky Legislature petitioned President Johnson to pardon Breckinridge so he could return to Kentucky. In January 1868, the Louisville city council asked the state's Congressional delegation to demand that the Administration permit him to return to his home: "The name and face of the Hon. John Cabell Breckinridge are dear, and his counsel considered valuable as to the concerns of both the State and the Republic." The Lexington *Observer and Reporter* wrote: "The day when General Breckinridge can return to us in safety, will not be more joyful to him than to the thousands who love and honor the exiled soldier and statesman. Kentucky, the South, the Democratic party, the whole country sadly needs the aid of his eloquence and counsel."

At Christmas 1868, a General Amnesty Proclamation issued by President Johnson finally ended Breckinridge's exile. He attempted to return inconspicuously to avoid demonstrations, but he was recognized on March 9, 1869, on the train from Cincinnati to Lexington. Cheering crowds turned out at every station in heavy rain. Many entered his car to shake his hand. "Gentlemen," he said, "you must excuse me for being quiet. I am here by permission and it is my request that I be allowed to pass quietly."

At Lexington, at the home of his cousin and wartime comrade, W. C. P. Breckinridge, he was welcomed by a great celebration of bonfires, fireworks, and band music. The strains of "Dixie" echoed with Rebel yells. Breckinridge thanked the crowd for their welcome, "purely personal and containing no particle of political significance," and expressed a hope that old animosities be forgotten. Even these mild remarks brought enthusiastic cheers from the crowd. Oratory was a fine art in the nineteenth-century South, and Breckinridge was a master of it. "Breckinridge," Basil Duke recalled, "had no peer as a stump speaker in Kentucky. Those who never saw or heard him can form no conception of his wonderful imagination. It resided as much in his look and gesture as in his voice. Often a mere glance over the crowd, while he remained seated and silent, would elicit wild cheers and a tumult that could with difficulty be stilled."

In June, a few months after Grant had been inaugurated President, Breckinridge, on a visit to Wisconsin, told a New York *Times* correspondent that he thought "Grant smart enough to take care of himself. His Cabinet, while none of the best, was just such an one as Grant needed, and was better for his purposes than one of more talent would be." This remark, though hardly complimentary, was much milder than the comments most Southerners were making at the time. The report from Wisconsin concluded with the observation that Breckinridge was "an attractive man, a gentleman of mind and culture, and we are pleased to believe that he will hereafter work zealously for the good of the whole Republic."

By October, Breckinridge was speaking more freely, and at the Owen County Fair, he made one of the strongest and most persuasive of his appeals for national peace and harmony:

The great contest of arms, at least, is over. I have heard that during the progress of hostilities the "State of Owen" was never wholly conquered. However this may have been, I am sure that now we all desire amity and peace. The growth of a kind and genial nature has effaced the material ravages of war; it will be well if other scars can be covered by the verdure of the heart. If, with minds elevated by experience and chastened by misfortune, and with spirits free, on the one hand, from base subserviency and the cowardly abandonment of our honest convictions, and on the other from an irrational obstinacy, we address ourselves to the duties of the future, what brave and true heart can doubt that there yet remains for us and our children a career full of prosperity and honor.

A few days later at Nashville, Breckinridge told Confederate veterans he "could say nothing that would be more useful than to express the hope that we are all busy and doing something—to express the hope that we all feel that an idle, whining, repining man demands neither the respect of gods, men, or women."

Breckinridge rigidly held to his policy of avoiding public controversy the rest of his life. Cassius M. Clay, an ardent Kentucky Unionist and a vigorous political foe of Breckinridge, admitted, "He was foremost wherever fortune led him. He never was at heart a secessionist." It was Breckinridge who "denounced and effectively killed in Kentucky, at least, the remorseless Ku Klux Klan," like the militant neutralist he was.

He refrained from public political activity and office-seeking as assiduously as did General Lee. There was a close friendship between the two men, as well. Lee had written inviting him to come to Washington College as Professor of Law. He declined the offer but visited Lee at the college where his sons Clifton and Owen were enrolled.

Following Lee's death in 1870, one of many memorial services was held in Louisville. There Breckinridge made one of his rare post-war speeches. The South had fought hard and well in a cause it believed just. But, "being overcome," he said, "they accepted the results of their defeat and yielded a calm yet proud submission."

Breckinridge devoted himself to law and private business, but many urged his election to office. The Louisville *Courier* had already asked, "Could a better, and abler, or a more gallant man be sent to the United States Senate than John C. Breckinridge? Would he not honor that body more than it could possibly honor him? Would he not stand there without a peer in everything that constitutes greatness?"

President Grant himself would have liked to see Breckinridge return to public life. "Breckinridge was most anxious to restore the Union to good relations," he said. "He was among the last to go over to the South, and was rather dragged into the position. . . . I thought if we pardoned Breckinridge, he would become a candidate for Governor, not on the Republican, but on the Anti-Bourbon ticket. The influence of a man like Breckinridge, at the time, would have been most useful." But Grant soon discovered that Radical Senators were generally opposed to giving Breckinridge the required Congressional pardon. Breckinridge himself did not want the office.

"I would not accept any office within the gift of the people, if I could get one," he said in 1866. "If I could be returned to my old place in the Senate, and should be permitted by Congress to take my seat, I would not consent to go back to Washington." General John Gordon remarked in his reminiscences, "No man in the Confederate army had surrendered a brighter political future, sacrificed more completely his personal ambition, or suffered more keenly from the perplexing conditions in his own State."

Breckinridge was never blind to Southern faults or to weak-nesses in Southern argument and attitudes. Colonel John S. Mosby, the famous partisan ranger, one of several prominent Confederates to embrace the Republican party after Appomattox, recalled that he heard Breckinridge say at a dinner in Baltimore, soon after returning from exile, that if the Southern Confederacy had survived, "there would have been such a spirit of local self-assertion that every county would have claimed the right to set up for itself." Certainly this "spirit of local self-assertion" had its effect in hastening Confederate defeat.

Breckinridge not only worked quietly to create conciliatory hearts and minds among his fellow Kentuckians, but he also participated, as did many former Confederate leaders, in the postwar encouragement of business and industrial expansion, especially the building of railroads. Not all these business efforts were successful, not all the railroads materialized, but they showed a willingness to look not only back to glory but forward, as the South slowly and steadily emerged from the ruins. He supported the construction of a railroad from Cincinnati to Chattanooga, and he served as vice president of the Lexington, Elizabethton and Big Sandy Railroad. "We have now in Kentucky," said Breckinridge in 1870, "more railroad Charters and fewer miles of railroads than any other State in the Union." This was a situation he helped to remedy.

Breckinridge was undoubtedly the most beloved and popular man in Kentucky. He remained quietly active until his health began to fail.

In 1875, Breckinridge underwent two operations for a liver condition. The operations were not successful. He died in Lexington at 5:45 p.m. on May 17, at the age of 54. He was conscious, propped up in bed, almost to the end, talking cheerfully to his family and friends, though often suffering great pain. With him were his wife, his two daughters, his son Clifton, and other relatives.

The New York *Times,* not overly sympathetic to Confederate "Brigadiers" as a rule, observed that "The General, in his last hours, awaited death with wonderful composure, passing away quietly and peacefully." The *Times* praised Breckinridge for having "since the collapse of the rebellion . . . maintained an absolute reserve; and his life closes unmarred by any of the public follies with which several of his companions in arms have been chargeable."

The Louisville *Courier-Journal* termed him Kentucky's "bravest, noblest, soldier-statesman." The Governor and local mayors issued proclamations expressing sorrow. Stores and public buildings and many homes throughout Kentucky were closed and draped with black. Extra trains brought friends of Breckinridge, many of them companions of the Mexican and Civil Wars, to Lexington to the funeral. Thousands followed the procession, the largest ever seen in Lexington, as it moved from the First Presbyterian Church to the cemetery. Soldiers, civilians, public officials—some on foot, some in carriages—moved in a mile-long entourage. At the head of the procession as chief marshal was General Basil Duke, Breckinridge's old friend, whose men had guarded the Confederate Cabinet in its long flight through Virginia and the Carolinas and had been among the last to surrender.

In January 1876, memorial services were held in both houses of the Kentucky Legislature, "feeling no apprehension that posterity will deprecate or underestimate the exalted virtues we know him to possess." Republicans and Democrats joined in praising one who had struggled to maintain the Union as a "confederacy of states under the Constitution," and, when that failed, had fought no less staunchly to create a Southern nation on the same basis, taking part in more battles in more parts of the Confederacy than any other commander. The words of tribute have a somewhat more convincing ring than legislative eulogies usually do—perhaps because the speakers believed what they were saying.

"Representative at 28, in Congress at 30, Vice President at 36, a Senator and candidate for President at 40," one speaker said. "Companionable and fascinating in society, successful beyond precedent in politics, brilliant and argumentative in debate, digni-

fied and impartial as a presiding officer, competent to the discharge
of duties assigned him. . . . Kentucky could but mourn her loss
and teach her sons to imitate his virtues."

"I think," said George B. Hodge, who had served in the Confederate Army with him, "he felt that the purpose for which he
was sent upon earth was accomplished. I think his refusal to
emerge from the reticence of his last years was owing to the feeling that the consistency of his career would have been marred by
any addition; and that, while honestly recognizing the decrees of
Providence as adverse to the political creed he professed and illustrated, he was willing that his life should go down to posterity
as an example of steadfast purity of principle and integrity of
conviction."

In 1886, a statue of Breckinridge by Edward Valentine was
erected opposite the courthouse in Lexington by the state. The
famous Kentuckian stands straight and tall, in the role in which
he was best known and most admired by his fellow citizens,
statesman and public speaker. Senator Joseph C. S. Blackburn, in
his address at the unveiling ceremonies, reviewed Breckinridge's
ante-bellum and Civil War career and said:

His own dignity, in the light of his antecedents, precluded any slavish
appeal for pardon. He never asked and never received the right of citizenship. He came back with the consent of the Government to live and die
an exile in the home of his fathers, to obey the laws that had been made
and to respect the authorities that had been established. Faithfully he observed the Constitution. Never obtruding himself upon public notice,
taking no part in the controversies pending; in the quiet of home and
friendship's circles he patiently waited the end that was so near.

Breckinridge would have been pleased to know that his sons
continued the family tradition of public service—winning elections handily when necessary. Clifton, a successful Arkansas
planter, served six terms in Congress and was appointed Minister
to Russia. Owen became a district attorney and legislator in California. Cabell was named Surveyor General of the Washington
Territory by President Cleveland.

In January 1958, a Circuit Court judge in Kentucky, at the

request of the Commonwealth's Attorney dismissed an 1862 indictment for "treason and conspiracy" against John Cabell Breckinridge and sundry other Kentuckians. The shade of Breckinridge could take at least some comfort from this long-delayed reprieve—and from the fact that no Confederate leader was ever, anywhere, at any time, actually tried for treason. In this sense at least, the irrepressible conflict can be pronounced a draw. Breckinridge lived and died believing that, in the words of Davis, "the war showed secession to be impracticable, but this did not prove it to be wrong." Indeed, Breckinridge was really saying the same thing when he told a group of Confederate veterans in Nashville in 1869, after returning from his exile, "I am the same man that I was." Those who heard him knew what he meant and cheered him to the echo. They were the same men, too.

Yet Breckinridge accepted verdicts, whether the Compromise of 1850, the Dred Scott decision, or Appomattox. If the verdict were a vindication of his own personal views, he was delighted; if it were not, he was acquiescent. In any case he doubted not the validity of his arguments—only their efficacy. He might lose a case; he might even lose a war; so far as he was concerned, he never lost his argument. Like Confederate money, the argument was good only to those who accepted it. Beyond that point it was a matter for memoirs and museums. All this Breckinridge knew. In fact, when he returned from exile, it was as if he, too, were a museum piece. He would not resurrect his former political and public self; instead he placed himself deliberately on the shelf, in the glass case, no longer militant—only moderate.

But, amazingly enough, from the "museum" he exerted more influence than some of the "Bourbons" and "Brigadiers" who chose involvement rather than retirement. From his glass house no stones were thrown, as Davis and others were wont to do. Thus no one cared to toss a stone at Breckinridge. So he died as Lee had—in losing his war gracefully, he lost his enemies, too.

4

Man on Horseback
NATHAN BEDFORD FORREST

"A man I have never seen . . . his name is Forrest." Thus, on April 9, 1865, at Appomattox, General Robert E. Lee is said to have revealed the name of the man he considered the greatest soldier under his command. Perhaps Nathan Bedford Forrest also represented a South many Southerners had never seen.

Here was the irony. The man whom the greatest Virginian recognized as his greatest soldier had not fought for an inch of Virginia soil during the whole war. It wouldn't have been fitting, anyway, for Old Nathan and his critter company. He didn't belong where wars were fought like tournaments, not this foot soldier on horseback. He didn't belong up there with the professional blue-bloods and the professional soldiers. He was the apotheosis of Southern yeomanry, a bearded handsome man, standing six feet two, with iron-gray hair and gray-blue eyes—generous and gentle, yet fierce and terrible in anger.

Yeomen like to defend their own firesides; they like to fight close to home; and that Forrest did—mostly in Tennessee, where he was born, and Alabama and Mississippi—and a little bit in Georgia. Never Virginia, for Forrest had been much too busy trying to hold together the Confederacy's poorly defended western outposts. This War had been fought over Virginia—except in Forrest's case. And that was as it should be.

Only a wise man like Lee could realize that Forrest was the real stuff of the Confederacy; the real stuff of the Old South—the reality that was, not the legend that never was. Like his South, he was self-made. Socially he became a gentleman, but it was a title that ill suited him. His parents, like Adam and Eve in the Lollard rhyme, were plain folk who had to delve and spin; and so were the parents of most Southerners of his day. Like his Confederacy, he was also a self-made contender who never dreamed he would or could be defeated.

The solid strength of the Confederacy was not the handful of generals but a nation full of sturdy privates. Forrest became a general, even though he had originally enlisted as a private. As far as he was concerned, he was a private all the way through the war.

If there ever were a citizen army, it was Forrest's men; if there ever were a citizen's general, it was Forrest. Few men of the day realized all this (Lee was one who did). The next generation forgot it, if they ever knew it. Instead, they read the memoirs of the literate generals (Forrest was *not* that kind of general) and imagined it was a war fought out of a book and not out of the hearts of men. There was even an attempt to turn old Nathan into a plumed knight and to transfuse his veins with blue blood to replace the red blood he was born with. Fortunately, the real Forrest survived all this humbug; fortunately also, the real South survived it, too, if with greater difficulty.

The real South, like the real Forrest, was something down underneath, where the man is; something that may be hidden but not destroyed by the superficialities of epaulettes and braid, of colonnades and moonlit verandas. All of these things Forrest came by in his lifetime, as did most ambitious and successful men of his day. He became a gentleman, and the South where he had his being was a South where for every person who was born a gentleman there were a thousand gentlemen who had been made.

Despite the fondness of the latter-day South to enjoy the luxury of ancestors, Southerners in the nineteenth century rarely inherited anything that was worth much, not even land. All these Southerners ever had, they had to get by the sweat of brows and anguish of soul. All they inherited was themselves. They had ancestors, but one single generation was enough to forget most of their names.

Whether they were well born or not mattered very little so long as they were born well on land they could live on and in a country they could live in. They took names not only from the grandparents whose names were perchance remembered but also from the country itself—a stream, a town, a county, a governor, or a President. Perhaps these latter were the more fitting namesakes. Appropriately enough, Nathan Bedford Forrest bore a family name, Nathan, taken from his grandfather, and the name of the Tennessee county where he was born—Bedford. And he liked to be called by the latter.

Genealogists dug up a Sir Thomas Forrest, a Jamestown pioneer, but Forrest himself could remember his lineage only as far back as Old Shadrach, the great grandfather who left Virginia for the "Valley of Humiliation," as Virginians dubbed North Carolina, four decades before the American Revolution. Settling in Orange County, the Forrests could well have been among the Regulators of the 1760's, who revolted against their corrupt officials and might have humbled the mighty royal governor of North Carolina had they known enough about military protocol to recognize the sound of truce beaten by the governor's drummer. Instead, they kept on fighting and were defeated. Orange County was good training ground for Bedford's ancestors. In 1806, the Forrests went across the mountains into Tennessee, where Nathan's father, William, plied the trade of a blacksmith and presently married a Scotch-Irish Presbyterian lass, Miriam Beck.

"I was borned in Marshal Co. Tenn. on 13th day of July 1821." These words were written by Nathan Bedford Forrest in his own hand on December 11, 1864, in the journal of Charles Todd Quintard, Connecticut-born rector of the Church of the Advent in Nashville, a Confederate chaplain, and later Bishop of Tennessee. (The "uncut diamond" of a general had spent the night with the learned rector and had consented to write in his diary.) What schooling he received was at a log school taught by John Laws, who apparently used the rod frequently on the boy, a fact to which both attested when they met at Corinth during the Civil War.

Bedford learned to read and write after a fashion, although to the end of his life he employed his own spelling—such as using "know" for "no"—and his speech abounded in archaic colloquialisms like "mout" for "might." In time, his misuse of the language engendered a picturesque legend that had enough truth in it to make it plausible. Antecedents meant as little to him in a sentence as they did on a family tree.

Little is known of his youth. Perhaps apocryphal but at least true to the later character of the man are several stories of unusual bravery, almost foolhardiness—battling a rattlesnake, diving for a lost knife, and dispersing a crowd of drunks at his uncle's tavern. At thirteen he was gathered up and taken by his father on one more pioneering venture—to settle newly-opened Chickasaw Indian lands in northern Mississippi. The homestead was in Tippah County, near what was then Old Salem. The soil was blessed with fertility, but less so than its inhabitants, who produced families as methodically as crops. In fact, children were to become a major export crop, for the area eventually produced more children than it could use and became a steady provider for the neighboring towns, especially cities like Memphis, Tennessee.

When Bedford was pushing sixteen, his father died, leaving him to assume the headship of the family. He now settled down earnestly to farm labor, and things were going well enough in 1841 for him to leave home with a company of volunteers from near-by Holly Springs formed to help the Texans, who reputedly had been attacked by the Mexicans. The expedition to Texas ended in a fiasco, for Texas proved to be in no apparent danger; and presently young Forrest was back home ready to settle down again, his roving spirit becalmed for the time being.

Now he turned to mercantile activities. At Hernando he became a horse trader in a firm operated by his uncle. There was an opportunity to show his mettle when his uncle Jonathan was attacked and slain in the village square by a band of four men. Forrest arrived just in time to take up the fight, felling two of the attackers with a pocket pistol and putting the other two to flight with a Barlow knife someone in the crowd of onlookers had handed him.

Another of Forrest's conquests was that of the hand of Mary Ann Montgomery, 1845. Miss Montgomery was a genteel lady of the plantation set. The first meeting came about when he pulled the Montgomery family carriage from a mudhole, while an ineffectual driver and two "suitors" stood around and watched. Needless to say, Forrest sent the suitors packing, not only then but later when he called at young Miss Montgomery's home to court her. Bedford and Mary Ann were married that fall, although her foster father, a Cumberland Presbyterian parson, objected. "You cuss and gamble," he complained to Forrest, "and Mary Ann is a church girl."

A married man with responsibilities, Forrest sought new directions for his enterprise. He opened a brickyard and even obtained a commission to build an academy, but this project failed as miserably as his own scant childhood educational efforts—thanks in this case to the perfidy of a partner.

In 1851, Forrest took his business operations to Memphis. There his mercantile ventures soon went beyond cattle trading and eventually embraced plantation real estate and cotton. Next he undertook to operate a slave market. Apparently he did not share the Southern yeoman's inborn dislike of Negroes. He was considered more benevolent than harsh in the treatment of his slaves, never separating families and refusing to sell to persons known to be severe.

After he purchased several plantations in Mississippi and Arkansas, he became at least technically a member of the plantation oligarchy. He, however, had earned his way into the elite class; and those who had inherited still looked down their aristocratic noses at him.

In Memphis Forrest continued to be something less than a quiet spectator of the city scene. In 1858, he was elected alderman, thanks in part to the courage he had displayed against a lynch-bent mob. A year later, he resigned this office and gave up his mercantile operations in Memphis. He now became a full-fledged Mississippi Delta planter. In 1861, he realized better than $30,000 from his cotton crop. As the records went, he had now arrived at the El Dorado of ante-bellum Southern enterprise. In fact, he estimated himself as being worth "a million and a half of dollars."

Soon Forrest was to arrive at the gentlemanly estate through another avenue—the military. On June 14, 1861, he volunteered as a private in the Seventh Tennessee Mounted Rifles, six days after his home state of Tennessee left the Union. Reputedly a Unionist, he had had no truck with the violent Secessionists, but once his own state was out of the Union, he was ready to do battle for the Southern cause.

The Civil War gave him a chance to exercise his talents for getting things done. Sheer persistence and dogged courage had transformed him from a yeoman farmer into a merchant, a slave trader, and finally a planter. Had he been given a major role in assisting the Confederacy in making something out of its nothing, the story might have been quite different. He could recruit an army out of almost nobody, he could arm it with almost nothing, he could subsist it from almost nowhere. The only thing he did not know about logistics, perhaps, was how to spell it. He could perform impossible marches, he could cross unpassable streams, he could defeat unconquerable opponents. If there were ever a case of native military genius, Forrest was it.

Unburdened by a knowledge of military book learning, he was a genius at improvisation, one of the first soldiers to realize that the cavalry could someday become obsolete. He used it, of course, for what it was worth, but he would gladly have exchanged a horse for an able-bodied soldier. The horse was a beautiful thing to behold and it was an intelligent animal withal; moreover, men looked impressive, indeed, astride this noble mount. But Forrest never failed to see the soldiers for the horses. He used his horses just as any good planter would have—as a means of going places and of getting things done. Often in battle Forrest would have his men dismount and fight as foot soldiers; for it was, indeed, his men that won battles, not his horses.

Forrest had been a private for less than a month when he was detached and given the rank of lieutenant colonel, with a commission to recruit and organize a mounted battalion for Confederate service. He set out for Kentucky, where the best horses were raised, to do most of his recruiting, and along with his troops he obtained supplies, including arms, for his men. He paid for things out of his own pocket. From then on, he fought the War very much on his own, supplying his men with practically no help from the Confederacy but with much unintentional help from the Yankees in the form of captured supplies and equipment. His strategy was his own, too—mostly his own invention, in fact. He could rout gunboats with rifles or horse-troops with dismounted cavalry, whichever the occasion warranted. Certainly he never fought by the book, for he hadn't read it.

Book or no book, Forrest rose rapidly. By July 1862, he was a brigadier general. When he gave General Braxton Bragg a piece of his mind in 1863, he was not punished; instead, he was transferred and promoted to major general, where there would be fewer superiors to curse. Before the War was over, there were few men high or low who had not received his chastisement. His particular ire was directed at idlers and at officers who took themselves too seriously or overdid the privileges of rank. One story tells of a persistent soldier who had submitted a third letter requesting leave. The irate Forrest scribbled his own answer on the back: "I told you twist, Goddammit know." And when his cavalry turned amphibious for a hasty crossing of the Tennessee River, the general interrupted his own efforts at the poles to toss a do-nothing lieutenant overboard. "Now, damn you, get hold of the oars and go to work!"

Although Forrest anecdotes are legion, most of them are word-of-mouth tradition, taken down sooner or later by more literate folk than he. There are extant, however, a few authentic examples of his own handwriting (together with a host of forgeries). One is a letter written from Corinth, Mississippi, in May 1862, to a friend in Memphis. It is highly original in its spelling:

Sir your note of 21 Ins is to hand I did not fully understand the contents and ask for Information the amount you ask for is it for a publick
contrabution or is it for my dues due the lodge I wish you to give me
the amt due the log [lodge] from me as you did not State it in your
notice or the amount asked for I had a small brush with the Enamy on
yesterday I Suceded in gaining thir rear and got in to thir entrench-
ments 8 miles from ham burg and 5 behind farmington and Burned a
portion of thir camp at that place they wair not looking for me I taken
them by Surprise they run like Suns of Biches I captured the Rev Dr
Warin from Ilanois and one fin Sorel Stud this army is at this time in
front of our Entrenchment I look for a fite soon and a big one when it
coms off Cant you come up and take a hand this fite wil do to hand down
to your childrens children I feel confident of our success

your Respect
N. B. Forrest

Any combat with Forrest was likely to be a tale to be handed
down to one's "children's children." This the Federals knew no
less than the Confederates. Defeating him proved to be the most
difficult job the Union generals ever tackled. At Fort Donelson
he took his own men out almost singlehanded, although the rest
of the garrison surrendered. After defeats at Shiloh and Vicksburg
had all but left the Mississippi Valley to the Federals, he maneu-
vered brilliantly in northern Mississippi and western Tennessee
to frustrate the forces of occupation. Every Federal army sent out
to destroy "that devil Forrest," as Union General William T.
Sherman called him, came to grief.

During the siege of Atlanta, he so demoralized Sherman's
supply lines in eastern Tennessee, that the Yankees found it more
expedient to march to the sea rather than back to Tennessee.
When Confederate General John B. Hood invaded Tennessee
while Sherman was marching in the opposite direction, it was
Forrest who skillfully commanded Hood's cavalry forces around
Franklin and Nashville and maintained a brilliant rearguard
action to enable his superior to escape complete annihilation. In
February 1865, he was rewarded with the rank of lieutenant
general.

Not till the War was nearly over did Jefferson Davis realize the greatness of Forrest. But in the last anguished moments of the Confederacy, it was Forrest that Davis hoped might serve as a leader to carry on the struggle in the west. For a man whose shrewdness and foresightedness had enabled him to win battles by getting there "fustest with the mostest," this must have been ironic indeed; for if Forrest knew how to win, he also knew when he was licked. Nevertheless, it was the same Forrest who had refused to surrender at Donelson who doggedly outlasted the Confederacy by a whole month and became the last Confederate general east of the Mississippi to lay down his arms.

The month between Lee's surrender at Appomattox and Forrest's surrender at Gainesville, Alabama, found Forrest attempting to hold off the penetration of southern Alabama by the Union cavalry under General James H. Wilson. Wilson, an engineering officer with West Point training, was the antithesis of the untutored Forrest; yet by the end of the war even the book generals had learned how to get there "fustest," and Wilson was now penetrating Alabama with a swiftness Forrest could appreciate. Perhaps only the capture by Wilson of Forrest's dispatches prevented a showdown combat between the two on equal terms. As it was, the Confederates lost Selma, the last battle of any consequence in the war. And Forrest, repeating his usual tactics, managed to ride out of the falling city with his men.

The two men finally met at Cahaba on April 8 under flag of truce. It was the day before Appomattox. They dined and discussed an exchange of prisoners, acting withal as if they were "old acquaintances." There were to be further friendly relations between Forrest and Wilson after the War.

On April 9, while Lee was in the process of surrendering to Grant, Wilson was preparing to set out the next day on a triumphal march to Montgomery, where the United States flag was raised on April 12, the fourth anniversary of Sumter. Forrest remained behind, still hoping to rally his forces, making his base at Gainesville. Rumors of Lee's surrender were now rife; meanwhile, Sherman and Johnston had negotiated a peace in the Carolinas on April 18. On April 25 Forrest charged his men to "stand firm" and remain "true" to the colors, but General Richard Taylor was preparing to yield to Federal General E. R. S. Canby, ending all fighting east of the Mississippi. On May 4 Taylor and Canby agreed upon terms of surrender, and two days later Taylor declared Confederate resistance under his command to be at an end.

Would Forrest acquiesce? There were rumors that he would become the last protecting arm for Jefferson Davis, now in flight somewhere in the Carolinas. Ironically, it was General Wilson who captured the fleeing Confederate President. Meanwhile there was talk of continuing resistance across the Mississippi. There was strong sentiment, too, for taking refuge in foreign lands. Many of the younger men hotheadedly favored a Mexican venture and doubtless would have undertaken it had Forrest given any encouragement.

Forrest pondered all prospects. Conferring with his aide, Major Charles W. Anderson, the general gave bent to his deep despair when, as the two reached a crossroads, he observed that he cared little which way they went. "If one of them led to hell and the other to Mexico, I wouldn't care which one I took."

In the end Forrest chose the road to hell. Apparently many of his men would have gone with him to Mexico; but some would have remained behind. He chose that all should remain, and that he should "share the fate of my men." On May 9, at Gainsville, Alabama, he issued an address calling upon his soldiers to accept the outcome peaceably. The words were written out by Major Anderson, but history has taken it as pure Forrest, as it essentially was. It read:

That we are beaten is a self-evident fact, and any further resistance on our part would be justly regarded as the very height of folly and rashness. The armies of Generals Lee and Johnston having surrendered, you are the last of all the troops of the Confederate States Army east of the Mississippi River to lay down your arms. The cause for which you have so long and manfully struggled, and for which you have braved dangers, endured privations and sufferings, and made so many sacrifices, is today hopeless. The government which we sought to establish and perpetuate is at an end. Reason dictates and humanity demands that no more blood be shed. . . . It is your duty and mine to lay down our arms, submit to the "powers that be," and to aid in restoring peace and establishing law and order throughout the land. The terms upon which you surrendered are favorable to all. They manifest a spirit of magnanimity and liberality on the part of the Federal authorities which should be met on our part by a faithful compliance with all the stipulations and conditions therein expressed. . . .

Civil War, such as you have just passed through, naturally engenders feelings of animosity, hatred and revenge. It is our duty to divest ourselves of all such feelings, and, so far as it is in our power to do so, to cultivate friendly feelings toward those with whom we have so long contested, and heretofore so widely but honestly differed. . . . The attempt made to establish a separate and independent confederation has failed, but the consciousness of having done your duty faithfully and to the end will in some measure repay you for the hardships you have undergone. . . . I have never on the field of battle sent you where I was unwilling to go myself, nor would I now advise you to a course which I felt myself unwilling to pursue. You have been good soldiers, you can be good citizens. Obey the laws, preserve your honor, and the government to which you have surrendered can afford to be and will be magnanimous.

N. B. Forrest, *Lieutenant-General*

It was now time to be a good citizen, and he must set the example. Symbolically, the battle flag of the 7th Tennessee Regiment —made from the bridal dress of a Southern belle from Aberdeen, Mississippi—was cut into pieces and carried home by the men. This was the relic of a crusade. The battle flag was irreparably sundered; so was the resistance of the last troops east of the Mississippi.

Forrest's moderation was somewhat unexpected, particularly as far as the Yankees were concerned. Sherman had taken it for granted that men like Forrest would organize bands of desperadoes or guerillas and offer continued resistance to both the Federal government and civilian ways of life. "They will not work and their Negroes are gone, plantations destroyed, etc.," observed Sherman.

Of course, what really happened Sherman hardly expected. The Southern cavalry raiders, who had given the Northerners something to invent atrocity stories about, were no more inclined to turn into peacetime desperadoes than was the South's own candidate for atrocity legends, Sherman himself.

It was, of course, the peculiar fate of both Forrest and Sherman to engender atrocity propaganda against themselves. Usually, both Forrest and Sherman had better sense than to believe their own propaganda, unless they wanted to; and in their case we may depend upon professional rivalry to ensure enmity. They were happy, indeed, to believe their own lies against each other.

Forrest did not, however, live up to the reputation with which Sherman and the Northerners had endowed him. He had not been brought up to practice that military protocol which dictates honor among generals of opposing armies, but Forrest learned it quickly. He surrendered in good faith, calling upon his men to forget past bitterness and accept the outcome without reservation. Henceforth he felt it incumbent upon himself to "cultivate friendly feelings toward those with whom we have so long contended." We may be assured that these words, though written by his scribe Anderson, were Forrest's own conviction, even if they were expressed in more gentle prose than the general himself would have used.

That Forrest sincerely meant what Anderson said for him is best indicated by subsequent actions, which spoke louder than words. In fact, Forrest so completely accepted the new order that occasionally doubts were raised as to his loyalty to the South. What Forrest did was what any practical man was disposed to do, acting in accordance with the first law of nature. He set out promptly to recoup his fortune, which had been largely wiped out by the War.

Forrest had used his own resources to fight, including some forty-five of his slaves, who accompanied his army as orderlies, teamsters, and laborers. He had told the Negroes that this was a war upon slavery, that if they went with him and the South lost, they would be free, that if on the other hand the South won, he would set them free. A year and a half before the War ended, he became convinced the Confederacy would lose; and, fearing that he might be killed, he prepared emancipation papers for these Negroes.

War ended; Forrest's slave "soldiers" were now free; but most of them chose to return with their former owner to work his Mississippi plantation lands. In the last week of May 1865, he was in Grenada with his slaves, preparing to go to his plantation in Coahoma County. Accompanying him were seven young officers of the United States Army. One of them became a partner of the general. To these officers he rented land, on his own and neighboring plantations. During the next year these Union men made a crop, the Confederate general and the Union officers helping one another. In fact, Forrest used them to get laborers for him, among which were around 200 Negroes who had served in the Union army.

Apparently Forrest maintained the most cordial social relations with the Yankee farmers. They even made his house "their home on Sundays." In the Congressional investigation of the Klan in 1871, Forrest was asked whether he had more confidence in these Northern men "than others down there had"; he replied laconically, "I think I had," and then went on to point out that all Northern men in the postwar South were not necessarily regarded with disfavor. "Some men go down there and go to planting, and do not have anything to do with politics, behave themselves, and do not mix with the Negroes more than white people. They are looked upon as a different class of people." Were they called "carpetbaggers"? Forrest replied, "I do not know that they are called anything except Southern citizens. I know some men who stand as fair . . . as anybody we have there." So Bedford Forrest was practicing what he had preached at the end of the fighting.

Only Bedford's horse, King Philip, seemed to be unreconstructible. In 1865, he charged a company of blue-coated Federal soldiers who visited Forrest's plantation. Several years later, he also routed a group of blue-coated Memphis policemen.

For two years following the War, Forrest "planted," working as diligently as he had done thirty years before when his family had to start from nothing in Tippah County. He now described himself as a "beggar." This he hardly was; for whatever he did, he refused to depend upon others to succor him. Instead, he busily set about recovering his fortune. When, in 1867, he decided to give up planting and return to Memphis, he was able to sell out at a substantial price.

Forrest's relations with his colored workers had on the whole been good. As before, he was a hard but fair master. Once, when he stopped a Negro engaged in wife-beating, he was attacked by the enraged man; but the general managed to seize an ax and split the Negro's head. The incident brought an angry mob of 200 Negroes, mostly former Union soldiers, to his door. Armed with two pistols, the old general came to the porch. Nobody but Forrest would have had the presence of mind to think of his stratagem. It was simple. He merely shouted in succession the orders "Halt! . . . Order arms! . . . Ground Arms!" All were obeyed. He next ordered the men back to work, and they went. Shortly afterward, Forrest was acquitted in a court presided over by a Negro judge.

Later, after Forrest had left his plantation and entered the railroad business, he managed to quell a race riot at Crawford, Mississippi, where a crowd of 800 Negroes were laying siege to the town after an incident between a white man and a group of marching Negroes. He arrived in the midst of the excitement. First he undertook to quiet the whites by promising to appeal personally to the Negroes. "I then got a horse," reports the general, "and rode over to the Negroes and made a speech to them," whereupon they dispersed and the incident was over.

Surprisingly enough, Forrest was apparently far less perturbed over the enfranchisement of the Negroes than many of his compatriots were. He opposed Negro suffrage but was willing to accept it if the Negro-Radical regime in Tennessee would also return the vote to the white Democrats who had been disfranchised. Meanwhile, he made no effort to prevent his colored railroad hands from voting, if they could qualify to do so.

Forrest enjoyed, of course, a formidable reputation, particularly in the North, as an abuser of Negroes. Actually, he was grossly misrepresented. Much of this ill fame derived from his supposedly wanton massacre of a Negro garrison at Fort Pillow in 1864. A Congressional investigation in that year accused him of butchery, but the evidence of more sober times largely discredited the story. General Sherman himself, among others, was indisposed to blame him. Nevertheless, much was made of this atrocity story both during the War—particularly in the election year of 1864—and afterward.

Since Forrest was to the North as Sherman was to the South, an excellent subject to be lied about, his name continued to be anathema to many Northerners. Only Jefferson Davis—perhaps not even he—enjoyed more figurative hangings from sour apple trees. Once when Forrest journeyed into Northern country, he was accosted at a small town station by the local bully who had promised to give him a licking. Remaining on his train, as requested by the conductor, he waited until the giant appeared at the door of the car demanding "that damned butcher, Forrest." Whereupon he rushed forward, eyes ablaze. "I am Forrest," he answered, "what do you want?" The bully suddenly turned and fled, a crowd of onlookers enjoying a huge laugh at the expense of his challenger.

Later in the same trip, Forrest was greeted in his hotel room by an irate lady who demanded to know whether he had "murdered those dear colored people at Fort Pillow." The reply was instant: "Yes, madam, I killed the men and women for my soldiers' dinner and ate the babies myself for breakfast."

Despite his poor standing with the Northern public, Forrest set out after the War to prove himself a good citizen. As early as July, 1865, he applied in Mississippi for a pardon. This he was to be denied for nearly three more years. Nevertheless, he urged his Confederate compatriots to seek pardons. That such gestures were not completely rejected in the North is evident from the fact that some friendly hands were extended by prominent Northerners. One of these was a Missouri Unionist, Frank Blair, who "conceived a very great personal attachment" for the general and personally interceded with President Johnson in Forrest's behalf. Blair commended Forrest's "noble bearing" in accepting without complaint the result of the War and in encouraging others to "accept it in the same spirit." All this was significant, said Blair, in view of the fact that his influence was "more powerful than that of any man in West Tennessee."

Despite high hopes and noble talk, the disposition of men like Forrest to forget and be forgiven was not reciprocated by the Radical Republicans in power. It was difficult enough for the wartime soldiers to become good citizens; it was next to impossible for the wartime politicians to do so. From the latter he expected reprisals. In fact, when Confederate Admiral Raphael Semmes, of raider *Alabama* fame, was arrested, General Dabney Maury, who had a talk with Semmes at New Orleans, became convinced that Forrest would be next; so he hied himself to Memphis to warn him. Forrest was still at his plantation, but Dabney despatched a letter by messenger, advising escape to Mexico, and even arranged with Forrest's business partner, Colonel Sam Tate, to send letters of credit so that he might make a speedy departure. His reply was characteristic: "This is my country. I am hard at work upon my plantation, and carefully observing the obligations of my parole. If the Federal government does not regard it, they'll be sorry. I shan't go away."

His reply was followed by a visit to the Federal commander at Memphis, who reassured him as to his parole. But after a celebrated raid into Memphis in 1864, Forrest had been indicted for treason, and in the spring of 1866 he undertook to clear this charge by making a $10,000 bond in the Federal court in Memphis, but the charge was not pursued.

All things considered, it was indeed nothing short of miraculous that Forrest did escape imprisonment. Perhaps it was the realization on the part of even his worst enemies that he was thoroughly honest about his loyalties. Once the War was over, he was ready to be "reconstructed." In fact, in 1871 he told a Congressional committee: "I have said, and have always said, that there was no time during the War that I would not have been willing to have taken up the old flag with the northern people and fought any other nation, and give the last drop of blood I had. I have said that, and I say it yet."

Such Unionist sentiment was no pseudo-patriotic humbug. Here was the same intense nationalism that had moved the American yeoman since the birth of the Republic. It had resisted nullification (the doctrine that the states could nullify Federal acts deemed unconstitutional) a generation earlier, when Southerners talked of ignoring the tariff law of 1832 as "null and void"; it had looked askance at secession in 1861; and it had provided the solid core of reconstructibility in the war-torn South of 1865. It had always been quick at the trigger, but it preferred fighting foreigners to fighting Americans. It even made the fighting of a civil war somewhat casual at times. For men who usually ate the same victuals, drank the same spirits, chewed the same tobacco, sniffed the same snuff, sang the same war songs, told the same jokes, and "cussed" in the same language, it would have been usual to have common enemies, and not one another. No wonder fraternizing on the battle ground was a frequent occurrence. Fraternizing after the war should even come more easily.

Disposed to render unto Caesar the things that were Caesar's, Forrest was willing to accept the Reconstruction governments of the South, even their Fourteenth and Fifteenth Amendments. "I told the people," he remarked, "that they were inevitable and should be accepted." Forrest did not, however, condone the wholesale disfranchisement of the white Democrats under the Reconstruction program of the Radicals. In Tennessee, in 1865, the vindictive old Unionist, Parson William G. Brownlow, had become Governor. By the time Forrest moved to Memphis in 1867, he had become convinced that Radical Reconstruction was designed to destroy the South.

Neither a "scalawag" nor a "carpetbagger," Brownlow, like President Andrew Johnson of Tennessee, had remained during the War a continuing Unionist, secession or no secession. With Confederates excluded from voting, Brownlow easily got control

of the Reconstruction government of Tennessee and in 1866
brought the state back in the Union ahead of all of its Confederate
sisters. Using the militia, which contained many Negroes, Brownlow now proceeded to "police" the state, creating a reign of terror
for those who had served the Confederacy. It was at this point
that the white man chose to fight back, using a most unique
agency, the newly organized Ku Klux Klan, of which Forrest was
to become the leader. Forrest's associations with the Klan seem
to have begun not long after his return to Memphis in 1867.

At Memphis he at first followed the example of practically
every Confederate general of the day; he went into the insurance
business, casting his own lot with the Planters Insurance Company,
of which he became president. Of course, Confederate generals
had scarcely more than their names to contribute toward the operation of an insurance company, but that was enough. Often the
money came from Northern sources, but the name of a reputable
Southern general was sufficient to decontaminate the lucre.

Insurance was highly popular after the war. In fact, with war
widows and war orphans much in evidence, no better dramatiza-
tion of the need for insurance could be found. Forrest's flyer into
insurance was vigorous but brief. His company was soon in trouble,
and he blamed it all upon the disturbing influences of Radical
Reconstruction. He wrote to a friend in Mississippi:

I have no business, nor do I no of any by which you could find employment in this City at any price. I have sold out all the contracts I have
had on hand and am now settleing up my affairs as rapidly as possible,
believing as I do that Everything under the laws that will be inaugurated
by the military authority will result in ruin to our people.

In February 1868, Forrest ended up in bankruptcy. Once more
he was back where he had started thirty years earlier. In his
despair he pondered a filibustering expedition to Mexico; some
of his compatriots had already gone to that country to found
colonies under Emperor Maximilian. He imagined that with
30,000 men he could conquer Mexico in six months and become
its "King or President." This new country he would open to
European and Southern immigrants. He did not think the United

States would interfere, as it would be glad to get rid of him. Actually, he had no time to take his proposed venture very seriously. In fact, as a friend remarked who had heard him recite his filibustering pipe dream, "from the appearance of things at Washington, if Mr. Forrest would just keep quiet a little while he can get enough fighting in this country."

Indeed, new versions of "riding with Forrest" were about to be born. Before the year 1868 had ended, Forrest was busy building railroads; he was also busy directing the affairs of the Ku Klux Klan. In fact, his railroad activities formed a better cloak than a Klansman's hood for his maneuvers against the reign of terror created by the Radicals in the South.

Forrest's railroad ventures involved the presidency of the Selma, Marion, and Memphis Railroad, a combination of the two roads in Alabama, Mississippi, and Tennessee, which are now parts of the Frisco and Southern lines. He traveled far and wide peddling stock in his railroad, selling it not only to individuals but also to counties and cities, which voted by public election to purchase stock. The sales campaigns were vigorous enough. Using his name and his reputation, which were about the only assets the company had, he sold large quantities of stock in the enterprise, only to have the company go down in collapse after the panic of 1873 and the yellow fever epidemic that ravaged Memphis in that year. Once more he was bankrupt, and the waning years of his life were plagued with the painful memories—not to say litigation—engendered by the collapse of the company.

If Forrest's railroad ventures were destined to come to grief, the other project in which he had become involved by 1868 also ended in dissolution; but before it did so, it had done much to change the face—or at least the color—of Southern politics. It was the Ku Klux Klan, of which he became the Grand Wizard. Forrest conceived of this organization more as a means of economic and social than political control. Indeed, Forrest was rarely interested in politics except where the economic and social order was concerned. Forrest apparently accepted, if reluctantly, the political restrictions placed upon him and other ex-Confederates; but what disturbed him deeply was the reign of terror occasioned by the advent of carpetbag rule.

Forrest was troubled by the prevalence of "disorders, particularly by the blacks." There was even fear of a revolution such as had occurred in Santo Domingo—a "war of races." As he said later to a Congressional committee:

During the war our servants remained with us, and behaved very well. When the war was over our servants began to mix with the Republicans, and they broke off from the Southern people, and were sulky and insolent. There was a general fear throughout the country that there would be an uprising, and that with those men who had stopped among us—those men who came in among us, came there and went to our kitchens and consulted with the negroes—many of them never came about the houses at all.

Specifically, the Klan was the Southern white man's answer to the Loyal Leagues, secret political societies which promoted the Negroes' interests and were generally credited with encouraging organized violence by Negroes. The Klan was only one of a number of organizations with similar purposes, including the Knights of the Golden Circle, the Order of the Camellia, and the Pale Faces. In fact, Forrest himself belonged to the last before he joined the Klan. But the Klan became the supreme agency of resistance to Radical Reconstruction, and at the appropriate time it took unto itself as its leader Nathan Bedford Forrest.

The Klan first organized innocently enough. It began as one of the countless secret societies of a purely social nature that were forever appearing in the heyday of fraternalism, the late nineteenth century. It all started on a December day in 1865 at Pulaski, Tennessee, when a group of six young war veterans decided to relieve their boredom by forming an "order." Since this was an era of Greek fraternal names, the members hit upon the word *Kuklos,* or "circle," to which they added the alliterative word "clan." From here it was an easy step to Ku Klux Klan, which made as likely a set of initials as could be found anywhere. Outlandish costumes were not unknown in such societies; and the hood and sheet of the Pulaski organization attracted considerable attention in the town, particularly among the superstitious freedmen. Almost overnight, the Klansmen realized that in their horseplay they had stumbled upon a tremendously effective agency for terrifying Negroes, particularly the more difficult ones, into circumspect behavior.

Born in middle Tennessee, the Klan spread so rapidly in that area that soon it numbered at least 40,000 state members. Its rapid growth can be accounted for in part by the fact that Tennessee, being the first state to become "reconstructed," was experiencing the most serious disturbances. In particular, the Klan's activities were designed to thwart Parson Brownlow's efforts to use the militia against the rebellious white Democrats. Speaking at the Congressional investigation of Klan activities in 1871, Forrest said that he thought the Klan arose

. . . about the time the militia were called out, and Governor Brownlow issued his proclamation stating that the troops would not be injured for what they should do to rebels; such a proclamation was issued. There was a great deal of insecurity felt by the Southern people. There were a great many Northern men coming down there, forming leagues all over the country. The Negroes were holding night meetings; were going about; were becoming very insolent; and the Southern people all over the State were very much alarmed. I think many of the organizations did not have any name; parties organized themselves so as to be ready in case they were attacked. Ladies were ravished by some of these Negroes, who were tried and put in the penitentiary, but were turned out in a few days afterward. There was a great deal of insecurity in the country, and I think this organization was got up to protect the weak, with no political intention at all.

The Klan was not long in expanding beyond its Tennessee locale. Similar organizations appeared in nearly every spot in the South where there was a large Negro population. Actually the whole thing was almost spontaneous in development. The whites were casting about for a secret organization to combat the work of the Loyal Leagues. The Ku Klux Klan of Pulaski was simply a timely naming of a baby that was already born. Any other organization might have provided the name and suddenly found itself a purpose. Fate and alliteration gave Pulaski the priority. The original Klan had as its chief officer the "Grand Cyclops." Its meeting place was the "den." These terms survived. Soon state and regional organizations appeared, and superior offices, those of "Grand Dragon" and "Grand Wizard," were created. In Tennessee, where the organization first achieved notoriety, Confederate General George W. Gordon served as the first Grand Dragon of the state. Under Gordon a "prescript," or constitution, was drawn up at a convention held in Room 10 of the new Maxwell House at Nashville in April 1867. In this outline of purposes and organization the name of the Klan never appeared; instead the body was identified only by asterisks. The prescript began with an acknowledgment of the supremacy of United States law. Early in 1868 the statement was revised to include a declaration of the Klan's "character and objects":

This is an institution of Chivalry, Humanity, Mercy and Patriotism; embodying in its genius and its principles all that is chivalric in conduct, noble in sentiment, generous in manhood and patriotic in purpose; its peculiar objects being

First: To protect the weak, the innocent, and the defenseless from the indignities, wrongs and outrages of the lawless, the violent and the brutal; to relieve the injured and oppressed; to succor the suffering and unfortunate, and especially the widows and orphans of Confederate soldiers.

Second: To protect and defend the Constitution of the United States, and all laws passed in conformity thereto, and to protect the States and the people thereof from all invasion from any source whatever.

Third: To aid and assist in the execution of all constitutional laws, and to protect the people from unlawful seizure, and from trial except by their peers in conformity with the laws of the land.

The Klan made a special effort to identify itself with Southern tradition, its knights often referring to their nocturnal apparitions as the ghosts of the Confederate dead. Certainly the majority of the members were live Confederate veterans. In its best days, it seems to have been highly selective as to membership, carefully avoiding irresponsible elements. Forrest testified before the Congressional committee investigating the Klan:

My information was that they admitted no man who was not a gentleman, and a man who could be relied upon to act discreetly; not men who were in the habit of drinking, boisterous men, or men liable to commit error or wrong, or anything of that sort; that is what I understood.

There is a story, once widely believed, to the effect that Robert E. Lee was approached to serve as Grand Wizard of the Klan. Pleading ill health, Lee refused but supposedly wrote a letter giving his blessing to the movement, even though his role must remain "invisible." Hence the term "Invisible Empire" came to be applied to the organization. Lee was also said to have approved the selection of Forrest in his stead. Whether Lee did all this— and he probably did not—makes little difference. His "letter" was accepted as valid by those who wanted to believe it.

Forrest was not one of the earliest Klansmen. But already in Memphis he had organized a group of "secret police" immediately after the War to function on election day, and later he had joined the Pale Faces. Apparently he was the one to whom the troubled whites intuitively turned in the first disturbing days of Reconstruction. Forrest later recalled that he "was getting at that time from fifty to one hundred letters a day, and had a private secretary writing all the time. I was receiving letters from all the Southern States, men complaining, being dissatisfied, persons whose friends had been killed, or their families insulted, and they were writing to me to know what they ought to do."

In this state of affairs he was a natural leader. The story goes that he soon decided to take himself to Nashville to join the Klan. This was not, of course, the first time he had set out to join an army. In Nashville he sought out his old chief of artillery, John W. Morton, who headed the local den. Morton reportedly took him into a secluded spot beyond the city and there gave him the oath. "The worst swearing I ever did," Forrest said. That night he was initiated in Room 10 of the Maxwell House.

He promptly became the Grand Wizard, being elected apparently sometime in May 1867. The fighting South was once more alive; its greatest man on horseback was at the helm of the "invisible empire" of the embattled postwar South. Although he used the Klan as a political force, particularly against such Radical governments as that of Parson Brownlow in Tennessee, there was still a sort of political detachment in what he was doing. Once more he was the general in the field, not the politician in the council chamber. Many of his operations were in fact somewhat strange for a Klansman. Republicans were not, for example, anathema to him. As he said with respect to his canvassing of the area through which his new railroad was to go: "I said when I started out with my roads that railroads had no politics; that I wanted the assistance of everybody; that railroads were for the general good of the whole country. We have had no political discussions along the line of my road; we have had no difficulty."

In Hale County, Alabama, when the scalawag probate judge, Joseph Blackford, who had "given a great deal of bad advice to the Negroes, and kept them in confusion, and off the plantations," was set upon by Klansmen, Forrest gave the victim protection. Blackford had held "large meetings of Negroes at his house," but Forrest chose to give him sanctuary because "he and I had canvassed two counties together" in behalf of the railroad! "He assisted me in my elections," Forrest observed. "In fact I had the assistance of Republicans in all the elections I held in each county, except Greene County."

This was the Grand Wizard of the Klan, meeting the enemy under flag of truce, as it were, so that railroads could be built. Yet, at the same time, Forrest was organizing dens and directing Klan activities wherever he went. But whether he recruited for the night riders or for the iron horse, he acted with a Machiavellian sense of expediency. Each was a job to be done, and he was military man enough to see that policies were carried out, even if dubious means might sometimes become involved in the achieving of ends.

Wherever Forrest went, the Klan was sure to abound. When he campaigned for railroads in northwest Alabama, there followed a concomitant spurt of Klan activity. Similarly, in Mississippi did

Klan and Forrest ride at one and the same time. When his railroad company headquarters were temporarily located at Aberdeen, the night riders were soon in evidence, taking their vengeance out chiefly on Negro schools. Also in Georgia, North Carolina, and Arkansas, the arrival of Forrest and the Klan were significantly related events.

In the year 1868, when the Klan was probably at the peak of its influence, its leader, Nathan Bedford Forrest, was in the thick of public affairs, coming indeed as near to complete political involvement as he ever did.

It was the year for a Presidential election, the first since the war ended. The Democrats held their convention in New York, and Forrest was a delegate. Naturally, he attracted much attention, particularly in the New York press, which for the most part eyed him suspiciously, muttering reminders of Fort Pillow. However, the *Herald* described him as "one of the best reconstructed rebels." The convention nominated a New Yorker, Horatio Seymour, whom Forrest actively supported once his own candidate, Andrew Johnson, failed to muster sufficient votes to win.

The campaign that followed was a "bloody shirt" affair, in which most Southern leaders, particularly Forrest, came in for severe treatment. "There were a great many things said in regard to myself," he remarked later, "that I looked upon as gotten up to affect the elections in the North."

In Tennessee the situation quickly reached the ultimatum stage. On August 1, his name appeared on a list of thirteen Tennessee leaders, all generals in the Confederate army, who filed a protest against the Brownlow regime, particularly its militia policies. This protest was drawn up at a "Council of Peace" in Nashville. Forrest, arguing the matter before a legislative committee, warned the Radicals: "Abolish the Loyal League and the Ku Klux Klan; let us come together and stand together."

In a speech delivered subsequently at Brownsville, he did not mince words. "I for one do not want any more war," he argued. He had, indeed, seen all the bloodshed he cared to. He implored his fellow Democrats to avoid giving the Radicals any excuse for bringing on war. But, he warned, "if they bring this war upon us, there is one thing I will tell you—that I shall not shoot any Negroes so long as I can see a white Radical to shoot, for it is the Radicals who will be to blame. . . ."

Late in August, a reporter from the Cincinnati *Commercial* attempted to interview him about the Klan and political issues in the South. Forrest, not one to enjoy being interviewed, was uncooperative and, to make matters worse, ill with a "sick headache," the result of an illness he had contracted at the New York convention. In fact, during the interview he spent "part of the time vomiting," and after twenty minutes ended the conversation and offered to talk further in the evening. The reporter did not return. On September 1 an account of the interview was published.

The article in the *Commercial* proved to be sensational, for in it Forrest was quoted as revealing certain information about the Ku Klux Klan—its size, its objects, and its activities. He was so troubled by the article that he wrote a letter refuting certain parts of it. Nevertheless, it is apparent that in the original interview Forrest had come dangerously close to revealing his own connections with the Klan. The general was quoted as saying:

If they attempt to carry out Governor Brownlow's proclamation by shooting down Ku Klux Klansmen . . . if they go to hunting down and shooting these men, there will be war, and a bloodier one than we have ever witnessed. I have told these Radicals here what they might expect in such an event. I have no powder to burn killing Negroes. I intend to kill the Radicals. I have told them this and more. There is not a Radical leader in this town but is a marked man; and if a trouble should break out, not one of them would be left alive. I have told them that they were trying to create a disturbance and they slip out and leave the consequences to fall upon the Negro; but they can't do it. Their houses are picketed, and when the fight comes not one of them would ever get out of this town alive. We don't intend they shall ever get out of the country. But I want it distinctly understood that I am opposed to any war, and will only fight in self-defense. If the militia attack us, we will resist to the last; and, if necessary, I think I could raise 40,000 men in five days ready for the field.

In the midst of the excitement, Forrest found himself on the verge of a duel. One of his most choleric critics in the North was General Judson Kilpatrick, a veritable collector of atrocity stories about Forrest. Forrest ended by demanding satisfaction and named a friend in Kentucky, General Basil Duke, as his second. Kilpatrick demurred under the pretense that the Forrest of the Fort Pillow massacre was no gentleman and need not be given satisfaction. So there was no duel.

Scarcely anything is known, of course, of the Klan activities in which Forrest participated or which he directed. It was generally thought, however, that he played a prominent part in a Klan raid in the dark of the night in September 1868, when the steamer *Hesper,* which had been chartered by Governor Clayton of Arkansas to bring arms to bolster his Radical regime, was set upon and all its cargo of arms dumped into the river.

The 1868 election placed General U. S. Grant in the Presidential office. Both Forrest and Grant had a high regard for each other. In fact, Forrest undertook to exonerate Grant for a supposed theft of pianos at Holly Springs, near his family home, during the War. "I said I did not believe it," Forrest stated, adding "that I had talked with parties . . . who denied it." Shortly after Grant's inauguration, a rumor began to circulate to the effect that Forrest had paid a secret visit to Grant, during which the President had promised to restore civil government in the South provided Forrest would dissolve the Klan. The story of the meeting between the two was probably a fabrication; no such bargain was carried out if it were made. About this time, however, Forrest disbanded the Klan. This step does not seem to have had any connection with national politics or with supposed Presidential guarantees.

When and why did Forrest order the Klan to cease operations? The date is uncertain but it was probably sometime in 1868 or 1869. One thing seems to be clear. He did, according to his own testimony in 1871, "suppress" the Klan, which means that he sent out the order to destroy regalia, burn records, and disband completely.

In part his action seems to have been dictated by the intervention of Northern moderates who pleaded with him and other Southern leaders to "try and restrain everybody there from difficulty and violence, to let this thing blow over, work itself off in that way." At the same time, it was apparently becoming obvious to Forrest that the secrecy of the organization was both its strength and its weakness. As it grew in numbers, it became the haunt of lawless elements—"wild young men and bad men," as Forrest called them—who perverted the original objectives of the Klan by engaging in wanton violence and terrorism. At first, an effort had been made to screen carefully all prospective members so that "rowdies and rough men" would be excluded. As Forrest himself testified in 1871, those who joined the early Klan were "worthy men who belonged to the southern army; the others were not to be trusted; they would not fight when the war was on them, and of course they would not do anything when it was over."

When disorderly elements began to run rampant, Forrest found himself in an embarrassing position. He repudiated those who resorted to violence. He told the Congressional committee in 1871, "I am disposed to do all I can to try and fetch these troubles to an end. . . . I want the matter settled. . . . I want our country quiet once more."

His orders to disband the Klan were buttressed by the precept and practice of the Grand Wizard. Time and time again when called upon for advice in the handling of some critical situation, Forrest counseled restraint and peaceful measures. To a man who asked Forrest's advice in the case of a murdered brother, Forrest wrote:

Dear Sir: Your favor of the 26th instant has been received. While I sympathize with your desire to bring those who were guilty of murdering your brother to justice, and would willingly do anything in my power to aid you in this, I cannot consent to become a party, either directly or indirectly, to any act of violence, or to the infringement of any law. On the contrary, all my efforts have been, and shall be, exerted to preserve peace and order, and to maintain the law as far as possible.

It is especially incumbent upon all good men at this time to keep the peace. Every act of violence, no matter by whom or for what cause committed, works an injury not only to the persons engaged in it, but to the community in which it occurs, and through it to the whole South. Our enemies gladly seize upon such acts as the pretexts for further oppressions, and hence it becomes, more than ever before, the duty of every man to refrain from them, no matter how great the provocation he may have received. I beg, and insist therefore, that you abandon the purpose you indicate, and hope that no one will be so unwise as to aid you in carrying it out.

By February 1869, Parson Brownlow was ousted and a moderate governor replaced him, removing the last necessity for Klan activity in Tennessee. Henceforth the Klan survived independently in a number of areas; but it was in the guerrilla manner only, for the general of the armies had declared the fighting at an end. He was, of course, to be subjected to an inquisition in 1871 at the hands of a Congressional committee investigating the Klan. There he did a magnificent job of obfuscation. His memory failed him at the crucial moments; he contradicted himself with the straightest of faces; occasionally he all but admitted his close relationship with the Klan. But throughout it all, he pleaded his case of gentlemanly detachment from the excesses that had been committed in the name of the Klan.

The inquisitors were unable to prove Forrest a Klansman, much less that he was the Grand Wizard; but the committee strongly hinted that the ties existed. That the old general did some gentlemanly lying before the committee he reputedly admitted to his friends; but the admission was totally unnecessary. It should have been obvious to anyone that there was no Klan and Forrest was its prophet.

By the time Forrest was called in by the Congressional inquisitors he had indisputably repudiated the Klan as a continuing agency for dealing with the South's problems. The Klan's biographer, Stanley F. Horn, is certain that Forrest had disbanded the Klan by the expiration of his constitutional term as Grand Wizard in May 1870. Forrest's "outlaw years" were over once the whites began to regain control in the South. He would lead no perpetual underground, no lawless guerrillas. The early Klan had emphasized loyalty to the United States Constitution and the faithful execution of the law. It had relied upon discipline. As long as Forrest could lead a mounted troop that he could see, that could be counted upon to follow his orders, he might head the Klan; when lawless elements arose in his command, he could not tolerate either them or the organization any longer.

But there was still another horse to mount—the iron horse. Riding this horse had already taught him the virtues of order and moderation. When he told the investigating committee that railroads had no politics, he meant what he said. Books have been written to prove the obvious fact that it was railroads that licked the South and saved the Union for Lincoln. Some day perhaps it will also be found that railroads had reunited the country. To Forrest the railroad was a marvelous thing. It was still another way of getting there "fustest with the mostest."

Forrest was busy with his railroading from 1869 on. His public gave the project enthusiastic financial support. The city of Memphis, Shelby County, the north Mississippi counties through which the line was to pass, and the sovereign state of Alabama all came to the aid of the general. What better investment could there be than Nathan Bedford Forrest's peacetime cavalry? His army of investors was not, however, destined to "ride" with him—the road was never finished.

There was one enemy with which not even the great Forrest could contend—economic depression. It hit in 1872-1873; and here was a battle from which Forrest could not emerge without surrender. The result was bankruptcy and humiliation. He could not, like some of his contemporaries, bail himself out by writing his memoirs. So it was back to the land for him; but even here there was a touch of the Forrest ingenuity. He gave up his Memphis home and went to President's Island on the Mississippi in sight of Memphis. There he leased land and worked it in cotton with convicts hired from Shelby County at ten cents a day. President's Island had been a Union refugee camp for Negroes during the war. Now he operated it as a sort of "penal plantation," and he made money, with yields of as high as 500 bales on his 800 acres. He could now go about making peace with his creditors.

He also chose at this time to make his peace with his Maker. In November 1875 he joined the Court Street Cumberland Presbyterian Church in Memphis. His health had now become increasingly precarious. He got about infrequently. Yet in September 1876 he attended the reunion of the 7th Tennessee Cavalry. There he spoke bluntly:

Soldiers of the Seventh Tennessee Cavalry, Ladies and Gentlemen:—I name the soldiers first, because I love them best. I am extremely pleased to meet you here today. I love the gallant men with whom I was so intimately connected during the late war. You can readily realize what must pass through a commander's mind when called upon to meet in reunion the brave spirits who through four years of war and bloodshed fought fearlessly for a cause that they thought right, and who even when they foresaw, as we all did, that the war must soon close in disaster, and that we must surrender, yet did not quail, but marched to victory in many battles, and fought as boldly and persistently in their last battles as they did in their first. Nor do I forget those many gallant spirits who sleep coldly in death upon the many bloody battlefields of the late war. I love them too, and honor their memory. I have often been called to the side, on the battlefield, of those who have been struck down, and they would put their arms around my neck, draw me down to them and kiss me, and say: "General, I have fought my last battle, and will soon be gone. I want you to remember my wife and children and take care of them." Comrades, I have remembered their wives and little ones, and have taken care of them, and I want every one of you to remember them too, and join with me in the labor of love.

The master of President's Island was declining rapidly. He had told the soldiers in September that he had barely been able to meet with them. At his office in Memphis he was visited by General Dabney Maury. "General," he said, "I am completely broke up. I am broke in fortune, broke in health, broke in spirit." On Sunday, October 28, his condition was recognized as hopeless and he was brought into town to die. The next evening he was dead. Among those who arrived in the last moments was Jefferson Davis, who was to remain as one of the pallbearers.

In Memphis on that 29th day of October was the writer Lafcadio Hearn, who viewed it all as a "stranger in a strange city may observe the last of a long chain of unfamiliar events."

Upwards of 20,000 people watched the funeral procession. As it moved slowly toward the cemetery, Jefferson Davis ate humble pie before Governor Porter, confessing to the lack of foresight and understanding that had caused the Confederate government to underestimate Forrest.

In the entire procession only Forrest wore his Confederate uniform, though there were countless old soldiers there. But the War was over, and Reconstruction was nearly so. There were doubtless many there who had ridden with him as Klansmen; but there was not a hood or a sheet in sight, for it was not the Grand Wizard there in the casket—only the grand strategist in his battling uniform. The clothes which had once "made" him a soldier did so no longer. He accepted the war's outcome, and he had learned in the end to accept Reconstruction. The men who now rode with Forrest down Main Street knew that no matter whether he was buried in a Confederate uniform or not, Old Bedford had turned out to be reconstructible.

So had Forrest's South, in fact; for between the extremes of Radical Reconstruction and irreconcilability, Bedford Forrest and most of his fellow Southerners had chosen to pursue the sober tactic of reconciliation. Forrest, then, had proved to be a sort of typical Southerner: the indestructible pioneer, the shrewd moneymaker, the self-made planter, the spirited fighter, the inspired tactician with a flair for strategy, the defeated Confederate who was willing to endure punishment but not persecution. Forrest had the virtues as well as the faults of the Southerners of his day; he was cut from the same cloth as they—the Southern yeomanry. Most other leaders were something special and unique—a race apart, almost. Not Forrest, for he was, like most of his fellow Southerners, a man of action—of considerable passion, too. His cause, and theirs, had been defeated; but neither he nor they had been defeated. He, like they, had a tremendous talent for survival. Reconstruction and what followed it was his and their story.

5

The South's Conscience
ALEXANDER H. STEPHENS

On that Sunday morning in April 1865, when Lee surrendered at Appomattox, Alexander Stephens was far from from the field of battle. He was waiting quietly at Liberty Hall, in Crawfordville, Georgia, for the news that he had known for months—or was it years?—must inevitably come.

Already Stephens had become somewhat of a legend. His size was a joke, but his "stature" was not. He was "Little Aleck" to those who weighed his body and not his intellect. When a political *bombastes* offered to grease Stephens' ears and swallow him whole, Aleck only replied that his opponent would then have more brains in his stomach than in his head. Here was a man whose sickly body and healthy brain were a power in American politics for fifty crucial years that began in the 1830's and ended in the 1880's. A model of integrity and an apostle of moderation, he fought Know-Nothings, Fire-Eaters, carpetbaggers, and Klansmen with equal fervor. This "bodyless brain," as they called him, was as Southern and as Georgian as one could be. But he was not the physical South, loving a fight; he was the spiritual South—loving peace.

Little Aleck had surrendered long before 1865. He had never had his heart in that War. He had known that the War would be near suicide, so far as his beloved South was concerned. The sooner it was over the better. At least, Stephens had not waited until he was licked to surrender. In a way he had surrendered before the fight began. He had felt that though secession was right as theory, it was wrong as strategy. He was certain it would bestir the North to coerce the South in order to hold it in the Union, and such a step could lead only to war.

These convictions he had aired without hesitation in the troubled weeks when his own state stood on the brink of secession. The Fire-Eaters despised him for it, but that was what he thought and nobody in all the state of Georgia could silence him. "I am afraid of nothing on the earth, or above the earth, or under the earth—except to do wrong," he had said back in 1856, when the anti-Catholic bigotry and hatred fostered by the American party threatened his Georgia and he had dragged his ailing body from one of his many retirements to run for Congress so that he might destroy what he called "a disease, not for plasters, but for the knife."

If ever man acted from honest convictions of right and wrong, it was Alexander Stephens. That was why two years before his routing of the Know-Nothings, he had defended Stephen A. Douglas' Kansas-Nebraska Bill as a triumph for popular sovereignty. That was why, in 1852, he had fought for the independent Whig ticket with Daniel Webster as its candidate—the Webster who with courageous disregard for his own political welfare had called for moderation in sectional animosities back in 1850. Webster died before the 1852 campaign was over, but Stephens voted for him anyway! That was why, back in 1850, he had supported Henry Clay's compromise designed to heal the Union's bleeding wounds; and that was why, in 1851, he had led his Georgia in repudiating the Fire-Eaters who demanded secession because this compromise was not to their liking. Finally, that was why back in 1844, the year he first set foot in Congress, he had favored the annexation of Texas but refused two years later to condone the war with Mexico that followed; for much as he loved the South, he would not further the cause of Southern expansionism by what he regarded as General Zachary Taylor's unwarranted invasion of Mexican territory.

Folly and injustice Stephens would condemn, even if it were in his own kith and kin. If his South was wrong, he would not coddle it. In his own peculiar way, without even intending to be, he became the South's conscience. Others might be its sense of pride and the embodiment of its glory, but he was its inward sense of shortcoming and its outward act of penance. He was the South few Northerners heard above the shouting of the Fire-Eaters. And somehow he realized that there were also quieter voices in the North than those of the screaming Abolitionists— that on both sides there were more men of good will than there were wilful men.

There was some sort of fitting irony in the fact that the Confederacy chose two such opposites as Alexander Stephens and Jefferson Davis to head its government. But it has always been the manner of American politics to tie ideological tails together. Both South and North had known and practiced the fine art of American political compromise ever since a "bundle of compromises" became a constitution in 1787. The North of the sixties was a divided nation, even as it pointed its guns at Southern disunionists; the embattled South was also.

There was the South's ego, Jefferson Davis, resolute and headstrong, determined to fight it out even to the last man; and there was Stephens, its alter ego, also resolute and headstrong, determined to talk it out, so that not even the first man should have had to fall. And when all the shooting of war and Reconstruction had ended, when Lee and Grant, Klansman and carpetbagger, Tildenite and Hayesite had muzzled their guns, it was men talking the calm words of peace in 1877 that really brought the Civil War and Reconstruction to an end. Little Aleck, as usual, was right.

Henry Clay had insisted he had rather be right than President; Stephens settled for being right—and Vice President. That this "bodyless brain" ever survived the ravages of nearly five decades of physical frailty and wretched health to assume the Vice Presidency of the Confederacy is almost unbelievable. That he was to survive two decades more through Civil War and Reconstruction and live to become governor of Georgia before he died in 1883—this was in the realm of miracles.

Stephens was born in Wilkes County, Georgia on February 11, 1812. His British grandfather, Alexander, had supported the Stuart Pretender against the House of Hanover and had left England in time to fight as a Pennsylvanian in the French and Indian War and the American Revolution. In the Revolution, he rose to captain. Tradition has it that the Stephenses and Stevenses of Pennsylvania were kin. This would have made the Thaddeus of the Congressional Radicals a kinsman of Alexander of the defeated Confederates. At any rate, grandfather Alexander left Pennsylvania in 1795, to settle in Georgia, where he leased at first but finally became owner of the land which in the course of time was to be remembered as the family homestead.

Alexander's youngest son was Andrew, who farmed and taught an oldfield school, held in an abandoned plantation house. Andrew's first wife, Margaret Grier, bore three children. The youngest was given the name of the grandfather, Alexander. In a second marriage, Andrew became the father of one more daughter and four more sons; the youngest of these, Linton, was to be the favorite and confidant of his half brother Aleck.

Andrew Stephens was a Puritanical sort of person, either from his nature or because of his school teaching. Drinking and dirty jokes he despised; and although he never became a member of any church, he permitted no foolishness on the Sabbath, even driving off visitors by regaling them with the reading of sermons on Sabbath-breaking. Yet Andrew was a lenient and civilized schoolmaster who taught manners as well as the three "r's"—though he kept Alexander so busy hauling manure and working in the pasture that the boy had little time for the classroom.

When young Alexander was only fourteen, he lost his father and his stepmother within a single week; the children had to be parceled out among their kin. Alexander went with his brother Aaron, to live in Taliaferro County with their maternal uncle, Aaron W. Grier, a general of the militia in the War of 1812 and a "scientific" farmer with a fondness for livestock. Uncle Aaron gave Alexander bed and board. With the interest at 8 per cent on his portion of the proceeds of the sale of the family homestead, Alexander could pay tuition at school and buy a minimum of clothing. In summer, he worked on his uncle's farm.

The large families of those days were well used to death, which visited young and old with reckless abandon, breaking up families and redistributing kin. Alexander Stephens was not to be pitied; in fact, he could hardly have been better off. Soon his brilliance, particularly as a Bible scholar, had so impressed his Sunday school superintendent, Charles C. Mills, that that kindly gentleman lent the boy the money to attend the academy in the town of Washington.

At Washington, young Stephens lived in the home of the Reverend Alexander Hamilton Webster, who got him into the Presbyterian church and hoped to bring him into the ministry. Webster offered to prepare Alexander for college and secured for him financial aid from the Georgia Education Society's funds for ministerial training. Webster, however, was soon taken away with a vaguely defined ailment known as "malignant autumn fever"; in gratitude to him, Alexander adopted a middle name, Hamilton.

Ready for college in nine months, he entered Franklin College at Athens, Georgia (now the University of Georgia), but soon realized that he was to be no clergyman and diverted his patrimony of $444 to complete his schooling, arranging after graduation to pay off his indebtedness to the Society. He was quite popular in college. "My intimates and associates were a strange compound," he admitted. To his room, boys came "who never met nor recognized each other elsewhere; the most dissipated young men in college . . . and . . . the most ascetically pious," and he offered as attraction neither liquor nor tobacco nor cards.

He finished first in his class and taught school a few years to pay back his debts. On May 26, 1834, he bought a wallet to hold papers—and money if he had any—and moved into a courthouse office at Crawfordville, where he was supposed to be on call as legal aide to the sheriff. Here he read law alone and in less than two months was admitted to the bar. In 1836, he won a seat in the Georgia Legislature as a Whig. By all odds he should not have done so, for he was well known as a strong opponent of the popular nullification doctrines of John C. Calhoun and had successfully argued against the formation in Taliaferro County of a vigilance committee to ferret out suspected stirrers-up of slave revolt.

Yet Stephens won and spent four years in the Legislature. Later, he went to Congress in 1843, where he remained until he decided to retire in 1859. By that time, his Whig party had fallen to pieces and his Union seemed ready to. He was firmly convinced that "the Union cannot last long." When he was asked if he planned to return as a Senator, he barked: "No, I never expect to see Washington again unless I am brought here as a prisoner of war." In this prophecy he was all too right; he next saw the city on his return from prison at Fort Warren in 1865.

By 1859, there was nothing left for Stephens to be but a Democrat, even though he distrusted most Democratic politicians. He was even pushed as a party candidate for the Presidency in 1860, but would have no part in the move. After the Southerners walked out on the party in 1860, he doggedly remained loyal to Douglas, the Democratic nominee, and insisted that the demand of the South for a plank assuring the integrity of slavery in the territories was unnecessary, as the Constitution by its very nature made such guarantees under its "great principles of self-government."

In the summer of 1860, Stephens was predicting the history of the next five years. "Men will be cutting each other's throats in a little while," he cried. In less than twelve months "the bloodiest war in history" would be underway, he was convinced:

What is to become of us then God only knows. The Union will certainly be disrupted; and what will make it so disastrous is the way in which it will be done. The Southern people are not unanimous now, and will not be, on the question of secession. The Republican nominee will be elected. Then South Carolina will secede. For me, I should be content to let her have her own way and go out alone. But the Gulf States will follow her example. The people are by no means unanimous; but the majorities will follow her. They are what we will start off with in our new nation—the Gulf States following South Carolina. After that the Border States will hesitate, and their hesitation will encourage the North to make war on us. If the South would unanimously and simultaneously go out of the Union we could make a very strong government. But even then if there were only slave States in the new Confederacy we should be known as the Black Republic, and be without the sympathy of the world.

Lincoln's election still did not convince him of any need to leave the Union. He was firmly dedicated to the South and its rights. He was certain that "slavery was not in violation of the laws of nature, the laws of nations or the laws of God," and he had no intention of submitting to hostile legislation against the South. Yet he did feel that the South should not secede just because it had lost an election. On December 14, he spoke before the Georgia Legislature in opposition to secession. In the crowd was Robert Toombs, as much of a Fire-Eater as Stephens was a Unionist. In tribute to Stephens, Toombs rose to demand "three cheers" for "one of the brightest intellects and purest patriots that now lives." Georgia respected its statesman's position, but it went on to secede on January 21, 1861. Alexander Stephens cast one of the eighty-nine votes against his state's secession; over two-thirds of Georgia's delegates voted to leave the Union.

About secession he had not had his way; he was destined nevertheless to have much to say about the formation of the new government. He was a delegate to Montgomery, where he made the rules for the Provisional Congress and saw to it that the Confederate Constitution was largely a carbon copy of that of the United States. He was even boomed for the Presidency of the republic he had not wanted; but that would never do. So the Vice Presidency it was.

At first, Stephens did yeoman service for the Confederacy. At Savannah he made a fiery speech proclaiming the fact that the "cornerstone" of the Confederacy rested upon slavery as the "natural and normal condition" of the Negroes—an assertion that was as much out of character for him as it was a shock to the

Fire-Eaters themselves. Next he was sent to hasten the progress of the Virginians out of the old Union and into the new.

During the war Stephens was often at odds with Jefferson Davis and the Confederate Congress. He opposed conscription and gave encouragement to the attempts of Governor Joseph E. Brown of Georgia to thwart its operations. Stephens denounced the suspension of habeas corpus, and when General Braxton Bragg appointed a military mayor of Atlanta, Stephens insultingly wrote the new official that the "office is unknown to the law. General Bragg had no more authority for appointing you civil governor of Atlanta, than I did and I . . . have no more authority than any street-walker in your city."

Before the war was half over Stephens and Davis were barely on speaking terms. Whatever the President did seemed to be wrong, and Stephens was soon convinced that there was nothing left to do but negotiate peace. When, in the summer of 1863, Davis sent him to discuss an exchange of prisoners of war with the North, the Washington government refused to meet Stephens. Had Davis allowed him to do so and had Lincoln agreed to hold the negotiations, Stephens was disposed to talk terms of honorable peace and restoration of the Union. By 1864, he had the situation sufficiently in hand in Georgia to get its legislature under Governor Joseph E. Brown's whip to pass resolutions opposing the suspension of habeas corpus and a recommendation to the Confederate government that after each Southern victory a peace offer should be made to the North on the terms of the Declaration of Independence.

The fat was now in the fire. Stephens was denounced by the Davis adherents in Richmond as a traitor. Nevertheless, he stood by his peaceful guns. He hoped for McClellan's victory in the Presidential election of 1864, for the Northern Democrats had extended peaceful gestures toward the South. He had also, in the same year, been approached verbally by a representative of Union General William T. Sherman, but had rejected such irregular talks. At the end of 1864, he returned to Richmond, which he had previously abandoned. There he presided over the Confederate Senate. It was considering extending the suspension of habeas corpus, and only a last-minute change of one senator's vote prevented Stephens from breaking a tie by voting down the measure.

Stephens was now just about ready to resign. Nevertheless, he had much support in the Confederate Congress, and a resolution he had drawn up calling upon Davis to appoint peace commissioners to confer with the Federal government seemed at times close to passage. Meanwhile, Francis P. Blair came down "unofficially" from Washington attempting to sell the Confederate government on a joint expedition against Napoleon III's puppet Emperor of Mexico, Maximilian. Davis conferred with Stephens on the scheme and appointed him one of three commissioners to pursue the matter. Stephens did not want to go, for he knew that Davis was really trying to silence him. But there was no refusing, and on January 29, 1865, he journeyed to Hampton Roads, Virginia, where on February 3, the Confederate commissioners talked with Lincoln. Stephens, who had amazed the Northern onlookers by his tiny size, renewed acquaintance with Lincoln, who on watching him unwrap his many shawls and coats, cracked, "Never have I seen so small a nubbin come out of so much husk."

The conference reached no conclusions. Stephens found Lincoln extremely uninterested in Mexico and insistent upon a return of the South to the Union as the basis for any further talks. Back at Richmond, he convinced himself that Davis had stacked the cards against him, that there was no desire on the part of the Confederate President to do anything but fight on recklessly to the bitter end. Davis made a "bold and undaunted" public appeal at a huge demonstration February 9 in Richmond. Stephens was present but not participating. On the same day he took leave of Davis and set out for Crawfordville, "a lonely and bewildered figure," who, as his biographer Rudolf Von Abele observes, wandered "through the twilight of the Confederacy with a copy of its Constitution in his hands."

Liberty Hall was a pyramid where Stephens, like a shawl-wrapped mummy, enjoyed an immortality that allowed him to remain longer on this earth than by right his body ever deserved. "He's dead now but he don't know it," a Yank had remarked as the Vice President of the Confederacy went to the Hampton Roads meeting. Somehow there was always new life back there in the house at Crawfordville.

Fortunately, there is a contemporary record of the life at Liberty Hall. It was the work of Henry Cleveland, who visited Stephens before writing *Alexander H. Stephens, in Public and Private,* which appeared in 1866. Liberty Hall stood on an elevation at the edge of the town, surrounded by a "plain, high board fence, not painted, with large white gates." In the front hall were an iron hat rack and a huge barometer, in the parlor family paintings and a bust of Stephens done in 1859, in the dining room a silent mantel clock without hands. Two annex rooms were his holy of holies. One was his library, the other was his bedroom.

There is a pretty carpet of green and flowers. Low French bedstead draped in white. The walls too are white. There is a bureau and mirror, cot-bed for waiting-boy "Tim," wash-stand and toilet furniture. Over the mantel, Brady's imperial photograph, taken in 1855. . . . It is flanked on the right by the picture of "Faith at the Cross," given while at Fort Warren, by a much valued lady friend. On the left by an embroidered watch-stand, and a pair of lamps. Then a bookcase with broken glass, and bundles of papers in great seeming disorder.

Two miles away was the old homestead, which Stephens had bought back with his first earnings as a lawyer and had added to until it was 1,000 acres in size. Although the soil was poor, it was fertilized and made into productive orchard land. There were also the usual unpainted main house and Negro cabins. At this time, he also owned another 250-acre plot of fine grazing land.

His slaves, who ran his places for him without benefit of overseer, stood by him, even as the Confederacy fell to pieces; and they continued as his loyal servants afterward. Nothing was really changing except the outside world. Early in May, his nephew, Lieutenant John Alexander Stephens, C.S.A., arrived at Liberty Hall bearing a letter written by Lincoln on February 10. Carrying out a promise made to Stephens at Hampton Roads, the President had released John from a Federal prison and had given him a photograph and a letter to "Hon. A. H. Stephens." By the time the letter reached Liberty Hall, Lincoln was dead and the Confederacy was dying. "Please, in return," wrote Lincoln, "to select and send me that officer of the same rank, imprisoned at Richmond, whose physical condition most urgently requires his release." Stephens cried as he read the words of the dead President.

On May 2, Stephens was visited by his good friends Robert Toombs and Governor Brown. By now, what was left of the Confederate government was fleeing through Georgia. It passed a few miles east of Crawfordville, but for all Stephens cared it might as well have been a continent away. Then, on the morning of May 11 the arrest came. Stephens was playing cassino with a visitor, when news arrived that the Yankees were in town. "I expect they have come for me," he said calmly, and went to his bedroom. When the troops arrived, he was in the library. He surrendered quietly, and it was all over.

He packed and in fifteen minutes was at the railway station ready to go to Atlanta, arriving with a bad cold and sore throat. On Sunday the 14th, he was sent under guard to Augusta but stopped briefly in Crawfordville to obtain clothes and bid farewells. At Augusta, the captured Confederate government, including President Davis, were already in custody, and Stephens was put aboard a tug for Savannah. On deck, Monday morning, Davis and Stephens met for the first time since Stephens had left Richmond. "As much as I had disagreed with him," wrote Stephens in his diary, "I could not but deeply sympathize with him in his present condition. His salutation was not unfriendly, but far from cordial. We passed but a few words, and they were commonplace." At Savannah, the party was put aboard the *Clyde* whose captain undertook to chide Stephens for not adhering to his anti-secession doctrines; but Stephens promptly answered that all he had done was oppose secession, not as a right, but because he considered it bad policy. Davis and Stephens saw much of each other on shipboard.

Stephens was finally placed on board the *Tuscarora,* whose captain gave up his own bed to the frail little man "in consideration of his age and past services to the country." Arriving at Boston harbor on May 23, Stephens was placed in an underground cell at Fort Warren. His poor health quickly became worse, despite the fact that he was soon given considerable freedom of the post during the day. Finally, on August 20, he was moved to a better room, under orders from President Johnson, and on September 1 his beloved half-brother Linton came to stay with him. At first Alexander had been fed soldier's rations, but later he was given permission to purchase food from the outside. During the long hours he read and wrote a great deal. One of the results was a lengthy prison diary.

On June 9, Stephens had applied for a pardon from the President, but hearing nothing, he asked for a personal audience with him. Pressure was being exerted in Georgia to obtain a release, and General Grant, too, conferred with Johnson about him. Newspapers like the Louisville *Courier-Journal* insisted that "a release of Stephens would have the happiest effect." Finally, on October 12, a parole was granted, and Stephens started home for Georgia. In New York, he was feted by a large crowd who came to honor him at the Astor House. At Washington, he called on the President. Back in Georgia, he observed "how changed are all things here." His friends in Atlanta saw that he had changed, too; "his hair was turned quite gray since his imprisonment." He was then fifty-three.

At Liberty Hall, Stephens found his Negroes as usual looking after things for "Mass' Alic." Several of his oldest servants, Uncle Dick, Aunt Mat, and Uncle Ben he maintained without requiring them to work. The major-domo of Liberty Hall was the everfaithful Harry, whose wife and five children lived there. Stephens was always mindful of his charges, and even as he ate his meals, "fat Negro children [were] looking into the door or boldly entering for the bread and butter which they like best from his hands." In tune with the times, he was insisting that these children be educated, even though they were taking their learning "in broken doses." He now paid wages but fed and largely maintained his servants without charge. His plantation he left in the hands of his former slaves, who operated it for him under contract.

Stephens' only white household companion was his nephew, John Alexander Stephens, now serving as Alexander's secretary and practicing law in Crawfordville, where he enjoyed the benefits of his uncle's brains, books, and fame. Of all Alexander's family, though, Linton, now a prominent lawyer and politician, was his closest confidant. Linton's first wife, Emmaline, had died in 1857, and to keep his brother from destroying himself from grief, Stephens had demanded more and more of Linton's attention. "I have no mortal on earth I can unbosom myself to," he had written at that time; and all through the War and the imprisonment at Fort Warren, it was Linton who protected and looked out for his half-brother. Soon Linton was to fall in love with Mary Salter, a girl half his age, and in 1867, they were to be married. Linton was still Alexander's dearest kin and Mary herself proved to be a favorite of her brother-in-law.

Georgia set about its own reconstruction in the fall of 1865. Acting under the Presidential scheme, whereby a provisional governor was appointed by Johnson to call a convention to revise the state constitution, Georgians held a convention in October and in mid-November elections were held for state officials and the Legislature. At once Stephens' name was mentioned for governor, even though as a high Confederate official he was obviously ineligible, except by special act of Congress. "It seems to be a hard matter for our people to realize the fact that old things have passed away," wrote Stephens. He announced that he was not available. His political friend former Governor Brown, though itching for the job, also abstained. Charles J. Jenkins was elected without opposition.

In November, while the gubernatorial canvass was under way, Brown had written Stephens, "It is now hoped by May that you will consent to accept the position of Senator in Congress." Stephens' determination not to become involved in politics wavered. Discreet feelers were even sent out to determine the possible reaction in Washington. President Johnson argued it would be "exceedingly unpolitic," but there was some encouragement elsewhere at the capitol. There is little doubt that when the Georgia Legislature convened in December, Stephens, then at Milledgeville, was still loath to accede. Word of the prospective senatorship somehow reached Brown, who had now fled to Cuba and was contemplating a new home in Mexico. On December 12, the wartime governor wrote him expressing deep regret over "your purpose to go back to the Federal counsels." But Stephens was still holding out. In January, he announced that he was not a candidate. But under pressure he later admitted that he could not "imagine any probable case in which I would refuse to serve . . . the people of Georgia." That was enough; on January 31, 1866, he won the race by a vote of 152 to 38.

Several weeks later the Legislature called upon him to speak on Washington's Birthday. Here was his first real opportunity to offer his "mite of counsel" on the state of the South and of the nation. "The great object with me now," he began, "is to see a restoration if possible of peace, prosperity, and constitutional liberty in this once happy, but now disturbed, agitated, and distracted country." The first duty of the people, he observed, must be patience. "It will not do to make too much haste to get well," he cautioned. "One thing is certain," said Stephens, "that bad humor, ill-temper, exhibited with restlessness or grumbling, will not hasten it." The second duty was "the exercise of a liberal spirit of forbearance amongst ourselves." In no wise should the old differences of the prewar and war periods be agitated. "Great disasters are upon us," he said, "and upon the whole country, and without inquiring how these originated, or at whose door the fault should be laid, let us now as common sharers of common misfortunes, on all occasions, consult only as to the best means, under the circumstances as we find them, to secure the best ends toward future amelioration." After all, the conflicts of past years had arisen out of a common desire for good government, even if there was disagreement as to "the best means to be used." It would be unfair, he insisted, to accuse the South of disloyalty to the principles of self-government embodied in the Constitution. Secession was tried in an effort to follow these principles; but the result was that instead of bettering itself, the South came "well nigh losing the whole of the rich inheritances with which we set out."

Stephens concluded that the South's "surest hopes" lay in Johnson's "restoration policy." The only way through the bitterness of the times was for the American people to "conquer their prejudices," just as Daniel Webster had told the people of Boston in another period of unreasoning hate. Then next to the conquest of prejudice he placed "the indulgence of a Christian spirit of charity." For Georgians there was another duty: "We should accept the issues of the war, and abide by them in good faith. . . . The whole United States . . . is now without question our country, to be cherished and defended. . . ."

Slavery was now abolished. "The change should be received and accepted as an irrevocable fact," he warned. There were new racial problems to be solved. "Our present duty on this subject is not with the past or the future; it is with the present." Dealing with this matter involved "not only the best interests of both races, but it may be the existence of one or the other, if not both." The Negro should therefore be assured that he would "stand equal before the law, in the possession and enjoyment of all rights of person, liberty, and property." The existing inequality between the white man and the black in intelligence and moral culture would "not lessen the moral obligations on the part of the superior to the inferior; it rather increases them," he said. With the freedman, "school, and the usual means of moral and intellectual training, should be encouraged amongst them." They should not be allowed to grow up "in ignorance, depravity, and vice."

In facing the days ahead, it was Stephens' desire then, as it had been before and during the War, that "whatever might be done, might be peaceably done; might be the result of calm, dispassionate, and enlightened reason, looking to the permanent interests and welfare of all." If, instead, "passion and prejudice" should prevail and the "embers of the late war shall be kept a-glowing until with new fuel they shall flame up again," the fate of the great nation of the West would be calamitous.

In conclusion, Stephens quoted a verse written by his friend and biographer, Henry Cleveland, for the occasion. Stephens, altering it slightly, warned of the end that might befall this country. "Some bard" might then sing:

> The star of Hope shone brightest in the West,
> The hope of Liberty, the last, the best.
> That, too, has set upon her darkened shore,
> For Hope and Freedom light up earth no more.

He had gone about his oration with thoroughness. It was the second time in his life he had written out a political speech in advance. He had it printed prior to delivery, and it was given verbatim. There was to be no mistaking what he had said. The address was "unanimously indorsed" by both houses of the Georgia Legislature and published in their journals. All this was intended to establish beyond a doubt the attitude of Georgia and of her leading statesmen in the Reconstruction controversy.

The New York *Times,* a pro-Johnson newspaper, printed the speech in full by telegraphic report at considerable expense, enthusiastically praising Stephens as "a representative southern Man." The New York *Tribune* called the address "the best yet proceeding from any citizen south of Mason's and Dixon's line." The Louisville *Courier-Journal* characterized the speech as "most appropriate, most loyal, most national," and hoped it would be printed in "every paper in the country." The address also received notices abroad, where the London and Paris *Cosmopolitan* described it as "such a political address as is, we take it, not often heard in America. It is an effort that recalls the first race of American statesmen."

Stephens' statesmanship made no impression upon the Radical Republicans in Congress. They refused to seat him or any other delegates from those states that had reconstructed themselves under the Johnson plan. Stephens remained in Washington to watch the Radicals triumph over the President by passing the Civil Rights Bill over Johnson's veto. That night the Grants gave a reception and he attended. Strangely enough, he had a profound admiration for Grant:

> He is an unsophisticated, honest, and, I think, as yet unambitious man. There is a great deal of development for Grant yet. He is young, and will yet have a more important destiny than he has had thus far. I do not doubt that he is a patriot. The Radicals pretend to claim him; but they know that he is not with them. He says little about politics, but what he does say is to the point. For instance, one day when I called to see him, he was speaking about the Radical policy, and said, "The true policy should be to make friends of enemies. The policy of the present majority is to make enemies of friends." One of the party asked him if it was true that he had been fined for fast driving on the street. He answered, "Yes, I was. I expect the next thing will be that they will take me before the Freedmen's Bureau."

Stephens was called to testify on April 16, before the Reconstruction Committee, set up by Congress to investigate the attitudes and sentiments of the South. The Radicals had made much of a stir over vagrancy laws passed by many of the Southern state legislatures to force Negroes to sign work contracts instead of waiting for the "forty-acres-and-a-mule" that were supposed to materialize somehow out of Washington. In the North, there had been an outburst of protest against these measures. The South was attempting to restore slavery! So, Congress investigated.

The main purpose of the Committee was witch-hunting. Southern leaders who appeared before it kept their tempers and stood their ground. Stephens was no exception. He had already written a letter to Senator William M. Stewart of Nevada two weeks earlier, enclosing a copy of the Washington's Birthday address. The unanimous approval of Stephens' remarks by the Georgia Legislature was, said the Georgian, "a better and more reliable index of the feelings and views of the people of the state . . . than any bare individual opinion I might entertain or express." He also offered as an exhibit of Georgia's good faith a legislative enactment "to declare the rights" of Negroes.

To a query about "relations subsisting between the whites and blacks, especially with respect to employer and employee," Stephens replied that while conditions had been disturbed in the previous fall by the refusal of freedmen to go back to work, by the first of the new year contracts were generally being made and affairs had since that time "in the main, moved on quite smoothly and quietly."

Would Georgians consent to Negro suffrage? Stephens felt that they would not; it was a matter that should be left up to the state. Should Georgia's Congressional delegation be reduced to exclude the Negro population from the basis of representation? Again he objected, and he insisted that Georgians would never ratify the proposed Fourteenth Amendment which would have enforced Negro suffrage under penalty of a reduction of representation in Congress. Should the Radicals persist in excluding the South from the Union on grounds that were not to apply in the other parts of the country, said Stephens, the North, not the South, would be opposing Union. "The former disunionists would thereby become unionists, and the former unionists the practical disunionists."

Stephens' testimony was praised enthusiastically by the newspapers that supported Johnson against Congress, including the Washington *National Republican,* the Baltimore *Sun,* and the New York *Times.* The *Times* found an interesting contrast in the comments of Stephens and Robert E. Lee:

Lee declined to indulge in speculative fancies; refused to go below the surface, or to set forth any thing that was not quite palpable upon the face of it. He could hardly be drawn into the answering of questions involving political views, and was cautious to the last degree as to the force and bearing of every word he uttered. Stephens was more open and free, more explicit and exact, as well as more rhetorical, less dubious, and less fearful; and was not backward in exhibiting what of course he possesses—a far more thorough knowledge of political influences and laws, and a far more extensive apprehension of the springs of human action and the forces that govern the popular will.

The two names just mentioned are those of the two foremost men in the Southern States. The testimony of no other party or parties could be of equal importance or historical value, unless it were that of Jefferson Davis.

During the summer months of 1866, the struggle between President Johnson and Congress went on unabated. Amid the political maneuvering, the idea of a "Union Convention" at Philadelphia was promoted by Johnson and the Democrats. Here would be a great show of national unity to contrast with Radical Republican "disunity." Stephens felt that if Northern Democrats gave it their loyal support, the convention might offer some hope; so he became one of the delegates from Georgia. In the end, illness prevented his attending the sessions, though he went to Philadelphia. Nearly 15,000 men participated in this "arm-in-arm" convention, where Yank and Rebel delegates walked down the aisles with arms joined. But the Radicals were still in the ascendancy, no matter what else happened in the City of Brotherly Love; and Stephens went home in despair, both of his own health and of that of the Union.

One good thing came out of Philadelphia for Stephens. He was approached by a publisher who wanted him to do a history of the War. He agreed tentatively. His health was now wretched, and further to darken his days, his old servants Mat and Dick died. His country, too, he felt, was *in extremis.* "We are," he said, "now just entering that dark region in our future . . . to which we have been tending for years. . . . Our political doom is sealed: the great and dreaded night has come upon us. My soul is in anguish at the death of American Constitutional liberty!"

By now, Congress had passed the Fourteenth Amendment, and the states—except the Southern ones—were busily ratifying it. It was December before Stephens could finally force himself to make firm his commitment to write the history; as the tragic year of 1867 dawned, he was seeking physic in the pen.

In March, Congress put into effect its Reconstruction Plan, intended to force the South to accept Negro suffrage and at the same time to eliminate most of its white voting strength, for practically every participant in the "Rebellion" would now be disfranchised. To enforce compliance, Congress placed the South under military rule; and in April, 1867, General John Pope took command in Georgia. Governor Jenkins was removed in January

1868, but former Governor Brown, now back in the States, knuckled under to the new regime and became a Republican "collaborator."

Stephens had decided it was his duty to write his book but not to speak his mind in public. He did, however, feel that the few whites who could qualify should vote, for "by taking part they may secure control, and thus save themselves from domination by the black race." He wrote that the Congressional plan could not be successfully carried out, that "the two races can not coexist . . . on this basis." He would not attempt to obstruct it, but he took a dim view of the whole sorry business. As for himself, he insisted that he was not taking "any active part on public questions and I do not intend to mingle in public affairs ever again." A few days later he wrote another friend: "I do not see the slightest prospect of my being able to tender the public the least possible good."

Stephens was an eloquent person even when he was silent. Soon his failure to speak was interpreted as submission, and words were being invented and attributed to him to bear out the rumors of his defection to the Radicals. All that Stephens had done was, in his words, to "express the opinion in Atlanta that it would be best for the state and for the whole country that the Radicals in the Legislature should adopt" the Fourteenth Amendment. He advised Democrats not to vote for it and said that were he in the legislature he would not vote favorably, for he regarded the measure as unconstitutional. He would refrain from voting if the Amendment might thus be allowed to pass, for he feared that hard as the Amendment was, it was not so bad as the military rule that would remain in Georgia until the wishes of Congress had been carried out.

Stephens would have no part of the setting up of a new state government. Elections for a convention to fulfill the demands of Congress were under way in the fall of 1867, but he joined the Democratic leaders of Georgia in urging the white men "to have nothing to do with it," to boycott the election. Brown did not boycott it, and, to do him credit, he managed to prevent white disfranchisement at the same time that Negro suffrage was adopted by the convention. Apparently, Stephens felt that Brown had saved the state from a worse fate, for in 1868, he said that despite the Radicals, Georgia white men would be able to vote in the Presidential election of that year.

In December 1867, he set out for Philadelphia to see his book through its last stages. There he lived with his publisher, J. R. Jones, and, in one of his few ventures out into the icy streets, fell and was painfully hurt. He left Philadelphia, visited briefly in New York, where he talked with Henry Ward Beecher, and in Boston, where he was visited by Dr. Oliver Wendell Holmes and spent several days with Mrs. Salter, the mother of Linton's bride of the previous summer. In April 1868, Stephens returned and supported the Democratic gubernatorial candidate, John B. Gordon, but disagreed with his party. He was willing to accept Brown's proposed constitution—for fear of a worse one. The Democrats lost, of course, for the Negro was voting in Georgia, and the Radical candidate, Rufus B. Bullock, was elected.

The Legislature elected under the new constitution came close to sending Stephens to Washington as a Senator. On the first ballot he was only six votes behind the leading candidate, Brown. Then the Stephens supporters joined with other anti-Brown men to thwart Brown, thus giving the senatorship to Joshua Hill. Stephens was deprived of the chance to take a seat in Congress to which, if elected, he would doubtless now have been admitted. His political eclipse seemed complete.

The first volume of *A Constitutional View of the Late War Between the States* had come from the press. It was well received in many quarters but denounced by Dr. A. T. Bledsoe in the *Southern Quarterly Review*. Stephens interrupted his work on the second volume to reply to Bledsoe in the Baltimore *Statesman*. However, the fact was that his lengthy book expounding his ideas about secession and state rights seemed more like that of a frustrated man than the daring thinker who had spoken so brilliantly for the moderate South in the crises of War and Reconstruction. It was like an old statesman mouthing again and again his old oratorical harangues. "Writing is not my forte," Stephens once wrote in disgust to his brother Linton. He tried to disprove the point in the second volume of the *Constitutional View*, which so far had been a considerable success financially, thanks to the author's fame.

In December 1868, Stephens got a letter from his old friend Robert Toombs announcing that he had been unanimously chosen to a "chair of history and political science" at the University of Georgia. The salary was to be $2,000 a year. Stephens was flattered but pleaded ill health and rejected the post. He confided in a letter to a friend: "I could not live upon the salary." He was now painfully afflicted with rheumatism and could barely get about. His appetite, too, was poor, and he subsisted mainly on coffee and chicken wings.

Stephens went out walking one February day in 1869, and pulled a large iron gate down upon himself. Now a hip injury was added to a body already ruined. For the rest of his life he moved with wheel chair or crutches. He doubted that he would live to see another book in print, but redoubled his literary efforts all the same. He could still write—and the writing of the great orator was pedestrian.

Georgia's Congressmen elected under the Radicals' plan had been seated, and in the State Legislative elections, white Georgia Democrats, enjoying the voting privilege held by a few of their peers elsewhere in the South, had won sufficient power in the Legislature to expel most of the Negro members and replace them with whites. As a result, the Congress changed its mind, and in December 1869, all legislators from Georgia were ordered to take an oath that they were not ineligible under the Fourteenth Amendment. The state was required, in addition, to ratify the Fifteenth Amendment before her Congressmen could be re-seated.

Military rule was briefly restored in Georgia, and in the legislature Negroes replaced the whites who had earlier replaced them. The two Amendments were ratified. Governor Bullock, afraid of an election, tried to prolong his term until 1872 but yielded to the regular democratic processes and allowed elections in the fall of 1870. Guided by Stephens' genius at political strategy, the Democrats won again, assuring the "redemption" of Georgia. Linton caused the arrest at the polls of a number of Negroes who had not paid their poll taxes, whereupon he was himself arrested and taken to jail by the Federal Marshal. At his trial, Linton spoke so effectively, with the ghost-voice of his brother, that the case was quashed.

Even President Grant came to the rescue of the "Redeemers." He said bluntly that "the people of Georgia may govern themselves as they please, without any interference on my part, so long as they violate no federal law." In October 1871, Governor Bullock resigned, and his successor, the Radical president of the senate, was thrown out of office in December, making way for a Democrat, James M. Smith, the speaker of the house, to take over in January, 1872. Now the "redemption" was completed.

Life was by no means calm during these years of the "redemption." Stephens even became a party, unwittingly, to a railroad fraud involving Joseph Brown, Ben Hill, and other prominent political leaders of Georgia. The state-owned Western and Atlantic Railroad had been leased to a company in which a number of state politicians were stockholders. It was fairly clear that there were shenanigans afoot, but Stephens had obtained half a share in the enterprise quite innocently. When the venture collapsed, the list of shareholders was printed. Stephens promptly explained everything in the Atlanta *Constitution* and turned over his half share to the state.

He settled for a newspaper instead of a railroad. For a time he wrote for the Atlanta *Intelligencer*. In 1871, he purchased half-interest in the Atlanta *Southern Sun,* buying it out completely in December and selling it to the *Constitution* two years later. Stephens used his paper as a personal and egotistical medium, signing his editorials. Toombs joked that Stephens, who painstakingly suffered over every jot and tittle of make-up and editing, would even insist on correcting the proofs of his own obituary. Some time later, when he was apparently at death's door, the *Constitution* prepared an obituary, only to be foiled by the many-lived statesman. Shortly afterward he did correct his own obituary, for future use!

His role as an editorial writer gave him an opportunity to speak his piece in 1872 about the Democrats' "New Departure" program. They had proposed to join with Horace Greeley's Liberal Republicans of the North to unseat the Radicals and accept the constitutionality of the Fourteenth and Fifteenth Amendments. This Stephens would never do. Stephens' irrepressible constitutionalism restrained him, and for once he was not found among his submissionist friends. Instead, the tables were turned. Fire-Eaters who in 1860 refused to vote for Douglas were now "huzzahing for Greeley" for President and presumably accepting the dictates of Reconstruction. Stephens, who had once called for such a surrender, now counseled against it! He had lost faith in Grant. Stephens prophesied that Greeley would not carry a single Northern state, and he didn't.

Stephens and his *Sun* stood by the "straight" Democratic candidate, Charles O'Conor, even though this estimable gentleman had refused to run. Stephens had never shied from voting for nonexistent candidates, including the dead Webster in 1852. Greeley carried Georgia with 75,896 votes to Grant's 62,485 and O'Conor's 3,999. Grant won in Stephens' own county. The next year, Stephens' shortlived *Sun* would set.

Meanwhile, he had passed through "one of the bitterest agonies" of his life. In July, while the Presidential election campaign was raging, his beloved half-brother Linton died. For several months Stephens was inconsolable; but by fall he was drowning his sorrows in the only spirits for which he had much of a taste—politics. While his Presidential "candidate" was going down in defeat, he decided to become an active candidate for the United States Senate. He put the issue squarely: "Either the 'New Departure' or I shall die, politically, in Georgia." Stephens met defeat when the Georgia Legislature convened in 1873, thanks to his "straightism" and his shrewd enemy, Ben Hill. He did decide to run for Congress to fill a vacancy and was elected without difficulty, campaigning by wheel chair and reviving his energies during his speeches with sips of brandy, each prefaced with a toast to "Jeffersonian democracy."

Once more life was worth living. In April, he wrote a friend boasting of being terribly busy. Old politicians never die, not when they can get elected to Congress! Some professed patriotic horror that the "second Rebel" should be back in Congress. "Let him come back," said a Georgia newspaper, though it chided Aleck for a new arrogance: "Alexander H. Stephens does not emulate the modesty of the rose. He positively refuses to 'pine upon the bush.' He is not only ready to be plucked but means to oblige somebody to pluck him. He feels that his dear Georgia cannot get along without him at Washington."

The "little irrepressible steam engine, with a big brain and scarcely any body," as a newspaper writer described him, came to Washington in the autumn of 1873. He arrived in time to speak against a civil rights bill guaranteeing to the Negro the use of certain public places and transportation facilities. Stephens described the measure as unconstitutional and inexpedient. At the same session, he bravely flouted public opinion by opposing the repeal of the "salary grab" law of 1873, whereby Congressmen had voted themselves a raise. Stephens felt they needed it; that settled the issue as far as he was concerned. Stephens was backed by the new Democratic Congressman from Mississippi, the rising statesman L. Q. C. Lamar, a former Confederate officer.

While in Washington, Stephens became embroiled in a hot controversy in the Georgia press with his old enemy, Ben Hill. In a statement purporting to be an "Unwritten History of the Hampton Roads Conference," Hill had declared that malcontents like Stephens were "not fit" to write books about or deliver speeches on the Confederacy or to "pass judgment on the faithful." Stephens and his ilk, by attacking President Davis, promoting peace movements, and raising constitutional doubts about Confederate laws, he said, had assured the defeat of the South. Stephens replied in kind, and for months to come there were charges and countercharges. Stephens returned home in 1874 to stand for re-election, but the Hill campaign did not hurt him;

the opposition quickly fled the field and Stephens was returned to Washington.

Stephens was ill often during his term in Congress, being scarcely able in the midst of constant pain to enjoy a moment of repose. In 1876 he caught pneumonia and for nine months hovered at the edge of death. He soon became almost constantly dependent upon drugs, so great was his suffering. Only at Liberty Hall was there release. Once three thousand Negroes from the Sunday schools nearby marched from a meeting to his home to serenade the ill old man with hymns and spirituals. Touched deeply, he spoke briefly and advised his visitors to educate themselves that they might better undertake their new responsibilities. The Negroes filed past him and each touched his hand. He said afterward he "could have almost wished to die while listening to that music."

In Philadelphia, it was Centennial Year, the hundredth anniversary of the Declaration of Independence. Stephens had favored the celebration as a healthy counterirritant to the sectional animosities of the day, and before he became ill, he had agreed to make an address in New York honoring the occasion.

Stephens joined the forces of moderation in the contested Presidential election in 1877 between Tilden and Hayes and voted for acceptance of the political compromise of the electoral commission that Congress had set up to settle the dispute. When a bargain was agreed to between leaders of the contending sides, he was the first to acquiesce; he knew that with the agreement would disappear the last vestiges of military control and carpet-bag rule in the South.

He refused to give up politics, though he did very little in Congress, held no important committee assignments, and was absent for weeks at a time. When he did gather his bones together to come into the House, people knew he was there, even if he did not speak. A newspaper description at this time has become a classic:

A little way up the aisle sits a queer-looking bundle. An immense cloak, a high hat, and peering somewhere out of the middle a thin, pale, sad little face. This brain and eyes enrolled in countless thick-nesses of flannel and broadcloth wrappings belong to the Hon. Alexander H. Stephens, of Georgia. How anything so small and sick and sorrowful could get here all the way from Georgia is a wonder. If he were to draw his last breath any instant you would not be surprised. If he were laid out in his coffin he needn't look any different, only then the fires would have gone out in those burning eyes. Set, as they are, in the wax-white face, they seem to burn and blaze. Still, on the countenance is stamped that pathos of long-continued suffering which goes to the heart. That he is here at all to offer the counsels of moderation and patriotism proves how invincible is the soul that dwells in this shrunken and aching frame. He took the modified oath in his chair, and, when he had taken it, his friends picked him up in it and carried him off as if he were a feather. So old Thaddeus Stevens used to be picked up and carried in and out when this same man, of the same name and an opposite lineage, was the Vice-President of the Southern Confederacy. The old lion of Pennsylvania rests from the fight; and the great "rebel" of Georgia, with the very shadow of death upon his face, lifts his failing voice in behalf of moderation and peace.

The "death upon his face" was no understatement. In 1877, when he was sixty-nine, there was another attack of pneumonia. News of his death was actually put on the wires. Newspapers printed extended obituaries. Homes even in Crawfordville wore mourning drapes. But he would not die. He got to read his obituaries and did the *Constitution* the honor of making the corrections that enabled that journal six years later to scoop the country with the only personally approved version of Alexander H. Stephens' death notice.

In February 1878, he paid homage to Lincoln at the presentation in the House of F. B. Carpenter's painting of the signing of the Emancipation Proclamation. It was a sentimental speech, closing with the verses he had recited at Atlanta in 1866. His remarks brought tears from those who heard it, jeers from those in the South who were sick of Stephens' kind words for Lincoln, and complaints from some Yankees who were irritated that he had some kind words to say for slavery.

By 1882, Stephens would no longer consent to return to Congress. He wanted to live out his remaining days in peace. But the temptations of office snared him once again and at 70 he became a candidate for governor.

Internal state politics had always been his challenge, even when he was far off in Washington. In his own peculiar and headstrong way he had taken the vicissitudes of Georgia politics seriously. He could out-faction the factions, turning from one to another with ease and impunity. In the late seventies, Stephens had even made friends with one of the more colorful Independent leaders, old William H. Felton, a doctor-preacher of tremendous agrarian appeal, who deviled the machine Democrats of Georgia in the seventies. With unusual perspicacity, Stephens seemed to understand the nature of the problems disturbing the agrarian population. "If ever there is another war in this republic," he observed, "it will not be sectional but social." He felt that the American system of "class legislation, taxes and finance" could lead the "masses" to "trenchant reform or frightful revolution."

Felton had talked to Stephens in terms of the governor's race. At first, he would not hear of the idea. Yet, by 1882 the Independents were out to draft him, and in a weak moment he apparently consented to their demands. At any rate, he had their nomination. The regular Democrats now wanted to capture him, too; and the confused old man turned his back on Felton to accept the Democratic nomination.

Stephens' election was a certainty. On November 5, 1882, he was inaugurated. Indeed, his corpse had to appear before the hosts of Georgia like that of the Spanish Cid before the embattled Christians, so he attended the sesquicentennial of the city of Savannah in February. He spoke, he shook hands, he was seen.

After that he just wasted away, dying by inches—the few inches there were of him. By the first day of March, he was critically ill, but this was not news—he had died so many times already. But on March 3, 1883, he was indeed dying. Toward midnight, in his dreaming, he was campaigning again. Somewhere he had carried a box or a district "individually by a six hundred majority." At 3:24 A.M. on March 4, he assumed that office—whatever it was. Two days later the governor was back in the capitol lying in state—a wheel chair, a casket, and a small bundle of a man.

There were times when Little Aleck had felt along with Toombs that both had "outlived the Constitution." Now, he was gone, but he had lived long enough to know that the spirit of moderation and political compromise which had produced that Constitution had at last reasserted itself. The days of the "bloody shirt" were numbered. Reconstruction was over; it had ended in 1877 as Stephens wanted it to, with men burying their hatchets somewhere else than in one another.

A large bundle of compromises born in 1787 had survived a Civil War and a Reconstruction; a tiny bundle of compromise born in 1812, Alexander Hamilton Stephens, had lived to see all this happen.

6

Artificer of Reconciliation
L. Q. C. LAMAR

"I shall stay with my people." With these simple words Colonel Lucius Quintus Cincinnatus Lamar, young judge advocate of the Third Army Corps, announced his decision to share the fearful consequences of what happened at Appomattox on that Sunday morning in April 1865. He would devote his life "to the alleviation, so far as in my power lies, of the sufferings this day's disaster will entail upon" the people of the South.

Lamar meant what he said. He would stay with his people and put into their mouths the gentle words of peace. He would show Northerners that a Southerner could lead not only his own people but all the people of the nation. He would become the artificer of reconciliation.

The Civil War had already given this brilliant young man an opportunity to practice his gift of oratory. His fellow Mississippian, Jefferson Davis, President of the Confederacy, had sent him off to Georgia to battle administration critics like Alexander H. Stephens. And when he spoke in January 1865, to the tattered men of Harris' Brigade while shells crackled about him, he so stirred the desolate soldiers that they burst into cheers. The Federals "shot at the noise," but Lamar continued, though splinters flew from the stump on which he stood. Later, in Reconstruction, he would, as the lone Democrat in Congress from his home state, speak boldly on, even though some of the irreconcilable Radicals were disposed with no less success than before to "shoot at the noise."

When Lamar signed his parole at Appomattox, he was attached to the First Corps, which had absorbed what was left of the old Third Corps of General A. P. Hill. He was married to Virginia Longstreet, a cousin of his new commander, James Longstreet. In the grueling postwar years that were to agitate the South and the nation, both these men played prominent and significant, but very different, roles. In the end they were to become symbols of a nation's reunification.

Lamar resigned from Congress in 1861, to return to Mississippi to draft his state's Ordinance of Secession. He served as lieutenant colonel and colonel of the 19th Mississippi Regiment in the Peninsula fighting before Richmond in 1862, was three times cited for bravery and outstanding leadership. Then two attacks of a recurrent illness, a "violent vertigo . . . something like an apoplexy," put an end to his military service.

The same year he was appointed Confederate minister to Russia (though he never reached Russia) and special envoy to England and France. "Lamar struck Paris as an imposing, even picturesque personality," one writer said, "and in his broad-brimmed hat, tight buttoned coat, and hirsute luxuriance he cut a striking figure on the boulevards." A French lady praised the courtly Southerner as the only diplomat at the French court "who fully recognized and endeavored to utilize the power of the women there." He made friends also with the French poet, A. M. L. de Lamartine, who in a manner to warm the Southern heart turned out to be a distant relative.

In London Lamar stayed at Thackeray's home. Henry Adams, who was in England with his father, Charles Francis Adams, the United States Ambassador, found Lamar "quite unusual in social charm," and felt that "he would have done better in London, in place of Mason [James Mason, the Confederate minister]. London society would have delighted him; his stories would have won success; his manners would have made him loved; his oratory would have swept every audience."

Lamar spoke persuasively on the South's position to British groups. On the question of slavery he said that the South had not introduced the African to slavery, but in the South, under slavery, "the white race had been the guardians, the protectors, the benefactors of the black man; that they had elevated him in the scale of rational existence, and that they had Christianized him to a state to which he has never before attained."

To those who might say that "the South owed it to Christendom to emancipate him," Lamar replied that the Negro was not ready for emancipation. "So many and so great were the boons the South had already conferred on the negro race, that the world had ample guaranty that if the time should ever come for the South to believe that liberty would be a boon, and not a curse, then she would be prepared to confer that boon upon them. . . . If that time should ever come, they would be capable of asserting their own claims; and the whites could not, if they would, withhold the boon."

Returning home, he ran the Union blockade in a ship that was pursued and wrecked. Back in Georgia, in 1864, he spoke effectively for Jefferson Davis' administration in the hostile bailiwick of stubborn Governor Joseph E. Brown and sulking Vice President Alexander Stephens.

Georgia was Lamar's native state. He had been born there, in 1825, at the family's homestead near Eatonton, Putnam County, in the prosperous, cultured plantation country of central Georgia. The Lamars, of Huguenot origin, had spent a generation in England before settling in Maryland in the late seventeenth century. Within another century branches of the family had become well established along the South Atlantic seaboard. In the first years of the nineteenth century, a grandfather of Lucius, John Lamar, had settled at the Eatonton plantation, where he became a wealthy and successful planter, the owner of many slaves.

Among the famous Lamars whom Lucius knew as a boy were his uncle, Mirabeau Lamar, President of the Republic of Texas; Gozaway B. Lamar, who had left Georgia for New York to become president of the Bank of the Republic; and Henry G. Lamar, a Georgia Congressman. There was nothing provincial about these Lamars.

Lucius' father was a brilliant lawyer, educated for the bar in Connecticut. When he was only twenty-two, the Georgia Legislature asked him to compile the first digest of the laws of Georgia. At thirty-three, he was made a judge of the highest court in the state, the youngest man ever to hold this office. Four years later, on July 4, 1834, this greatly respected, prosperous and successful jurist, happily married and the father of five children, returned from a public meeting, kissed his wife and children, went out into the garden and shot himself. The reason was never known. Something of his high intellectual quality, brilliance in argument and judicial interpretation, combined with sensitiveness and inner questioning, were later revealed in the personality of his famous son.

Young Lucius was nine years old, eldest of three brothers, when his father died; his grandfather had also died less than a year before. The golden, happy plantation days were over. Removing to Georgia, where a Methodist boys' school had just opened, Lamar studied Greek, Latin, history, the natural sciences, and declamation.

As the boys approached college age, the family moved to nearby Oxford, site of Emory College, which Lamar entered in 1841. An important influence on his life was the college's new president, Augustus Baldwin Longstreet. A Georgian who had gone to school in South Carolina with John C. Calhoun, he had graduated at Yale and served in succession as lawyer, judge, Methodist minister and author of one of the South's first books of local color sketches, *Georgia Scenes*. A strong state rights advocate and a political disciple of Calhoun, Judge Longstreet's memorial to the General Conference of the Methodist Episcopal Church in 1844, split that church over the questions of slavery and state rights.

To Judge Longstreet Lamar once wrote, "I am indebted to you for ennobling influences from my boyhood up to middle age. . . . For many years I have loved you as few sons love a father." As for Lamar, no spot on earth had "so helped to form and make me what I am as this town of Oxford." He meant not only the town, for the town was the college and the college was Judge Longstreet.

Two years after graduation Lamar was admitted to the Georgia bar and married Judge Longstreet's daughter. They settled in Covington, but when Judge Longstreet accepted the presidency of the University of Mississippi, Lamar and his wife moved to Oxford, Mississippi, also. Lamar practiced law and taught as Adjunct Professor of Mathematics at the University—a prosaic and uncongenial activity for his own imaginative intelligence. "It may be a great accomplishment, that of putting truths all in a row 'Each holding to the skirts of the other,' " he wrote, "but in my opinion if Newton's *thoughts* had been compelled to go through the process which is now employed in the *demonstration* of his binomial theorem, the world would never have heard of its discovery."

When Lamar was only twenty-six, he took his first public part in politics. Supporting Jefferson Davis' gubernatorial campaign in a joint debate, he bested Davis' opponent Senator H. S. Foote. The University students bore their young professor off in triumph on their shoulders. Davis lost the election to Foote, but Lamar's political future was assured.

In 1852, the family returned to Georgia. The Whigs normally controlled the county, but Lamar was elected to the Legislature as a Democrat. "He was then young, not more than 27," a contemporary described him, "with a handsome face, a full head of dark hair, brilliant eyes, in figure rather below the medium of height, handsomely dressed, with fine musical voice. . . . In a short speech of not more than thirty minutes he captured the whole assembly. . . . Such an excitement as was produced by his speech I never saw in that body . . . a remarkable exhibition of the power of the orator and the logician."

In 1855, Lamar was back in Mississippi, where he bought a plantation, "Solitude," of more than a thousand acres, located on the Tallahatchie River between Oxford and Holly Springs. There he became the Southern gentleman. To his slaves, he was at once "master, guardian, and friend." He was "loved and petted by his women folk and his children." He was frequently visited by "cultivated and attractive friends for days and even weeks," and he visited them in turn. A planter with a feeling for diversification, his "summers were devoted to the growing of cotton and corn, while the winters were occupied in killing hogs, curing bacon sides and delicious hams, making sausages, and trying out snowy lard." Thus his son-in-law, Edward Mayes, described the life at Solitude.

Soon Lamar was also cultivating politics. In 1857, he ran for Congress under the sponsorship of Jacob Thompson of Oxford, Secretary of the Interior in President Buchanan's cabinet, and a potent figure in Democratic circles. Thompson had discovered Lamar to be "a man endowed by genius and culture with the qualities that make a politician and a statesman . . . gifted with eloquence and of scholarly attainments, with no political or moral sins to answer for."

Lamar won, and as a young Congressman in the turbulent atmosphere of Washington he had need for all his talents. One of many who now began to despair of a peaceful solution of the slavery question, he foresaw the dissolution of the Union, and— as many did not—that a break-up of the Union meant war. "Dissolution cannot take place quietly," he wrote. "The vast and complicated machinery of this government cannot be divided without general tumult and, it may be ruin. When the sun of the Union sets, it will go down in blood."

Although Lamar was a firm supporter of state rights and of the theoretical right of a state to secede, he was not an extremist, and he worked always for honorable compromise on disputed issues. He was considered a conservative and a peacemaker. "I am no disunionist *per se,*" Lamar told the Congress. "I am devoted to the Constitution of this Union; and so long as this Republic is a great tolerant republic, throwing its loving arms around both sections of the country, I, for one, will bestow every talent which God has given me for its promotion and its glory."

Writing his friend, Dr. F. A. P. Barnard, who succeeded Judge Longstreet as President of the University of Mississippi and later became President of Columbia University, he expressed regret that "the sectional war rages with unabated violence . . . brought about by ultra party leaders and deluded fanatics." He longed for a leader who, "rising above the passions and prejudices of the times," would "speak to both sections in a spirit at once tolerant, just, generous, humane, and national." Little did he realize that he was describing himself two decades hence.

Lamar spoke out eloquently when he felt the position of the South was threatened. He could also resort to more elementary eloquence. In February 1858, when debate over the explosive Kansas situation led to a fight on the floor of the House between Pennsylvania's Grow and South Carolina's Keitt, it was reported that "even Lamar of Mississippi and Parson Owen Lovejoy had a little set-to in the course of the passing gust."

Mrs. Clement Clay, wife of the Senator from Alabama, described Lamar as the most "affectionately held" of any Southerner in Congress. "Moody Lamar," he was sometimes called, "for he was then, as he always was to be, full of dreams and ideals and big warm impulses, with a capacity for the most enduring and strongest of friendships, and a tenderness rarely displayed by men so strong as was he."

His firm but moderate course was fully approved in Mississippi. He and Jefferson Davis had become the state's most prominent figures, and both were greatly in demand for speeches and public appearances. Even Lamar's political opponents recognized his ability and took pride in his conduct on the state and national scene. "In our judgment," said the Vicksburg *Whig,* an opposition paper, "Mr. Lamar is the ablest man in either branch of Congress from this State. . . . There is hardly a question of governmental policy on which we do not differ materially with him; but if his side is to have the Congressman, we at least feel a sort of State pride that such a man as L. Q. C. Lamar is made the recipient of the honors of his party."

Like most Southern leaders, Lamar would have preferred to avoid secession, but he had come to feel that this was impossible. Secession, said Lamar, "was the culmination of a great dynastical struggle, an 'irrepressible conflict' between two antagonistic societies. . . . This culmination was a result of the operation of political forces which it was not within the power of any individual man or set of men to prevent or postpone."

Lamar was fully convinced that the South's position was proper and constitutional. He wrote the Ordinance of Secession adopted by a State Convention at Jackson in January, 1861. The ordinance proposed that another federal union of seceded states be set up on "the basis of the present Constitution of the United States." Lamar was, in fact, ready for the Southern states to re-adopt the United States Constitution and all existing Federal laws, exactly as they were. It was his view, and that of many other Southern leaders, that there was nothing wrong with the Federal Union that a conscientious adherence to the laws and Constitution as written could not cure. He had become convinced, however, that such a course was not to be expected from a government dominated by Northern Republicans.

In the War that Lamar had foreseen, his family, like most others in the South, suffered grievously, not just financially and materially, but in the death of its members on the battlefield. Thirteen Lamars closely related to Lucius are known to have been killed. Both of Lamar's brothers were killed—one at Crampton's Gap, Maryland, in 1862; the other at Petersburg, Virginia, in 1864.

As Lamar made his way southward after Appomattox, through the devastated countryside to Mississippi, he fell in with another veteran, Major General Edward C. Walthall, who had distinguished himself at the battles of Chickamauga, Missionary Ridge, Nashville, and Franklin. Walthall, born in Virginia, had been reared in Holly Springs, Mississippi, where Lamar had practiced law before the War. Walthall, too, was a lawyer, and the two men decided to open an office together at Coffeeville, near Oxford. Thus began a close relationship that was to have a profound effect upon the political events of Reconstruction and after.

Lamar was soon hard at work at his law practice and in his modest home. "We keep no man servant," Mrs. Lamar wrote her mother in February, 1866. "Lucius has been working about the fences and gates and locks to his outhouses. He feeds his cows and helps cut the wood and does a great deal of work. If he can only have good health, I feel as if we would be happy under almost any circumstances." In June of that year he became Professor of Ethics and Metaphysics at the University of Mississippi and the next year Professor of Law.

During the first years of Reconstruction, Lamar believed, with General Robert E. Lee, that the best former Confederate leaders could do was to obey the law, work to rebuild the South and remain out of the limelight. "I have thought and still think," he wrote in 1870, "that all such a one can do, or should do, is not to uphold or approve, but quietly to acquiesce in, the result of the wager of battle."

Lamar "acquiesced" by giving up his post at the University after the carpetbag and Negro regime had triumphed in Mississippi and the "Black and Tan" Constitution had been adopted in 1869. Lamar even considered leaving Mississippi. He was discouraged enough to write in May 1870: "The state of things is permanent. The Negroes have a large and increasing majority. I must take my property and family from the state." Moreover, his wife's mother had died in 1868, and Judge Longstreet a year later—two of the strongest links that had bound him to Mississippi. After some hesitation, he decided to remain, encouraged perhaps by the marriage of his daughter, Fannie, to Edward Mayes, later to become Chancellor of the University of Mississippi and Lamar's biographer.

In the years following the Radical triumph, the white Democrats of Mississippi took to the underground. Many turned to the Ku Klux Klan as a means of fighting carpetbag and Negro rule. Federal efforts to suppress the Klan brought lawyers like Lamar into the courts to defend his accused friends and neighbors. Oxford, as a Federal court town, was the scene of many "Klan" trials, filled with Federal troops, prisoners, and a large number of government witnesses and hangers-on.

On June 22, 1871, Lamar became embroiled in a courtroom roughhouse with a disreputable government witness, a former counterfeiter, embezzler, and murderer, who interrupted and threatened him, even starting to draw a pistol conspicuously displayed at his waist. Lamar picked up a chair and declared that if the judge wouldn't make the witness sit down, he would. In the confusion Lamar knocked down and broke the jaw of a well-meaning Federal marshal who attempted to intervene. Federal troops stationed in the building were called in. Lamar spoke bitterly to the judge for permitting the situation to develop and denounced Federal officers who were threatening to arrest him. Finally order was restored without further violence. "We never saw a better fight or heard a better speech," said one of the Federal soldiers.

Lamar apologized for his part in the disorder, especially to the marshal whom he had knocked down, but the judge temporarily disbarred Lamar from practicing in his court. The injured marshal testified for Lamar, pointing out that he had prevented a threatened riot in Oxford during the 1869 election and had always been a force for law and order in the community. The Radicals, North and South, seized on the incident as an example of Southern troublemaking, part of a Ku Klux plot.

The state was now firmly in the grasp of carpetbaggers and former slaves. Throughout the South, the Negroes, thanks to the Thirteenth and Fourteenth Amendments and the presence of Federal troops, were now enfranchised, while numerous white leaders had been denied the ballot because of their efforts in behalf of the Confederacy. Many Northern states had not yet granted the suffrage even to educated Negroes, but the Radical Republicans were demanding that Federal troops guarantee the vote to the illiterate Negroes of the South. In states like Mississippi, where Negroes constituted a majority of the population, the effects of Negro voting were disastrous to the native whites, except, of course, for the few who like James L. Alcorn, became scalawags and co-operated with the carpetbag government.

Elected governor in 1869, Alcorn was a Mississippian who had been a member, with Lamar, of the state's secession convention of 1861 but after the War joined the Republican party. In 1869, there were thirty-six Negroes in the Legislature, few of whom could read or write, and sixty-four by 1873. Taxes were so high as to be almost confiscatory; the tax money disappeared in waste, extravagance, and embezzlement. Alcorn, who as a tax-payer resisted the upward tax spiral, was subsequently kicked upstairs into the United States Senate.

From his home in Oxford, Lamar had watched the degradation of his state with a sadness verging on despair. Late "upon almost any clement evening," wrote his son-in-law Edward Mayes, "if one should follow the plank walk until the picket fence which marked the premises of Col. Lamar should be reached, there he would be found; clad in a drab study-gown, somewhat frayed and stained with ink; his face long, massive, and sallow; bareheaded, with his long brown hair stirred by the breeze; his deep mysterious eyes fixed upon the yellowing western sky, or watching dreamily the waving limbs of the avenue of water oaks across the way; abstracted, recognizing the salutations of the passers-by with a nod half courteous, half surly, and yet obviously unconscious of all identities; a countenance solemn, sober and enigmatical."

The "grim despotism" of Radical Republican rule "glares upon us at every point," Lamar wrote to a friend. "Spies and secret detectives swarm through the country, dogging the footsteps of our best citizens . . . following up with arrests, arbitrary searches, indefinite and unexplained imprisonments, trials before vindictive and partisan juries picked for the purpose of insuring convictions." He felt that the Southern people had laid down their arms in good faith, had submitted, indeed, to the Northern interpretation of the Constitution. "Yet the administration of President Grant . . . has never ceased to treat them with contemptuous distrust, severity, and vengeance."

So keenly did Lamar feel the ordeal of his people that he ran for Congress in 1872. He did this reluctantly, for his law practice was prospering even if his party was not. "The time has passed with me for looking to political parties, Democratic or Republican, as a means of improving public affairs." He was particularly unenthusiastic about the Democratic acceptance of the Liberal Republican nominee for President, Horace Greeley. As a former Confederate officer and public official, Lamar was disqualified for office except by special act of Congress. He was elected, nevertheless—the first Democrat to be seated from Mississippi since Appomattox.

Lamar had been elected under unprecedented circumstances. He had announced before the election: "If elected . . . I will be in *one* sense a Representative according to the standard established in the purer days of the republic. Not a dollar will be spent, except for the printing of tickets in my district. . . . There will not be a vote bribed . . . and no *personal influence,* will, so far as I know, be brought to bear upon anybody."

Lamar's intellectual brilliance, his power as a speaker, his gentlemanly conduct to friend and foe alike, won him not only the normal Democratic vote but considerable Republican support as well—including the vote of the Republican United States marshal whom he had knocked down in the Oxford courtroom. When the time came to ask Congress for a removal of Lamar's political disabilities so that he could take his seat, his request was supported by Republican Governor Ridgley C. Powers as well as by three Republican judges of the State Supreme Court, the Negro secretary of state, and many Federal officers stationed in Mississippi. In December 1872, Congress passed a bill permitting him to take his seat.

In 1874, a former Federal officer from Maine, Adelbert Ames, was to become governor. The fact that he was a son-in-law of the well-hated Ben Butler (whose highhanded rule as military governor of New Orleans had incurred Southern wrath) did not add to Ames' popularity in Mississippi.

Lamar was present when the Forty-third Congress met in December. His course as a Congressman, he declared, would be marked "by moderation and reserve. If I say or do anything it will be to give the North the assurance it wants that the South comprehends its own great necessities, and wishes to be no longer the agitating and agitated pendulum of American politics." Pres-

The last photograph of Lee taken by Michael Miley, his official photographer,
January, 1870, in Lexington, Virginia
Courtesy of the Virginia Historical Society and Dementi Studio, Richmond, Virginia

ROBERT E. LEE

Photograph by Mathew B. Brady taken probably around 1860
Courtesy of The New-York Historical Society, New York City

MATTHEW FONTAINE MAURY

A copy by Nicola Marschall of an early postwar portrait by an unknown artist
Courtesy of The Filson Club, Louisville, Kentucky

JOHN C. BRECKINRIDGE

NATHAN BEDFORD FORREST

A postwar photograph by J. H. Moyston, Memphis, Tennessee
Courtesy of The New-York Historical Society, New York City

ALEXANDER H. STEPHENS

(Left) An early postwar photograph taken in Brady's studio. *(Right)* As an invalid from a fall in 1869. With his faithful servant, Tim, in Washington, D.C. *From the Mathew B. Brady Collection of the Library of Congress*

As Secretary of the Interior, photographed between 1885 and 1887 by C. M. Bell, Washington, D.C. *Courtesy of The New-York Historical Society, New York City*

L. Q. C. LAMAR

Photograph by D. J. Ryan, Savannah, Georgia, 1870 (Johnston is on the left)
(see page 49)
Courtesy of the Virginia Historical Society and Dementi Studio, Richmond, Virginia

JOSEPH E. JOHNSTON & ROBERT E. LEE

During his term as Governor of South Carolina, between 1876 and 1879
*Courtesy of the South Caroliniana Library, University of South Carolina,
Columbia, South Carolina*

WADE HAMPTON

Inauguration as Governor of South Carolina, December 14, 1876
*From "Frank Leslie's Illustrated Newspaper," December 30.
Courtesy of The New-York Historical Society, New York City*

Photograph taken in New Orleans around 1872
Courtesy of the National Archives

JAMES LONGSTREET

The metropolitan police under Longstreet attacking New Orleans citizens
near the Customs House *(see page 286)*
*From "Frank Leslie's Illustrated Newspaper," October 3, 1874. Courtesy of the
Howard-Tilton Memorial Library, Tulane University, New Orleans, Louisiana*

JEFFERSON DAVIS

With members of his household at his
home, Beauvoir, at Biloxi, Mississippi,
1885, photographed by Edward L. Wilson
*From the Collections of the Library of
Congress*

Davis leaving Richmond, Virginia,
Courthouse after his release on bail
(see page 321)
From "Harper's Weekly," June 1, 1867.
Courtesy of the New York Public Library

ently, Lamar was given an opportunity to practice these preachments.

On March 11, 1874, Charles Sumner, the Massachusetts Senator, Abolitionist and one of the chief architects of Republican
Reconstruction policy, died. A few days later, before a packed
gallery and a full House of Representatives, Lamar delivered a
eulogy on Sumner that astounded the nation. It was an ungrudging
acknowledgment of the sincerity and idealism of Sumner's career,
coupled with a plea for an end to sectional bitterness and strife.
"Let us hope," he said, "that future generations, when they remember the deeds of heroism and devotion done on both sides,
will speak not of Northern prowess and Southern courage, but
of the heroism, fortitude, and courage of Americans in a war of
ideas; a war in which each section signalized its consecration to
the principles, as each understood them, of American liberty
and of the Constitution received from their fathers." Then he
concluded with the memorable and historic phrase, "My countrymen, *know* one another, and you will *love* one another." So moving, so brilliantly delivered were Lamar's sentiments that Congressmen and spectators wept. In helping to heal the wounds of
a war that had rent the nation and desolated much of it, here
was probably the most important single speech ever delivered
in the House.

"It must begin to dawn upon even the most inveterate rebel
haters in Congress, and the press," said the Springfield (Mass.)
Republican, "that the war is indeed over." The speech "is instinct
with the patriot's pride and faith," said the Boston *Advertiser.*
"Evidence of the real restoration of the Union," was the verdict
of the Boston *Globe.* Two Boston papers, the *Transcript* and the
Herald, thought Lamar's generosity and tolerance proved that
Republican policy in the South had erred in not following a more
moderate course and working with such natural leaders as Lamar
rather than through carpetbaggers, scalawags and uneducated
blacks.

Southern papers praised Lamar no less. As Lamar himself said,
"I never in all my life opened my lips with a purpose more single

to the interests of our Southern people. . . . I wanted to seize an opportunity, when universal attention could be arrested, and directed to what I was saying, to speak to the North in behalf of my own people."

Congressman James G. Blaine of Maine, the Speaker of the House, later gave a shrewd and realistic, but no less complimentary evaluation of Lamar's achievement: "It was a mark of positive genius in a Southern representative to pronounce a fervid and discriminating eulogy upon Mr. Sumner, and skillfully to interweave with it a defense of that which Mr. Sumner . . . believed to be the sum of all villainies. Only a man of Mr. Lamar's peculiar mental type could have accomplished the task. . . . There is a certain Orientalism in the mind of Mr. Lamar, strangely admixed with typical Americanism. He is full of reflection; seemingly careless, yet closely observant; apparently dreamy, yet altogether practical."

Lamar was henceforth listened to with respect and consideration by all members of the House, including those of the dominant Republican party. In June 1874, he reviewed before the House the deplorable Reconstruction scandals in Louisiana relating to a contested election for governor, and at the same time coupled the Louisiana debacle with a general survey of Radical Republican excesses in the South. "No party supported by the moral sentiment of the American people," he said, "can long bear the responsibility of the infamy and disgrace which these grotesque caricatures of government have brought upon the very name of Republicanism."

Every one of these state governments, continued Lamar, "depends every moment of its existence upon the will of the President. That will makes and unmakes them. A short proclamation backed by one company determines who is to be the governor of Arkansas; a telegram settles the civil magistracy of Texas; a brief order to a general in New Orleans wrests a State government from the people of Louisiana." This speech, "though listened to by all the Republican leaders," reported one observer, was "neither answered nor contradicted and could not be, because the facts were indisputable."

Members of the House crowded around Lamar, however, to congratulate him after the speech, and papers, North and South, praised the address almost as highly as they had the one on Sumner. The Boston *Advertiser* declared that the "generous temper, the nobility of sentiment, and the moving eloquence of the present representative from Mississippi are doing more than anything else could to dispel unpleasant feeling and to promote good offices between sections of the Union." In Mississippi the Jackson *Clarion* called the address "a most triumphant vindication of a wronged people, executed in a style so knightly as to disarm opposition and compel attention and respect."

By the close of the session, Lamar had become in the eyes of his fellow Congressmen and of the nation, one of the leaders of the House. He had answered to his own cry of the 1850's for a statesman who could "rise above the passions and prejudices of the times." He was concerned only with the extent to which his efforts might serve to promote national harmony and hasten the end of the oppressive Reconstruction regimes in the South. He knew that in eulogizing Sumner, in speaking in conciliatory terms to the North and publicly accepting the political and constitutional results of the Northern victory, he was risking repudiation by the South, but he took this risk. On the whole, the people of his state supported him.

To a constituent who wrote urging that Lamar speak out to "expose the villainy and corruption" of the national administration and "the outrages upon our liberties," he replied that such an attack would only stir up sectional bitterness and strengthen the hold of the Radical Republicans. The Radicals, said Lamar, would gladly "raise a purse of $50,000" to reward any Southern leader who would so help their cause by making an intemperate and public attack on President Grant. The dominant party, he pointed out, "has even yet the power to inflict upon our defenseless people suffering or oppression which awakened resentments may invent. . . . The only course I, in common with other Southern representatives, have to follow, is to do what we can to allay excitement between the sections, and to bring about peace and reconciliation. That will be the foundation upon which we may establish a constitutional government for the whole country, and local self-government for the South."

"My recent speeches," he wrote a member of his family, "have not been prompted by self-seeking motives. It was necessary that some Southern man should say and do what I said and did. I knew that if I did it I would run the risk of losing the confidence of the Southern people. . . . Yet I loved my people more than I did their approval. I saw a chance to convert their enemies into friends, and to change bitter animosities into sympathy and regard. If I had let the opportunity pass without doing what I have, I would never have got over the feeling of self-reproach."

Republican misrule in the South, the scandals of the Grant Administration and—it is not too much to say—Lamar's own words and deeds, all contributed to a great victory for the Democrats in the national elections of November 1874. The House of Representatives went Democratic for the first time since the War. Papers in all parts of the country enthusiastically suggested Lamar for Speaker of the House, even for Vice President in the next Presidential campaign. Lamar declined to be considered for either post, believing that it was not appropriate or wise for a Southerner to hold such offices as yet.

He worked busily, however, to counteract a serious threat in the House from the lame-duck Republican majority, which sought to ram through various bills giving wide powers to President Grant to continue Republican Reconstruction in the South even after the Democrats took control of the House. Particularly obnoxious was the so-called "Force Bill," that would give the President dictatorial powers to control elections in Arkansas, Alabama, Louisiana, and Mississippi, states as yet under carpetbag rule, thereby helping to guarantee not only continued Republican control of those states but also the continuation of Republican occupancy of the White House after the next Presidential election. The Force Bill was so extreme and its constitutionality was so doubtful that some Republicans, including Speaker Blaine, gave support, open or tacit, to Lamar's extraordinary efforts to defeat it. In the end by parliamentary maneuvering and delaying tactics Lamar prevented the passage of the bill.

Lamar was also able to cause some tempering of a civil rights bill, a legacy from Charles Sumner. On many occasions he had avowed his acceptance of the postwar constitutional amendments granting full rights to the Negro and had urged his constituents to do the same. However, he felt that attempts to spell out by legislation in Washington the exact details of these rights was a mistake. Such a move would only create tension and imperil normal race relations—as, indeed, experience in the Reconstruction years had already proved. The Federal government, said Lamar, "by constituting itself as the Negro's sole protector in the State drives him to trust only its agents and partisans, often men of the vilest character, and rarely men who have any material relation to the State or to society among us. The Negro is thus isolated from the white people among whom he lives." And Lamar knew in the 1870's, just as many Southerners did nearly a century later, how disastrous this isolation could be for the Negro.

After the adjournment of Congress, Lamar made several speeches in New Hampshire at the request of the Democratic party, a move designed to convince Northern voters that the Democrats were truly a national party and that Southern Democrats were fully reconciled to the verdict of Appomattox. No better choice could have been made. He spoke to large audiences, made up of members of both parties, who turned out to hear this former Confederate officer and diplomatic envoy. Lamar spoke frankly of the "corruption, cupidity and graft, peculation and embezzlement, intimidation of voters, bribery, waste of public treasure, loss of public credit, fraudulent balloting, intimidation by the Federal military, taxation in all its grinding and diversified forms" prevailing in the South under the Reconstruction regimes. But he assured his hearers of the South's acceptance of the results of the war, including the rights granted the freed slaves, and he pleaded for understanding and justice. Lamar also spoke in

Boston, taking as his topic Daniel Webster and John Calhoun and praising both as men who loved and revered the Constitution, though they agreed to disagree on interpreting it.

The famous Southern newspaperman and inventor of the New South movement, Henry W. Grady, wrote of him at this period: "Mr. Lamar has all the physical characteristics of his knightly and illustrious family—that peculiar swarthy complexion, pale but clear; the splendid gray eyes; the high cheek bones; the dark brown hair; the firm and fixed mouth; the face thoroughly haughty and reserved when in repose, and yet full of snap and fire and magnetism. Added to these was that indefinable something which all great men carry about them."

At home in Mississippi, Lamar threw himself into the political campaign of 1875. He was a candidate for re-election, and public opinion in the state and nation were alike in demanding his return to Washington. But affairs in Mississippi had gone from bad to worse. The carpetbag governor, Adelbert Ames, was surrounded by an administration of corrupt officials maintained in office by armed Negroes and Federal troops. T. W. Cordoza, the Negro superintendent of education, was under indictment in New York for larceny. At all levels of government—municipal, county, and state—the stealing of public funds and falsification of records to cover the thefts were commonplace. Taxes had been increased 1,400 per cent in five years, with the result that in 1874, a total of 6,000,000 acres of land were forfeited for taxes—more land than there was in the states of Massachusetts and Rhode Island combined.

The bonded debt of the river town of Vicksburg (population 12,443), had increased from $13,000 in 1869 to $1,400,000 in 1874, most of the money finding its way into the pockets of county and city officials. In 1864, a Taxpayer's League organized to wrest control from the Negroes, cleaned house in the city and set about reforming the county. A riot followed. Many former Federal soldiers in the town fought with the whites against the armed Negroes. Sixteen persons were killed. There was another and bloody riot during the following summer at Clinton, near

Jackson, the state capital, and there were constant threats of out-breaks at other towns in the state.

In May 1875, representatives of the aroused and desperate white citizens assembled at Jackson and issued a memorial to the nation written by Lamar, listing their grievances. As one Mississippian expressed it, "We are fleeced and robbed on all sides, and we are powerless to prevent it, either by law or the force of public opinion." Lamar, aided by James Z. George, a rising leader in state politics, who had become chairman of the State Democratic Committee, mapped a strategy whereby organizations were set up in each county to work during the fall elections "by legitimate means to regain control of our public affairs, and thus secure to all classes, white and black, the blessings of a just and honest government."

He constantly decried the forming of parties on racial lines, but the whole policy of the Radical Republicans had been to ex-ploit the Negro vote by inciting the freedman against the native white man. Governor Ames had even sponsored an abortive scheme to reorganize Lamar's Congressional district so that it would be predominantly Negro, hoping thereby to defeat him. Before the State Democratic Convention in August, Lamar strongly opposed setting up the Democrats as a white man's party, and he urged that the rights of "the newly enfranchised race" be respected. In speeches all over the state, sometimes two or three a day, Lamar continued to appeal for and to the Negro, and the Democrats confidently expected to win over a sizeable colored vote. Many intelligent Negroes were themselves resentful of the corrupt Radical leadership and were tired of being herded to the polls and told how to vote.

If a really serious conflict in Mississippi had forced Grant to send in Federal troops, this would, of course, have strengthened the Radical position. "The blood of twenty-five or thirty Negroes," said Governor Ames, "would benefit the party in the State." Ames did indeed call on Grant for troops and used the Negro state militia to buttress his position. But Grant refused; the country, he said, was weary of these continued calls for Federal troops.

There is no doubt that Lamar's speech on Sumner and his other speeches, notably in New Hampshire and Boston, had helped to convince the rest of the country that the South was safely back in the Union and should be permitted the same freedom to control its affairs as other states had. Of Ames, the New York *Herald* said: "He has corrupted the courts, has protected criminals, and has played even with the lives of the blacks in a manner that, if this fall a good legislature should be elected, ought to procure his impeachment."

The election campaign, which had begun with both sides arming themselves to the teeth, ended in a somewhat less trigger-happy fashion. The contenders tacitly agreed to refrain from the use of bullets and to limit their attention to the ballot. Democrats wearing the characteristic red shirt that came to be symbolic of the "Redeemers" all over the South, did not necessarily abandon their sidearms. Rallies were noisy, excitement was unbounded, but shooting was generally into the air. Undoubtedly, the white Democrats, though they carefully avoided riots and incidents, engaged in a considerable degree of intimidation and economic pressure to frighten away or at least control the Negro voters. This policy of keeping the lid tightly sealed on the powder keg came to be known as the "Mississippi Plan," and it was imitated elsewhere, especially in South Carolina in the following year. Much of this strategy was conceived by Lamar.

The 1875 elections brought a resounding victory for the Democrats. The new legislature forthwith began to clean house. The Negro lieutenant governor, A. K. Davis, was immediately convicted of bribery and removed from office. The Negro superintendent of education, Cordoza, resigned to escape impeachment. In February, twenty-three counts of impeachment against Governor Ames were presented in the Legislature, but he agreed to resign if the charges were not pressed. His offer was accepted, and Ames left the state.

In the "redemption" of Mississippi, Lamar was indisputably the dominant figure. He had convinced the nation at large of the evils of Radical Reconstruction. He had also made clear his state's acceptance of the results of the War. At the same time he restrained extremists in his own party who would have resorted to violence and extraordinary measures that might have brought down new forms of oppression upon the state. His wise and moderate stand won support even from those of the opposition, including many Negroes.

The Forty-fourth Congress, meeting in December 1875, brought many more prominent white Southerners and former Confederate leaders to Washington. Lamar declined to be considered for Speaker of the House, but did serve as chairman of the Democratic party caucus, declaring the aim of his party to be "to restore the Constitution to its pristine strength and authority, and to make it the protector of every section and of every State in the Union and of every human being of every race, color, and condition in the land." To which the New York *Evening Post* replied: "A more genuine, conservative, comprehensive, sound politico-economic, and above all, Union speech could not have been made by Thomas Jefferson himself."

The good will and loyalty expressed by Lamar and other Southern leaders in the new Congress were well received in the North. Nationwide revulsion against the scandals of the Grant Administration endangered Republican control of the government. With a scarcity of things about which the party might boast, except that it had "won the war," Republican Congressional leaders were soon reduced to waving the bloody shirt in an effort to stir up for their own benefit the sectional animosities Lamar had so skillfully allayed. One such occasion was a violent interchange in the House between Blaine, who had Presidential ambitions, and Ben Hill of Georgia over a bill that would have provided amnesty to all ex-Confederates. By an impassioned and unusually effective speech, designed to counteract Blaine's maneuver, Lamar pleaded for harmony and "a restored and fraternal Union," thereby doing much to avert serious damage to the cause of reconciliation.

Meanwhile there were occasional outbreaks of violence in the South, caused by extremists on both sides. One such incident occurred in Hamburg, South Carolina, in July 1876, where several persons were killed. There was an attempt to make political capital out of the incident in the House, but here again Lamar's words had a calming effect.

Lamar shrewdly, and with justice, made a careful distinction between the carpetbag and Negro Republican state governments in the South and the Republicans of the North. The former were governments, he said,

which are called Republican governments; but it is a spurious Republicanism, which has no identification or sympathy with the views and purposes that have inspired the following of the great Republican party of this country. And, sir, those State governments have invariably encouraged these disorders and these murders by their inefficiency, by their imbecility, by their cowardice, and by their connivance; for they have in every instance not only failed to punish these murders, not only failed to administer justice, not only failed to execute the laws, but they have used the occurrences as occasions to appeal to Congress and the North for help in maintaining the power which they are so ruthlessly exercising.

Meanwhile there had been a growing demand that Lamar be advanced to the Senate to succeed James Alcorn. The movement grew so strong that a party caucus in Mississippi in January 1876, nominated Lamar unanimously, and a few days later a joint session of the two houses of the legislature elected him with only a scattering of opposing votes. He was to take his seat in 1877.

Lamar took a leading part in the Presidential campaign of the summer and fall of 1876 that found Democratic Governor Samuel J. Tilden of New York running against Republican Governor Rutherford B. Hayes of Ohio. It was the first opportunity since the War for Mississippi to participate freely in a Presidential election without the supervision of Federal troops. In Mississippi the Democrats scored a complete victory, winning all six Congressional seats and casting the state's electoral votes for Tilden.

In the contested Presidential election, Lamar, as a member of the House, did what he could to assure justice for Tilden. He voted to set up the nonpartisan Election Commission, but when its actions became obviously partisan, he voted against accepting the Commission's report in favor of Hayes. In the crisis that followed, Lamar was the leading Southern negotiator in drafting the bargain that saved the day for the nation—and for the South.

The diary and papers of Rutherford B. Hayes have shed considerable light on the origin and nature of the "Bargain of '77" and of Lamar's dominant role in it. In December 1876, Hayes wrote that he and Colonel William H. Roberts, a New Orleans editor, had discussed the matter. Roberts called upon Hayes to give him "the views of Lamar of Mississippi, Walthall, ditto, Wade Hampton of South Carolina, and probably General Gordon of Georgia." Then Roberts came to the point. "You will be President," he said. "We will not make trouble. We want peace. We want the color line abolished. We will not oppose an administration which will favor an honest administration and honest officers in the South." Not the least intriguing feature of the Roberts declaration is the reminder that the color line in Southern politics was invented by the Northern Republicans as a means of discriminating against the Southern whites.

In February 1877, in the final, critical stages of the bargaining, Hayes invited Lamar to a private meeting at his Ohio home, where mutual commitments were made. Lamar's support of the compromise and Hayes' acceptance of it created difficulties for both with their respective supporters. It was soon obvious in Mississippi, however, that Lamar had taken the best possible course for the South. Shortly after his election, Hayes, not without some sharp reminders from Lamar, was true to his promises. Federal troops were recalled from Florida, Louisiana, and South Carolina, and the carpetbag politicians were retired to private life, or at least to political offices elsewhere than in the states they had so long dominated.

Even after Hayes was inaugurated, there still remained the question of whether Lamar would be seated in the Senate. No former high-ranking Confederate had yet become a Senator. Georgia's Alexander Stephens, elected earlier to that body, had been denied his seat. Some Republicans were charging that the Mississippi elections had been marked by intimidation. Lamar, however, had strong support, both in Mississippi and in Washington, from Negroes as well as whites, Republicans as well as Democrats. Many Negroes had voted the Democratic ticket, and Hiram R. Revels, a former Negro Senator from Mississippi, had written to Grant and told him so. That should have satisfied all but the die-hards. In the end, after a brief dispute, Lamar was permitted to take his seat. Worthy of note is the fact that the Senator from Mississippi was aided by the timely parliamentary maneuvering of James G. Blaine, now a Senator from Maine and traditionally a Republican waver of bloody shirts.

Lamar spent the summer of 1877 resting at his Oxford home. In August he attended, as a delegate from his county, the Democratic State Convention at Jackson. His efforts, as usual, were directed toward party harmony, state and national, and he advised the party to permit Negro participation.

One of Lamar's greatest speeches offended many people in his own state. In 1873, Congress had suspended the coinage of the silver dollar, which had been out of circulation for forty years, thanks to a scarcity of silver. By the late seventies, the silver supply had greatly increased, and a restoration of the silver dollar would have resulted in the coining of dollars containing less than a dollar's worth of silver. This would have created inflation—something the debtor classes wanted. Such doings seemed to many, including Lamar, dishonest; it would have permitted the redemption of obligations in a devaluated currency. Times were hard, however, and many persons seized on the device as an inflationary, antidepression step.

The Mississippi Legislature requested the state's senators and representatives in Congress to support the bill for silver inflation. Lamar's speech came when he informed the Congress of his instructions and then proceeded to state his reasons for not following them. While his vote against the bill drew an implied rebuke from the Legislature, which passed a resolution praising the Negro Senator, Blanche K. Bruce, for his support, there was general admiration for Lamar's integrity. There was irony in the fact that he endangered his political career to support payment in gold of

Federal war debts incurred in crushing the South, while many Northern Senators, with an eye on the ballot box, heeded popular clamor and pushed the bill through to passage. Already the "Redeemers" seemed to be turning into "Bourbons," as the conservative pro-industrial element in the South soon came to be called.

Lamar did not find his course easy. In a private letter to a friend he wrote, "It is indeed a heavy cross," he said, "to lay upon the heart of a public man to have to take a stand which causes the love and confidence of the constituents to flow away from him. But the liberty of this country and its great interests will never be secure if its public men become the mere menials to do the biddings of their constituents instead of being representatives in the true sense of the word, looking to the lasting prosperity and future interests of the whole country." Nearly two decades later, Lamar's party was going to heed another leader who spoke of a cross—"a cross of gold." He was young William Jennings Bryan, who had gone all the way for free silver to the horror of the Southern conservative element but to the delight of the rising Southern Demagogues.

The South was slowly regaining its position in the government and the nation, but there were periodic flare-ups in Congress of sectional feeling, often as a cloak for political scheming. Lamar stood firmly for his section but worked for harmony. His ability to think on his feet in extemporaneous Congressional debate frequently enabled him to repulse fierce attacks. He defeated an attempt by Maine's Republican Senator Blaine to revive the question of Negro voting and Southern election practices. Blaine's action arose from a Northern uneasiness at the emergence of the Solid South—solidly Democratic, that is. The blame, of course, was correctly laid at the door of the Republican party and its Radical Reconstruction policies. In a fierce barb directed at the Radicals, Lamar observed that Blaine would have done the race problem service had he and the Republicans proposed "some well-devised scheme of public education by which this newly enfranchised race may be fitted to exercise their great duties as freemen and citizens and as participants in the sovereignty of Commonwealths."

In March 1879, Lamar reacted swiftly to a bloody-shirt speech
by Senator George F. Hoar of Massachusetts comparing Jefferson
Davis to Aaron Burr and Benedict Arnold. "Jefferson Davis,"
said Senator Lamar, "stands in precisely the position that I stand
in, that every Southern man who believed in the right of a State
to secede stands. The only difference between myself and Jefferson Davis is that his exalted character, his preeminent talents, his
well-established reputation as a statesman, as a patriot, and as a
soldier, enabled him to take the lead in a cause to which I con-
secrated myself. . . . Jefferson Davis is honored among the
Southern people. He did only what they sought to do; he was
simply chosen to lead them in a cause which we all cherished. . . .
The people of the South drank their inspiration from the fountain
of devotion to liberty and to constitutional government." Later in
the same debate Lamar expressed his gratitude for the generosity
"of the victorious section in its treatment of the section that was
conquered." The reunited nation was a "great, imposing and inspiring spectacle." Shrewd Southern orators like Lamar had long
ago learned that the best answer to the waving of the bloody
shirt was the waving of the flag.

Later in a bitter senatorial debate on a military appropriation
bill to forbid use of Federal troops in controlling Southern elections, Lamar tangled with Senator Roscoe Conkling of New York.
Conkling replied angrily, "Should the member from Mississippi,
except in the presence of the Senate, charge me, by intimidation or
otherwise, with falsehood, I would denounce him as a blackguard,
as a coward, and a liar." To this Lamar answered, "I have only to
say that the Senator from New York understood me correctly. I
did mean to say just precisely the words and all they imported. I
beg pardon of the Senate for the unparliamentary language. It
was very harsh; it was very severe; it was such as no good man
would deserve, and no brave man would wear."

"In the dead silence that followed Lamar's subtle and fatal
stab," reported the Washington *Capital,* "Conkling was to the last
degree unnerved and confused. . . . The point to the whole
affair, however, is the fact that the terrible thrust came from the

coolest, politest, and most self-controlled member of the Senate. Lamar, of Mississippi, has been noted for his courteous bearing in both public and private life." Lamar was indeed slow to anger, but under attack he could be deadly. No longer did he wave aloft pieces of furniture, as he had done in the Oxford courthouse during a Klan trial in 1871. He had now learned to flail with words.

Yet Lamar could still go beyond verbal combat. On one occasion Senator O. D. Conger of Michigan made an insulting personal reference to him in a speech. The next day Lamar walked over to Conger, looked him straight in the eye, and said, "Conger, you are always talking about fighting, but never fight; that's where you and I are a good deal unlike. I don't talk about fighting, but I am ready for it any time." Conger said nothing and Lamar walked back to his seat. Senator Conger's subsequent references to Lamar were remarkably temperate.

While Lamar was vigilant in the Senate in upholding the position of his state and region in a restored Union, he labored in Mississippi when Congress was not in session to keep peace among the divergent elements in his party and to create national as well as sectional unity. In 1879 there was real danger that some of the "unreconstructed" Bourbon Democrats would not only precipitate a split in the party (with the result that the Republicans might regain control) but provoke a revival of sectional feeling. In many respects Lamar was a Bourbon of the Bourbons, but he parted company with them when they forgot their moderation of '76. The Bourbons, he said, "unwisely invite upon themselves and the State a restoration of the evils from which, since Democratic supremacy was established, we have been slowly recovering by means of conservatism and moderation." For the time being, his influence was strong enough to keep his party united and the conservative faction in control of the state.

In 1879 the strain of a summer of campaigning and speech making, followed in October by the death of his mother in Macon, Georgia, caused Lamar to suffer from one of his periodic apoplectic attacks. He did not take his seat in the Senate until February

1880. Even then he wrote his wife, "I am easily fatigued, and writing makes my head swim. My arm is heavy and weak, but I have thrown aside my crutches and walk with a stick."

In Washington the artificer of reconciliation had an opportunity to launch an attack on an attempted revival of the racial issue, specifically in a speech by Senator William Windom of Minnesota. Lamar's rebuttal Senator Hoar of Massachusetts called "the very best speech that could possibly be made on that side of the question." A Washington correspondent observed:

The influence wielded in Congress by Colonel Lamar is peculiar and wonderful, and it is fair to say that no man's utterances are so attentively regarded and considered by the members of all parties in both Houses. . . . If it is known that he is to speak, the galleries are crowded; every official of the capitol deserts his office for the Senate Chamber; while all the members of the House of Representatives who can get away from their own hall are found on the floor of the Senate . . . each man feeling that, in the remarks that are falling from the lips of the distinguished Mississippian, his peculiar political faith or belief is receiving the strongest possible support, or is being entirely undermined and crushed.

That summer Lamar rested at Oxford. His health was poor. "I am so liable to attacks of vertigo that I cannot prepare a detailed speech. I cannot study documents without a painful swimming in the head, nor bend over to write without a rush of blood to the brain."

More serious, his wife was quite ill with tuberculosis. "I have been in the room of my invalid wife for twenty-one days," he wrote "scarce an hour of which she has spent in freedom from pain." Yet he took part in the election campaign of 1880, in which the Democratic Presidential candidate, W. S. Hancock of Pennsylvania, was defeated by James A. Garfield of Ohio. Whatever the fortunes of his party, Lamar, as a Mississippi newspaper observed, stood as "a great, central, conservative power in himself, able to repel force with force when the attack is directed against his people, able to restrain impolitic impetuosity when his own people rush to the attack. In heart, in interest, in high commission, a Mississippian, he is a great national conservator of the peace, whose sphere and influence are almost limitless."

Yet Lamar had some opposition, especially from extremists who opposed his moderate attitude toward the North. These hot-heads still remembered his active role in the Bargain of '77 that had made Hayes President and his conservative stand in the silver coinage controversy. In 1881, he voted to give a pension to General Grant. In fact, Lamar was the only Southern Democratic Senator to speak in support of the bill. In the state legislative elections of that year Lamar's Senate seat was at stake. Had he alienated his Mississippi constituents? The answer came in unmistakable terms. His supporters were swept into office, and Lamar was re-elected when the Legislature convened in January, 1882. Among the legislators who voted for him was the Negro Republican, J. A. Shorter.

Lamar returned to the Senate to become embroiled in the first sustained Democratic attack on the protective tariff since the hegemony in national affairs of the prewar Democrats. In the sixties the Republicans had risen to power in the industrial east with promises of a high protective tariff. Once levied, the tariff not only remained, it increased; for Big Business would not hear to a curtailment.

By 1883, when the Democrats won control of the House of Representatives, Lamar was ready to launch a vigorous attack. The New York *Evening Post,* reporting the substance of Lamar's first oratorical assault on the tariff, pointed out how Lamar had sarcastically observed that the United States was "probably the only country in the world whose people were severely and superfluously taxed . . . because their rulers were unable to devise a mode of reducing that taxation." Lamar also denounced the practice of "paying bounties to certain business interests" in the form of the tariff, thus making American industry "dependent for existence, not upon the natural development of resources and the natural growth of industries, but upon taxation by the government."

Perhaps no less fateful than the tariff speech in its significance was Lamar's forthright defense of Federal aid to public education in an address on March 28, 1884. It is startling to note that the

South, which in the ante-bellum period and again in the troubled mid-twentieth century would have few words of favor for Federal aid to education, should produce vigorous affirmation of such a policy in the 1880's by a supposedly conservative leader. Lamar spoke enthusiastically for a bill to permit temporary aid to public schools, mostly in the South. Constitutional objections he cast aside in welcoming what he felt would bring "unspeakable benefits" to the entire population of the South, white and black.

Prior to the Civil War the South's system of private colleges, schools, and academies had made public education a sometime thing. But the double economic blows of War and Reconstruction had pulled the financial rug out from under private schooling in most parts of the South. When carpetbag governments forced public schools upon the South, there was at first bitter resistance. Schools were burned and schoolmasters driven out of town, for the public schools set up by the Radicals were largely for Negroes and the white taxpayer had to foot the bill. Then, when Reconstruction was ended, the destitute Southerner suddenly realized that if he were to educate his children at all, the task had to be performed at public expense. Not always were these schools, either for Negroes or whites, given adequate financial support, for money was lacking. But public schools were almost universally accepted, and became the educational novitiate for Southern whites of all classes: the tenant farmer and the planter, the worker and the industrial leader.

Probably never in the turbulent history of American public schooling had democracy in education come nearer achievement among the whites. In the eighties a Massachusetts educator described the Southern public school as "the most favorable, the most persistent, the most devoted public school now in any part of the world." The first school integration ever to be known in the South was not a racial one but a social one. Wherever else the Southerner maintained his sense of class, he lost it in the public school as few Americans ever had before him or have done since.

Not many Southerners were conscious of what was really happening. As much as anything else it was a matter of an economic determinant known as "impoverishment"; but it happened. Cer-

tainly L. Q. C. Lamar must have understood. "Now," he observed in his remarks to the Senate, "the common school system
has become the indispensable factor in diffusing education generally throughout the South." And Lamar felt that universal
schooling could do for the Negro what it was doing for the white.
Actually his support of the Federal subsidy was predicated largely
upon the aid it could give the white man in the financial support
of Negro schools. "In my opinion," said Lamar, "this bill is a
decided step toward the solution of the problem of race."

Back in Mississippi, Lamar's personal affairs were complicated
by the worsening condition of Mrs. Lamar. She died at Oxford in
December 1884, before Lamar could reach home. He wrote to his
sister: "The present is a dark period of my life. The pale face of
my wife is ever before me, and my grief seems to have fixed itself
in my heart." Two years later, in January 1887, Lamar was married to Henrietta Holt, widow of General William S. Holt, former
president of the Southwestern Railroad Company. The second Mrs.
Lamar, wealthy and socially prominent in Washington, was a
native of Macon, Georgia, and Lamar had known her since boyhood.

Lamar returned to Washington in 1885, to find he might be
appointed to the Cabinet by the incoming President, Grover
Cleveland, the first Democrat elected to the office since the Civil
War. Lamar did not seek the post—that of Secretary of the Interior—and he accepted it with some reluctance, knowing full well
that President Cleveland by appointing a Southerner would probably join Jeff Davis on the "sour apple tree." But Cleveland was
not a man to be deterred by fear of public reaction, especially from
the die-hard Radicals.

Lamar wrote Davis:

I hope that the step I am about to take will meet your approval. It
certainly proceeds from no motive of ambition; but when pressed by my
friends in the Senate and in the House, and through the country, and
by those nearest to the President-elect, to take a position in his Cabinet,
I have hardly felt at liberty to decline. If, by conducting the affairs of
the executive department prudently and honestly and fairly to all sections, I may serve the interests of a common country, I may do more

good than I have ever yet been able to accomplish. . . . Recent events have crushed out all ambition in my heart, and I now have no other desire connected with public affairs except to serve to the best the interests that our people have entrusted to me so often. . . . I am inclined to think that I ought to have retired when I saw the South restored to her Constitutional position in the Union. . . . I have always thought it was a serious blemish, or rather defect, in our American statesmen, that they always cling to office too long.

The Senate confirmed Lamar as Secretary of the Interior, despite some opposition, and most Northern newspapers approved, with the New York *Times* commending Lamar's "original and thoughtful mind, conservative habit, and sobriety of judgment," and observed that in the new Cabinet member "the President secures a good adviser and an administrative officer whose deep-rooted aversion to such doubtful and devious ways as have of late caused the Interior Department to be made the subject of unfavorable comment cannot fail to have a wholesome effect."

Lamar soon impressed the nation with the efficiency of his administration. He had the Southern Redeemer's sense of economy. He even cut down sharply on the numerous horses and carriages maintained for the use of Department employees. Lamar was conscientious in the administration of public lands, and he vigorously pushed civil service reform. He scrupulously backed the actions of his subordinates, even if he questioned their judgment. The Mississippi Negro ex-Senator Bruce later recalled how Lamar for some time paid from his own pocket the salary of a Negro cleaning woman who had been discharged by the Department and for whom Bruce interceded. Lamar did not want to interfere in the handling of the incident by a Department official, but he was anxious that the woman should not be in want.

Lamar's administration of the Interior Department received national acclaim. The Washington *Post* called him "the brainiest, most logical, and clear-headed" Secretary ever to fill the post. The Augusta (Georgia) *Constitutionalist* described him as "the most fascinating member of the Cabinet, the most active, hard working and industrious. So far he has completely put to the sword all predictions that he would be a scholastic dreamer and moody talker."

One of Lamar's best known addresses he made in April 1887, at Charleston, South Carolina, on the occasion of the unveiling of a monument to John C. Calhoun. Into the speech Lamar poured all of his lifetime study of the Southern viewpoint on the American political system as enunciated by Calhoun, together with the conclusions appropriate to the facts of American history since Calhoun's death. It was, in a way, Lamar's valedictory political speech. It was heard and applauded by thousands and read by other thousands over the nation. In his address Lamar paid tribute to the accomplishments of the "lion-hearted" Wade Hampton and felt that old John C. Calhoun would be happy to see South Carolina restored to "dignity and equality in the Union." South Carolina would sacrifice no principle and falsify no sentiment "in accepting the verdict" and would "henceforth . . . seek the happiness of her people, their greatness and glory, in the greatness and glory of the American Republic."

In December, President Cleveland nominated Lamar to the United States Supreme Court. It was an honor that had been rumored for some months and had at first been almost universally applauded. A small group of extremist Republican politicians and newspapers, however, sought to make political capital of the matter and gained some support from party members. Lamar did not wish to continue in the Cabinet while his nomination was being considered, lest it be thought he was in position to influence Senators about to vote on his confirmation; so he resigned.

The Republican Cincinnati *Commercial-Gazette* declared that "the Supreme Court is in danger as well as the Senate of the United States." Similarly, the Cleveland *Leader* argued: "Little ground now remains for the South to win back in order to regain all its lost prestige and posts of honor and emolument. The Army and Navy will doubtless soon be attacked by the Democrats in behalf of ex-Confederate officers." Some of the opposition to Lamar came from extremists in his own party. The Jackson *New Mississippian,* an unyielding, unreconstructed paper, complained of "the extraordinarily conservative course which he had pursued at Washington, the preference which he has shown to the Grand Army of the Republic, and the tenderness with which he has dealt with the negro Republicans from Mississippi."

The Richmond *Whig* characterized Lamar as "the peer of any man upon the Supreme Bench," despite the "silly charges that have been made against him by malignants." He was "equal to any of them in patriotism and devotion to the Union and the Constitution." When Lamar was finally approved in January 1888, a few Republicans actually joined the Democratic minority in order to make the confirmation possible.

Nevada's Senator William M. Stewart was one of the Republicans who voted for Lamar's confirmation. "The beneficial results of that action of the Senate," said Stewart, "were immediately felt both North and South. Confidence, respect and good fellowship were increased in every section of our common country. It was an object lesson for the world. It marked the contrast between the methods of despotic governments, which never forgive a fallen foe, and our own free government, which, entertaining malice toward none, has charity for all."

Lamar's characteristic modesty caused him to write his son-in-law that he hesitated to accept the nomination, feeling unequal to the position. "I had no more idea of it than I had of the dukedom of Argyle. . . . I have been too long out of the atmosphere of practical jurisprudence, and my misgivings are so painful that I have sleepless nights."

From the day in January 1888, when he assumed his place on the Court at the age of sixty-three, Lamar took an active part in its work. He early attracted attention by the courage and wisdom of his opinions and the force and clarity with which they were expressed. Chief Justice W. M. Fuller said Lamar's was "the most suggestive mind that I ever knew, and not one of us but has drawn from its inexhaustible store." For two years Lamar applied himself vigorously to this new role, and even after 1890, when he was increasingly troubled by illness and failing strength, he conscientiously continued to serve.

Lamar and his wife set out in December 1892, to visit Pass Christian on the Mississippi Gulf Coast. Enroute he suffered a heart attack. At the home of Captain W. H. Virgin, a son-in-law of Mrs. Lamar, in Macon in his native state of Georgia, among friends and relatives, he died quietly on January 23, 1893. He was buried in Macon. Later his body was moved to the cemetery of St. Peter's Episcopal Church in Oxford, Mississippi.

To the grave he bore in his right hand a copy of the United States Constitution he had carried with him for many years. To many that document had been a holy thing. Some had worshipped it; some had called upon it, as to a saint, to do their special bidding; some had presumed to interpret it as they would Scripture; and some had considered it entirely capable of working miracles. Perhaps all were right. Certainly Lamar's veneration for it was something more than a lawyer's quest for ultimate law or a politician's last resort for winning arguments. For Lamar it could work miracles—miracles of reconciliation. It was itself a "bundle of compromises," as any student of the founding of the Republic knows. It had been begotten in reconciliation of faction with faction; and there its strength and its inspiration to Americans, North and South, would lie. Lamar had lived with this Constitution for years, carrying it as it were, next to his heart, as soldiers do Testaments to ward off bullets. When the Union was sundered in '61, he would have no new constitution, only the old one kept inviolate like a cherished relic. When the Union was restored in '65, he could see no other course but a rigid adherence to the ancient gospel which had reconciled a disunited Republic in 1787 and must become the only workable basis for the reconciliation of a divided Union scarcely a century later.

Lamar had not only *lived* with this Constitution; he had become like it. "Until the hour of his death," said the New York *Illustrated American,* "Lamar meant to the South the voice that had stilled faction, restored Constitutional right; to the North the intellect that had penetrated the darkness of Northern doubt. . . . It is as the inspired pacificator that Lamar will stand out unique, almost incomprehensible, to other times. . . ." Like his Constitution, he had become the artificer of reconciliation.

7

Subdued but Unrepentant
"OLD JOE" JOHNSTON

On the April Sunday in 1865 when Lee's Army of Northern Virginia rested finally from its warring, "Old Joe" Johnston's 25,000 men were still fighting stubbornly and well in North Carolina. For most of the war Joe had been battling not only Yanks but Jefferson Davis also; and he had been engaged in almost constant strategic retreat before both of them. At last he had conquered Davis. In February, the Confederate President, against his will, had restored Johnston to command of the old Army of Tennessee. Davis had removed him on the eve of the battle of Atlanta, and General John B. Hood, a favorite of Davis', turned Johnston's orderly retreat before Sherman into a rout, and then foolishly ran away. He lived to fight another day, but only to be defeated at Franklin and Nashville in Tennessee.

And now the peppery, indefatigable Johnston was back, and the remnants of his old Army of Tennessee, augmented by troops from the eastern Carolinas, were standing 25,000 strong against Sherman's 80,000 Yanks near Bentonville in North Carolina. The Confederacy might be dying, but in the Carolinas it would die with its boots on; and Johnston, who would live to be a pallbearer of his chief wartime enemies, Grant and Sherman, would now see that his Confederacy had decent burial.

Almost happy were these last days for Johnston's men. For months they had sung a stanza of their own to "The Yellow Rose of Texas":

And now I'm going Southward,
For my heart is full of woe,
I'm going back to Georgia
To find my "Uncle Joe."

Find him they did. And in less than two months after resuming command, Johnston had instilled renewed confidence in the scattered Confederate troops in the southeast. Reuniting them in the Carolinas, he had slowed General Sherman's heretofore almost unopposed drive north to meet General Grant in Virginia. At Bentonville, on March 19, in the largest battle ever fought in North Carolina, Johnston delivered a severe check to Sherman. It confirmed the Northern general in the high opinion he had held of "Old Joe" since the Atlanta campaign. It was one point, at least, on which Sherman agreed with most Southerners. General Lee himself, in opposing Johnston's removal in 1864, had told Secretary of War J. A. Seddon that if Johnston could not stop Sherman in Georgia, no one could.

Back at the head of an Army, Johnston showed all his old courage and skill in opposing a large and powerful force with a much smaller one. His plan was to slow Sherman in North Carolina and eventually to join with Lee's forces for a blow at Grant or Sherman before the Federal armies could unite. But early on the morning of April 11, he received a dispatch from President Davis, who had come to North Carolina when Richmond was evacuated, that Lee himself had surrendered.

Johnston was summoned to meet Davis at Greensboro. Here were gathered with the Confederate President his Cabinet members and various officers, including General P. G. T. Beauregard. Davis, unyielding to the last, was all for continuing the war, but most of the others, including Johnston, Beauregard, and recently appointed Secretary of War John C. Breckinridge, advised negotiating for peace. On the 13th, a message dictated by a reluctant Davis and signed by Johnston was dispatched to Sherman, asking for an armistice "to permit the Civil authorities to enter into the needful arrangements to terminate the existing war." Sherman, however, agreed only to negotiations affecting the two armies. A meeting was arranged between the commanders for April 17, at a point near Durham.

Johnston rode out to meet Sherman accompanied by his chief of cavalry, General Wade Hampton, and other officers. The two generals—strangers—shook hands and set about the business at hand. Johnston, at fifty-eight, was thirteen years older than the Federal commander. He was erect and military in his bearing, rather small in stature, his complexion florid, his gray eyes bright and flashing. "He was dressed," as an eyewitness observed, "in a neat, gray uniform, which harmonized gracefully with a full beard and mustache of silvery whiteness." The two leaders, still conversing, rode to the near-by farmhouse of one James Bennett to discuss the details of surrender.

Sherman had momentous news for the Confederate general: President Lincoln had been assassinated. Johnston was appalled and in the name of the Confederate government disclaimed the deed, which he called "the worst possible calamity to the South." No Confederate army officer would resort to assassination, Sherman said, but he could not say the same of Southern political leaders. Both men realized that the task of making peace and restoring the Union would now be much more difficult. Sherman did not even inform his own army of Lincoln's death until after he returned from his first day's negotiations; he feared his soldiers would wreak vengeance on Southern homes and on civilians.

The terms were written by Sherman himself after two days of discussion. The combined arguments of Johnston and Breckinridge, who sat in on the meeting on the second day, won from Sherman concessions that went beyond those granted Lee by Grant. Soldiers and officers would be paroled and freed from punishment for participating in the War (as had been agreed at Appomattox), and Confederate arms would be turned over, not to the Federal forces, as Grant had decreed in Virginia, but to the various state governments set up under the relatively mild Lincoln plan for Reconstruction. Sherman reported to Washington that he thought the states should have the means of maintaining order and suppressing possible guerrilla activity. He was convinced, he said, "that all the men of substance" in the South "sincerely want peace."

One Confederate, W. H. Swallow, who was with the troops accompanying President Davis and Cabinet, rode over to see Johnston and was deeply impressed with his kindness, intelligence, and soldierly qualities. "Nothing could have passed off more graciously than these negotiations," he wrote later. "General Johnston impressed all with his superior knowledge of the law of nations in time of war. He was one of the best conversationalists."

For several days, Sherman and Johnston held their armies in their respective positions, awaiting acceptance of the peace terms by President Johnson and his advisers. Both generals feared that bitterness over the death of Lincoln might produce a demand for a less generous settlement. The word came on April 24—Washington had rejected the terms. Moreover, General Grant, commander of all the Union armies, was dispatched to North Carolina to supervise negotiations. Under new instructions, Sherman warned that he would be forced to resume hostilities unless Johnston accepted the terms of Appomattox "purely and simply." Johnston urged Jefferson Davis, now at Charlotte and still calling for last-ditch resistance, to move away speedily to the south or southwest with an escort of cavalry. He himself prepared to meet Sherman once again at the Bennett house and accept the North's new terms. This he did on April 26, and the two generals signed a second agreement for ending hostilities. This peace was approved the next day.

Despite the restlessness of the Confederate troops in these final days of uncertainty, their loyalty to "Old Joe" kept them under control. He set about attending the manifold details of the peace terms in his usual efficient, methodical manner. He had $39,000 in silver coin from the Confederate treasury. This he distributed to his soldiers—$1.15 to each man. He sent reports on the surrender to the governors of states in his command (North and South Carolina, Georgia, Florida), and issued an account for the newspapers. He saw to it that the archives of the Confederate War Department, which had been brought from Richmond when the capital was evacuated, were turned over to Federal forces for safe-keeping.

On May 3, after signing their paroles, the men of the Army of Tennessee started their last march together. Johnston rode with them as far westward as Salisbury, where the men separated to go home. They carried with them the words of the commander whom they had fought under all across the Confederacy, from Chattanooga to Vicksburg, to Atlanta, and the Carolinas. It was a brief, straightforward farewell order, affectionate and spirited. Johnston expressed no bitterness at defeat and looked forward to a strengthened and harmonious reunion of the states:

> Comrades: In terminating our official relations, I most earnestly exhort you to observe faithfully the terms of pacification agreed upon, and to discharge the obligations of good and peaceful citizens at your homes as well as you have performed the duties of thorough soldiers in the field. By such a course you will best secure the comfort of your families and kindred and restore tranquility to your country.
>
> You will return to your homes with the admiration of our people, won by the courage and noble devotion you have displayed in this long war. I shall always remember with pride the loyal support and generous confidence you have given me.
>
> I now part with you with deep regret—and bid you farewell with feelings of cordial friendship and with earnest wishes that you may have hereafter all the prosperity and happiness to be found in the world.

So ended the military career of the brilliant, energetic strategist who had won honor and respect in the Seminole War, the Mexican War, and finally in the Civil War. In each conflict he had fought with great courage with his men, in the thick of battle, and had been grievously wounded. At the battle of Seven Pines on the Virginia Peninsula in 1862, where he was opposing General George B. McClellan's push toward Richmond, he had been wounded so severely that his command had been given to his fellow Virginian Robert E. Lee, with whom he had graduated from West Point in 1829.

Johnston was born in 1807 in southwestern Virginia. His father, a prominent lawyer, had fought in the American Revolution; his mother was a niece of Patrick Henry. After West Point, Johnston had advanced steadily in the Army, early gaining a reputation for thoroughness, hard work, and ambition. He continued to study both professionally and otherwise while in the Army, earning for himself the reputation of being the best educated officer in the service. In the fifties, he was in western service as a lieutenant colonel of the U.S. First Cavalry. Among his friends were Lee, Albert Sidney Johnston (no relation), and George B. McClellan, all in the cavalry.

In 1860, while on detached service in Washington, Johnston was suggested for a vacancy in the post of Army Quartermaster General. It was said that the Secretary of War, John B. Floyd, preferred Joe Johnston to Lee and Albert S. Johnston, and that Jefferson Davis, Chairman of the Senate Military Affairs Committee, supported Albert S. Johnston. In June, the position went to Joe Johnston and with it came the rank of brigadier general. This was not the first time, and it was far from the last, that Johnston and Davis were in opposition, or were presumed to be.

The following year, when Virginia seceded, General Winfield Scott, about to retire from the U.S. Army, urged Johnston, as he had Lee, not to resign from the Federal service. Scott was also a Virginian and a long-time friend, but Johnston believed, as did Lee, that he had no choice but to go with his state. He had taken no part in the sectional controversy or in politics; undoubtedly he would have preferred that the differences be settled peacefully and secession avoided. But he knew he could take no part in a war against Virginia.

Johnston has stated Virginia's position (which was also his own) clearly and succinctly in his *Narrative of Military Operations,* written after the war:

The composition of the convention assembled in Richmond in the spring of 1861, to consider the question of secession, proved that the people of Virginia did not regard Mr. Lincoln's election as a sufficient cause for that measure, for at least two-thirds of its members were elected as "Union men." And they and their constituents continued to be so, until the determination to "coerce" the seceded States was proclaimed by the President of the United States, and Virginia required to furnish her quota of the troops to be organized for the purpose. War being then inevitable, and the convention compelled to decide whether the State should aid in the subjugation of the other Southern States, or join them in the defense of principles it had professed since 1789—belong to the invading party, or to that standing on the defensive—it chose the latter, and passed its ordinance of secession. The people confirmed that choice by an overwhelming vote.

Johnston's wife was the former Lydia McLane of Maryland, daughter of Louis McLane, Senator, Minister to England, member of President Andrew Jackson's Cabinet, and president of the Baltimore and Ohio Railroad. Although she supported Johnston's decision to resign from the United States Army, she had misgivings about his future in the Confederacy. General Scott had talked to her about her husband's resignation.

"Get him to stay with us. We will never disturb him in any way," Scott said.

"My husband cannot stay in an army which is about to invade his native country," she replied.

"Then let him leave our army, but do not let him join theirs."

"This is all very well," she answered. "But how is Joe Johnston to live? He has no private fortune, or no profession but that of arms."

To her husband she was less confident. Not only was she reluctant to leave "home & family & all," but she assured him that Jefferson Davis "hates you, he has power & will ruin you." When the decision was made, however, she was uncomplaining, and there was never any doubt of her loyalty to her husband or to the Southern cause.

On April 22, Johnston walked to the War Department and handed his resignation from the United States Army to Lincoln's Secretary of War, Simon Cameron. The next day the Johnstons left Washington for Richmond. Johnston, in civilian clothes, carried with him the sword used by his father in the Revolution. He was to wear it all during the war—though it was nearly lost in the fighting on the Peninsula (a fellow officer returned to the battlefield under fire and retrieved it after Johnston was wounded). Even before he resigned from the U.S. Army, Johnston had been offered a Confederate commission of equal rank, brigadier general. In Richmond he was given this rank in the Virginia forces at Lee's recommendation and was placed in charge of organizing and instructing the troops pouring into the Virginia capital from all over the Confederacy.

Early in the war General J. E. B. Stuart, the brilliant cavalry leader of the Army of Northern Virginia, described Johnston as "in capacity, head and shoulders above every other general in the Southern Confederacy." "Old Joe" was "erect, alert, quick and decisive of speech," wrote General Richard Taylor, brother-in-law of President Davis, "the beau idea of a soldier . . . brave and impetuous in action . . . a master of logistics."

Lydia Johnston proved correct in her forebodings about her husband's relations with Jefferson Davis. There is a story that ill feelings between the two men stemmed from rivalry over a girl during West Point days, and there may have arisen other points of difference during Davis' ante-bellum tenure as Secretary of War and Senator. Although Johnston was the highest ranking United States Army officer and the only general to join the Confederacy, Davis, in August 1861, placed him fourth in rank among Confederate generals and contrary, as Johnston interpreted it, to "solemn legislative and executive action." He wrote Davis a strong protest, which the Confederate President thought "unbecoming," and Johnston later blamed this letter for Davis' "animosity" during the war and after.

Eventually, Mrs. Davis and Mrs. Johnston, both proud and clever women, also took part in this personal feud, something of a scandal in the Confederacy. Johnston stood his ground with Davis, Secretary of War (later Secretary of State) Judah P. Benjamin, and others who made his military role difficult, but he waged no vendetta. Opponents of Davis used Johnston's cause as a rallying point for their attacks on the Confederate administration. After the War, Johnston did write to a friend: "With any

other President than Mr. Davis the South might have won. . . .
It was from no want of courage, constancy, and zeal that the
Southern people were overcome, but from their want of discretion
in selecting a leader."

When Confederate armies took the field, Johnston was placed
in command of troops in the Shenandoah Valley in Virginia. One
of his subordinates was General Thomas J. Jackson—"Stonewall"
Jackson—and Johnston is given credit for early recognizing the
talents of this tough, God-fearing soldier and encouraging him in
his often unconventional but successful maneuvers. Johnston, with
Beauregard, was the chief architect of the Confederate victory at
Bull Run (First Manassas), in July 1861, the first large-scale
battle of the war. During the four years of conflict, he commanded Confederate armies in each of the great theaters of war:
in Virginia, in the West during the Vicksburg campaign, in the
center at Chattanooga and Atlanta. After First Manassas, Johnston
won no great victory, but he suffered no serious defeats, either.

Fighting usually with forces inferior in numbers and equipment, he consistently inflicted much greater losses on his opponents than he himself suffered. Even when forced back by
superior numbers, he was so tenacious and skillful in maneuver
that General Winfield Scott commented, "Beware of Lee's ad-
vances and Johnston's retreats." Another Federal officer described
Johnston as "the foremost man among the Southern leaders in
point of general ability and military genius. A man eminently
brave, energetic, and ambitious; capable of enlarged views in war
or politics, and one who will take the highest position in case the
rebellion succeeds. Cold and concentrated in manner, of un-
movable self-possession, he will exhibit great vigor in the field."

Though a master of tactics and strategy, Johnston never risked
the lives of his soldiers needlessly. He was trusted and revered
by his men and thoroughly respected by his opponents. Two of the
most eminent of these—Grant and Sherman—considered him
the ablest of Confederate generals. In the Atlanta campaign, Sherman's casualties were greater than Johnston's entire force, and
when Johnston was removed from command, both Sherman and

his superior, Grant, heaved a sigh of relief. Grant told Episcopal Bishop Henry C. Lay of Arkansas that the move was the equivalent of giving Sherman an additional army corps. Johnston was stubborn and tenacious in all things, as his military record and his often rocky relations with both Jefferson Davis and civilian advisers prove. It was said that Johnston disliked "to be beaten even at a game of billiards." Even so, those who knew him spoke also of his kindliness, consideration, and sense of humor.

G. Moxley Sorrell, Confederate General James Longstreet's aide, recalled seeing Johnston at First Manassas, "full bearded, dusty and worn from long marching; a high-bred, stern-looking soldier of faultless seat and bearing in the saddle." General Edmund Kirby-Smith wrote his wife from Virginia in December 1861, marveling at his spartan life and wholehearted attention to duty. The general, who like any private, slept rolled in a blanket on the cold ground, was to Kirby-Smith a "true patriot, sensitive and retiring, and with an abnegation of self which ignores all personal grievances and slights in his great sense of duty & devotion to his country."

After Johnston was wounded at the battle of Seven Pines in 1862, the Richmond *Examiner* wrote, "He is the only commander on either side in this contest that has yet proven, beyond all question, a capacity to maneuver a large army in the presence of one yet larger; to march it, fight it, or not fight it, at will, and while so doing, to baffle the plans of the ablest opponents in every instance. Time may yet produce another, but no living man in America is yet ascertained to possess a military knowledge so profound, or a decision of character so remarkable."

Johnson's wound was severe, the eleventh in his long military career. As late as 1863, in the Vicksburg campaign, it was necessary for a physician to go with him everywhere. Mrs. Johnston stayed near him, too, when she could, sharing the wartime austerities of life in the little towns and villages of the Deep South as the general moved back and forth across the Confederacy. In July 1864, she came out from Atlanta to Johnston's headquarters north of the town to be with him on their nineteenth wedding anniversary. Only a week later President Davis relieved him of his command.

"Johnston," wrote the British observer, Colonel A. J. L. Fremantle, after a visit to his headquarters during the Vicksburg campaign, "talks in a calm, deliberate, and confident manner; to me he was extremely affable, but he certainly possesses the power of keeping people at a distance when he chooses, and his officers evidently stand in great awe of him. He lives very plainly, and at present his only cooking utensils consist of an old coffeepot and frying-pan. There was only one fork (one prong deficient) between himself and Staff, and this was handed to me ceremoniously as 'the guest.' He had undoubtedly acquired the entire confidence of all the officers and soldiers under him. Many of the officers told me they did not consider him inferior as a general to Lee or anyone else."

Fremantle was also impressed by the fact that when a locomotive on which he and a group of Confederates, including Johnston, were riding ran out of fuel, the general hopped off to gather wood with the others and "worked with so much energy as to cause his 'Seven Pines' wound to give him pain." When the group later had to leave the engine and set out on foot, Johnston carried Fremantle's cloak, in addition to his own and that of another officer.

Johnny Green, a Kentucky soldier of General John Breckinridge's Orphan Brigade, serving with the Army of Tennessee, wrote in his diary early in 1864, "The army has been enthused by the fact that Genl Braxton Bragg, relieved at his own request. Genl Johnston took command Dec. 27th 1863. I saw him at the Episcopal church last Sunday, or rather at church where an Episcopal preacher conducted the service and preached. Genl Johnston is not a large man except in brain & ability but is every inch a soldier in fact & in appearance. A number of us stood on the pavement and lifted our caps in salute as he passed. He saluted in response and said 'Good morning my men, I am glad to see you at church.'" Later in the year, when Johnston was himself replaced by Hood and the Orphan Brigade was bottled up in

Atlanta, Johnny wrote: "The boys with dejected spirits say you would never have caught Genl Joe Johnston in this trap."

Wade Hampton, Johnston's chief of cavalry in the final weeks of the War, felt that he was "equal if not superior to Lee as a commanding officer." Vice President Alexander Stephens and Generals Beauregard and Longstreet were among those urging Lee to restore him to command after Lee was appointed commander of all Confederate forces in 1865.

Even though the fortunes of the Confederacy declined and Johnston's own difficulties, both in the field and with the Davis administration, increased, the brisk, efficient little general never really lost heart and certainly showed no loss of self-confidence. When he resumed command in the dark days of 1865, in the face of Sherman's overpowering array of men and material, he showed the same zeal and determination that had distinguished him at First Manassas. Knowing that he could only delay Sherman, not defeat him, he put his heart and mind into the effort and, never doubting himself or his men, was well pleased with the results. In that final campaign in the Carolinas, as in all his others, the verdict of history has largely come around to Joe Johnston's own opinion: he accomplished much against great odds. Back in 1863 after he had failed to lift the siege of Vicksburg, he wrote his wife that he was conscious "of doing my best manfully and loyally." He was confident that history "will accord me the only reputation I have ever coveted—that of a brave, & honorable soldier, & disinterested Patriot." Somehow, with Johnston, those words were not so bombastic as they would have sounded from another.

Probably no Confederate leader accepted the verdict of Appomattox more readily than Johnston and no one was more willing to forget the animosities the war had aroused. "We of the South," he wrote, in August 1865, "referred the question at issue between us and the United States to the arbitrament of the sword. The decision has been made and is against us. We must acquiesce in that decision, accept it as final, and recognize the fact that Virginia is again one of the United States. Our duties and our interests coincide. We shall consult the one and perform the other by doing all we can to promote the welfare of our neighbors and to restore prosperity to the country."

When a bellicose young man announced that the South had been "conquered but not subdued," Johnston asked in what Confederate command he had served. Unfortunately "circumstances made it impossible" to be in the army. Johnston said grimly, "Well, Sir, I was. You may not be subdued but I am."

For all Johnston's willingness to accept an end to the conflict of North and South, there remained for him the problem of earning a living. What Mrs. Johnston had told General Scott in 1861 was still true. Her husband had "no private fortune or no profession but that of arms." His profession he could no longer practice in the United States, and he does not seem to have considered expatriation, as did his cavalry chief, Wade Hampton, Matthew Fontaine Maury, Breckinridge, and others. He did seek and obtain permission to visit Canada, but he did not go.

Mrs. Johnston, who had been in Lincolnton, North Carolina, in order to be near her husband during the final months of the War, was not well. Strain and privations had seriously undermined her health, and soon after the surrender the Johnstons went to Buffalo Springs, near Danville, Virginia, for a rest. Later in the summer they visited Mrs. Johnston's family in Maryland.

Johnston applied to President Johnson during the summer for amnesty and removal of restrictions placed on him as a high-ranking Confederate officer. He wrote the President, "I regret to be unable to advance any special claim for indulgence. Perhaps, however, Your Excellency may think it worth consideration that while an officer of the United States Army I served faithfully for many years & gave my blood & offered my life in that service many times."

To Confederate Admiral Franklin Buchanan, who said he had not asked for amnesty because he could not express regret for joining the Confederacy, Johnston replied, "You don't have to express any regret. I have asked pardon and have expressed no regret. Oh, yes, I did, too. I requested that His Excellency would grant me a pardon, and expressed regret that I could offer no reason why he should." His Excellency, in any event, was not granting amnesty to any high-ranking Confederates in the summer of 1865.

"Old Joe" found much to praise in the conduct of the Federal officers and men stationed in the South during Reconstruction. "I passed the month of May, 1865," he wrote, "in the middle part of North Carolina—in Charlotte, Greensboro and Raleigh—in which there were not less than 20,000 federal troops . . . these men conducted themselves precisely as if they had been in towns of Ohio, Pennsylvania or Massachusetts—believing that the only object of the war on their part was the restoration of the Union, and that as that had been accomplished by the result of the war, the Southern states were again in their old places, and the people around them their fellow citizens. And so they treated them. Such conduct was fully appreciated by our people. . . . And this gave them a kinder sentiment for their late antagonists than had existed among them since 1849."

Johnston regretted that similar understanding and good will was not apparent in the actions of "Northern politicians who had staid at home and inspired in those who had staid with them, strong hostility. . . . Although we were re-admitted into the Union, the dominant Northern party does not admit that we occupy places in it equal to theirs." Even Lincoln, whose plan for Reconstruction was so much more moderate than the one Congress imposed, found little favor in Johnston's eyes. "I can say nothing in his praise," he wrote. "The Southern people think him good natured and kindly. I believe that he never valued human life when it was in the way of his objects."

Johnston had accepted the terms of surrender in good faith and expected the North to do the same. When word came that some Federal authorities in the South were not abiding by the terms of the paroles given his men in North Carolina, he called on General Grant in Washington and insisted that the matter be corrected.

Grant promised to write a letter to the President asking that the injustice be remedied. And as Johnston rose to leave, Grant asked if he might introduce his staff officers, who, on hearing that "Old Joe" was in the building had gathered to pay their respects. Bradley Johnson, Johnston's biographer, who was present, described the scene as "a curious and interesting one, but the most impressive part was the manner in which Johnston bore himself— the dignity, the grace, the grave friendliness, with which he received this superb overture of respect. He seemed to tower above the crowd, although he was hardly of the average height, and I believe every man present that day left deeply impressed that he had met a very great man."

Attempting to earn a living in the depressed postwar South, Johnston went first to Richmond as president of the National Express and Transportation Company, which he helped organize and which promptly failed. Later, in 1866, he and Mrs. Johnston moved to Selma, Alabama, where he took over the presidency of a small railroad, the Alabama and Tennessee River, reorganized in 1867 as the Selma, Rome & Dalton; but the venture was unsuccessful.

The Johnstons had taken an active part in social and community life in Selma, and "Old Joe," who had been baptized during the Atlanta campaign, as had Generals Hood and W. J. Hardee, by Episcopal Bishop and General Leonidas Polk, was confirmed by Bishop Richard H. Wilmer of Alabama in St. Paul's Church. Johnston treasured all his life a blood-stained copy of Charles Todd Quintard's *Balm for the Weary and Wounded,* inscribed to him by Bishop Polk and found on the Bishop's body after his death by cannon fire at Pine Mountain, Georgia. Quintard, the Connecticut-born physician who became a Confederate chaplain and later Episcopal Bishop of Tennessee, saw much of Johnston after the war. "More and more," wrote Quintard, "Johnston entered into the religious life, illustrating in his daily walk and conversation the highest type of the Christian gentlemen." He considered him "a charming man . . . of perfectly simple manners, of easy and graceful carriage and a good conversationalist."

Johnston found hard times and lack of capital to be handicaps. Some time later he wrote:

The consequences of the war were far more disastrous to us than to the Northern people. One of them was the destruction of the capital of banks, planters and merchants. If at the close of the war, the benefits of good government had been granted, they would, probably, have gone to work to make new capital or increase what was left, by judicious industry. But the rule of carpet-baggers and the military (the latter much preferred by the subjects) offered little inducement for such courses. Four or five years of misrule put an end to hopefulness in all who were wanting in force.

Certainly Johnston himself was never one "wanting in force." He was undaunted by the failure of his express and railroad projects and traveled to England and the Continent, in 1868, stopping in New York on the way to urge delegates arriving for the Democratic National Convention to nominate Francis Blair of Missouri, a former Union general, for President. Blair did win the nomination for Vice President on the ticket with Horatio Seymour of New York. Johnston visited abroad with numerous expatriate Confederates and returned to organize Joseph E. Johnston & Co., in which he served as agent for English and New York insurance companies. Former Governor Benjamin G. Humphreys of Mississippi and Livingston Mims, both ex-Confederate officers, joined in the venture. Humphreys handled company business in Mississippi, with an office at Jackson. Mims operated in Atlanta and later became mayor of that city. The Johnstons chose to settle in Savannah, where he was a familiar and prominent citizen until the late seventies.

In 1870, Johnston was among those who welcomed Robert E. Lee to the seacoast city and shared the plaudits of the crowds who turned out for the event. In a very unmilitary way, history has memorialized the occasion in the familiar photograph of the two grizzled old warriors sitting tranquilly in civilian clothes at a small table. This encounter was in April; in October, Lee was dead.

After Lee's death, Johnston offered to raise a fund for the assistance of Mrs. Lee, but she declined this help. He did serve as president of the Lee Memorial Association, which built an extension to the Chapel of Washington and Lee University in Lexington, Virginia, and provided a mausoleum for Lee and his family together with the famous recumbent statue of Lee.

In 1875, Johnston was offered the presidency of the Arkansas Industrial University, later the University of Arkansas, which had recently been opened; but he turned it down. He did accept many invitations to speak at public gatherings in the South: in May 1874, he spoke in Richmond at the celebration of Queen Victoria's fifty-fifth birthday, and in October 1875, he was marshal of the parade preceding the unveiling of Richmond's monument to "Stonewall" Jackson, who had died at Chancellorsville in 1863.

The insurance business seems to have supplied Johnston with at least a living, which in the Reconstruction South was about as much as a former Confederate general could hope for. But business and the social life of Savannah did not occupy all of his time. Like most generals in all wars, those who led the armies of North and South could not resist the temptation to put pen to paper in defense of their generalship. At least as early as 1867, Johnston began to consider writing an account of his campaigns. He was especially anxious to give his side of the controversies involving Jefferson Davis and to defend his part in the Vicksburg and Atlanta campaigns. He had corresponded with several former Confederates and some Northern officers on the subject even before he moved to Savannah, and he continued to gather material for several years. Characteristically, he refused to publish anything or make any public comment regarding his differences with the Confederate President as long as Davis was being held prisoner at Fortress Monroe.

Johnston's book, *Narrative of Military Operations Directed During the Late War Between the States,* was finally published in April 1874. Ever the practical man, Johnston not only received an author's royalty of 10 per cent but acted for a period as Southern agent for the book, with a commission of 50 per cent.

The *Narrative* was written in his typical straightforward, unadorned style. "I offer these papers," he wrote, "as my contribution of materials for the use of future historians of the War between the States." As such, the book is, indeed, useful, and it makes a good case for his 1863-64 military strategy in Mississippi and in Georgia. Though his book was criticized by friends of Davis and provoked some rejoinders from other Southern generals (notably Beauregard, for the treatment of that general's part at First Manassas), his comments were no more outspoken than they had been during the War. He attributed the final failure of the Confederacy not to inferiority in numbers or resources but to the failure to make full economic use of the South's cotton in the early months of the War. We see him here as the practical man of affairs, the close student of economics as well as military tactics. Not for nothing had he been chosen in 1860, to be Quartermaster General of the U.S. Army.

Johnston's version of several important Civil War incidents was also recorded in four articles for the series, "Battles and Leaders of the Civil War," sponsored by the *Century Magazine* in the 1880's. These were: "Responsibilities of the First Bull Run," "Manassas to Seven Pines," "Jefferson Davis and the Mississippi Campaign," and "Opposing Sherman's Advance to Atlanta." These articles emphasize especially his defense against the criticisms made by Jefferson Davis. The recurrent Davis-Johnston controversy, never resolved, flared up also in 1881, as a result of an interview with Johnston that appeared in the Philadelphia *Press.* The interview linked Davis with the disappearance of Confederate funds following the evacuation of Richmond. Johnston insisted he was misquoted, as he probably was. But Davis would not be appeased and he refused to make the featured address at the dedication of the Lee Memorial at Lexington in 1883, when he learned that Johnston was to preside.

Late in 1876, Johnston, who had never severed his ties with Virginia, moved his insurance business to Richmond, where he and his wife had many friends. He now found himself more and more drawn into participation in political affairs. In the Presidential campaign of 1876, he had taken an active part in support of Samuel Tilden, the Democratic candidate for President, although he thought earlier that as a reform governor, Tilden "had made enemies of so many New York scoundrels" that he could not even be nominated.

When the contested Presidential election was finally resolved in favor of Hayes by the Bargain of '77, Johnston was considered, along with some other Southerners, for a place in the President's Cabinet, perhaps as Secretary of War. This was a part of Hayes' general plan for a moderate course toward the South and also very good practical politics, for it would help to salve the feelings of those Democrats who were angry over the election "bargain." However, it was probably too early for an ex-Confederate of Johnston's rank to take a place in the Cabinet, and General William T. Sherman, now commanding the U.S. Army and Johnston's friend, so advised Hayes.

Perhaps it was just as well. Johnston did not share the satisfaction of other Southerners with the political arrangements that put Hayes in the White House and took Federal troops out of the South. He thought that if Tilden "had the heart of a dung-hill hen he would have claimed the Presidency and been inaugurated." Northern Democrats, he said, were not intimidated by President Grant's "700 infantry in Washington and 5 iron-clads on the Potomac" and "were in favor of meeting those threats with expressions of our intention to see the President whom we had elected inaugurated." But "such a course was prevented by Mr. Tilden." As for President Hayes' moderate policy toward the South, Johnston thought this was motivated more by a Democratic majority in Congress, including many Southerners, than by a desire for conciliation.

Johnston's political disabilities as a high-ranking former Confederate officer were removed by Congress in 1877, and in the following year his Richmond friends prevailed upon him to run for Congress on the Democratic ticket. He took a dim view of campaign ballyhoo and the sometimes dubious methods deemed necessary to win an election. He almost withdrew from the race at one point when his supporters seemed to be presenting him in one locality as a supporter of free trade and in another as a believer in a protective tariff. Nor would he countenance the solicitation of funds to wage an elaborate campaign.

Finally, one of his baffled supporters approached Mrs. Johnston with the dilemma about funds. She, at first, was as little interested in political realities as her husband. "It's all your fault," she said. "You got him into this thing, and it's shameful, a man of his age and reputation, going around to your cross roads, like a common member of Congress. I do hope he'll be beat. That'll serve you all right." When informed that, as things were going, Johnston undoubtedly *would* be beat, Mrs. Johnston, as usual, rose spiritedly to her husband's defense. "If he's beat it will be simply disgraceful and shameful! It will kill him! He shan't be beat; you must not allow it. I will not permit it." Mrs. Johnston then insisted on contributing from her own resources toward the campaign. This contribution was returned to her after his victory, and the general was none the wiser.

When he took his seat in the Forty-sixth Congress, on March 4, 1879, he joined a considerable number of other former Confederates, who made up a formidable bloc in both the House and Senate. In their journey to their Congressional posts these Southern members had followed various political paths—from frank cooperation with the Republicans to fervent loyalty to the Democratic program. But they were united in devotion to their section and in a determination to restore it to its former prosperity and position in the Union.

Among the Confederate luminaries in Congress were Senator L. Q. C. Lamar of Mississippi and the Georgia Senators, John B. Gordon and Ben Hill. Lamar and Gordon had both served under "Old Joe" in the Confederate army, and Hill had been a Confederate Senator. Also in the Senate were Zebulon Vance, who had served under Johnston before becoming Confederate Governor of North Carolina, and Wade Hampton of South Carolina, his brilliant cavalry leader. In the House with Johnston were the former Confederate Vice President, Alexander H. Stephens of Georgia and Confederate Postmaster General, John H. Reagan of Texas. Two of Johnston's kinsmen were there also—his brother-in-law Robert M. McLane, a member of the House from Maryland, and his nephew, John W. Johnston, a Senator from Virginia since 1870.

Johnston served conscientiously during his one term; he did not seek re-election. During this period he was appointed a member of the Board of Visitors of the College of William and Mary in Williamsburg, Virginia. The president of the school was his old friend, Colonel Benjamin S. Ewell, who had served as adjutant general for the Army of Tennessee. "I have been much interested," wrote Johnston, "in the old college of William and Mary of late. Partly on account of our old friend Ewell. It being almost entirely ruined by the war, Ewell used most of his means, certainly $15,000 of them, in endeavors to save it." Johnston's letter books and other papers were given to the college after his death by his nephew, Robert M. Hughes of Norfolk, Rector of the Board of Visitors and author of a biography, *General Johnston,* published in 1897.

In 1880, Johnston attended the ceremonies marking Nashville's centennial. There he unveiled a statue of Andrew Jackson and was wildly acclaimed by a great throng of his former soldiers of the Army of Tennessee. One old veteran, after cheering lustily and waving his hat in greeting to "Old Joe" with the one arm that had survived the war, brushed the tears from his eyes and exclaimed to another, "By heaven, that is the old, noble General sure enough! Say, I'd fight for him again, wouldn't you?"

After his term as Congressman, Johnston maintained his home in Washington, though he kept his insurance business and legal residence in Richmond. He was unwilling to run a second time for Congress—he had only agreed to be a candidate originally "because assured that I would not have a canvass to make. But it was greatly required and would be again. In my estimation the game is not worth such a canvass." He continued his keen interest in national affairs, however; and his freely expressed opinions, always firmly conservative and realistic, were heeded by his fellow Virginians and by influential friends in both North and South. He was a loyal Virginian, but he had, indeed, many friends in the North, and he was devoid of state or sectional prejudice. "As a man," he could truthfully say, "I have mixed almost equally with the people of the two sections . . . my observation has brought me to the conclusion that the only well-founded sectional prejudice was that in favor of Virginia hams."

Although he supported the Democratic party, which he considered more likely to help the South and the nation than the Republican, he did not do so blindly. For one thing, he distrusted the party system as putting too much power in the hands of "a few Managers pretty much self constituted . . . not generally of the best class of our people." "This political machinery," he wrote, "has made our political ruin—by bringing the people to the belief that the machine is to make the government—and not they." He recalled that "in my boyhood party candidates were not nominated. Any one who pleased might 'offer.' " This earlier system, he believed, produced better candidates and therefore better government.

In the summer of 1880, Johnston wrote, "I am confident that our party is not much better prepared to make the administrative reforms required than the Republicans." Still, the Democrats "would correct the most glaring abuses, and especially repeal unconstitutional and obnoxious laws, and impose proper limits to executive power." He was sure that "if the Republicans should win in the coming election, we shall see or feel no more of political liberty. Our republican *form* of government may be retained a little while, but none of the Substance." He particularly feared the Radical Republican tendency to strengthen the central government.

A Democratic victory in the elections would, said Johnston, "put an end to the oppression in the weaker Southern states; and, I believe, restore such purity of administration as the state of public morals will permit." Clearly, he did not think the state of public morals would permit much purity. But since the Republican party was "the most corrupt that has ever existed," a Democratic victory could only be better. As late as 1888, when the excesses of Reconstruction seemed safely curbed, he still dreaded lest a Republican election victory would bring "Negro supremacy" to all the former slave states.

Grover Cleveland, elected President in 1884—the first Democrat since before the War—appointed Johnston Commissioner of Railroads in 1885, a post later to be held by two other well-known former Confederates, James Longstreet and Wade Hampton. The job called for pleasant traveling about the nation, occasional speech-making and attendance at public and semi-public gatherings. While he was on a railroad inspection trip to the West, he received word of the death of General Grant. Each had often expressed respect for the other's military achievements. Grant "was the best fighter" in the Federal army, "Old Joe" had said; and Grant had thought that no soldier, North or South, could have handled the Confederate side of the critical Georgia campaign of 1864 so well as Johnston.

The seventy-eight-year-old Johnston traveled from Portland, Oregon, to New York to serve as pallbearer at Grant's funeral in July of 1885. Among the pallbearers selected by President Cleveland were another former Confederate general, Simon Buckner of Kentucky, and Grant's old lieutenants, William T. Sherman and Philip Sheridan. *Harper's Weekly* marveled at the sight of "Confederate generals with arms locked in Union generals' arms— Johnston with Sherman, Sheridan with Buckner . . . a picture of American fraternity astonishing almost to ourselves who remember the terrible conflicts within the present generation."

Then, in November, another former high-ranking Union officer died, George B. McClellan. Johnston attended his funeral services in the Madison Square Presbyterian Church, New York, and at Trenton, New Jersey. He was particularly moved on this occasion, for his friendship with "Little Mac" had been close, going back to prewar days in the United States Army in the West. After the funeral he wrote, "This death has been to me like the loss of my

last brother. That of no other man could have been so afflicting.
. . . He will appear in history an exemplary Christian, noble
gentleman, valiant soldier and wise leader."

There was a similarity in the personal and military character
and history of the two men. Both were conscientious, hardwork-
ing, and careful commanders, indisposed to reckless ventures or to
risking the lives of their men needlessly. Both were unmoved by
political pressures in determining military strategy, and both suffered reprisals at the hands of politicians and influential, self-
appointed civilian military experts. Johnston was, perhaps, somewhat blunter in his expressions of opinion to Richmond authorities than McClellan was to Washington; but the effect was very
much the same.

The Johnstons often journeyed to the spas and summer resorts
of New York and New England as well as the South, partly in an
attempt to improve Mrs. Johnston's health, permanently affected
by the worries and privations of the War. But in February 1887,
she died in their Washington home. The Johnstons had no children; her devotion and affection had always been centered upon
her husband and his welfare.

General Dabney H. Maury, a nephew of Captain Matthew
Fontaine Maury and a long-time friend of the Johnstons, said,
"I have never known two people more devoted to each other
than they were. Her health was not robust, and he watched over
her in her illness with the greatest tenderness, and at all times
paid her the delicate attentions of a lover." Maury remembered
a number of pleasant incidents from the family life, not omitting
mention of a noble mint julep served him by General and Mrs.
Johnston at White Sulphur Springs.

A glimpse of the Johnstons at home came from John S. Wise,
a former Confederate officer and prominent postwar Virginia
Republican, who called on them one cold winter night in Richmond. Johnston was seated in an armchair in his library, "dressed
in a flannel wrapper," recovering from "an influenza." By his
side, upon a low stool, stood a tray with whiskey, glasses, spoons,
sugar, lemon, spice, and eggs. At the grate a footman held a brass

teakettle of boiling water. Mrs. Johnston was preparing a hot
Tom-and-Jerry for the old gentleman, who thoroughly enjoyed
the attention and the drink.

"It was snowing outside," Wise recalls, "and the scene within
was very cozy. As I had seen him in public, General Johnston was
a stiff, uncommunicative man, punctilious and peppery, as little
fellows like him are apt to be. He reminded me of a cock sparrow,
full of self-consciousness, and rather enjoying a peck at his neighbor. That night he was as warm, comfortable and communicative
as the kettle swinging on the hob."

It was on this occasion that Johnston told Wise about General
John Breckinridge's indignation, during the 1865 surrender negotiations in North Carolina, when General Sherman failed to offer
the Southerners more than one drink. Later, Wise says, he told
the story to Sherman, who was vastly amused. "I don't remember
it," said Sherman. "But if Joe Johnston told it, it's so. Those
fellows hustled me so that day, I was sorry for the drink I did give
them."

In conversation and letters to her friends, Lydia Johnston had
fought her husband's battles against his opponents in the Davis
administration and elsewhere as stubbornly as she knew how.
After her death, he is said never to have trusted himself to mention her name. He kept their Washington home exactly as she left
it, permitting nothing to be changed.

His wife's numerous relatives were attentive to the lonely old
general, and a number of his Confederate army friends holding
public office in Washington came to visit frequently—among them
two men who had served him as chief of cavalry: Joseph Wheeler,
now an Alabama Congressman, and Wade Hampton of South
Carolina, now a Senator. Another, Bradley Johnson, with Johnston's permission and assistance set about the writing of his life;
the book, *A Memoir of the Life and Public Service of Joseph E.
Johnston,* appeared in 1891.

In 1890, Johnston attended a great Confederate Memorial Day
gathering of Confederate leaders and veterans held at Atlanta,
the city where, above all others, perhaps, the "Old" South began

to turn into the "New." Johnston stayed with Livingston Mims, Mayor of Atlanta and Johnston's partner in Joseph E. Johnston & Co. The chief purpose of the meeting was to lay the cornerstone of a home for Confederate soldiers. The campaign for funds had been spearheaded by Henry W. Grady, newspaper editor and apostle of the New South. The occasion, besides, paying tribute to the Confederate dead, was in the words of Grady's paper, the Atlanta *Constitution,* "to renew old memories and associations." The *Constitution* called it "the largest and most enthusiastic reunion of Confederate veterans that has taken place since the war."

Johnston, here in the city he had not been permitted to defend, was given a rousing welcome that touched him deeply. "The rattle of the drums and the roll of the music," reported the *Constitution,* "were drowned by yells of the old soldiers; they were wild, mad with joy; their long pent-up love for the old soldier had broken loose." Some of the veterans, seeing "Old Joe" and many of their comrades for the first time since the surrender, "made no effort to conceal their emotions, but literally fell on each other's necks and wept."

As he drove in procession through the city, his flower-bedecked carriage in which he was riding with General Edmund Kirby Smith was seized, the horses were unhitched, and the enthusiastic veterans themselves pulled the carriage to the opera house, where further ceremonies were scheduled. Only Johnston's age and infirmity kept them from carrying him on their shoulders into the building.

"Never again, perhaps," said the *Constitution,* "shall we see such a gathering of the Confederate veterans. They compose an army that must march on without recruits. The veterans and their leaders are growing old. Overwhelmed in the field, they have had a hard fight with fate and circumstance since the war. In this fight they have won a glorious victory, and in both struggles they have received honorable scars."

In May, Johnston was in Richmond, where he unveiled the great equestrian statue of Lee on Monument Avenue. It was on one such visit to Richmond that Johnston served as godfather to a granddaughter of Dabney Maury, who said, "I have rarely seen the general brighter or more cheerful. He played with the little child, ran up and down the halls with her, and held her in his arms during the entire service." He later told Maury it was his happiest week in many years.

In February 1891, once again he went North to attend the funeral of a great Federal general of the Civil War. This time it was William Tecumseh Sherman. First Grant, then McClellan, now Sherman—"Old Joe" had lived to bury them all.

The funeral was held from the family home in New York on a raw and windy day. Johnston, now eighty-four, stood bareheaded in the February cold with the other pallbearers. A spectator urged him to put on his hat. As usual, "Old Joe" needed no advice, least of all from a civilian. "If I were in his place and he were standing here in mine, he would not put on his hat."

On his return from the funeral, Johnston was confined to his Washington home with pneumonia and never left it alive. He received Holy Communion from the rector of St. John's Church, and on March 21, died quietly, with his brother-in-law, Robert McLane, a former Governor of Maryland, at his bedside. Maury describes a visit made to the old general a few days before his death: "As I bade him farewell, I said, 'Good by,' as cheerfully as I could, adding, 'I go to Texas tomorrow. We will soon meet again.' 'Yes,' he replied with marked emotion, 'we surely shall meet again'; and drawing me to him, he kissed me twice."

Johnston had asked for a simple funeral, and his wish was granted. After a service at St. John's, he was buried in Greenmount Cemetery, Baltimore, beside his wife. At the funeral was a delegation of Union soldiers of Baltimore, who paid their respects to a one-time opponent, just as he had to Grant, McClellan, and Sherman.

Memorial services were held in many parts of the South. One of these was in the Church of the Holy Communion in Charleston, South Carolina, on April 26, the twenty-sixth anniversary of Johnston's acceptance of Sherman's terms. The sermon was preached by the Reverend A. T. Porter, former Confederate chaplain with Wade Hampton's cavalry and a member of Johnston's staff at the surrender. His text was from the Thirty-seventh Psalm: "Mark the perfect man, and behold the upright, for the latter end of that man is peace."

Johnston would have scorned the flatterer who dared call him either perfect or upright—though he was obviously more so than many of his contemporaries. But indisputably his latter end had been peace, a peace which he had won in 1865 while a war was being lost, a peace he had labored to preserve through a quarter of a century when many men, North and South, were still crying war when there was no war.

8

Redeeming Arm

WADE HAMPTON

"Old Hampton is playing a bluff game, and he don't mind old Sherman will call him." That was how a gunner put it when Wade Hampton's cavalry was covering "Old Joe" Johnston's last retreat —the last of many retreats—through the North Carolina low country into the Piedmont. On the day of Lee's surrender—April 9, 1865—Wade was still playing the same game. Yet it was not just bluff.

Wade Hampton would have been the last person to pretend he was something that he wasn't. He was a man of his word and a man of action. There were many Southerners like him. During the Ku Klux Klan hearings in Washington in 1871, Hampton was taunted with the old canard that "one Southern man could whip ten Yankees." "I did not put the numbers as large as that," said Hampton, but "the result of the war proved that we were not so very far wrong, so far as the fighting was concerned."

Hampton was the stuff of which good soldiers are made, even though his talent for soldiering had never asserted itself in the ante-bellum years. Hampton's civilian experience with horse and gun had been extensive; the Civil War turned his talent into military channels and taught a planter to beat his plowshare into a sword. He became a general long before the War was over; but he had been a leader of men—his Southern fellow citizens—before it started. After he had led his soldier compatriots in war, he would be ready to lead them again in peace—for a third of a century of Reconstruction and Redemption—into a promised land, the "New South."

It is hard to believe that this Southerner of Southerners ever existed, for he was too true to a legendary pattern, too much like a hero created by Walter Scott for the South to emulate. Or was he indeed a legend, invented by the tellers of tall tales? Alfred B. Williams, who knew him, described him as

. . . a big, powerful, athletic man, with rather small dark blue eyes, the face of the good humored, self confident, fearless fighter. . . . When in the saddle he looked as if he and the horse were one. His vanities were manly. He was proud of his horsemanship and never felt so much at home as when on a strong, spirited horse and was frankly vain of his skill as fisherman and hunter. He had a record of more than eighty black bear killed in the Mississippi swamp with the hunting knife—going in on them when they were brought to bay and pitting his strength and activity against theirs. . . .

Now, in the April of Appomattox, Wade Hampton was still fighting. He could not do otherwise: he hardly knew how to abandon any assigned task. As Robert E. Lee's army crumbled before the massed Union armies of General Grant, remnants of the old Army of Tennessee were making a last-ditch stand against Sherman's forces in North Carolina. In command was General Joseph E. Johnston, at long last called upon to pull Jefferson Davis' chestnuts out of the fire, although the President heartily despised this popular, brilliant, headstrong general.

From South Carolina, in the eastern sector, came troops from Charleston under General W. J. Hardee and from Wilmington under General Braxton Bragg, one of Davis' now humiliated favorites. Hampton, commanding the horse troops, had fought most of this War in Virginia but had been hurried into the Carolinas in January 1865, to cover the Confederate withdrawal in the face of Sherman's swift march from Georgia. Hampton had seen his beloved city of Columbia, South Carolina, put to the torch, either by the carelessness of Sherman's men, or, as Sherman later claimed, by Hampton himself.

When Sherman entered North Carolina, the demoralized army of resistance, now commanded by Johnston, was marshaled against him. While the lines formed and wavered, Hampton's cavalry busily protected the flanks and the rear. For three days Yank and Reb had at each other at Bentonville. On the eve of the engagement, Hampton's cavalry had delayed Sherman's advance by occupying a commanding position on the road to Bentonville—a position stronger than the forces defending it. But the "bluff" worked. After Johnston's inevitable retreat began, it was Hampton's cavalry which had to cover the flight of the master of retreats. Since the situation in Virginia had become desperate for the Confederates, Sherman did not press his advantage. He marched on westward toward Goldsboro. Johnston, too, marched, moving westward—toward Raleigh and Durham Depot, while Hampton's cavalry hovered protectingly over his charges. That morning in April when Lee surrendered in Virginia, Sherman knew of the end; Johnston's army did not. There were rumors, the men had become restless, but Hampton sturdily discredited the surrender story. He was even unaware that the message to Sherman, which he carried at Johnston's orders on April 13, initiated the second surrender.

Hampton, of course, was not ready to surrender. He planned, instead, to escape to Texas, serving perhaps as a guard to the fleeing President, now in Charlotte. Twice he wrote Davis offering assistance; finally he went in person. The President expressed his willingness to have Hampton join him with the proposed escort. But while Hampton visited Davis, Johnston surrendered the army. Hampton felt that his own absence had excluded him from the terms of capitulation and that he was therefore free to go to the aid of his President, who was already fleeing southward. Hampton set out alone from Charlotte on April 28.

Hampton visited his wife at Yorkville, South Carolina. She dissuaded him from going with Davis; but, nevertheless, he was the last of Johnston's generals to ask for parole. It was proper that he was; for he symbolized the unyielding Southern spirit. Hampton could not, as Davis did, become a professional "man without a country"—the unrepentant, the unredeemed, who could save neither others nor himself. Hampton, whose swiftness of movement and quickness of wit had saved many a day for the

fighting Confederacy—all the way from Manassas to Mill Creek
—would lay down his arms, would presumably repent and seek
pardon, and would even do his stint of penance in the early days
of Reconstruction when his leadership was repudiated. But this
was for the sake of salvation: in due time penance would be done
and redemption would come. South Carolina—the whole South,
in fact—would in the end look to Hampton for peacetime generalship.

Wade Hampton was a proper South Carolinian, having even
taken the trouble to be born in Charleston. The Hamptons had
settled first in Virginia, but the father of the first Wade Hampton
had moved to the South Carolina back country, where he built his
cabin near the site of present day Spartanburg. The first Wade—
his name came from the surname of his mother—lost his father,
mother, and four other members of his family in 1776, when
Cherokee raiders burned the Hampton cabin and scalped its occu-
pants. Wade and three brothers were away from home at the time
of the massacre. The raiders were overtaken and most of them
killed with Hampton thoroughness.

During the Revolution, the Hampton boys fought for the patriot
cause, and the first Wade became a lieutenant colonel in the horse
troops. When the war was over, he began to build his estate
"Millwood," a few miles from the new town of Columbia, which
became the state capital in 1786. Old Colonel Taylor, who owned
most of the town site, argued that "they are ruining a damned
good plantation to make a damned poor town."

At his own plantation, a few miles from Columbia, Hampton
began to prosper. The Whitney gin had made cotton a desirable
money crop. Soon Wade I had created a "tradition" for his family:
he hunted, raced horses, attended militia muster, and got into
politics, as any planter of his day should. He read books and,
although he had had precious little formal education himself, he
contributed liberally to South Carolina College and served as one
of its charter trustees. Both he and his son Wade were active in

the War of 1812. Wade II was the first to take the news of the victory at New Orleans to Washington.

By the end of that war, the Hamptons had purchased more estates, this time in the burgeoning wilderness of the Old Southwest—"The Houmas" in Louisiana and "Wild Woods" in Mississippi. The family could now be considered landed gentry. In 1838, Wade II helped things along financially by marrying the daughter of Christopher Fitzsimmons, a rich Charleston merchant shipper. Wade III was born at Charleston, in 1818, but grew up at "Millwood," spending many summers at "High Hampton," a family estate in the North Carolina mountains. In 1838, two years after graduating from college, young Wade married his half-cousin, Margaret Preston, and moved to "Sand Hills," next door to "Millwood." There a fourth Wade was born in 1840.

Wade III followed an established pattern for a young planter. He had studied law in South Carolina College, but he had no intention of entering the bar. In 1846, he made the required grand tour of Europe. Back home, he visited the family plantations in Louisiana and Mississippi. When his wife, Margaret, died in 1855, he rallied quickly and soon became business adviser for Mary McDuffie, orphaned daughter of a former South Carolina governor. In June 1858, he married her.

Meanwhile, in the manner of the English gentry and of the Americans who aped them, Wade III had got into politics. Wade II consorted with politicians, entertained men like Henry Clay and was considered somewhat of a "great Warwick of South Carolina," holding aloof from office-seeking. He was determined that his son should enter politics; and in 1852, young Wade had got himself elected to the state house of representatives. In 1856, Wade went to the state senate and remained there until his resignation in 1861, to raise his "Legion" of volunteers. He was at that time at the height of his fame and affluence—renowned for his culture, his hospitality, and his uncompromising honesty. He was, as his biographer Manly Wade Wellman avers, "probably the wealthiest Southerner alive."

In the ante-bellum Legislature, Hampton exhibited the conservatism one would expect of a cultured, well-to-do slave owner, who could dare to talk objectively about slavery without being branded an Abolitionist. He knew that his wealth was built upon a system of forced labor, yet he was intelligent and objective enough to realize that it was both morally wrong as a way of life and outdated, not only as a social but also as an economic institution. He knew enough about balance sheets to realize that ultimately slavery would lose its economic advantages. Had he been able to chart a course for the future, he would have worked toward gradual emancipation. In no case would he have approved the sudden casting of helpless and destitute freedmen upon a society unready to cope with the problems of emancipation.

Of one thing Hampton was certain: he would have no part in a movement that was gaining strength in the late fifties to reopen the African slave trade. At that time, the scarcity of slaves had forced prices to a prohibitive level, and desperate planters were seeking relief by a legal reopening of the slave trade, which had been outlawed since 1807. He stood resolutely against such a proposal in the Legislature; so did the conservative element of his own state and the remainder of the South. Fearing that slavery might well be the "rock on which the Constitution would be wrecked, and the Union shattered," Hampton pleaded with the legislators and with the South to avoid "making any new issue that might avert her from the only true one, which is *the union of the South for the preservation of the South.*"

Hampton encountered strong opposition in the Legislature, but he did manage to secure a postponement of action on the question of reviving the slave trade. South Carolina, hitherto always in the forefront of Southern pro-slavery extremism, for once faltered. Other states of the Deep South passed favorable legislation; South Carolina never acted.

The strident Abolitionist editor of the New York *Tribune,* Horace Greeley, characterized Hampton's calm and unspectacular appeal to the legislature as "a masterly piece of oratory." But many Yankees, and even some Southerners—including a Virginian, of all people—thought Hampton proud and intolerably haughty. Apparently, in South Carolina even those who disagreed with his policies refused to share these judgments. He was simply playing the role that God and Carolina meant for him to assume. If that was arrogance, there was nothing to do but make the most of it.

As the South trod nearer and nearer to the brink of secession, Hampton became disconsolate. He entertained no reservations about the constitutional right of a state to secede. He opposed secession in 1860, just as he would have opposed it in 1814, when New Englanders talked of it at Hartford. It mattered little to him from which side of the Mason-Dixon line the secession talk came; to him disunion was unwise—"inexpedient," was the way he put it. Moreover, Hampton could never convince himself that the South had suffered "sufficient provocation." He was wise enough to know that if nobody listened to the hotheads, they would soon wear themselves out and be forgotten. He would have dismissed both the Abolitionist of the North and the Fire-Eater of the South.

Hampton was not even present when South Carolina voted herself out of the Union in December 1860. He cordially disliked the Fire-Eater governor, Francis Pickens, and would have no part in the folly that was being perpetrated by the hotheads. Out of the Union went South Carolina, and for several months Hampton did little but "sit it out." Early in April 1861, he was at his Mississippi plantation worrying over his cotton, but not particularly worried, tolerant man that he was, over the fact that his local parson was considered to be a bit "Yankeeish."

Fort Sumter changed things, though. The how's and why's no longer mattered, once a war had begun. Secession was inexpedient, indeed; but so was disunity, now that South Carolina was at war. Hampton would have entered as a private, but the Governor chose to call upon his distinguished enemy from "Millwood" to accept a commission as a colonel and assemble a legion consisting of six companies of foot soldiers, four of cavalry, and one of artillery for service in the Confederate army.

Hampton had no difficulty recruiting his men, for he was

immensely popular. Of course, he possessed almost no military knowledge; but he was skilled at woodcraft and adept at horsemanship. "The Hamptons," remarks William W. Ball, "scarcely looked at home except on horseback." But Wade Hampton knew precious little about organized combat. Nevertheless, he surrounded himself with able subordinates who could teach him their military book learning, and from them he learned fast.

Purchasing some of the equipment for his men out of his own pocket, Hampton soon had his Legion outfitted and ready for service at the first major engagement of the war, Bull Run, or Manassas Junction, in Virginia. Here he was wounded for the first of five times in his first two years of combat. Thereafter, Hampton was always in the thick of the struggle, getting himself not only wounded but also promoted with startling frequency.

Rarely, except toward the end, did Hampton leave the stage of combat in Virginia. He saw infantry action during most of the Peninsula Campaign, being wounded at Seven Pines and subsequently promoted to the rank of brigadier general. In July 1862, he became commander of the First Cavalry Brigade of the Army of Northern Virginia, second in command only to General J. E. B. Stuart. Here Hampton easily distinguished himself. What he lacked in formal military apprenticeship he made up for in leadership. Stuart considered him "brilliant." The border actions of 1862 and 1863 found Hampton in the thick of the fighting, and he was wounded at Gettysburg.

After Stuart's death in May 1864, Hampton gradually eased into the position of cavalry commander, although personal rivalries among his fellow generals delayed his receiving recognition. His courageous and brilliant turning back of General Philip Sheridan at Trevilian Station and Samaria Church in the Shenandoah Valley, in June 1864, assured his official elevation to chief cavalry commander in the Army of Northern Virginia. On August 11, he took charge, and for the remainder of the year his job was chiefly to keep open the supply lines from Virginia southward, without which the fall of Richmond and the surrender of Lee would have been immeasurably hastened.

Hampton had few peers at defensive tactics; his own judgment proved to be his strongest asset. When mounted troops were not needed, like Forrest he did not hesitate to turn his cavalry into foot soldiers. Indeed, as horses became scarcer and scarcer, Hampton found that the use of dismounted cavalry was hardly more than a realistic acknowledgment of the facts of military life in the faltering Confederacy.

In January 1865, Hampton was dispatched to South Carolina with a division of dismounted cavalrymen. Sherman was preparing to march through the Carolinas, and both President Davis and General Lee felt that Hampton could "be of service in mounting his men and arousing the spirit and strength" of South Carolina. Hampton's transfer proved to be a fatal blunder, insofar as the defense of Richmond was concerned, as Lee himself later admitted. The return of the native was not without some dramatic impact on the beleaguered state of South Carolina, but Hampton had little success either in mounting his men or inspiring the spirit of his fellow Carolinians. The cause was already lost.

By now South Carolina, penetrated by Sherman's army, had been all but abandoned by the high command, and General P. G. T. Beauregard had received orders to rally all forces across the border in North Carolina. Hampton, promoted to lieutenant general on February 14, remained helplessly behind with almost no troops. He watched his state's capital, Columbia, captured and burned.

The responsibility for the burning of Columbia became one of the great controversies of wartime and after. Sherman blamed it on an ill-executed Confederate attempt to burn all the city's cotton. Sherman said that "the smoldering fires, set by Hampton's order, were rekindled by the wind, and communicated to the buildings around." Hampton insisted that he had given specific orders that the cotton "should not be burned." Recriminations echoed on both sides for years to come, but the prevailing opinion of the scholars is that Sherman's charges were intended to serve the purposes of propaganda rather than historical accuracy. "I distinctly charged it to General Hampton," he wrote later, "and

I confess I did so pointedly to shake the faith of his people in him. . . ." Actually, it would appear that the fire was set by drunken soldiers of the invading Union army. It is doubtful that Sherman ordered the applying of the torch. He did, however, on his own admission, gain considerable satisfaction from the sight of the holocaust, from the fact that Columbia was "utterly ruined."

On the night of the same day—February 17—Charleston was abandoned. South Carolina had lost its "holy city" and its capital in one single day. Possibly Sherman could have been stopped had anyone in authority listened to Hampton's plan to concentrate forces at Branchville, the railway junction between Columbia and Charleston. But South Carolina had been abandoned to the enemy. The Army of Tennessee, Hardee's Charleston forces, and Beauregard's troops from eastern North Carolina were assembling far away to the north under Johnston to make a last-ditch stand.

Time was running out for the Confederacy. Within a matter of weeks, first Lee and then Johnston had surrendered their armies, and Wade Hampton was back home in Columbia. The city was blackened rubble; so was his home at Sand Hills, for it, too, had been fired by the invaders. For all he knew, he had lost his fortune, too: his Negroes were now free and his plantations likely to be seized for indebtedness. Hampton, like most of the antebellum plantation aristocracy, had managed to get himself into debt, despite his cotton profits. With irresponsible zealots in the North crying for the heads of Confederate leaders, and the new President, Andrew Johnson, withholding amnesty from the Confederate ruling class—all high officials, generals in the army and citizens worth over $20,000, as he put it—Hampton was desperate. He could have said with the Carolina poet, Henry Timrod, that the future along with the present was "Beggary, starvation, death, bitter grief, utter want of hope."

But Hampton kept quiet and bided his time. No man with the stellar reputation he had earned during the War could have failed to distinguish himself also in peace. "In all the high companionship of knightly men," wrote the historian Douglas Southall

Freeman, "none had exemplified more of character and of courage and none had fewer mistakes charged against him. Untrained
in arms and abhorring war, the South Carolina planter had
proved himself the peer of any professional soldier. . . ." In
time he would have an opportunity to demonstrate his talent for
making "fewer mistakes."

Undoubtedly Hampton's record of successes was possible
largely because he never lost his head in a crisis and was content
often to watch while others wore themselves to frustration in a
futile effort to do *something*. In the summer of 1865, Hampton
observed and kept exceedingly quiet, at least insofar as public
pronouncements were concerned. In June, President Johnson,
taking advantage of the fact that Congress was not in session,
went ahead with his and Lincoln's benevolent policies of Reconstruction, which looked toward a quick reorganization of the
seceded states.

The President appointed Benjamin F. Perry as provisional
governor to proceed with the Reconstruction of the state government. Perry, a former judge, was a well-known South Carolina
Unionist and a friend of Hampton. Both Perry and Hampton had
high hopes for a rapid return to stability in their state under the
Johnson plan. Hampton, in fact, was disposed to extend suffrage
to the upper-class Negroes. Perry agreed, but, fearful of opposition, did not recommend this action in the Constitutional Convention held in September 1865, a blunder, he later felt, that
only hastened the subsequent atrocities of Radical Reconstruction
dictated by Congress.

Hampton had been elected to the Constitutional Convention
of 1865 but did not receive notice of this in time to attend. It
is doubtful whether he would have attended anyway, for he
wished in no way by his presence to jeopardize the orderly process
of South Carolina reconstruction by giving the Northern Radicals
an opportunity to accuse him, still under Johnson's restrictive
interdict against high Confederate officers, of trying to meddle in
the affairs of the new regime.

Hampton had to be extremely cautious; as a correspondent of

the *Nation* observed in the fall of 1865, he and Lee were "the two most popular and best loved men in the South today." If either of these "should raise the standard of revolt tomorrow, thousands upon thousands would flock to their support."

Some indication of the Hampton spell had been apparent during the summer, when a rash of colonization projects for Confederate *émigrés* had broken out in South Carolina, as it had elsewhere in the South. The promoters of a colony in Brazil attempted to make him their head. He refused, and advised his fellow Southerners to stay home and see their South through its difficult years of Reconstruction. "All who can do so," he counseled, "should take the oath of allegiance . . . so that they may participate in the restoration of civil government to our state." Although he advised against colonization, he obtained data on Brazil from the Consul General at New York and made it available to his correspondents. Meanwhile, his fellow Confederates flocked in large numbers to Hampton's summer home in the mountains, seeking aid and advice. Rumor had it that he would promote a scheme to revive the Confederate struggle, a piece of news calculated to excite the Radicals of the North. He had no such intention.

Hampton was still playing the cautious role. The September convention had seriously considered drafting him as candidate for governor under the new constitution. Hampton asked his supporters not to consider him, feeling he would jeopardize the South's cause by becoming a candidate, particularly since he had not yet been pardoned by Johnson. The convention, aware of his reluctance, gave its blessing to a Confederate Congressman and a leader of the wartime peace movement, James L. Orr. The election was, of course, none of the convention's business, anyway. Stubborn Carolinians persisted in their desire for Hampton, and they voted for him in such large numbers that for some days after the election he seemed to have won. In a final recount, however, Orr, who had practically conceded the election to Hampton, was declared the winner by 9,928 to 9,185 votes.

It was Hampton's own home district that gave Orr the victory, for there the voters, knowing they had better take Hampton at his word, dutifully trooped to the polls and voted for Orr. So the first Reconstruction government of South Carolina went into effect, and at its head was a man of much smaller stature as a statesman than Hampton. Orr was soon being denounced as an opportunist. As a matter of fact, he did change principles and policies rather frequently.

Hampton set out for Mississippi toward the end of the year to attend to the family properties there. He stopped at Montgomery, where he was feted by the Alabama Legislature. He spoke in response, and his harmless remarks were taken in the North as the next thing to incitement to further rebellion. When he arrived at New Orleans, he also "met with great attention."

On his Mississippi plantation, Hampton was delighted to find many of his former bondsmen ready to go back to work. He argued that since the Negro had been faithful to the white man as a slave, the white man should treat him as a friend now that the slave had become a freedman. He wrote that he had taken in some Yankee tenants—as Forrest had done. "It will be a good thing for my Negroes to have Yankees so near them, and this will be sure to make them more contented."

Hampton attempted unsuccessfully to recoup his fortunes, yet he was luckier than many of his fellow Carolinians. Despite relief funds and moratoriums on debts, there was much stark suffering. In Charleston a white woman who had been wealthy at the outbreak of the War was seen standing in the ration line with Negroes seeking charity handouts. The cashier of the Bank of Charleston turned to relief agencies. Confederate officers took jobs as streetcar drivers. At the same time, Carolinians, who had survived the plundering and destruction of wartime, were greeted with the plundering and destruction of postwar carpetbaggery. Even the Reverend and Mrs. Henry Ward Beecher journeyed to Charleston, where they picked up a few choice "relics," including a panel from the pulpit of St. Michael's church. To be fair to the lady, the panel was eventually returned.

Presidential Reconstruction under Orr was far from satisfactory to either South Carolina or Congress. By 1866, many who had looked to Johnson as the South's hope felt disillusioned. Among these was Hampton. In August 1866, he wrote an open letter to President Johnson excoriating him and Congress for not living up to the terms of surrender but instead subjecting the South to all sorts of unreasonable new demands and humiliating persecution at the hands of Northern occupation forces.

That fall, before a group in South Carolina, Hampton was almost defiant:

It is full time that some voice from the South should be raised to declare that, though conquered, she is not humiliated; that though she submits, she is not degraded; that she has not lost her self-respect, that she has not laid down her arms on dishonorable terms; that she has observed these terms with the most perfect faith, and that she has a right to demand the like observance of them on the part of the North.

Yet Hampton was not willing to throw caution to the winds. As he had written at the conclusion of his letter to the President, Hampton was willing—and so was his South—to accept "the situation." Speaking further, he observed:

Everything that she [the South] has done has been done in perfect good faith, and in the true and highest sense of the word, she is loyal. By this I mean *that she intends to abide by the laws of the land honestly; to fulfill all her obligations faithfully and to keep her word sacredly,* and I assert that the North has no right to demand more of her. You have no right to ask, or expect that she will at once profess unbounded love to that Union from which for four years she tried to escape at the cost of her best blood and all her treasure. Nor can you believe her to be so unutterly hypocritical, so base as to declare that the flag of the Union has already usurped in her heart the place which has so long been sacred to the "Southern Cross." The men at the South who make such professions are renegades or traitors and they will surely betray you if you trust them. But the brave men who fought to the last in a cause which they believed *and still believe* to have been a just one, who clung to their colors as long as they waved, and who, when their cause was lost, acknowledged their defeat and accepted the terms offered to them, as they were true to their convictions in the one case, they will prove true to their obligations in the other.

As if the South's woes were not enough under Johnson's plan of Reconstruction, the triumph of the Radicals in Congress during 1866 brought a Congressional demand that the conquered states ratify the Fourteenth Amendment, which undertook to guarantee Negro suffrage. South Carolina rejected the Amendment. So did the remaining Southern states, except Tennessee. The Radicals now swooped down upon South Carolina and the other obstinate states and placed them under military rule, pending their reorganization under the Congressional plan allowing suffrage to the Negro. South Carolina swept the moderate Orr government out of office and ushered in the troubled years of Radical Reconstruction.

Some Carolinians had considered the wisdom of acquiescing to Congressional demands. Governor Orr was willing to do so, "humiliating as they may be"; for he was ready to yield to what he felt was the inevitable. Hampton was unwilling to surrender completely. For public purposes he would accept the Fourteenth Amendment, but he would promptly set up the machinery for controlling the Negro vote. If the Radicals could, why couldn't the Southern whites? He appealed "to the blacks, lately his slaves, as his political superiors, to try the political experiment of harmonizing with their late white masters before going into the political service of strangers." Only by racial cooperation and harmony could Hampton see a resolution of the South's problems short of a "bloody conflict."

Hampton outlined a course for the South in a letter to a friend:

Now all the dirty work is taken off our hands by this Sup. Bill, and it seems to me that but one hope is left to us and that is to direct the Negro vote. I advocate a warm protest from the South against all this legislation of Congress, but protests can do us no good. We must meet it, as a *fact;* one we have to deal with and on the solution of which depends the very existence of our country. . . . Now how shall we do this? Simply by making the Negro a Southern man, and if you will, a Democrat, anything but a Radical. Beyond these motives for my action I have another. We are appealing to the enlightened sense and the justice of mankind. We come forward and say, we accept the decision rendered against us, we acknowledge the freedom of the negro and we are willing to have one law for him and for us. We are making up our record for posterity and we wish no blot or flaw to be found there.

Hampton lost no time in promoting his scheme of taking over the Negro votes before the carpetbagger could get at him. He spoke at public meetings of Negroes, including one at Columbia, in which he promised the freedmen that even should the Reconstruction Acts be ruled unconstitutional, he would advocate state legislation to give the suffrage to all persons, white or black, who could measure up to certain minimum literacy and property qualifications. He minced no words:

The Supreme Court has decided that a Negro is not a citizen of the United States, and Congress cannot reverse that decision by an act. The states, however, are competent to confer citizenship on the Negro, and I think it is the part of wisdom that such action be taken by the Southern states. We have recognized the freedom of the blacks and have placed this fact beyond all possibility of a doubt, denial or recall. Let us recognize in the same frank manner, and as fully, their political rights also.

Altogether, Hampton and the proponents of his plan strove diligently to win over the Negro with arguments, parades, and barbecues. Neither the Negro nor the white man was disposed to follow the sweet reasonableness of Hampton—not yet, at least. The Radicals could offer the freedman far more than conservative white Southerners could. The average white South Carolinian was still inclined to agree with one of Hampton's critics that "General Hampton and his friends had just as well try to control a herd of wild buffaloes as the Negro vote." Soon Hampton himself recognized that compromise was for the moment out of the question. "Recent events," he wrote in August 1867, after the Radicals had completed drafting their program of army-controlled Reconstruction, "show that there is no longer a possibility of that entire harmony of action among our people for which you and we have heretofore hoped and striven."

Hampton found that the impact of Radical Reconstruction had divided Southern whites, also. Some of them, like former Confederate General James Longstreet, attempted to work with the Republicans and were subjected to "virulent attacks," which moderates like Hampton deprecated, even though he had no inclination to compromise with the Radicals.

The crux of the scheme of Reconstruction was a convention to draft a new constitution which should give the vote to the Negro. The constitution must be sanctioned by the electorate. Hampton's reaction to all this was to advise the white man to exercise "the right accorded to all by these military bills, to oppose their adoption by all lawful means. . . . Let every man register and cast his vote against the Convention."

Hampton even preferred that his state continue under military rule rather than "give its sanction to measures which we believe to be illegal, unconstitutional, and ruinous." During the fall, the wholesale registration of Negro voters in the convention election was completed. Whether the white man would try to interfere with the Negroes at the polls was a moot question. Already the Ku Klux Klan was active and it undoubtedly had membership in South Carolina. But the Democratic leadership, under Hampton's moderating influence, had no desire to see violence injected into the situation. In October 1867, Hampton wrote an open letter reiterating his peaceable intentions, and he and other Democrats actually drafted a proclamation for Governor Robert K. Scott (a former Union officer from Ohio) to sign, calling upon all parties to "bear and forbear." As a result, the campaign ended on a peaceful note.

Certainly one reason for the orderliness of the election was the fact that few white men even bothered to vote. On November 6, one week before the voting, the whites had held their own convention at Columbia. Wade Hampton was one of its vice presidents. The white man "would never acquiesce in Negro equality or supremacy," the convention declared and it counseled against voting at all in the forthcoming election, hoping that enough Negroes would join the whites in abstaining to void the election for a lack of a majority of the participating electorate. But such was not to be the case. The whites stayed away in large numbers, but many Negroes voted, and the constitutional convention won by 66,490 votes for to only 2,272 opposed. More than 52% of the total registered voters had gone to the polls, so the convention had won. By abstention most of the whites, except scalawags and carpetbaggers, had removed themselves from its councils. A new constitution was drafted which dutifully conferred upon the Negro the suffrage, free of any restrictions; Hampton's suggested educational and property qualifications had mustered only two votes.

Now the white Democrats realized that willy-nilly they would have to participate in elections; in April 1868, they held a convention before the balloting on the new constitution and the election of new state officers. Hampton was made chairman of the Democratic state executive committee, but despite fervid appeals to Negro voters, the constitution triumphed by 70,758 to 27,228. The Democratic candidate for governor went down in defeat, although so far as he was concerned he never ran: he refused to accept the nomination of a convention that had tolerated Negro voting.

In June, a Democratic convention opposed to Negro suffrage in any form met and repudiated the action of the earlier convention. The new convention proceeded to choose delegates to the National Democratic Convention in New York. Hampton's efforts at conciliation brought the two groups together to form a joint delegation. The Fourteenth Amendment prevented Hampton from holding office, but he was not barred from politics, and this he engaged in vigorously.

Hampton, a delegate to the National Convention, carried with him the memory of a visit with Robert E. Lee at Washington College. Lee admitted to the students that he would act in "precisely the same manner" were the issue of secession and war to be "done over again." Knowing that he had the support of the only other man in the South whose words carried as much weight as his own, Hampton spoke out with vigor at New York. As a member of the committee on resolutions he was responsible for a plank in the party platform denouncing Congressional Reconstruction as "unconstitutional, revolutionary, and void."

Much was made at the Democratic Convention of the fact that soldiers of both North and South extended and accepted "the right hand of fellowship." Hampton made the seconding speech to the nomination for the Vice Presidency of General Francis P. Blair, who had marched with Sherman through Georgia and the Carolinas. Here was more than a demonstration of honor among generals; it was a burying of hatchets. Only a man of Hampton's stature and reputation could have accomplished it.

The Radicals now made sneering remarks about the "Southern chivalry who ran the late Democratic National Convention." Hampton was denounced as a traitor who "rode into the Rebellion to trample out a nation's life . . . under the hoofs of his horses," but he worked vigorously all the same for the ticket of Seymour and Blair. During the campaign, Hampton asked the intrepid Charles Francis Adams to speak in Carolina. Adams came at the call of a rebel whom he described as "just such a rebel as I am and no more." The Democrats lost, of course, for the Republicans were well in control of the situation in most of the Southern states.

Meanwhile, Hampton's personal affairs were in grievous state. At the close of the War, he had had 12,000 acres and 900 Negroes. He lost most of both. He had incurred in the fifties a considerable indebtedness, mortgaging his Mississippi plantations. After the War he tried to pay off his debts, but failed miserably. On the day before Christmas 1868, he was forced into bankruptcy to the tune of $1,041,991, in a case filed in the U. S. Court in Mississippi, where the ante-bellum family property Wild Woods was. He had lost most of his South Carolina property, except a portion of his Sand Hills estate and a small farm at Columbia, but managed to hold part of his Mississippi holdings, though lawyers argued bitterly whether he had failed to acknowledge all his assets to the court.

Meanwhile, Hampton never forgot that he was still a planter at heart, and always would be. But he found other responsibilities to engage his attention, including a brief presidency of the Baltimore Fire Extinguisher Works.

These were years of wild government spending and mounting

state debts. The white Democracy of the South was almost in complete eclipse. During this era, Hampton spent much of his time in Mississippi, where he struggled to operate the few acres the War and the courts had left him. He was forced to establish legal residence there to salvage what he could of the family property by homestead right. These Mississippi ties embarrassed him when he returned later to South Carolina to run for governor.

Meanwhile, Hampton's concern over Radical excesses caused him to write to President Grant warning of the danger of a "collision of the races" in South Carolina. Soon there was a revival of Ku Klux Klan activity in that state. "Rifle clubs" appeared to combat the Negro practice of carrying guns. Yet the incitement for the Klan was not the armed Negro citizen but the Negro soldier clothed with the authority of an army of occupation or the Negro militiamen organized by carpetbag Governor Scott of South Carolina during the state election campaign of 1870. The whites' reply was to organize companies and tender their services also to the Governor; but he accepted only one or two of these groups. Hampton likewise counseled the whites to join the Negro companies. Apparently the advice was not taken, but the idea of boring—or perhaps we should say, shooting—from within was characteristic of this resourceful and realistic leader, who in the end would redeem South Carolina for the white Democrats simply because he took advantage of every legal means at his disposal to effect his ends.

In 1871, Hampton told the Congressional Committee investigating Klan "outrages" that the movement was directed not against the "General Government" but against corrupt state and local governments. He felt that on the whole there had been little Klan activity in the state of South Carolina. "I have never seen any man that was identified with that organization, if one exists. I have never been approached upon the subject at all, and I do not know that there is an organization of that kind at all." He admitted that there had been violence; but "whether this is done by any organization extending through the state or merely from some local outbreak, I do not know; but I am inclined to think it is the latter." He personally "always expressed" his opinion "very decidedly" against the "outrages." One cannot doubt his honesty on this point. In fact, the evidence as sifted by the historians of South Carolina's reconstruction, Francis B. Simkins and Robert H. Woody, tends to show that in that state the Klan movement was weak and was "for the most part composed of low-type men." Its only strength was apparently in the backwoods and hill sections; aristocrats like Hampton would scarcely have deigned to consort with these yokels and "reckless young men, without a great deal of standing."

It seems unlikely that Hampton belonged to the Klan. Whether he was as ignorant of its operations as he pretended to be during the Congressional investigation may be open to question. On the other hand, when anti-Klan laws were passed in Washington and at Columbia, Hampton was ready to resist with "some concert of action among us." "We should," he observed, "engage the service of some Northern lawyers to defend our Ku Klux cases. They would have more weight than our own advocates and could speak more freely."

Hampton was now emerging as the strategist of the "Redemption." In the first several years after the War, he and Lee had been recognized as the most potent leaders of the South. In 1870, Lee had died, and Hampton was called upon to deliver a memorial address at Baltimore. Lee was "no longer with us," he said, but "his example, his fame, and his virtues are still left to us, and he is not dead."

No, Lee was not dead; he lived on in Wade Hampton. A Richmond editor, E. A. Pollard, described him as "representative of a class," the calmly defiant, old conservative leadership of the South. *Harper's Weekly* called it "the most perilous element in this country." Northern critics spoke ominously of these "Wade Hamptons of the South." The old bluff was working still.

Hampton's next step toward leadership in the South came with his pardon, after the Amnesty Act of 1872, just in time for him to enter the Presidential campaign. Many Southerners would have no part of Horace Greeley, the joint nominee of the Liberal Republicans and Democrats, but Hampton supported him with vigor. South Carolina and all of the South save Georgia, Texas, and Tennessee went over to Grant, who was re-elected.

Hampton's campaign activities brought vituperation from the North. In December 1872, the old issue of responsibility for the burning of Columbia was revived and unofficial hearings were conducted in Washington to attempt to fix the responsibility. The matter of ultimate blame was left undecided. Hampton's enemies enjoyed a field day at his expense, but their glee was short-lived. His influence in the South grew as the attacks from the North increased.

One of the carpetbag winners of the 1872 elections had boasted that there were "still five years of good stealing in South Carolina." But it was not the bankruptcy of morality but of finances that was to bring about the revolution that drove the Radicals out of South Carolina. Hampton had told the Congressional investigators in 1871, that South Carolinians would have tolerated the Radical regime had it not dipped thieving hands into the public purse.

Even in the Radical camp, some Republicans—the scalawags in particular, for they were usually Southern property-owners and taxpayers—were beginning to complain of the spiraling public debt and the concurrent burgeoning of tax levies. To men like Hampton, excluded for a time from public office, it smacked of representation without taxation, for most of the freedmen and many of the carpetbaggers owned no property and paid no taxes, leaving a tremendous burden upon the property-owners, most of them white Democrats who had incurred civic disabilities because they had fought in the War. By 1871, the disgruntled property owners had begun to hold taxpayers' conventions. In 1874, Daniel H. Chamberlain, a Radical who promised reform, was elected governor. It was Chamberlain that Hampton two years later succeeded in defeating to bring about the overthrow of the Negro-carpetbag regime.

Since the Radical triumph in 1868, South Carolina Democrats had scarcely bothered to maintain a party organization. The term

"Conservative" was used to embrace all the critics of the regime at Columbia—both Republican and Democratic. Chamberlain was even disposed to talk with this Conservative group about putting up a candidate for lieutenant governor, who would probably fall heir to his place should he be sent to the Senate.

But sentiment gradually grew for a "straightout" Democratic slate of candidates, and vigorous steps were taken to revive the party. Hampton held with the "Straightouts" and this was good news to old "Bald Eagle," Martin W. Gary, inventor of the "Straightout" name, who had been unable to find a proper candidate for governor.

On a train returning from the centennial celebration of the battle of Fort Moultrie at Charleston, Hampton, who had been grand marshall of the parade, and Gary struck up a conversation. Gary had been somewhat cool toward Hampton, but he changed his attitude completely and in a matter of minutes had talked Hampton into the candidacy.

Gary set about master-minding the campaign strategy. To the Straightout name he contributed an effective symbol, the red shirt, soon worn by every member of the Democratic Clubs. Meanwhile, the National Democratic headquarters and its Presidential candidate, Samuel J. Tilden of New York, preferred "some man of less prominence" than a Confederate general, and Hampton would have quit in a huff had Gary let him.

The strained relations with the national party created many charges and countercharges. Some of Hampton's enemies felt he had deliberately alienated Tilden. Before the campaign had proceeded far, Hampton was apparently ready to withdraw support from the Tilden electoral candidates. He reputedly told one audience as he pointed northward, "Vote for Hayes and Wheeler, if you like. That big fight is up yonder."

Mississippi had freed itself of carpetbag control by a strenuous campaign of red-shirt wearing and military drilling, which intimidated Negro voters and kept large numbers away from polls. Now South Carolina seemed certain to take a leaf from the Mississippi book. There had been incidents with Negro militiamen in the summer of 1874, and in January 1875. In July 1876, came the Hamburg riot. A company of Negro militia were beseiged in the town armory by a group of angry white citizens, and a few Negroes and white men were killed. Governor Chamberlain threatened militia action.

In August, the Straightouts broke up a Chamberlain campaign speech at Edgefield by ascending the rostrum and seizing "equal time." When the State Democratic convention met on August 15, Hampton's name was placed in nomination for Governor. Hampton responded: "I have not tried to influence this convention. . . . I came here only to pour oil on the troubled waters, if necessary, and to promote unity and harmony if I could." He said he had refused a wartime invitation to run because he would not leave the battlefield. When the War was over, he had felt that his "day was past." He had been disposed "to lay his weary bones" in his native state, claiming only "a grave in yonder churchyard [Trinity Church]." If his candidacy would "jeopardize the general Democratic party," he would "gladly decline." But his next words made his nomination inevitable:

Besides this, there are men in South Carolina who think I possess a disqualification of which I cannot divest myself. I mean what they call my war record. This is the record of fifty thousand South Carolina soldiers, and if I am to forfeit that, and say that I am ashamed to have been one of them, all the offices in the world might perish before I would accept them.

Hampton had learned the merits of the "bloody shirt" technique himself. He was nominated by acclamation. A list of candidates for state offices was picked—every one of them a former Confederate officer.

There were tremendous crowds every time Hampton appeared. Usually the day of the rally was known as "Hampton Day." There were mammoth parades and noisy processions, with platoons of Democrats, black as well as white, decked out in red shirts and other appropriate regalia. Women attended many of them wearing

Red ribbons round their waists,
Red ribbons in their hair,
Red ribbons to their tastes,
Pinned to them everywhere.

Hampton's platform was simple: "Reconstruction, Retrench-ment, and Reform." He appealed to the Negro for support, and many of his former slaves rallied behind Hampton. "I write to say," said one, "that I will vote for you and will get all the black men I can to do the same." The Negro red-shirts were often given "front seats at the stand." Some of the Negro Democrats suffered from a Republican terror no less frightful than that attributed to the Klan. Nevertheless, approximately 7,000 or 10,000 Negroes joined the Democratic Clubs. Hampton's pleas to the Negro were unequivocal. As governor he would under no circumstances grant "privileges and immunities" to white men that he would not give to Negroes, and this he meant.

A number of prominent Radicals also "crossed the Jordan," as the saying was, to join the Hampton forces. The white voters were almost solid for Hampton, while Chamberlain probably had fewer than 500 white supporters, office-holders excepted. Every-where the invariable words of greeting and farewell identified the supporters of the Straightout ticket: "Hurrah for Hampton!"

Everybody—white and black, Republican and Democrat—was armed; some wore as many as three pistols. The Democratic arms were intended more to be seen than heard—or if heard, the firing was into the air. Yet the freedman did not fail to observe that the sights could easily be lowered. As William Watts Ball put it, "the strategy was to hold up to the gaze and din into the ears of the Negroes the picture and sound and menace of war against them without committing overt acts of war."

Hampton himself went about unarmed. He said later he had not seen more than twenty pistols in the whole campaign and had noticed no "armed body of men" at any of his "fifty-seven large meetings." He had promised that there would be no intimidation and had declared if there were, he would "withdraw from the canvass." Hotheads like Gary, knowing that Hampton meant what he said, were careful to confine the antics of the rifle clubs and such to spots where Hampton was not campaigning at the moment. Hampton thought that his own persuasion was winning the Negroes. Gary did not bother to disillusion him.

There were numerous "strikes" of Negro workmen during the summer; Governor Chamberlain hurriedly broke up one. There were also riots—at Charleston, at Ellerton, at Cainhoy. In October, Chamberlain ordered the rifle clubs disbanded. Then came a similar proclamation from President Grant, and Federal troops in the state were ordered reinforced. Yet for the most part the reinforcements proved to be white men, who fraternized with the Hamptonites.

The rifle clubs now changed their names but not their purposes, masquerading under such titles as the Allendale Mounted Baseball Club, Mother's Little Helpers, the First Baptist Church Sewing Circle, and the Hampton and Tilden Music Club. The last had "four twelve pounder flutes" with which they welcomed Hampton to one rally. Hampton announced that Grant's injunction to disperse and retire peaceably to their respective abodes could not be obeyed "because we are not gathered together." Hampton insisted his supporters were already in their "homes in peace, disturbed only by the political agitation created by the governor and his minions."

Election day was relatively calm. In many counties there were more ballots than voters. Fraud was charged by both sides, and the charges were doubtless true. Hampton had apparently won by 92,261 to 91,127, but the five-man State Board of Election Commissioners, three of whom were candidates for office, threw out enough Democratic votes to give the Radicals the victory in the state campaign. At the same time, the Republican Presidential electors had apparently won by a very narrow margin.

Hampton, of course, refused to accept defeat. On the day Chamberlain was "inaugurated," he announced: "The people have elected me governor, and, by the Eternal God, I will be Governor or we shall have a military Governor." Most people knew, and Chamberlain feared, that Hampton meant what he was saying. The state high court had taken sides with the Democrats; so there were two Legislatures, each claiming to be the properly authorized one. On December 14, a week after the induction of Chamberlain, the Democrats inaugurated Hampton, to a lively cannonade from the Hampton Saluting Club, erstwhile Columbia Light Artillery Club.

The State Supreme Court, though Republican controlled, subsequently gave *de facto* recognition to Hampton's claims, not solely for legal reasons but undoubtedly because the justices knew and respected him. Chamberlain's treasurer was immobilized by an injunction against withdrawals from the public depositories. Hampton informally called for a token payment of taxes (ten per cent) to keep his government in operation. Nearly the entire tax was contributed willingly. Almost nothing came into the Radical-controlled treasury.

The dual governments continued for several months. Hampton seems to deserve most of the credit for keeping the peace in these tempestuous weeks. "Do nothing to provoke a riot," he had counseled his supporters. "We trust to the law and the Constitution, and we have perfect faith in the justice of our cause." This he had said in November, when Gary wanted to let the Red Shirts storm the state house and Hampton dispersed a violent mob of 5,000 "within three minutes." According to the New York *Herald,*

> He had only to lift his finger, he had only to signify the slightest assent, and the State house would have been rescued from the Federal soldiers and his supporters would have controlled the organization of the Legislature. The Federal troops were only three hundred, and there were at least eight thousand Democrats present in Columbia, accustomed to the use of arms and with arms probably upon their persons, who could have crumpled and annihilated the small Federal force had they given way to their indignation and to their sense of wrong. It is fortunate that they have a leader so strong, so sagacious, so self-possessed and so thoroughly trusted as Wade Hampton.

Hampton's enemies attempted to embarrass him with the accusation that he had deserted Tilden and secretly supported

Hayes. He was pictured as ready to turn South Carolina over to Hayes in return for recognition of the Democratic gubernatorial claimant's rights to the chief magistracy of the state. Fuel for these flames was provided by some Hampton correspondence with Hayes. In March, President Hayes called Chamberlain and Hampton to Washington for a conference. "I go there," said Hampton, "to say to him that we ask no recognition from any President. We claim the recognition from the people [of South Carolina]." To Hayes he wrote:

> I shall avail myself of your invitation, so that I may reiterate in person what I have the honor to submit in writing: That in my judgment all impediments to the objects so earnestly desired by yourself and so anxiously expected by the people of this State can at once be removed by the withdrawal of the federal troops from the State House. . . . Whatever grievances exist, whatever wrongs we suffer, we propose to redress them, not by a resort to force, but by legal and constitutional agencies. In seeking such redress I feel sure that I represent fully the determination of the thoughtful and conservative portion of our people when I give the assurance that no proscription shall be exercised here on account of political opinions; that no discrimination shall be made in the administration of justice; and that all citizens of both parties, and both parties and both races, shall be regarded as fully protected by and amenable to the laws.

Hayes told the two rivals that Hampton would be recognized as governor, in line with the "bargain" already made on the national level to let Hayes have the Presidency while the Democrats kept their state governments. At any rate, Federal troops were removed from South Carolina on April 10. On April 11, the state had only one Legislature and only one governor—Wade Hampton.

To most white Carolinians their state had been "redeemed." Not till 1879, after Hampton was chosen United States Senator, a post that Gary coveted, did animosity reappear. Gary was a rabble-rouser—"the people's man"—a sort of forerunner for the budding Demagogue Ben Tillman. In his disappointment Gary revived the story of the alleged Hampton trade of the South Carolina Presidential vote for a guarantee of the governorship. The attack proved a dud, and Gary's death in 1881 brought an end to the campaign of vilification.

Hampton had waited a decade, until his state was ripe for the "Redemption," and until "he was called upon," as he liked to put it. But his silence had been as eloquent as the few addresses he had made. He was the politician's dream of the perfect candidate—a man who could be in politics but not of it.

And now in the twenty-five years of life remaining for him he was to be the apostle of the Redemption. Hampton quickly set about the task of restoring his state to peace and prosperity. A few of the swindlers were brought to justice—"two or three of the most important," as Hampton put it, but punishment was tempered with mercy. The tremendous public debt was reduced, but Hampton and the conservatives would not hear of a proposed scaling down which might have caused certain bonds of doubtful validity to be repudiated to the detriment of the bankers of Charleston. South Carolina also committed itself to stand behind nearly five million dollars in ante-bellum railroad bonds, which might have been repudiated had the state been controlled by the bond-hating hillbillies. Hampton would not establish solvency at the expense of the Reconstruction-born public school system, for he believed in it and fought for its improvement. He also encouraged industrial development in his state.

Some carpetbaggers fared well under Hampton's rule. A. J. Willard was made Chief Justice, much to the disgust of the more partisan Democratic elements. Hampton was even accused of having sold out to the Republicans, so co-operative was he. On the other hand, he was probably too radical to suit some of the conservatives. He was also subjected to criticism for his appointment of friends, mostly veterans.

Hampton was more disposed than his associates to keep his campaign promise to give "equal rights and full protection" to "our citizens of all parties and all races." The new governor's first official act was to appoint a Negro as Jury Commissioner in Abbeville County. Usually, however, Negro Democrats were appointed to menial offices; and though no wholesale effort was made to disfranchise Negro voters, the numbers of qualified voters and of officeholders dropped constantly. In 1878, Hampton warned his party:

> You have it all in your hands. You carried your election by an over-whelming majority, because you came before the people, white and black, recognizing the right of every citizen and saying, "you shall all be equal under the law." You went to the colored people and told them that their rights would be protected. . . . You appealed to them to come and help you work out the redemption of the State. They came by hundreds and did help you. And now would you turn your back upon them, and after trying for ten years to convince the colored man that his true interests lay with the Democratic Party, would you say, "Now we have no use for you. . . ." If this is to be the policy of South Carolina, then am I sadly mistaken in the people of South Carolina and the peoples are mistaken in me, because I can carry out no such policy as that. I stand where you put me in 1876.

Aristocrats like Hampton often felt that the Negro could be controlled sufficiently well to prevent any serious threat to white supremacy. In fact, as time passed, it became apparent that the Negro voter was essential to the supremacy of the aristocrat in many of the Southern states, for it was largely the planter's con-trol of Negro votes that enabled the aristocratic "Brigadiers" to run the South for nearly two decades after the end of Reconstruc-tion, while the dirt farmer complained bitterly over his political subordination to the overlords and their serfs. Before the War, the plantation economy had survived, thanks to the Negro slave. Now not only the economy but also the political hegemony of the planter depended upon the Negro freedman. The fate of these two was irrevocably linked together.

When a post-Reconstruction Legislature undertook to force able-bodied county prisoners to do road work, Negroes felt that the scheme was designed to produce a black chain-gang system. Hampton agreed, vetoed the legislature act, and his veto held. Certainly Hampton's popularity with the Negroes was no figment of his imagination, though he may have magnified the numbers of the faithful. He was touched when some of them pleaded with him to run for re-election in 1878, and when on one occasion he was welcomed to town by a torch procession of Negroes.

In 1878 Hampton dined with two Negroes at Claflin University in Orangeburg, in the home of a white professor. He had accepted the invitation without knowing that a Negro professor and ex-Supreme Court Justice Wright, also a Negro, would be present. Hampton was too much of an aristocrat to create a scene. South Carolinians seem to have been bothered about the incident until rabble-rousers, like Gary and Tillman, passed the story around to embarrass Hampton and discredit him and the conservatives.

Toward the North Hampton presented a friendly mien. In June 1877, he was invited to speak at Auburn, New York. He recognized Union General James Shields in the audience. "He wore the blue," said Hampton, "and I wore the gray, but we can let the curtain drop over those years, and go back to the time when that flag borne by him waved alike over the men of the South and the men of the North, and we can look beyond to the future, when through all time that flag shall float over a free and prosperous and reunited country."

In the fall of 1877, Hampton was included by President Hayes in a party touring the South. The old rumors of a sell-out were revived. Hampton had developed rather close ties with Hayes, even helping the President battle the corruption of New York's irascible Senator Roscoe Conkling. "You can strengthen my hands . . . greatly," said Hampton to Hayes, "by the exercise of executive clemency in behalf of these who are charged with the violation of U. S. laws. . . . There are but three men from this state now in the Albany Penty [penitentiary] on Ku Klux charges and I have asked you to pardon them. . . ." Hampton had no love for the Klansmen, for they were among the "extreme men" he was constantly battling in an effort to keep the peace. For him, however, their freedom was merely a matter of principle— state rights, or individual rights, perhaps.

"Brother Wade seems to have won golden opinions everywhere," wrote Kate Hampton in 1878. Although there were enemies in his party, men who felt that the general was "blending the executive with the legislative . . . too closely," they were soundly squelched, and in that year he was renominated and over-whelmingly re-elected. But the victory had hardly been won when Hampton broke his leg while out hunting and lay undis-covered for hours. The wound became infected, and the leg had to be amputated.

While Hampton lay seriously ill, the South Carolina Legislature elected him to the United States Senate. Equipped with an arti-ficial limb, he took his seat. For the next decade, Hampton pursued an uneventful Senate career, ruling state politics, however, with an iron hand as the "grand mogul" of South Carolina Democracy. He was aging fast—he was now sixty—and he recovered slowly from personal blows like the death of his son Wade Hampton IV in 1879. "Life seems closed for me," he wrote then, "and I have nothing but duty to live for."

It was soon to be his "duty" to fall out with the "people's" man, "Bald Eagle" Gary. "I have," he wrote, "always regarded his views as narrow, unwise and dangerous." Gary to him was worse than a Radical. It was Gary's followers whom he accused of at-tempting to substitute "the policy of Ku Kluxism" for the "policy of peace, good-will and harmony" that had prevailed in the jubilee year of 1876. In 1880, he succeeded in wrecking Gary's candidacy for the governorship and was being spoken of as a possible Democratic candidate for Vice President, balancing the prospective Presidential candidacy of Yankee General Winfield S. Hancock. The proposal came to naught, but Hampton's national reputation was something to reckon with.

As an elder statesman, Hampton apparently exerted great in-fluence among his Senate colleagues. One Carolinian insisted that Hampton had "more influence in the Senate than any other man." Hampton, who found Grover Cleveland's administration of 1885-89 to his liking, was a friend and advisor of the Presi-dent. Both had strong convictions about the holding of a public office as a public trust. Both were conservative on the money issue, though it would have been far better for both of them politically had they gone overboard for cheap money, as their party was soon to do.

Hampton continued to be in dire personal financial straits. His senatorial income was all he had. Yet he could never refuse a loan to a needy veteran or a handout to a begging Negro. Dirt farmers were seeking to resolve their financial plight by inflation; Hampton was too much of a man of honor to cheapen the dollar, even if he did not have one to his name.

Back in South Carolina, the up-country farmers were restive. The Redeemers had fallen far short of bringing prosperity. Bad crops, low prices, and grasping creditors soon reduced many of them to tenancy—or nearly so. The Brigadier leadership was either too proud or too callous to cope with the problem. Then, in 1885, a farmer named Benjamin Ryan Tillman set out to do something about the situation; he launched the Farmers' Movement. Tillman, who liked to be known by the nickname "Pitchfork Ben," attacked not only the old ruling class but all the forces of Bourbonism, especially the industrialists, bankers, and railroad magnates—many of them Yankees—with whom the Southern aristocrats had co-operated. Tillman would place the dirt farmer in control of the South and drive out all the money changers.

With Tillmanism Hampton was completely out of sympathy, if he understood it at all. To him the lower classes should not lead but be led—led not by their own kind but by their betters. In 1886 and 1888, the Tillmanites made a bid for control of the state Democratic convention, and failed. But the farmers would not be silenced and demanded a state primary which would have taken party control away from Hampton's Bourbon "machine." Even without a primary, the Tillman group won control of the state house of representatives in 1888.

Two years later, Tillman was out to get the governorship—and Hampton. The farmers' movement had by now infiltrated the Democratic party. The state committee allowed joint debates in each county, so the Hampton conservatives and the Tillman radicals proceeded to talk it out with no holds barred. Brigadiers—

heroes of the War—were being shouted down and insulted on the stump. "I thought," Hampton said, "Good God, have all the memories of '61 been forgotten?"

The conservatives hurriedly assembled their forces. At Columbia they heckled Tillman, but that was his meat. He turned upon Hampton: "The Grand Mogul here who ruled supremely and grandly cannot terrify me. I do not come from such blood as that." At Aiken, where Hampton refused to ride in the same carriage with Tillman, the old man was treated to a "display of disgraceful blackguardism" which forced him to stop his address short. A new era of rowdyism in South Carolina politics had begun.

In September, the party convention was captured by the Tillmanites, and Tillman was nominated for governor. The conservatives attempted to set up a splinter convention, declaring the nomination of Tillman "illegal and void." With amazing unawareness of the facts of politics, the old Brigadiers sought to win the Negro vote without promising any offices to Negroes. There was a revival of the "spirit of '76"—the red shirts, the "Straightout" title, and such. The candidate, Colonel A. C. Haskell, had been a friend of Hampton. Hampton refused, however, to bolt his party, saying he would cast his vote for Tillman. At the same time, Hampton refused to speak against Haskell, "who was my comrade in war."

Tillman's inauguration in 1890 and the installation of another Tillman-controlled Legislature meant one thing to Hampton: the end of his political career. Tillman had warned that should Hampton fail to be re-elected to the Senate, the conservative leader could "attribute his defeat to his own acts."

There was no stopping the Tillmanite Legislature. Hampton was replaced by John L. Irby in a landslide vote of 157 to 43. "It was a hard thing to do," explained Tillman, but he made no effort to save the old man from humiliation. Hampton and the conservatives would try desperately in 1892 to effect a comeback, but their cause was lost. The Redeemers had been utterly repudiated.

There is uncomfortable irony in the fact that in the early months of 1891, while Hampton was marking time as a lame-duck Senator, he should have made the most effective speech of his Congressional career—the only one, as a matter of fact, that achieved any widespread publicity or had any recognizable influence on legislation. The speech was against the Force Bill, one of the last-ditch measures of the old Radical Republican element designed to reinstate Federal intervention in elections in the South. He pleaded that the South cherished "no animosity toward the Negroes"; responsible Southerners were not practicing unfair and illegal discriminations against Negro voters. The American people, he said, "do not desire a Force Bill, but a bill that shall be enforced, not for the advantage of any party, nor in the interest of any section, but for the good of the whole country. . . ." The bill failed; many gave the credit to Hampton.

The speech was his swan song, and a fitting one it was. For years to come the solemn guarantees that Hampton made in this speech were accepted in good faith by the moderates of the North, with whom he was still a prophet not without honor. Only in his home state had he been forced to the conclusion "that gratitude is short-lived."

Tillman had often directed his vitriol at a stereotype he liked to call the "broken-down aristocrat." After losing his senatorial salary, Wade Hampton was just that. But after Democrats were returned to power nationally in 1892, with the second election of Cleveland, the President, at the suggestion of Senator Vest of Missouri, appointed Hampton U.S. Commissioner of Railways, a post now vacated by the death of "Old Joe" Johnston. When in 1898 President McKinley fired him (despite the unsolicited intervention of Ben Tillman) it was to make room for a better Republican but hardly a better conservative, Confederate General James Longstreet.

Hampton returned to Columbia to live out his last years. There he was when the Spanish-American War broke out in 1898; he was for it. From Columbia he journeyed occasionally to veterans' meetings, and at the Charleston Survivors' Association convention in 1899 he rode a spirited horse at the head of the ranks of the Army of Northern Virginia.

The assassination of McKinley in 1901 placed the redoubtable Theodore Roosevelt in the Presidency and overtures were made by the new President suggesting Hampton's appointment as post-master of Columbia provided the old Confederate would join the ranks of the South Carolina Republicans. "The people of South Carolina know me well enough," was Hampton's answer, "to be certain that I cannot be bought."

At a reunion at Charleston's South Carolina College late in 1901, Hampton caught a stubborn cold. By spring his eighty-four-year-old heart was in trouble. On April 4 he took to his bed for good. To Episcopal Bishop Ellison Capers he spoke characteristically. Whether he asked absolution for his own sins or not we have no record, but he did absolve those of his enemies. "From my heart I forgive my enemies if there are any men in South Carolina who are my enemies." By now even Tillman, a Senator since 1895 and very much of a conservative, had forgotten the old bitterness and was taking his place in a second-generation-poor-relation sort of way. Presently the two of them would be facing each other in stone on the state house grounds.

It was April 12, 1902. Forty-one years ago the guns had begun firing at Sumter; thirty-seven years ago the guns had fallen silent at Appomattox and Wade Hampton was about to offer himself as the Confederate President's escort across the Mississippi; twenty-five years ago the Straightout governor of South Carolina was taking over the state house in Columbia after the occupation troops had marched away. . . . But this day Wade Hampton was back among his slaves. . . . Then he was on the battlefield, and he cried out as two Hampton sons went down in battle. . . . Then the war was over, and he was the apostle of the Redemption: "God bless all my people, black and white," he murmured.

The funeral was held on April 13. Columbia teemed with 20,000 mourners, many of them black in skin as well as in attire. The general had demanded that there be no military funeral. In the War Hampton had fought his cavalry on foot, just as Forrest had—now the mourners, too, were dismounted. No salutes were fired—there was only the sound of taps punctuating the last words of the ritual.

In the crowd was Edward Wells, who would become the author of two eulogistic and undistinguished books about Hampton's feats in war and peace. The funeral over, Wells sat down and wrote to the Charleston *News and Courier:*

As we passed by the pretty residences and charming grounds, evidences of thrift and prosperity, and remembered that if it were not a Sunday, the air would be throbbing with the hum of thousands of busy spindles, I thought, if it had not been for Hampton in the crisis of Reconstruction, these things would not now be.

And I could not help thinking of a bright moonlight night many, many years ago, when, with one comrade only, I rode through the deserted streets of Columbia, the only sound that of our horses' hoofs, the only sights naked chimneys against the sky, and blackened ruins, and I reflected, *that* was Sherman's work, "War is Hell"; *this* is Hampton's work, the peace of God . . .

Thinking of all these things, I realized that others too—thousands— were then having similar thoughts, and that the memory of Hampton was a mutual bond between us all, a common ground upon which all good men can meet in sympathy, whatever may be their politics. . . .

Already the century had turned. Now only Longstreet remained—Longstreet the "turncoat," whom Hampton had refused to denounce. By 1902, the South, too, had ceased to denounce; it had forgotten all except "the memories of '61." Perhaps by now the South had found a common ground upon which all good men might "meet in sympathy." Perhaps the redeeming arm of Wade Hampton had been raised not for South Carolina alone, but for the whole South.

9

The Reconstructed
JAMES LONGSTREET

"General, unless he offers us honorable terms, come back and let us fight it out." It was April 9, 1865, and Lieutenant General James Longstreet was giving a final piece of advice to his superior, Lee, now preparing to meet Union General Grant at Appomattox for the surrender of the Army of Northern Virginia. Longstreet, who commanded the First Corps, the last effective fighting unit in Lee's army, had fought stubbornly and effectively from Bull Run (First Manassas) to this moment. He was perfectly willing to fight a little longer. Two days before, Lee's chief of artillery, General William N. Pendleton, had asked Longstreet to speak to Lee about the hopelessness of the Army's position and the possibility of negotiating peace. Longstreet replied grimly, "If General Lee doesn't know when to surrender until I tell him, he will never know."

Longstreet had been commander of the First Corps and Lee's "Old War Horse" since his brilliant performance at the battle of Sharpsburg (Antietam) in September 1862, the bloodiest single day of the war, with 25,000 Union and Confederate casualties. After the death in 1863, at Chancellorsville, of "Stonewall" Jackson, who had commanded the Second Corps of the Army of Northern Virginia, Longstreet became increasingly close to Lee. They were constantly together in the field and on the march, and Lee was as ready to receive Longstreet's advice (though he did not always accept it) as Longstreet was to give it. To the soldiers Longstreet was "Old Pete," a rough-and-ready, very human leader, calmest when danger was greatest. Lee they revered. Jackson they had respected. But "Old Pete" was closest to them. He enjoyed smoking and card playing, took a drink now and then, and cussed a little when the situation seemed to call for cussing.

Careful in his arrangements for battle, concerned over his men, "Old Pete," when the fighting began, spared neither his men nor himself. "Everyone deplores that Longstreet will expose himself in such a reckless manner," wrote the British observer, Colonel A. J. L. Fremantle, in 1863. "Today he led a Georgian regiment in a charge against a battery, hat in hand and in front of everybody." "Difficulties," marveled Fremantle, "seem to make no other impression upon him than to make him a little more savage."

Even at Appomattox, while his chief went to meet Grant and the two armies faced each other in strange and uneasy quiet, Longstreet energetically prepared the Confederate forces for battle, in case the fighting should be resumed. He was interrupted by the sudden appearance of a Union cavalry officer, with flowing yellow locks, who charged through the picket lines into his presence and called out in a brusque, excited voice, "I demand the unconditional surrender of this army." It was Brigadier General George A. Custer in a typically dramatic and flamboyant gesture. Longstreet glared at Custer, and, according to one account, "simply cursed him out of his lines."

Longstreet's own version in his book, *From Manassas to Appomattox,* written years after the event and in a more tolerant mood, says Custer "was reminded that I was not the commander of the army, that he was within the lines of the enemy without authority, addressing a superior officer, and in disrespect to General Grant as well as myself; that if I was the commander of the army I would not receive the message." Custer, he added, "then became more moderate, saying it would be a pity to have more blood upon that field. Then I suggested that the truce be respected, and said, 'As you are now more reasonable, I will say that General Lee has gone to meet General Grant, and it is for them to determine the future of the armies.' "

Custer "was satisfied," says Longstreet, "and rode back to his command." But General E. P. Alexander, Longstreet's artillery commander, like several other observers, reported that Longstreet treated Custer "very roughly, far more so than appears in Longstreet's account of the interview." "Old Pete" was not easily pushed around, not even by men with a flair for "last stands."

When Lee returned to the Confederate lines after accepting Grant's peace terms, Longstreet was one of the three officers sent to arrange the details of surrender. Grant and Longstreet had been at West Point together (both were reluctant students and finished near the bottom of their class—though Longstreet had been voted the handsomest cadet in the Academy). After graduation, when they were stationed at Jefferson Barracks, St. Louis, Longstreet introduced Grant to his cousin Julia Dent, who in time became Mrs. Grant, with Longstreet as best man at the wedding. Longstreet himself had married, in Lynchburg, Virginia, Maria Louisa Garland, daughter of the colonel of his and Grant's regiment.

Both Grant and Longstreet had served in the Mexican War. Longstreet, severely wounded, had emerged a major, Grant a captain, who later was defeated by the bottle, resigned from the army in 1854. Longstreet later told how, on a military trip to St. Louis in 1858, he encountered Grant, "poorly dressed in citizen's clothes—really in needy circumstances." Grant, however, insisted that Longstreet accept $5 that he recalled as a debt from a card game in the Army fifteen years before. "Seeing the determination in the man's face," Longstreet said, "and in order to save him mortification, I took the money, and shaking hands we parted. The next time we met was at Appomattox."

In the weeks before Appomattox, Longstreet had sponsored a scheme for bringing the war in Virginia to a close. He proposed a conference between Grant and Lee (which would have involved a truce), then social visits between Mrs. Grant and Mrs. Longstreet. It was hoped that these events would bring about a permanent and painless end to the fighting and avoid the necessity of either side's surrendering. The political questions could then be settled by negotiation. Needless to say, while Confederate President Davis and Lee agreed to the proposal, Grant was forbidden by officials in Washington to take part in any such arrangement. Longstreet had broached a similar scheme to Union General John M. Schofield when both were in Tennessee in 1864. While these efforts came to nothing, they illustrate the familial and informal aspects of the war. They also illustrate Longstreet's characteristic blunt, unsubtle approach to a complex problem.

Longstreet undoubtedly wondered, as he approached the McLean house at Appomattox, how Grant would receive him. He soon found out. "As I was passing through the room, as one of the commissioners, General Grant looked up, recognized me, rose, and with his old-time cheerful greeting gave me his hand, and after passing a few remarks offered a cigar, which was gratefully received." The fighting over, Longstreet was already willing to resume prewar friendships and accept largesse from the victors.

The details of the surrender attended to and his own parole signed, Longstreet remained for the final assembly of the Army of Northern Virginia on April 12, then set off for Lynchburg, only twenty miles away. He had no job, no skills except those of the soldier (skills he could not use now unless he left the country), and little money—just before the surrender he had been offered $300 in United States currency as his share of the remaining funds of the army, but he had accepted only $100 and ordered the rest given to some of his men.

Longstreet, at the beginning of the War, was described by General Moxley Sorrel of his staff as, "a most striking figure, about forty years of age, a soldier every inch, and very handsome, tall and well proportioned, strong and active, a superb horseman and with unsurpassed soldierly bearing, his features and expression fairly matched; eyes, glint steel blue, deep and piercing; a full brown beard, head well shaped and poised." Longstreet, in 1865, had fought four arduous, bitter years. His appearance showed it: "The personal apperance of General Longstreet was not engaging," one account said. "It was decidedly sombre; his bluish grey eyes were intelligent—but cold; a very heavy brown beard was allowed to grow untrimmed; he seldom spoke unnecessarily; his weather-stained clothes, splashed boots and heavy black felt hat gave a certain fierceness of aspect to the man. His temper was high and combative." A near fatal wound through the neck and shoulder received at the Wilderness in 1864 troubled him the rest of his life. He never fully regained the use of his right arm and was forced to learn to write with his left hand.

Like Lee, and seemingly most other officers of the old prewar U.S. Army, Longstreet had once hoped that secession could be avoided. As he wrote later:

I was stationed at Albuquerque, N. M., as paymaster in the United States Army when the war-cloud appeared in the East. Officers of the Northern and Southern States were anxious to see the portending storm pass by or disperse. . . . But affairs continued to grow gloomy, and eventually came information of the attack upon and capture of Fort Sumter by the Confederate forces, which put down speculation and drew the long-dreaded line.

When secession came, Longstreet, like most Southerners, thought it was his duty to follow his state, Georgia. That a state, in an extreme situation, had the constitutional right to secede was a view that Longstreet had been taught at West Point.

In fact, it is doubtless true that many Northern officers fighting for the Union were motivated by state rather than Federal loyalty. They fought with the Union because their state fought with the Union. Longstreet recalled that at Albuquerque he was accosted by "a number of the officers of the post," who called "to persuade me to remain in the Union service." Captain Alfred Gibbs of New York, of the Mounted Rifles, "was the principal talker, and after a long but pleasant discussion," Longstreet bluntly asked him "what course he would pursue if his State should pass ordinance of secession and call him to its defense." The answer was "that he would obey the call."

After Appomattox, Longstreet stayed with his family in Lynchburg, where on June 1, a son, James Longstreet, Jr., was born. An earlier child with that name was one of three Longstreet children who died of scarlet fever in Richmond in 1862. In June, also, Longstreet learned of his indictment, with Lee, Jefferson Davis and others, for treason. Toward the end of the month, accompanied by his son Garland, Captain T. J. Goree (a Texan who had served with Longstreet all through the war), and a Negro servant, Jim, he set off toward the Deep South. Captain Goree urged Longstreet to go with him to Texas and start a new life.

Longstreet and Jim in an ambulance wagon, Goree and Garland on horseback, moved through North and South Carolina to Georgia, where Longstreet had spent most of his boyhood, though he had been born, in 1821, in South Carolina and appointed to West Point from Alabama. Longstreet's grandfather, born in New Jersey, of an old Dutch family, had gone to Georgia, where in 1787 he developed a steamboat that plied up and down the Savannah River. But Southern capital to exploit the invention was lacking, and Robert Fulton, of Pennsylvania, who had the backing, later received the fame.

From Georgia the four men went on toward New Orleans. In Alabama a drunken man on horseback accosted Longstreet, pointed a cocked pistol and threatened to shoot. Longstreet ignored the threat with his usual coolness in danger and, though his right arm was still lame from his wartime wound, wrenched the pistol from the man's hand. "Where-upon," wrote Captain Goree, "the man put spurs to his horse and made away as fast as possible."

The little party passed south of that spot near Chattanooga, where, at the battle of Chickamauga, Longstreet and a portion of his First Corps (temporarily detached from Lee's Army to aid the South's sagging fortunes in Tennessee) had won in 1863 the Confederacy's only large-scale victory in the West, a victory the dilatory Confederate commander, General Braxton Bragg, had characteristically failed to pursue. Chickamauga showed Longstreet at his bold and fearless best and suggests what might have been possible in the West had Confederate forces there had leadership of the quality available to the Army of Northern Virginia.

In New Orleans, Longstreet found many of his old wartime companions, including Generals P. G. T. Beauregard, John Hood, Simon Buckner, Braxton Bragg, Richard Taylor, and A. P.

Stewart. He decided to stay—a decision more fateful than he knew, for New Orleans became one of the most turbulent cities in the South during Reconstruction, and Longstreet was in the middle of it all.

He now returned for his family and saw General Grant in Washington. Grant urged him, as he had Lee, to apply for a pardon. Longstreet, blunt as always, told him he was unaware that he had committed any offense that required pardon. "Amnesty," said Grant, and Longstreet agreed to see the Secretary of War and the new President, Andrew Johnson. Grant offered to write a letter of recommendation to expedite the matter, but Johnson, who was being criticized as too lenient to the South, told Longstreet: "There are three persons of the South who can never receive amnesty: Mr. Davis, General Lee and yourself. You have given the Union cause too much trouble."

The New Orleans firm of Longstreet, Owen & Co., cotton brokers—with Longstreet and the three Owen brothers who had served with him during the war—began business in January 1866, and seems to have done well. In March, Longstreet was also elected president of a new insurance company at a $5,000-a-year salary, thus becoming one of the earliest generals to take a flyer in insurance. A letter to Longstreet, Owen & Co. from Robert E. Lee congratulated the partners and said, "I wrote to your senior [Longstreet] a few days since. . . . I do not consider my partnership with him yet dissolved, and shall not let go him during life."

Louisiana had been peacefully reconstructed under the moderate Lincoln-Johnson plan in 1864, before the War was over. The Radical Republicans, being unable to control the state, had become increasingly noisy and demanding. The result, in July 1866, was a New Orleans riot involving the Radicals and their opponents, the Conservatives, on whom General Philip Sheridan, the Federal Commander of the area, put the blame. The Congressional Reconstruction policy was completed in 1867. Sheridan was placed in command of the Fifth Military District, with wide powers he did not fail to use. He dismissed many officials, including the Mayor of New Orleans and the Governor. He dissolved the Legislature. His methods did nothing to make his actions more palatable. The state was soon in an uproar.

In June, before the rioting in New Orleans, Longstreet had said, "I must be content to remain on the fence." But as the situation grew more tense this proved to be impossible. A New Orleans editorial called on Longstreet, Beauregard, Hood, and other leaders for advice and help.

Longstreet was the first to respond, writing several letters for the local papers advising acceptance of Reconstruction as a necessary evil and support of the dominant Radical Republican party as the best means of gaining a moderate policy toward the South. In his usual blunt fashion he went to the heart of the matter: "The striking feature, the one that people should keep in view is that we are a conquered people. . . . Recognizing this fact, fairly and squarely, there is but one course left for wise men to pursue and that is to accept the terms that are now offered by the conquerors."

"Our duty resolves itself into two very simple propositions," argued Longstreet, "to relieve ourselves from our present embarrassments by returning to our allegiance, in good faith, to the General Government," accepting the procedure laid down by Congress, or "seek protection under some foreign government." Longstreet felt that those who chose to remain "should speed the work of reconstruction, and put our people in condition to make their own laws and choose their own officers for their execution."

In conclusion, Longstreet professed that he would be happy to work in "any harness that promises relief to our discomfited people and harmony to the nation, whether bearing the mantle of Mr. Davis or Mr. Sumner [the Massachusetts Senator and Radical leader]." The "military bill" and "amendments" he conceived of as peace offerings. "We should accept them as such, and place ourselves upon them as the starting point from which to meet future political issues as they arise." All of Longstreet's words and actions were related to what he called "a desire for practical reconstruction and reconciliation."

Longstreet was not only the first but the highest-ranking former Confederate publicly to counsel submission to the Reconstruction Acts and to urge support of the Republican party. Confederate General James R. Chalmers of Mississippi followed a similar course and soon became a Congressman; General William Mahone in Virginia became a United States Senator. The famous partisan ranger, Colonel John Mosby, also became a Republican. But New Orleans greatly resented Longstreet's advice. "Old comrades passed me on the streets without speaking," he wrote. "Business began to grow dull. General Hood (the only one of my old comrades who occasionally visited me) thought he could save the insurance business, and in a few weeks I found myself at leisure."

Then word came of Longstreet's pardon by the Federal government. It was the first amnesty granted to a former United States Army officer who had fought with the Confederacy, and it looked like a reward for his support of Reconstruction and the Republican party. Longstreet's stand put an end to his private business career in New Orleans. The cotton brokerage firm of Longstreet & Owen was dissolved.

Longstreet may have been surprised at the degree of animosity he aroused, but he had not taken his stand hastily. He had gone up to Oxford, Mississippi, to consult with his uncle, Judge Augustus B. Longstreet who, years before, had helped educate him. Reading one of Longstreet's proposed letters to the papers, the judge told him, "It will ruin you, son, if you publish it. We are not yet ready to hear such hard counseling."

To his sister in Mississippi Longstreet wrote: "For months I have prayed to God to guide me, and help me, to devise honorable means by which our people might be saved from the extremity of distress. The letters that are published are the result of my meditations, and His divine aid. They are written because I thought it a duty that I owed to our people."

Longstreet wrote Lee asking for an endorsement of his stand, but Lee declined, saying: "I have avoided all discussion of political questions since the cessation of hostilities. And have in my own conduct and in my recommendations to others endeavored to conform to existing circumstances. I consider this the part of wisdom as well as of duty. But while I think we should act under the law and according to the law imposed upon us, I cannot think the course pursued by the dominant political party the best for the interests of the country, and therefore cannot say so, or give them any approval." This was the last letter to pass between Lee and Longstreet. It brought to an end a lively correspondence.

In January 1866, Lee had written Longstreet asking his help in gathering material for "a history of the campaigns in Virginia." He added, referring to Longstreet's venture into the cotton and insurance business, "if you become as good a merchant as you were a soldier, I shall be content. No one will then excel you." In March, Lee wrote Longstreet thanking him for material sent via young Garland Longstreet, in school at Virginia Military Institute, in Lexington. Lee suggested that Longstreet also write *his* memoirs. Later in the month, Longstreet again sent Lee some material on the War and concluded with the words: "If you can come across my son when you have an idle moment, I hope that you will give him a few words of kindly advice and encouragement. He is taught to look up to you as superior to others."

However, after the estrangement, Longstreet did not attend the exercises at Garland's graduation from V.M.I. at Lexington on July 2, 1869, though he was then at Lynchburg, only fifty miles away. It is possible that the birth of his son, Fitz Randolph, on July 1, was the reason. It is more probable that Longstreet wanted to avoid a meeting with Lee, who lived hard by V.M.I., as president of Washington College, and doubtless would be present with other former Confederate officers. This cooling of relations with his former commander and other old comrades was but one of the penalties Longstreet paid for his support of the Republican party and that party's Reconstruction policy. There is no evidence that Longstreet ever saw Lee after Appomattox. Yet the next generation resumed the friendship: Robert Lee Longstreet served in the Spanish-American War on the staff of General Fitzhugh Lee, nephew of "Marse Robert."

But having made his choice, Longstreet stuck to it. He removed his family to Lynchburg in the summer of 1867, no doubt because of the tension in New Orleans. He supported Grant for President in 1868, partly because of their long and friendly relationship and because he felt that the general would be fair to the South. A special act of Congress, required under the Reconstruction Acts for the restoration of full political rights to Confederate leaders, was passed in June 1868, on Longstreet's behalf. There were rumors that he might run for the Senate.

The New York *Tribune* reported Longstreet had gone with General William S. Rosecrans to the August meeting in White Sulphur Springs, West Virginia, where Rosecrans got a conciliatory statement on Reconstruction from Lee and other Southern leaders. Rosecrans, who had been Longstreet's West Point roommate, was the Federal commander Longstreet had soundly defeated at Chickamauga. But Rosecrans was a Democrat, and the White Sulphur statement was designed to further Democratic Presidential hopes. It is not likely, therefore, that Longstreet attended the meeting. Certainly he did not sign the statement. He had already published words much stronger than those that came out of White Sulphur.

"On March 4, 1869," wrote Longstreet, "General Grant was inaugurated President of the United States, and in the bigness of his generous heart called me to Washington. Before I found opportunity to see him he sent my name to the Senate for confirmation as surveyor of customs at New Orleans. I was duly confirmed and held the office until 1873, when I resigned." In this brief, laconic statement he summarized his active part in one of the stormiest, most vicious chapters of Reconstruction. It should be added that there was almost as much outcry in the North over Grant's giving him the $6,000-a-year job as there was in the South over Longstreet's accepting it. The loudest Northern protestations came from the Senators from Pennsylvania, who had not forgotten the Army of Northern Virginia's invasion of that state in 1863, on the way to Gettysburg. Longstreet even considered refusing the appointment, not wishing to "compromise or reflect upon a too affectionate kindness of his illustrious kinsman and late antagonist, The President of the United States."

But in the end, Longstreet went to New Orleans, determined to restrain the excesses of Radicals on the one hand and recalcitrant Democrats on the other, hoping that the moderates in the two chief parties would draw together to restore order and prosperity to the city and state. For this stubborn hope Longstreet sacrificed much.

For eight years the blunt, honest soldier was caught in the swarm of unscrupulous swindlers, opportunists, political adventurers of both races, all party stripes and all degrees of honesty and dishonesty. Like Grant in Washington, he was largely helpless to control the bitter political in-fighting and financial corruption. Like Grant, his reputation, for the time, was diminished.

In Louisiana, there was, even from the first, a fierce contest for power not only between Democrats and Republicans, but between rival factions in each of the major parties. In some elections as many as five different sets of candidates of various splinter groups were on the ballot. At times there were also several sets of election commissioners, each determined to count the ballots and certify the results—all differently. Several candidates would then be declared elected for the same office. Rival legislatures frequently met at the same time, each declaring itself the legal one.

The first governor of Louisiana under the Reconstruction Constitution of 1868 was Henry Clay Warmoth, a former Federal officer. Warmoth's chief opponents, including J. F. Casey, collector of customs for the port of New Orleans and a brother-in-law of President Grant, were known as "the Custom House faction." Warmoth and his followers were not above reproach, but they were less tainted with scandal and corruption than the Custom House clique. The feeling between the two was bitter. In May

1870, Warmoth appointed Longstreet Adjutant General of the State with control of the militia. Longstreet and his militia (2,500 whites, mostly Confederate veterans, and 2,500 Negroes) were called out several times to put down rioting or enforce obedience to court orders and the law.

By the 1872 election, both Warmoth and Longstreet were so disturbed over the excesses of the Grant administration that they were at first willing to further the coalition between the moderates of the Democratic and Republican parties in support of the New York editor Horace Greeley's national Liberal Republican program. Greeley, in New Orleans in May 1871, conferred with Longstreet. The Liberal Republican movement in Louisiana was swallowed up by the Democrats by election time, however, and Longstreet supported Grant again. "There is more liberality in the Republican party," he wrote, "than has been developed by the move that has been called the Liberal movement." He did resign his position as Surveyor of Customs, stating he found it "inconsistent with my views of sound Republican philosophy to approve the efforts of prominent Federal officers in this city," meaning the corrupt Custom House faction. He resigned, also, as Adjutant General of Louisiana, but retained his commission as a Major General in the Louisiana militia.

Caught in the squabbling and election frauds, Governor Warmoth found himself impeached and out of office. The Negro lieutenant governor P. B. S. Pinchback sat briefly in the governor's chair, backed by Federal troops, until 1873, when the carpetbag senator, W. P. Kellogg, candidate of the Custom House faction and most other Republicans, was decreed by Washington to have been elected. Both Pinchback and Kellogg kept Longstreet in control of the militia. Kellogg also gave him charge of the New Orleans police, most of whom were Negroes, and appointed him president of the Levee Commission.

In the midst of the charges and countercharges, Longstreet struggled stubbornly to promote the rule of law and maintain Republican party integrity. At a Congressional committee investigation of disorder in New Orleans, someone asked the Federal

army commander, "Which side did General Longstreet repre-
sent?" The reply was: "I cannot say that he represented either."

Yet the outcry against Longstreet in the South grew in intensity.
Longstreet accepted without complaint his own social ostracism.
"I could see no other way," he wrote, "by which the Southern
people could re-instate themselves in proper sympathy and relations with the general Government and thus save themselves
greater losses and humiliation." Mrs. Longstreet spent much of
the year in Michigan, away from the South's hostility. There in
July, a daughter, Maria Louisa, was born, the Longstreets' tenth
and last child.

On September 14, 1874, Longstreet took part in one of the
bloodiest single pitched battles of the South's Reconstruction
period. Anger over the excesses of carpetbag and Negro rule—
the continued violence, crime and corruption (the state debt rose
from $10,000,000 to $50,000,000 in eight years), high taxes
(they were increased 450 per cent) and the looting of public
funds—had reached explosive proportions. The native whites
had begun to form armed White Leagues, determined to wrest
political control from the Radicals, by force if necessary, and to
oust Kellogg from the governorship, charging he had been il-
legally elected. An attempt by the New Orleans police to seize
the local League's guns and ammunition precipitated a battle.

Three thousand to five thousand citizens clashed on and near
Canal Street with a smaller, more heavily armed force of police
and militia led by Longstreet. The general courageously rode out
ahead of his men and called on the armed civilians to disperse and
return to their homes. Instead, he was greeted with the rebel yell
—and the sound of that fierce cry, echoing from Manassas,
Chancellorsville, Chickamauga, the Wilderness, caused him, it is
said, to betray signs of emotion. But he stood his ground. A
moment later, firing broke out. Each side claimed the other began
it. Over 100 were wounded, including Longstreet himself, and
more than 30 were killed. Federal troops restored order.

Moderation had been Longstreet's aim all along, and it is
ironical that his part, under the governor's orders, in a major

effort to maintain Radical Republican rule by force hastened the end of that rule in Louisiana and the nation. Longstreet's support of Reconstruction also cut the ground from under Radical Republican argument that there was no hope of reconciliation with former Confederates—an argument often used to justify the stern rule over the South.

In the New Orleans *Republican* of September 27, a reporter wrote:

I myself have heard men say that they "would shoot Longstreet on sight." The papers have demanded his life, and they call him "a recreant traitor," "the betrayer of the dearest interests of the South," and all that sort of thing. . . . So the old General has to keep pretty close. Did you ever see him? A tall, portly dignified gentleman of the old school, who wears ruffled shirts, and a fob chain dangling on his nankeen trousers. Grayish sandy side whiskers, and a head that is just bald enough to add to his dignity. A deep set, small blue eye, with bush eyebrows, and deep wrinkles running across from temple to temple, that look as if they had been cut there by a sculptor's hand. This is Longstreet. . . .

I was talking with him last night. . . . He sat in one chair, with his feet in another, his wrist bands and collar unbuttoned, waving a great fan . . . and I asked him—

"General, these people seem to be pretty savage on you, down there, don't they?"

"I don't know," he replied indifferently. "Maybe they do."

"Why, yes, they call you a recreant and a traitor, and they say you've betrayed the interests of the South."

"There exists a difference of opinion," he replied, "as to what the interests of the South are. I think they are one thing, they think they are another. That's the way we happened to get separated."

His old wound from the Wilderness often caused pain and discomfort, aggravated by his work in the swamps and marshes for the Louisiana Levee Commission, "the hardest work man ever did." "My comrades all died of it," he wrote, "and I was seriously injured." It was even rumored in New Orleans that he might be fatally ill.

His brother, William, urged him to return to Georgia, and he did. "I have worked myself completely down since I went to

New Orleans," Longstreet told Captain Goree, "and now have been laid up for the last six or eight months. . . . In Louisiana, particularly in New Orleans, the most violent Democrats admit that mine would have been the best policy. It is too late though now, and affairs will have to drag along in that state."

In the elections of 1876, the native whites were restored to power in the South and Rutherford B. Hayes was to win the contested Presidency over Samuel J. Tilden. Longstreet wrote to Grant about the election returns in Louisiana, advising that Democratic state candidates be accepted as elected. He urged that the Federal government refrain from installing by force the Republican slate headed by the Negro S. B. Packard. This was the will of the majority, said Longstreet:

I beg leave further to state that it will be better for the Republican party south if this idea can be adopted. For if the Packard government is forced upon this State, the greater part, if not all, of the Southern men who have been identified with the Republican party, in the hope that some day the party might be put upon a basis that might justify their efforts, in giving it permanent organizations, will be obliged to abandon their hopes.

In March 1877, Longstreet wrote General Benjamin Alvord, an old Army friend influential in the Hayes administration, asking for appointment to the post of Collector of Customs at New Orleans. Although Longstreet did not receive the appointment, General Alvord wrote a strong endorsement of him. "Since the war he has been consistently and perseveringly for the Union and the true interests of the South," Alvord said. "As fast as possible it is doubtless wise to utilize the brains, the pluck and the honor of the old rebels, who can do so much for permanent recuperation of their section. . . . I have great faith in the character and reliable qualities of General Longstreet."

At this time, Longstreet entered the Roman Catholic Church, under the tutelage of Father A. J. Ryan, the "Poet of the Confederacy" and author of such famous poems as "The Sword of Robert E. Lee" and "The Conquered Banner." An old friend and roommate at West Point, W. S. Rosecrans, was a Roman

Catholic, but Longstreet had been an Episcopalian. His wartime aide Sorrel wrote that the general's religion had deepened after the tragic deaths of three of his children in 1862, but he had never been as conspicuously religious as, say, Lee or Jackson. Some writers have said that Longstreet's fellow Episcopalians ostracized him for his support of Republican Reconstruction. Yet social pressure alone would not have moved a man as stubborn as Longstreet. Whatever the reason, Longstreet remained a faithful member of the Roman Catholic Church the rest of his life.

In his *From Manassas to Appomattox,* Longstreet records a conversation he had after the war with an old Negro who had looked after him as a boy.

"Marse Jim, do you belong to any church?"

"Oh, yes," Longstreet replied. "I try to be a good Christian."

The old Negro "laughed long and loud and said: 'Something must have scared you mighty bad, to change you so from what you was when I had to care for you.' "

Although Longstreet did not obtain an appointment in New Orleans from President Hayes, he was appointed Deputy Collector of Internal Revenue for Georgia in September 1878, and in January 1879, was made Postmaster at Gainesville. Longstreet was perhaps as surprised as anyone else to find himself appointed Minister to Turkey in May 1880. He spent only a few months in that country and resigned to accept the position of United States Marshal in Georgia, a post he held until 1884. Longstreet soon became a power to be reckoned with in Georgia politics, though never a dominant force. He fought there, as he had in Louisiana, to achieve integrity and respectability for the Republican party.

"There is an element of the Republican party . . . that may turn up as an important factor," the New York *Times* commented in 1882. "This element centers in Gen. James Longstreet, who is now U. S. Marshal in Georgia, and was at one time prominently mentioned for a Cabinet place under President Arthur, who took office in 1881. General Longstreet has been a consistent Republican since the war, was a Grant man in 1880 and since then has been working effectively in Washington through General [William] Mahone [Senator from Virginia], whose division was in Longstreet's corps in the late war. Longstreet is trustworthy, popular and strong and seems to have arranged very satisfactorily with the President for the encouragement of the Independent movement in Georgia."

Longstreet strove for twenty years to rescue the Republican party in Georgia from the unenlightened rule of two former Union officers who had settled in the state, A. E. Buck and John E. Bryant. These carpetbaggers sought only the short-term goals of immediate power and patronage. Longstreet's sights were fixed on a larger goal, a coalition of the best white and Negro voters into a responsible conservative party. "It has always been my theory that the Republican party to become practical and successful in this section must adopt some plan by which we may secure co-operation from a large part of the best citizens." He believed, as he said, "that it was the true policy of the South to accept Reconstruction and go in and control their own State Governments by acting in harmony with the Republican party, instead of being controlled by carpetbaggers and negroes, which resulted from their alliance with Democracy."

Longstreet worked with the respectable part of the Republican party (one faction ran him unsuccessfully for Congress in 1882, and even gave him a few votes in the Georgia Legislature for United States Senator). He also co-operated with the Independents, a group of dissatisfied Democrats and Republicans. The regular Democrats, headed by former Confederate General John B. Gordon and ex-Governor Joseph E. Brown (who had co-operated with the Republicans earlier), were in control of the state. Although Longstreet never built a coalition to defeat the regular Democrats, he achieved at least the threat of a two-party system.

Longstreet's carpetbagger opponents in Georgia eventually ousted him from his post as United States marshal on the ground that his accounts were in bad order—which they were, and had been, even before they were turned over to him by his predecessor.

Longstreet, no accountant, never got them straight. One of his supporters wrote President Chester Arthur: "General Longstreet has a stronger personal influence—not only in Georgia, but in the whole South—than any Republican in it, and has sacrificed more to his patriotism than any man in the South." As his one-time foe General William T. Sherman said, "Longstreet went into the Confederate army from an impulse—honest, enthusiastic and positive—and when the war was over . . . he stood up like a man to regain for his whole country the condition of law and prosperity which had been so foolishly jeopardized by the Civil War."

After 1884, Longstreet lived an extremely active life of writing and lecturing; he remained very much a public figure, active in politics. He earned money from his writing, received two small pensions—one for his Mexican War service and one from the state of Georgia for his Confederate service—and owned and ran at Gainesville a village hotel, the Piedmont House, where he and his family spent the winter months. Among those who stopped there were his old Confederate comrade General Joseph E. Johnston, the writers Henry W. Grady and Joel Chandler Harris, and a young student by the name of Woodrow Wilson.

A New York *Times* reporter who visited Longstreet wrote:

Does the old man regret the choice he made in 1861? No one ever heard him say so. In spite of his troubles brought on by his prompt acceptance of Reconstruction and his espousal of the Republican cause, General Longstreet has preferred to remain in the South, confronting opprobrium in many cases, but enjoying the personal respect of his neighbors, and always sure of the undying love of his army comrades.

It is during . . . summer . . . that one sees the grim old veteran at his best. He is the very embodiment of good humor. He tries to make every one comfortable, and as his hotel commands the best breezes from the Blue Ridge, he usually succeeds. He will mount three flights of steps to carry an apple to some little fellow who learns to know and love the bronzed face and white head of this Southern veteran.

If you go to Gainesville in the early spring, you will be told to secure a buggy and ride out two miles on the mountain road. General Longstreet seldom comes to town at that time. Somewhere in his country place, clad in a long duster and a broad-brimmed hat, you will find him clipping his fruit trees or trailing up the vines in his grape orchard. He will show you his turkeys with pride, and, like Cincinnatus, revels in his rustic surroundings and farm duties.

Then there are winter days, when he must not be disturbed. He is 75 years old, you know, and realizes that his book about the Civil War must be finished pretty soon. In it he hopes to vindicate his position at Gettysburg and account to unprejudiced posterity for his conduct in New Orleans. . . .

Since Longstreet's removal to Georgia his life has been smooth. He has regained much of his old popularity. Next to Stonewall Jackson, his people say, he was the most daring and persistent warrior on the Confederate side.

In 1886, he made a courageous and largely successful gesture to heal the rift with his friends and former comrades. There was a great gathering at Atlanta on May 1, for the dedication of a monument to the late Senator Ben H. Hill. Jefferson Davis was to unveil the memorial and speak. The Governor and many high-ranking former Confederates were to be present.

During the proceedings, the huge crowd (including 50,000 Confederate veterans) already in an uproar of enthusiasm at the sight of the President of the South's Confederacy, became still more excited when it saw a figure on horseback approaching the speaker's platform, dressed in the full grey uniform of a lieutenant general in the Confederate army. It was Longstreet. He had come, uninvited, determined to make it clear that his heart lay still with the Lost Cause.

The audience went wild, then grew quiet as Longstreet mounted the platform and moved toward the Confederate President. What would Davis do? Would he receive him as a friend or as an apostate from a sacred cause? "When General Longstreet was within about ten feet of the canopy where Mr. Davis sat," wrote an observer, "the old gentleman arose and hastened to meet the general. When the two came together Mr. Davis threw his arms around General Longstreet's neck and the two leaders embraced with great emotion. The meaning of the reconciliation was clear and instantly had a profound effect upon the thousands of Confederate veterans who saw it. With a great shout they showed their joy." It was said that no one had ever seen Mr. Davis so moved; the eyes of both men were wet.

It was Mrs. Longstreet who had urged her husband to make this dramatic appearance. She had faithfully stood by him in all the strenuous and difficult years of war and the almost equally distressing experiences since Appomattox. There is no record of any complaint—only love, sympathy, and loyal support. She died, December 29, 1889, three years later, the year in which Longstreet's country home near Gainesville burned, with the loss of "every relic that he had of the last war," including the Confederate uniform he had worn to Atlanta a few years before.

Henceforth, Longstreet was the old hero again. At a meeting of the Society of the Army of Northern Virginia at Richmond, the marching veterans left their ranks and almost broke up the parade when they saw Longstreet sitting in a carriage on the sidelines. "They shook my hand until they made my arm ache," he wrote. "At another time I was seized by a crowd of old soldiers and wrapped up completely in Confederate flags." From time to time, he attended Union veterans' meetings in the North as well and frequently was called on to speak. He would then reminisce about his friend General Grant, "my lifetime personal friend, kindest when I was most fiercely assaulted."

On St. Patrick's day, 1892, the Irish societies in Atlanta gave a banquet. Longstreet and General Daniel E. Sickles, a longtime friend and one of Longstreet's chief opponents at Gettysburg, came into the banquet hall arm in arm to the roar of the Rebel yell. It was an evening of great festivity, with numerous "potations of hot Irish whiskey." Longstreet led the singing of "The Star-Spangled Banner."

General Sickles describes the end of the evening:

We decided to go to our lodgings long before the end of the revel, which appeared likely to last until daybreak. When we descended to the street we were unable to find a carriage, but Longstreet proposed to be my guide; and, though the streets were dark and the walk a long one, we reached my hotel in fairly good form. Not wishing to be outdone in courtesy, I said,—

"Longstreet, the streets of Atlanta are very dark and it is very late, and you are somewhat deaf and rather infirm; now I must escort you to your headquarters."

"All right," said Longstreet. "Come on. . . ."

When we arrived at his stopping place and were about to separate, as I supposed, he turned to me and said,—

"Sickles, the streets of Atlanta are very dark and you are lame, and a stranger here, and do not know the way back to your hotel; I must escort you home."

"'Come along, Longstreet," was my answer.

On our way to the hotel, I said to him,—

"Old fellow, I hope you are sorry for shooting off my leg at Gettysburg. I suppose I will have to forgive you for it some day."

"Forgive me?" Longstreet exclaimed. "You ought to thank me for leaving you one leg to stand on, after the mean way you behaved to me at Gettysburg."

How often we performed escort duty for each other on that eventful night I have never been able to recall with precision; but I am quite sure that I shall never forget St. Patrick's Day in 1892, at Atlanta, Ga., when Longstreet and I enjoyed the good Irish whiskey punch at the banquet of the Knights of St. Patrick.

In 1896, Longstreet published *From Manassas to Appomattox,* eager to state once again his side of the controversy about his conduct at the battle of Gettysburg. It had been charged that Longstreet doubted the chances for victory and therefore delayed his actions on July 2 and 3, the two main days of the great battle, contributing to, or even causing, the Confederate defeat—and the loss of the war. Longstreet hotly denied the charge and sought by writing, correspondence, and speaking to disprove it.

Whether the hue and cry about Gettysburg were entirely based on the battle itself or were rather stimulated by Longstreet's support of the Republican party in Reconstruction is debatable. Whether the general fought with vigor at Gettysburg or not, no one can question the vigor with which for more than twenty postwar years he waged a battle of words to defend his military record.

It is certain that Longstreet was opposed to Lee's plan to attack Meade at Gettysburg in July 1863. Longstreet also disapproved of the strategy of that attack. Although there was a delay in the Confederate advance on July 2, the delay, it now appears, was not Longstreet's fault. Once begun, the attack was pressed, according to Longstreet's aide Sorrel, "in smashing style . . . Longstreet personally leading the attack with splendid effect. His fine horsemanship and martial figure, as he rode, hat in hand, were most inspiring."

Never one to conceal his opinion from his chief, Longstreet told Lee the next day, July 3, after Lee had ordered 15,000 men to make a new assault across the half-mile expanse of open fields separating the armies and up Cemetery Ridge: "I have been in pretty much all kinds of skirmishes, from those of two or three soldiers up to those of an army corps, and I think I can safely say there never was a body of 15,000 men who could make that attack successfully." The assault failed, but it failed so heroically that the charge of one of his generals, George E. Pickett, became perhaps the most famous in American military annals. As for Longstreet's part, Sorrel wrote, "While Longstreet by no means approved the movement, his soldierly eye watched every feature of it. He neglected nothing that could help it."

The battle was scarcely over before Longstreet had written his uncle, Judge Longstreet, a confidential letter alluding to "a sly undercurrent of misrepresentation" circulating about the events of Gettysburg. "The battle was not made as I would have made it. My idea was to throw ourselves between the enemy and Washington, select a strong position, and force the enemy to attack us. . . . I consider it a part of my duty to express my views to the commanding general. If he approves and adopts them, it is well; if he does not, it is my duty to adopt his views and to execute his orders faithfully." Certainly no sentiment of delay or disobedience is suggested by these lines.

"As we failed," Longstreet added, "I must take my share of

the responsibility. In fact, I would prefer that all the blame should rest upon me. As General Lee is our commander, he should have the support and influence we can give him. . . . I desire, therefore, that all the responsibility that can be put upon me shall go there. The truth will be known in time." But it was one thing to close ranks, support Lee, and maintain morale in wartime. It was another to accept criticism from former subordinates in peacetime, after the cause was lost and the great Lee was dead. That Longstreet was not prepared to do.

Soon after the war, Longstreet was interviewed by William Swinton of the New York *Times*. In a note in his book, *Campaigns of the Army of the Potomac*, Swinton said that a number "of the purposes and sentiments of Lee, I derived from General Longstreet." Lee, said Swinton, had "expressly promised his corps-commanders that he would not assume a tactical offensive, but force his antagonist to attack him." Also, "Longstreet, holding the right of the Confederate line . . . was really between the Army of the Potomac and Washington; and . . . could undoubtedly have manoeuvred Meade out of the Gettysburg position. This operation General Longstreet . . . begged in vain to be allowed to execute." Longstreet said very much the same things in his own later writings.

Confederate General Jubal A. Early, in an address at Washington and Lee University in 1872, widely distributed as a pamphlet, refuted Longstreet's remarks to Swinton and charged him with delay and disobedience at Gettysburg. The attack was renewed at Washington and Lee the following year by Lee's chief of artillery, General Pendleton.

The charges, made only after the death of Lee, have no support in any of Lee's own remarks or correspondence. Lee himself said, "It took a dozen blunders to lose Gettysburg, and I committed a good many of them." More importantly, the attacks arose only after Longstreet had embarked on his postwar political career. In 1875, Colonel Walter H. Taylor, of Lee's staff, wrote Longstreet, "I regard it as a great mistake on the part of those who, perhaps because of political differences, now undertake to criticize and attack your war record."

The war of words flared brightly for years. The controversy reveals once again Longstreet's pugnacity and fierce confidence in his own judgment. In *Annals of the War,* published in 1879, and *Battles and Leaders of the Civil War,* published in 1877-78, articles by Longstreet reassert his view.

In 1897, the year after the publication of his memoirs, Longstreet was a guest at the dedication of Grant's Tomb in New York City, a member of the party of Vice President Adlai E. Stevenson. That same year, a correspondent from the New York *Tribune* visited him near Gainesville, where he had built a small farmhouse to replace the house that burned:

I looked for a large, old-fashioned Southern place, with pillars and a wide hall. Instead, the house was an ordinary story-and-half farmhouse, such as a Northern carpenter might build. A board nailed to a tree offered wine for sale at a very low price, and I saw an extensive vineyard across the road. A lean, farmerlike person told me that General Longstreet was in his vineyard, and there I came upon him, scissors in hand, busily pruning his vines. He is a big old man, stooping a little now, and slow of gait. He wears long white whiskers cut away from his chin. His hair is white as wool, but his skin is ruddy as though sleep and good digestion were still his to command. We talked for a time about his garden and vineyard.

"I get out every afternoon," he said, "and work about. I find the sun and air do me good."

One of his arms is a little disabled, and he is quite deaf in one ear. He could not hear very well in the open air, and at his suggestion we returned to the house. "I live with my tenant. He is a veteran of the Northern Army," he said at the door, and there was a slight smile about his eyes.

One might have expected the seventy-six-year-old soldier to spend his remaining years peacefully tending his vineyard. But not Longstreet. He took a new wife that year, Helen Dortch of North Carolina, who had known him since her childhood, and also launched himself on a new career as a holder of public office, actively seeking the position of U. S. Commissioner of Railways, held by another former Confederate general, Wade Hampton. The Republican President William McKinley fired Hampton, a Democrat, and Longstreet got the appointment, confirmed in January 1898. When the Spanish-American War broke out later in that year, Longstreet offered to serve once again under the flag he had first followed. His age, of course, prevented him.

With his new wife and a new Confederate uniform his fellow veterans had insisted on having made for him (to replace the one burned in 1889), Longstreet took part in an enthusiastic United Confederate Veterans meeting at Atlanta in July. As Mrs. Longstreet recalls the occasion in her spirited biography and defense of her husband, *Lee and Longstreet at High Tide:* "During all his stay at that reunion the old soldiers flocked about him. . . . They went wild over him. When he went to the dining-room at the hotel, the doors had to be closed so that he could take his meals without interruption. . . . His old boys surged about him by the thousands for hours."

One afternoon while Longstreet was sleeping, "a one-legged, one-armed veteran, poorly clad, looking poorly fed," begged to see Longstreet, even asleep. "I haven't seen him since Appomattox. I came all the way from Texas," he said. "Without a word," wrote Mrs. Longstreet, "I opened the door, and as the worn veteran looked on his old chieftain we both cried. In the midst of it General Longstreet wakened and called the veteran to him. They embraced like brothers and wept together."

He attended the centennial celebrations at West Point in 1902, and, as a member of the class of 1842, was one of the two oldest graduates present. During the ceremonies, a great ovation broke out. "What are they all cheering about?" the white-haired old veteran asked. "They are cheering you, General," he was told. His face lit up with pleasure at this sign of affection and respect from his fellow graduates, most of them his opponents on Civil War battlefields.

He had hoped also to attend ceremonies at Gettysburg the

same year, but he was then suffering, as had his friend and kinsman, President Grant, from cancer.

When Longstreet died at Gainesville, on January 2, 1904, his remarkable and stubbornly pursued postwar political career had been forgotten and forgiven by most Southerners. He received a huge and impressive funeral, complete with a military escort. His casket was appropriately covered with a Confederate and a United States flag. Many high officials were there, and there was a vast assemblage of Confederate veterans. A Roman Catholic Bishop, who had himself served in Longstreet's First Corps, told the great crowd: "When the Southern States withdrew from the Union by reason of attacks on the reserved rights which were guaranteed by the Constitution, and were forced into the war between the States, James Longstreet offered his services and sword to the cause of self-government."

During the burial service an old soldier pushed his way to the graveside and asked that his Confederate enlistment papers and "old gray jacket" be buried with Longstreet. "I've served my time," he said. "And the General, he's served his time too. And I reckon I won't need my uniform and papers again. But I'd like to leave them with him for always." The request was granted. The jacket and the papers rest there in Longstreet's grave.

Editorials in the North and South praised Longstreet and defended him; veterans' groups and patriotic organizations passed resolutions commending him. Letters by the hundreds from old friends and total strangers poured in to Mrs. Longstreet. There was no doubt that the old soldier's lonely course had finally been understood. But a few could not forgive him, even in death: the United Confederate Veterans at Wilmington, North Carolina, declined to express regret at his passing, and the Daughters of the Confederacy at Savannah refused to send flowers to his funeral.

Shortly before Longstreet died, he had said, "I hope to live long enough to see my surviving comrades march side by side with the Union veterans along Pennsylvania Avenue, and then I will die happy." And of the Confederate defeat at Gettysburg, he wrote:

"It was the sorest and saddest reflection of my life for many years; but, today, I can say with sincerest emotion, that it was and is the best that could have come to us all, North and South."

There is something more than Southern rhetoric in the words of Mrs. Longstreet: "To me he has always been a figure of more sublime courage in the gathering storms of '67 and the years that followed than on any of the brilliant fields of the Civil War. And I love best to think of him, not as the warrior leading his legions to victory, but as the grand citizen after the war was ended, nobly dedicating himself to the rehabilitation of his broken people, offering a brave man's homage to the flag of the established government, and standing steadfast in all the passions, prejudices, and persecutions of that unhappy period."

History will probably think more kindly of Longstreet than did some of his contemporaries. There is no reason to believe that in his personal convictions he was any less dedicated to the cause that was lost than any other of the generals were. The War over, Longstreet seemingly had no different views with respect to the South's problems than obtained with Lee and Hampton and the others. He had surrendered, and like the military man that he was, he accepted the regime that inherited the postwar South— carpetbag, scalawag, Negro, and all. One thing is certain: it required somewhat more of courage for him to fire upon the White Leaguers at New Orleans than it took to belong to the White League—for his was the unpopular role.

Whether Longstreet ever fully realized it or not, he taught the Reconstructing South a lesson it needed to learn. The beleaguered Southerners were united almost too well by the woes of defeat and postwar persecution. They almost came to feel that there was only one side to the issues of the day, that there never had been, never was, and never would be any other *cause* than the one that had been *lost*. In its misery the South almost ceased to realize that all Southerners were not so noble as Robert E. Lee and all Yankees not so vindictive as Thaddeus Stevens.

The postwar South, in its tendency toward blind unity of opinion, almost forgot that the American political system was built on a diversity of ideologies, that Americans never really agreed on anything except their right to disagree—then, having disagreed, to work out a compromise whereby sensible men could live and let live. This made it inevitable that in America there must be a two-party system—that while some would be in favor, others would be out of favor; that while some would be "right," others would have the right to be "wrong."

In its postwar desperation the South came to be the "Solid South," and this South delivered itself to the party that was out of power during Reconstruction—the Democratic party. Only a handful of Southerners, and Longstreet was the chief, resisted this surrender to one-partyism, even though its effect was to be more fateful than that of the capitulation at Appomattox.

Perhaps it was best after all that James Longstreet took the course he did. Someone had to prove that the South's one-party system could be breached. Indeed, he proved more—that one could be a Republican in the South and survive the infamy, that the prodigal could return and fall upon the neck of Jefferson Davis.

Longstreet, the "Old War Horse," expressed it more simply, "I am not prompted by any desire to do, or to attempt to do, great things. I only wish to do what I regard as my duty."

10

The Unreconstructible
JEFFERSON DAVIS

On that Sunday morning in April 1865, when the guns turned quiet at Appomattox, President Jefferson Davis was attending church in Danville. The night before, Lieutenant John S. Wise had informed the President that Lee's surrender was "only a question of a few days." Just one Sunday earlier, the message announcing General Lee's abandonment of Petersburg had been brought to Davis as he sat in St. Paul's Church in Richmond. Hours later, under cover of night, the President of the Confederacy fled Richmond with a handful of Cabinet members and the gold from the Richmond banks and the Confederate Treasury.

Appropriately enough, Davis had to leave Richmond without his sword. It was at the armory for repairs; in his haste he forgot the weapon, and left it to suffer the ordeal by fire that consumed the building after its abandonment.

With only his Cabinet and the treasure to give him aid and comfort, he attempted to keep up appearances at Danville, where he had established a temporary capital. On April 5, he came forth with a fantastically unrealistic proclamation: "Relieved from the necessity of guarding particular points, our army will be free to move from point to point. . . . Let us but will it, and we are free." The man who all his life had been attempting to work miracles with his will, was almost the only person in Virginia who did not know that he and Lee and the Confederacy were beaten. Defeat was not Davis' will; therefore to him, it could not happen.

General Robert E. Lee, commander of the Confederate armies, was preparing to sheathe his sword at Appomattox, but under the terms of surrender, it would remain his forever. The sword of Jefferson Davis was still in Richmond, twisted and blackened by the armory fire; it ended up in a beer parlor, whose proprietor hoped to fetch a modest $200 for it. The nobility of one man's surrender was in tragic contrast with the ignoble fate of the man who could not surrender, who fled from Richmond, was soon to flee from Danville, from Greensboro, from Charlotte and Abbeville, only to be picked up in Irwinville, Georgia, as if he were a fugitive criminal.

From Danville to Irwinville took exactly one month. Davis had left his temporary capital on the Monday night of April 10, after W. P. Graves brought the noonday tidings of Lee's capitulation. Like his sword, the man taken in custody in Georgia had become but a twisted fragment of himself. He had been running away for so long now from the Union he had been loath to leave in 1861 and to which he was loath to return in 1865. To that Union he was soon returned and put in irons—but his will was still his own.

Of all Confederates, Jefferson Davis was the most willful, the most unreconstructible. Considered as an arch traitor by some Yankees, he was imprisoned but never tried. He refused to ask for a pardon, though he might eventually have obtained one. He could not accept the decision of the War. He was the unforgiving and the unforgiven. The *War* he had lost, though he could never imagine why; the *Cause* was never lost. Thus he came to symbolize the irreconcilable South, the willful, bitter, and frustrated South—the South that might some day forget but could never forgive.

Davis lived for nearly a quarter of a century after the fall of the Confederacy—as much of a mature lifetime as many mortals of his day could expect. In fact, he lived long enough for those Southerners who had come to despise him in wartime to forget the hatreds and bickering of a troubled people and a troubled President and to come to admire him for what he was—not a great man, but a man of great integrity; not a great soldier, but a man who in defeat was able to muster an amazing spirit of resistance among the people of his South; not even a great leader, but a man who because of his unique position found thrust upon him the role of chief custodian of the Lost Cause. He became its recognized apologist. At the same time, he became both the chief target of Northern contempt for the South and the chief repository of smoldering Southern hatred for the victorious North. In a manner which was more truth than pun, he had become the administrator of the Old South's last will and testament.

Jefferson Davis' will was born with him. Appearances changed, both with Davis and the world about him; but the same strong will went with him to the grave. It had been carefully husbanded, like the talent in the parable. In portraiture Davis fared best in stone. Granite and marble well befitted him, for though stone might crack or even crumble, it would never bend.

His willfulness produced a stereotype of Davis that often makes of him a cold forbidding person. But despite the fact that he was often criticized as humorless and undemonstrative, Davis could be the gayest and most personable of men, particularly among his friends and associates.

Davis was a man of will; but he could also be a man of good will. The two are not incompatible, and no Southerner who was anybody would have wanted Davis to be otherwise, since none was otherwise himself. For the South cultivated the virtue of sternness tempered by mercy and kindness; of austerity which presented a reverse side of relaxed jocularity. The Southerner did not deem this to be either inconsistency or hypocrisy. It was a form of *noblesse oblige;* it was just the way gentlemen did things. So Jefferson Davis was stubborn, but rarely did he lose his temper about it.

More than any man, perhaps, Davis *was* the post-bellum South. His reactions in war and reconstruction were probably typical of those of the average Southerner. Other Southern leaders were not the whole South, as Davis was. Lee was its spiritual quality—its soul. Alexander Stephens was its conscience. Davis was a bit of Lee, a bit of Stephens, a bit of all that was Southern.

Only when Davis was gone did the South or its history begin to change. He was born in 1808, when Southern nationalism was about to find itself in the voices of the War Hawks, who were itching to start a war for the South's sake. He died in 1889, when the fighting South had carried most of its swords and uniforms off to the attic and had become the "New" South of the Bourbons and industrialists.

Jefferson Davis was the tenth child of Samuel Davis and Jane Cook. Jefferson's paternal grandfather, Evan, had been born in Philadelphia but had removed to Georgia, where Samuel was born. Samuel had fought in the American Revolution as a commander of cavalry and had met a Scotch-Irish girl, Jane Cook, whom he presently married. The first child of this union was Joseph Davis, who was to become one of the South's richest men. In 1793 the children had increased to five and Samuel set his mind on the Kentucky wilderness, searching for better soil. Settling briefly in the bluegrass, the family next made its home in Christian County in the southwestern part of the state. It was there that Jefferson was born, the only Davis son not dubbed with a Biblical name. Instead, the Davises turned to the hagiography of American democracy.

While still a baby, Jefferson was carried off into the old Southwest, where his family had visions of becoming cotton barons. St. Mary's Parish, Louisiana, was picked first, but it was far too unhealthy; so the Davises turned next to Wilkinson County, in southwest Mississippi. There the small farmer Samuel Davis became a small planter with a dozen slaves to his name and a plantation with the high-sounding title of "Rosemont." Son Joseph went off to Natchez to practice law and was soon amassing his fortune.

Jefferson Davis was but a small child during the War of 1812, but he had already started going to neighborhood schools. The family unanimously agreed that young Jefferson had considerable promise; so when the war was over, Samuel wanted to send him off to a Roman Catholic boarding school in Kentucky. Brother Joseph, who was twenty-four years Jefferson's senior and as much a head of the family as the father, arranged for his brother to go up the Natchez Trace in the company of Colonel Thomas Hinds, who was journeying to Kentucky. It required courage for a lad of seven to take the thousand-mile trip through the wilderness, far from the arms of a doting mother.

Davis met Andrew Jackson at Nashville, then went on to St. Thomas College in Washington County, Kentucky. There he was the smallest boy in school and just about the only Protestant. His Baptist parents had taken a chance in sending their son off to a Catholic School. Indeed, he himself became so fond of the brothers and their religion that he would probably have become a Catholic had the Dominican father who headed the school not dissuaded him by refusing to talk about the matter.

After two years at St. Thomas, Davis returned home at his mother's insistence. He attended school in Mississippi, going for a short time to Jefferson College, at Washington. Once, revolting against an onerous assignment, he quit school and elected to work in his father's field with the Negroes. The "strike" lasted two days; then he was back at school.

In 1821, he went off again to school, this time to Transylvania University in Kentucky. He was a mere thirteen at the time. At the university he spent hours on end reading books, but he managed to practice the social graces, too. In his senior year he received an appointment to West Point and graduated in 1828. There he made many lifelong friendships, among them Albert Sidney Johnston, Joseph E. Johnston and Robert E. Lee.

For seven years after receiving his commission, Davis served at posts in Wisconsin and Illinois. At Fort Crawford, Wisconsin he fell in love with Sara Knox, the daughter of Brevet Colonel Zachary Taylor, who did not approve his daughter's sharing the transient life of an army officer. By 1835, he had decided to join his brother Joseph as a planter on Davis' Bend, south of Vicksburg; so he resigned from the army and married his beloved, despite her father's continued objections.

In the swampy lands of Brierfield Plantation, Davis and his young wife both came down with malaria. She died in September 1835. He, inconsolable, almost perished also. For the next few years he traveled, read omnivorously, and continued to operate his plantation. Like his father, he often worked in the fields side by side with his Negroes. His brother Joseph was his frequent companion in these years. In fact, after Samuel's death in 1824, Joseph had actually become "head" of the family. Upon him he now depended as upon a father.

In 1845, Jefferson Davis embarked upon two of the most influential phases of his career—his second marriage and his first political office. Varina Howell was the charming and intelligent young daughter of a wealthy Natchez family. She had first met Davis during Christmas holidays in 1843: "I do not know whether this Mr. Jefferson Davis is young or old," she wrote her mother. "He looks both at times; but I believe he is old. . . . He impresses me as a remarkable kind of man . . . and has a way of taking for granted that everybody agrees with him when he expresses an opinion . . . yet he is most agreeable. The fact is, he is the kind of person I should expect to rescue one from a mad dog at any risk, but to insist upon a stoical indifference to the fright afterward."

Varina did not fall in love immediately. She was seventeen and he was thirty-five. Her family were Whigs; he was a Democrat. But they soon found a common ground; both had a keenness of mind and a fondness for learning that drew them together. She was as much of an intellectual as he. They were married in February, 1845. Varina was the dutiful wife, but she was a person in her own right also. She could circulate in any company her husband kept, however sophisticated or however worldly. It was not just a marriage; it was a partnership of equals.

When Davis ran for Congress the summer after his marriage, Varina busied herself attempting to turn her Whig friends into Democrats. He campaigned vigorously, even keeping a speaking engagement the day after his mother's death. He swept his district; so now to Washington he went—he and Varina. They were scarcely settled when the Mexican War broke out, and Davis was off to command the First Mississippi Regiment, serving under his former father-in-law, General Zachary Taylor.

Davis proved a brilliant leader. His men were armed at his insistence with the new Whitney rifle. He was one of the commissioners receiving the surrender of Monterey and later, in the critical battle of Buena Vista, he deployed his men in V-formation at a critical ravine to hold back an enemy attempt to outflank Taylor. He was severely wounded in the foot, but he was a hero. The V-formation became the talk of military strategists for a generation.

Davis himself never got over the notoriety he achieved at Buena Vista, for ever thereafter he conceived of himself as a military genius. In the Civil War he constantly meddled with the strategy of the Confederate armies and even argued that were he and Lee able to take the field together, "we could between us wrest a victory from those people." Embittered Confederates meanwhile were predicting that if the South perished, it would die of a "V".

Taylor, Davis, and the Mississippi Rifles were to take second place to General Winfield Scott at Mexico City; so when the enlistment of the Rifles expired on May 29, 1847, Davis set sail for home—all his men, alive or in coffins, going with him. The quick and the dead arrived to an ovation at New Orleans, and soon Davis found himself appointed a Brigadier General by President Polk and a United States Senator by Governor A. G. Brown, filling out an unexpired term.

In Washington most of the time until his resignation from the Senate in 1861, he followed the unswerving line of the Southern Democrats on the slavery issue, insisting on the slaveowner's right to take his slaves into any free territory of the United States, even to northernmost Oregon.

Davis reluctantly voted against his former father-in-law for President in 1848, feeling that "the South should fraternize with the Democracy." He was one of the ten Senators who voted to the bitter end against the admission of California as a free state and opposed the principle of squatter sovereignty established by the Compromise of 1850. In 1851, he resigned from the Senate to go home and campaign for the governorship, in the face of certain defeat, after John Anthony Quitman withdrew from the race, leaving him to fight it out with a proponent of the Compromise, Henry Stuart Foote. In the fifties he became the unquestioned leader of the Southern proslavery element in his party, as he attempted to steer for the South a safe course between the shoals of nationalism and state rights.

Davis was a state-righter; but he was, ironically enough, somewhat of a nationalist. He knew that state rights could not exist in a vacuum, for states conceived of their rights only within a union, not out of one. To most Southerners the dread weapons of nullification and secession were to be resorted to only in desperation; surely they should never be fired at the Union except in the last ditches of self-defense. In fact, all things being equal—including, by the way, the states—Davis and a host of other Southerners preferred to live under a Union where the traditional checks and balances, separation of powers, and safeguards for minority rights prevailed. Under a Union so constituted, the South had become prosperous and potent. Under such a Union, the South had practically run the country since the days of the Virginia dynasty.

The Southerner in Washington was keenly aware of the virtues of Union, particularly if he were a member of Congress; for here the time-honored practice of political compromise was most conscientiously followed. In the 1850's, and again in the 1950's, political compromise, especially that practiced in the halls of Congress, seemed one of the few last hopes for sectional amity. So, a century ago, the Southerners stuck to their committees and exercised their seniority in Congress, just as they were doing a hundred years later, not in spite of, but because of, state rights. Knowing all this, Davis gave the Union some of his best years in the decade of the fifties.

In 1853, President Franklin Pierce made him Secretary of War. It is doubtful that any more energetic, progressive, and capable head of that department has ever graced it. In his high position he worked religiously for the promotion of the South's interests, and in 1854 vigorously supported the Kansas-Nebraska Act as a means of preserving the balance between North and South.

Meanwhile, the Davises had taken a prominent place on the social calendar of the capital. They were well-liked and exceedingly popular, and that in spite of Davis' continuing habit, criticized by Varina at first sight, of assuming that people agreed with him. That many people did not—that much of the Union did not —he seems not to have fully comprehended. After all, *he* was right; why should there be any question about it.

After the Cabinet years, Davis returned to the Senate. There he was at the time of the Dred Scott decision, whereby the Southern-dominated Supreme Court attempted to make the South's wishes the law of the land by guaranteeing the slaveowner's rights in the territories. There he was when this very issue sundered the Democratic party in 1860, thereby making it almost inevitable that the Republican candidate, Abraham Lincoln, would be elected. There he was when his state left the Union in 1861.

When the Southern states, one by one, began to secede, Davis was truly alarmed. He did not want the Union to fall apart. He was, in fact, terrified of the consequences. It was almost inevitable, he felt, that there would be coercion in an effort to return the seceded states to the Union. Should this happen, he anticipated that he might be placed in command of the South's forces of resistance. But he desperately hoped for peace. When he resigned on January 21, 1861, he was as inconsolable as if he had been "bending over his father, slain by his countrymen." He said:

> To argue that a man who follows . . . his state, resuming her sovereign jurisdiction and power, is disloyal to his allegiance to the United States, which allegiance he only owes through his state, is such a confusion of ideas as does not belong to an ordinary comprehension of our Government. It is treason to the principle of community independence. It is to recur to that doctrine of passive obedience, which, in England, cost one monarch his head and drove another into exile; a doctrine which, since the revolution of 1688, has obtained nowhere where men

speak the English tongue; and yet all this it is needful to admit before we accept this doctrine of coercion.

The time is near at hand when the places which have known us as colleagues labouring together, can know us in that relation no more for ever. I have striven unsuccessfully to avert the catastrophe which now impends over the country. For the few days which I may remain I am willing to labour in order that that catastrophe shall be as little as possible destructive to public peace and prosperity. If you desire at this last moment to avert civil war, so be it; it is better so. If you will but allow us to separate from you peaceably, since we cannot live peaceably together, to leave with the rights we had before we were united, since we cannot enjoy them in the Union, then there are many relations which may still subsist between us, drawn from the associations of our struggles from the Revolutionary era to the present day, which may be beneficial to you as well as to us. If you will not have it thus; if in the price of power, if in contempt of reason and reliance upon force, you say we shall not go, but shall remain as subjects to you, then, Gentlemen of the North, a war is to be inaugurated the like of which men have not seen.

Secession had proved to be a sobering experience, indeed, to Jefferson Davis. He had not wanted it—it was much better simply to threaten it. Yet there it was. In February, he was chosen President of the Confederacy. War was imminent, but Davis would try to make it a defensive one, arguing that the South was the injured party. On all these matters Davis had already convinced himself. Who would argue about it?

So war came, and Davis had to tackle the impossible task of winning it. He assumed the duty with confidence, for he knew all about strategy and he had utmost confidence in his talents as an administrator. Davis could see the victory. But defensive strategy proved of no avail and by the time Davis took the offensive, it was already too late. The War had to be fought by the South almost without money or industries or railroads—and in the end this determined the outcome even more than manpower. All the South had had was its fighting spirit and military leadership—and even these were often wasted.

Davis had undertaken the impossible, but he dared not admit it. One desperate measure after another he had attempted: conscription, impressment, the tax-in-land, suspension of the privilege of the writ of habeas corpus, and even the arming of slaves with the promise of emancipation. Inevitably his policies ran roughshod over state rights, even personal liberties; and the great state-rights advocate had to eat his ante-bellum words. Soon he was quarreling with the governors, as might well be expected.

But Davis' enemies were not merely the state-rights die-hards. There were many who felt his quasi-generalship left much to be desired. He meddled with the army; he sought to dictate strategy; and he had some fearful quarrels with and over his generals. By the time the War was half over, he had fallen out with his Vice-President, Alexander Stephens; and the Confederate Congress elected in 1863 was openly hostile to him. They even suspected him of planning a *coup d'état.* Yet he stood his ground. When peace movements sprang up in the last years of the struggle, Davis was determined to fight on, and so was the South. Even during the flight into the Carolinas and Georgia, he convinced himself that somehow he could revive the Confederacy's fortunes, either across the Mississippi or in Mexico—but somewhere.

The collapse of the Confederacy was something Davis was never prepared to accept. As he fled, he was the man who fights and runs away so that he can fight again another day. He had no intention of surrender—only strategic retreat. *His* will was not broken. Why should the will of the South be broken?

The flight from Danville into the Carolinas and Georgia began on April 10, the day after Lee's surrender. Davis' reception in Greensboro, North Carolina, was cold. The city had been a center of disaffection, and now with General Sherman's Union invaders likely to show up any minute, there was no disposition at all to give aid and comfort to the fleeing Confederate government. Mrs. Davis and the children had gone on to Charlotte, which was more hospitable. However, she had already decided to procede southward with the "treasure train."

Meanwhile, Davis met Generals Joseph E. Johnston and P. G. T. Beauregard at Greensboro. Without asking their advice, he told them how to continue the struggle. When he was finally informed cautiously that the two generals were ready to negotiate the surrender of their exhausted armies with Sherman, Davis still persisted; but finally Johnston told him point blank of the folly of continued resistance. Only then did Davis consent to negotiations. Davis was still unhappy. He felt that Johnston had cravenly given up the cause when it might have been salvaged.

While negotiations were proceeding, Davis and his Cabinet moved on southwestward. By April 16, Easter Sunday, they were at Salisbury. From there they pressed on to Charlotte, where Davis learned of Lincoln's assassination and the elevation to the Presidency of Andrew Johnson, a man who despised Davis and his aristocratic kind. More than ever was the willful Confederate President determined to resist; but little encouragement did he receive, except from the equally willful General Wade Hampton.

Urged by his Cabinet, Davis acceded, on April 24, to the peace terms Johnston had made with Sherman. However, the Confederate President had the last word. He predicted that the terms would be rejected in Washington; and, of course, he was right. On April 26, Johnston surrendered to Sherman under the same terms Lee did to Grant. Johnston did not, as Davis had charged him to do, "return with his cavalry" to defend the government and possibly help it escape to the west. For this action Davis never forgave the general.

The Federal government now concentrated its efforts on the capture of Davis and his Cabinet, together with the "treasure train," whose contents rumor had now inflated to the neighborhood of $10,000,000 and more—a wealth the Confederacy would have much preferred to be credited with in the lean days when the War was being fought.

As the Davis party entered South Carolina, it was royally received. Crowds cheered, flowers were strewn in the President's path, and food was offered in abundance. On May 2, the Confederate government reached Abbeville, where the treasure was turned over to Davis. On the same day, President Johnson offered a $100,000 reward for the Confederate President, under the assumption that Davis had been a party to a "conspiracy" that had brought about the assassination of Lincoln. But, as Davis later remarked, "Johnson knows I prefer Lincoln . . . to himself."

Davis, unaware of the price on his head, held a final council of war at Abbeville. He was still determined to fight on, but every one of his military leaders voted against further resistance. Chagrined, Davis still insisted he could escape to the west, where General Edmund Kirby-Smith remained under arms.

Near Washington, Georgia, the escort was dismissed, and Davis with a small party continued the flight. He moved southward, however, rather than westward, for he would not consent to go far from Varina and the children until he was certain that they had escaped to the Florida coast and safety. For most of the time Varina's entourage had traveled separately from that of the President, and both parties were deliberately kept small. "A small body of men elude the vigilance of the enemy easier than a larger number," Davis had observed, still the strategist in charge.

Nevertheless, Davis took chances. In fact, on the night before his capture, he rejoined Mrs. Davis; and unaware of his danger, he did not plan to part company with her until morning. Also, unknown to him, his remaining army east of the Mississippi had been lost with the surrender of General Richard Taylor on May 8. It was early in the morning of May 10 that Lieutenant Colonel B. D. Pritchard overtook the Davises at Irwinville, Georgia. As Davis told the story:

As it was quite dark in the tent, I picked up what was supposed to be my "raglan," a water-proof, light overcoat, without sleeves; it was subsequently found to be my wife's, so very like my own as to be mistaken for it; as I started, my wife thoughtfully threw over my head and shoulders a shawl.

I had gone perhaps fifteen or twenty yards when a trooper galloped up and ordered me to halt and surrender to which I gave a defiant answer, and dropping the shawl and raglan from my shoulders, advanced toward him; he leveled his carbine at me, but I expected, if he fired, he would miss me, and my intention was in that event to put my hand under his foot, tumble him off on the other side, spring into the saddle, and attempt to escape. My wife, who had been watching, ran forward and threw her arms around me. Success depended on instantaneous action, and, recognizing that the opportunity had been lost, I turned back, and, the morning being damp and chilly, passed on to a fire beyond the tent.

That was the end of it. Several days later the President and Vice President of the Confederacy met on their way to prison. The South's will and the South's conscience were united in the ignominy of the collapse of the Lost Cause.

The tense weeks after Lee's surrender had seen a tremendous outburst of anti-Southern sentiment in the North. The assassination of Lincoln on April 14 served to carry this feeling to the point of violent revenge. Already the Northern press had pointed the accusing finger at Davis as the guiltiest of the guilty. He had starved Yankee prisoners (Southern soldiers were under the impression he was starving them!) at Andersonville and other prisons. He was the arch war criminal; and as such he became a sort of scapegoat for the sins of the whole South. Somebody had to be hung to the sour apple tree. Who could better dangle from the limb than Jefferson Davis?

In much the same way Lincoln was to become to the Southerner the embodiment of the Northern spirit, even though the wartime president actually showed signs of being the most benevolent of conquerors. In like manner, Sherman was to be remembered as the pillager par excellence. No home had been really properly burned unless it was the work of Sherman. Like the Confederate "treasure," the Sherman loot—each heading in opposite directions in those last weeks of the struggle—reached astronomical proportions in the minds of those who were ready to make a good story of it. As Wade Hampton with straight face told a Congressional committee in 1871, Sherman carried off enough silver to pay off the entire debt of the state of South Carolina!

The postwar calumnies that were visited upon men like Davis and Lincoln and Sherman served to make popular saints out of every one of them. Lincoln was cordially disliked by a host of

Northerners, not the least of which were the vengeful Radical Republicans in Congress. His assassination, embellished with decades of posthumous and post-bellum denunciation heaped upon him as one of the South's favorite whipping boys, eventually caused the Northerners to forget that they had ever found anything to hate about Lincoln.

Sherman, who had been living in Louisiana and had owned slaves before the War sent him back to his native North, had offered Johnston's army terms even more generous than Grant's. He was consequently denounced by Radicals as a secret friend of the South; but the South's memory of Sherman's devastating raids turned him into a Southern scapegoat and assured his deification by the North. As for Davis, his unpopularity in the South in the last years of the war was widespread; but the North ran off with the South's chief object of derision and thereby quickly turned him into a martyr.

Davis was not ready to die when his Confederacy did, any more than the South was. This stubborn man had not given up the struggle yet. His dreams of a Confederacy across the Mississippi or in Mexico had come to naught. The fetters attached to his ankles by a half-illiterate blacksmith were enough to make him understand that from henceforth he was the prisoner of the United States, whether he happened to be behind bars or not.

After all, there would really be no need for setting up a Confederacy in exile. Instead, it was to be brought back into existence by the "reconstructed" South; for Radical Reconstruction policies unified the South more than it had ever been unified in wartime; and the South, its will no more crushed than was that of the leader of the Confederate cause, managed to recreate a Confederacy that, like St. Augustine's City of God, was eternal and indestructible, for it existed in men's minds and did not have to bother with corporeal trivialities.

It was to this new Confederacy that Davis devoted the last two decades of his life. His precept, example, and words became the gospel of the Lost Cause. His suffering, his humiliation, and his triumph over the grave of defeat became the burden of an amazing body of scriptures.

Prisons are potent breeders of martyrdom. They figured largely in the first wave of postwar reaction against the South and its leaders, particularly Davis. Already the South had observed the danger of creating saints by senseless persecution, as had happened when John Brown's body was sent to molder in the grave, thereby assuring him sainthood and a marching soul. The symbolic execution on a sour apple tree could but bring deification to Jefferson Davis, whose only crime was the crime of the Confederacy, which he bore vicariously.

The post-capture ordeal of Davis began with humiliation. The shawl and raglan of the escaping President became the major properties of a fantastic legend that Davis had tried to escape in his wife's clothes. As the story grew, a hoop skirt was thrown into the narrative for good measure. Immediately the Northern public burst out laughing, aided and abetted by cartoonists and showmen. P. T. Barnum did his stint to ensure the perpetuation of the story. Naturally, the tale humiliated the hero of Buena Vista, the man of strong will. Actually, Davis had conducted himself with dignity at the time of his capture; and when he tried to escape, it was as himself, not as his wife. Later, on the way to Savannah, he even refused an opportunity to escape that had been dreamed up by the impulsive General "Fighting Joe" Wheeler.

On May 22, 1865, Jefferson Davis arrived at Fortress Monroe, Virginia, where he was incarcerated in what the New York *Herald* described with satisfaction as a "living tomb." There he was to remain for just a few days short of two years. His treatment at first was intended to be harsh. He was ignominiously shackled, but not without a struggle in which he felled the blacksmith and tackled a sentinel and "four of the best men of the guard" that had been hastily summoned. The ordeal over, Davis wept at the realization of his having been visited with "such an indignity." That night, when the captain of the guard unlocked the harness to allow the prisoner to undress, Davis quietly obliged by "locking it again himself." The irons remained on Davis less than a week.

According to the blacksmith who forged them, "Dr. Craven . . . saiad the engered his halth." Actually, the public outcry at the shackling caused Secretary of War Edwin Stanton to order the fetters removed.

Dr. John J. Craven, the fort surgeon, befriended Davis from the start. Craven provided the prisoner with tobacco, and protested the maintaining of a twenty-four-hour guard inside his cell. Davis himself was almost driven insane by the light of the lamp, which was kept burning night and day. Finally, Craven managed to have him moved to a better room.

Craven and Davis discussed frequently and at length "topics of great public interest." Late in 1865, Craven was removed because he had defiantly purchased a winter overcoat for the frail prisoner. In 1866, now free of army censorship, he published a 377-page book entitled *The Prison Life of Jefferson Davis.* Here were recounted the sufferings of the prisoner, together with the substance of the numerous conversations. Davis had talked on practically everything under the sun—scientific matters, the fine arts, the postwar economy of the South, Fenianism, feminism, the Negro, the Southern aristocracy, and the leaders of the War and Reconstruction era.

When news arrived at Fortress Monroe of the energetic campaign then being conducted by Matthew Fontaine Maury and others to attract Southern immigrants to Mexico, Davis reacted negatively. Craven thus relates the conversation:

Mr. Davis spoke of the folly and something worse of those Southern leaders who had fled to Mexico. It was an act of cowardice—an evasion of duty only to be excelled by suicide. They had been instrumental in bringing the evils of military subjugation on the people, and should remain to share their burdens. The great masses of the people were rooted to the soil, and could not, and should not, fly. The first duty of the men who had been in command during the struggle was, to remain faithful fellow-sufferers with the rank and file. By doing so they could yet exercise a moral and intellectual, if not political, weight against the schemers of rapine and oppression now swarming over the Southern country; while by deserting, they abandon helpless ignorance to the sway of powerful craft, and confessed judgment to whatever charges might be brought against them. The scheme of a political settlement in Mexico was preposterous in practice, though tempting to wounded pride. Settlements and colonies were governed, or governed themselves, by laws of material interest, considerations of profit and loss; and no settlers could be imagined less fitted for the requirements of a new colony than a body of embittered politicians, still sore and smarting from a conflict in which they had incurred defeat. Patience, indomitable industry and self-denial were the necessities of every new settlement; and these—even were the colonists of a more suitable class—could scarcely be continued in Mexico, where languor, indolence and ease, are constituent portions of the climate.

Craven was succeeded by Dr. George Cooper, who likewise denounced the pointless impairment of Davis' health. Meanwhile, as Davis languished in prison, the question was being argued as to what should be done with him. President Johnson had borne ill-will against him since the forties, when, not knowing that Senator Johnson had once been a tailor, Senator Davis had in a speech made a casual but slighting reference to blacksmiths and tailors. Davis apologized publicly two times, but the angry Tennessean never forgot or seemed inclined to forgive. Thereafter he was obsessed with a loathing for "the illegitimate, swaggering, bastard, scrub aristocracy" to which Davis belonged; and at the end of the War, Johnson was talking bravely of giving "the head devil of them all" a well-deserved hanging.

When Lincoln's assassination suddenly precipitated Johnson into the Presidency, he began to relent. A Democrat at heart, his troubles with the Radical Republicans soon caused Johnson to change his tune. He even expressed a willingness to accede to Mrs. Davis' frequent requests for clemency for her husband. But Johnson was hardly in a position to do anything, for the Radicals were taking over, and not even the President could check them. Davis was, however, eventually allowed to have visits from his wife and friends and was given the freedom of the prison grounds.

Although Washington intrigues made it impossible to appraise the Davis case in any other fashion than a political one, the languishing Confederate soon enlisted the sympathy of a number of prominent Northerners. Charles O'Conor and George Shea, two of the most distinguished lawyers in the nation, were encouraged by a group of New Yorkers to volunteer as counsel for the defense. When O'Conor offered his services to Davis, the grateful letter of acceptance was never allowed to reach O'Conor. Nevertheless, he and other lawyers continued to occupy themselves with the case and demanded that the Confederate President be brought to trial at once.

Government lawyers, after "mousing among the archives," as Mrs. Davis described it, realized at once that the government would be "completely beaten" if an effort were made to prove in court any complicity on Davis' part in the assassination of Lincoln. Johnson, who had foolishly committed himself to the charges of Davis' guilt, became extremely loath to reveal the emptiness of the case; so there were endless delays.

Perhaps the most ludicrous development of all was an offer by Thaddeus Stevens, the arch enemy of the South in Congress, to serve as defense counsel for Davis. Of course, Stevens was acting to embarrass the Johnson administration, not to help Davis. At any rate, while Stevens denounced Davis as a public enemy and treated the South as "a conquered country," this Radical leader insisted that Davis was a gentleman, "incapable of being an assassin." Though never withdrawn, the charges were thenceforth not pursued. The government really wanted to forget about it all.

Meanwhile, some agitation had arisen to obtain an outright pardon for Davis from President Johnson. Although Johnson in an interview with Mrs. Davis had asked whether the prisoner had "thought of" asking for a pardon, neither Davis nor Johnson really wished to become involved in such a procedure. Johnson feared to eat crow by pardoning the man he had once assailed as an assassin. As for Davis, he obstinately insisted that he had done nothing to be pardoned for. Mrs. Davis' reply to Johnson was, "No, and I suppose you did not expect it."

After many delays, Davis was indicted for treason by a grand jury in Norfolk, Virginia, on May 8, 1866. That the action came in the civil courts rather than at the hands of a court martial (which some of the intransigents had proposed) was a victory for Davis and his counsel. Still there were delays. An attempt was made by his lawyers to force trial under the indictment, but the government managed to gain a postponement until autumn.

The next move of the defense counsel was to ask that Davis be released on bail. Here a coup was accomplished by the securing of the name of Horace Greeley on the bail bond. Greeley, the flamboyant editor of the New York *Tribune,* had long demanded that Davis be given a prompt and fair trial. So, Greeley signed the bond, even though he was advised that he would lose votes in his current campaign for the United States Senate, that his paper would lose subscribers, and that his recently completed history of the war would lose many orders. When he was subsequently brought up short by thirty-four members of the Union League Club, to which he belonged, Greeley launched an attack on the complainers as "narrow-minded blockheads, who would like to be useful to a great cause, but don't know how."

Not even the pen of Greeley could avail; the application for release on bail was rejected by the Federal court. In his paper Greeley now began to unleash bitter attacks on the government's policy. He also enlisted other offers of bail from notables like Cornelius Vanderbilt and even the Abolitionist Gerrit Smith.

Finally, early in May 1867, a writ of habeas corpus was issued to bring Davis from military prison to stand civil trial at Richmond, thus ending the first year of government dilly-dallying since the original indictment. His return to Richmond brought cheers from the crowds in the former Confederate capital. Already he had turned into a deity of the Lost Cause, thanks almost entirely to his persecution. The government, having decided on further delay, announced that it was "not its intention to prosecute the trial" at that term of court. He was released on $100,000 bail; and he walked out of the courtroom before cheering crowds, who met him with loud Rebel yells.

Davis' first action was to set out for Canada to visit his children. Then he spent some time in Havana, finally returning by way of New Orleans to his old plantation, Brierfield, which during the war had been seized by the Federal government, turned over to freed slaves and afterward sold to the Negroes.

In November, he was ordered to return to Richmond to stand trial; but the action was again delayed until March. One month before the scheduled resumption, came the impeachment of President Johnson; so further technicalities were dreamed up to delay trial. At this time a new indictment was produced, adding to the name of Davis that of Lee, together with most of the Cabinet and general officers of the Confederate government. Lee's reaction was to rush to Richmond to make common cause with Davis, although "a less able man," as Davis remarked, "might have availed himself of the opportunity to avoid danger by transferring this responsibility to one on whom it would certainly gladly be placed"—the former prisoner of Fortress Monroe.

The treason case was now postponed until June, then again until October, giving Davis time to make a summer trip to England to confer with a British commission merchant about a partnership offer. Although friends had contributed generously to him so far, Davis' pride would not let him accept charity indefinitely.

While Davis was in England, Federal lawyers worked rapidly toward the quashing of the old indictment. In the end, it was a fairly simple matter; Davis could not be considered a traitor if, as had been the case, the North had given *de facto* recognition to the South as a belligerent nation; an enemy cannot commit treason. The jurists further realized that there was little chance of getting a unanimous jury in this controversial trial.

Finally, irony of ironies, the lawyers for the defense, after having been prompted by the Chief Justice of the Supreme Court, resorted to the Fourteenth Amendment. Presumably passed for the aid of freedmen, it became the bulwark of the defenders of the "persons" of corporations in the age of rugged individualism. It also gave unwitting refuge to Jefferson Davis. Inasmuch as the Amendment had defined him as a traitor and had deprived him of citizenship as his punishment, the long-standing indictment in the courts had been automatically superseded. He had already been tried—by constitutional Amendment, absurd as it all was. Accordingly, he could not twice be placed in jeopardy for the same crime.

In the end, the matter was certified to the Supreme Court, where it was never brought up. Had any doubt remained, it was dispelled by a General Amnesty extending to Davis which Johnson proclaimed on Christmas day of 1868. In February 1869, the case was formally dismissed by the government attorneys. Davis was a free man at last, although a man without a country, for he never fully recovered his lost citizenship. He could vote but he could never hold state or federal office unless Congress should approve.

In his trip to England in 1868, Davis was welcomed by many loyal supporters, including the *émigré* Judah P. Benjamin, former Confederate Secretary of State. He also visited in France but refused to allow himself to be presented to Napoleon III, who had "played us false." The commission scheme had come to naught; so Davis had to cast about for another means of making a living. In March 1868, he had refused to accept the presidency of Randolph-Macon College in Ashland, Virginia, because he was still "a prisoner of state, released on bail" and would not imperil the "fortunes" of any institution "by inflicting it" with the "odium" that had been cast on him. In 1870, he was to be called to the presidency of the University of Alabama, but he declined because he had recently become president of the Carolina Life Insurance Company in Memphis.

In the Carolina company Davis sank all the funds he could command—$15,000 to be exact. In three years the venture failed. It was a familiar pattern: a fly-by-night affair would enlist the name and prestige of a prominent Confederate leader. Then, as the unsuspecting public and the unsuspected celebrity stood by, the whole operation would collapse, leaving the great man in the most embarrassing of positions.

But the Confederates went right on lending their seals of approval to the shaky insurance operations of the period. On one occasion, Stephen D. Lee had boasted that he was the only Confederate general who had not been drafted as an insurance company executive; in a matter of weeks he was an insurance company president himself. But soon the insurance speculators came to grief.

What next? Off and on Davis attempted to settle down and write his memoirs, but unwritten and unpublished books were not sufficient to maintain the solvency of the Davis family.

In 1869 his brother Joseph Davis died. Before his death, Joseph had recovered Hurricane and Brierfield, but in his will he did not leave Brierfield to his brother. In fact, Jefferson had never really been owner of the plantation, despite the fact that Joseph had promised it to him. Apparently Joseph had developed a considerable dislike for Varina Davis and had tried at one time to make Jefferson exclude her from any inheritance. The result was estrangement, and the brothers were only barely reunited before Joseph's death.

In his will, Joseph left $15,000 for each of Jefferson's children in lieu of Brierfield. Davis was furious and initiated a prolonged suit to recover his share of his brother's estate, particularly Brierfield Plantation. In the end he won Brierfield back, though it was an empty victory, for the place was almost worthless.

The flyer into the insurance business had not taught Davis much of a lesson. There was another ill-fated adventure in store— the Mississippi Valley Society, which sought to promote immigration into Mississippi and planned to operate a line of steamers from New Orleans to South America. Here again he failed.

Meanwhile, the family found a home at Beauvoir on the Mississippi Gulf Coast. A cottage on the estate was rented from Sara A. Dorsey, a staunch friend of Varina, who later sold Beauvoir to Davis, taking a mortgage on the property. At her death she generously canceled the mortgage, leaving him in full control. Davis at last got down to the task of writing. His *magnum opus,* on which he worked for years, assisted by Mrs. Dorsey, Mrs. Davis, and

Major W. T. Walthall, was the tedious *Rise and Fall of the Confederate Government.* The book was to reveal more about him than it did about the Confederacy. It would show him still to be a man of indomitable will, never admitting that secession was anything but constitutional, never conceding that he had done violence to the Union, never exhibiting the slightest inclination to admit any errors of judgment or administrative shortcomings as President of the Confederacy. Financially, the apologia was a failure, like its writer. There was a violent squabble between Davis and Appleton, his publisher; and the resultant court action was interminable.

Meanwhile, Davis was much sought after by the magazines, and his articles provided a modest income at a time when he sorely needed help. The American public wanted to know what he had to say, even if the saying was mostly in his own behalf. Mrs. Davis also took to her pen, preparing a voluminous *Memoir* of her husband's life and also writing occasional articles. It was the grand age of the recording of the Confederate scriptures. All over the South, the men, great and small, who had figured in the War were producing their literary testaments.

Not all these scriptures were dedicated to the greater glory of Jefferson Davis. In 1874 there appeared General Joseph E. Johnston's *Narrative of Military Operations Directed During the Late War Between the States,* which contained a venomous attack on his conduct of the executive office. In particular, Johnston denounced his failure at the start of the war to send the South's cotton abroad to be converted into money and munitions. Davis' explanation, of course, was that the Confederate government had no money to buy up cotton, much less export it. What he chose to forget was that at that time he was busily trying to create a cotton famine in Europe in order to force recognition of the Confederacy and secure aid for it from abroad.

Friends like General Jubal Early advised Davis to abstain from "personal controversy" with his detractors. After all, said Early, he must think of himself as "the representative of our cause." But Davis had not heard the last of Johnston. Only a few years later the General was quoted, he claimed, inaccurately, as wondering what Davis had done with the Confederate "treasure." The result was such a hue and cry that Johnston himself ran for cover.

Davis was in great demand at public functions. He made countless speeches, each carefully screened afterwards by the press for whatever of the sensational it might assay. His attitude toward the candidacy of Horace Greeley for President in 1872 was much discussed. Did his support of Greeley, despite the opposition of many Southerners, smack of "fidelity to a friend" who had signed his bail, or were his motives purely impersonal? Probably he himself did not know, but the Northern editor's courage and sense of justice had deeply moved him.

The speeches and articles of the Confederate President often revealed a persistent bitterness of soul that remained with him to the end of his life. At a historical convention he bluntly remarked, "We were cheated rather than conquered," a statement which stirred up a "great muss" in the North.

Even the prospect of an address by Davis on Northern soil could stir a number of die-hard members of the Grand Army of the Republic to threaten his life. In 1875, he was forced to turn down an invitation to speak at a Columbus, Indiana, fair. Later, after accepting a lecture engagement with the Winnebago County, Illinois, Agricultural Society, he was frantically implored to "decline in a statesmanlike manner," which he did.

Rarely was Davis a more convenient object of calumny than in the 1876 Presidential election, when the Republicans for lack of an issue resurrected the bloody shirt and attempted to revive wartime hatred. It began with an amnesty bill, drawn up with the intention of mollifying sectional animosity during the celebration of the centennial of the Declaration of Independence. James G. Blaine, the hand-picked prospective Republican Presidential candidate, led a successful attack on the measure by insisting that the Confederate President be excepted. Blaine, however, lost the nomination to Rutherford B. Hayes.

Later in the campaign, the embattled Republicans, embarrassed by the scandals of the Grant administration, continued to thrash their whipping boy; but Davis-hating was already becoming a tiresome pastime. The "Bargain of 1877" that followed the election and gave the Presidency to Hayes was to most Americans the official end of Reconstruction. The Southern states were now back under the control of the white Democrats, and the age of the "Redeemers" had arrived. At last North and South might be able to forgive and forget.

But Davis was not through his purgatory. In 1878, he was excluded from a pension bill that would cover veterans of the Mexican War. In 1879, there was another amnesty bill, but again the man who would not bend the knee to ask for a pardon was deprived of what he kept insisting he did not want. In fact, it was now a matter of honor *not* to take the oath, *not* to be forgiven. Rather, he would be lost along with his cause. Back in 1876, he had written: "I have no claim to pardon, not having in any wise repented. . . ." He never changed.

Reconstruction over, Davis entered upon the last stage of his progress toward deification. With the rank and file of Southerners he was now the man who could do no wrong—never had, for that matter. At last they saw him as he saw himself. When, in 1886, he appeared at the unveiling of a Confederate monument in Montgomery, Alabama, he was mobbed by his admirers. He was accepting a number of speaking engagements at that time, and all these he religiously kept in spite of failing health. Every journey was another triumphal entry. He could not have avoided it; nor did he really care to.

Davis had not invented the Confederacy, despite the insinuations of his Northern detractors. Instead, the Confederacy had invented him. It had chosen this essentially nationalistic Southerner to head the cause of the states against the Union. He had reluctantly acquiesced; but once having assumed the task of leadership, he took the entire burden of the South upon him and never laid it down, not even when the war ended. Peacetime merely replaced the epaulette with a chip.

Although now the South's idol, he could still engender controversy. He was constantly quarreling with his Yankee critics. In 1884, Sherman had accused him of harboring dictatorial aspirations back in the wartime days. All Sherman's barb did, of course, was to put Davis back on the front pages of the newspapers and into the magazines, where the old Confederate loved to be. Meanwhile, Davis had been somewhat benevolently inclined toward Grant, for although he considered the man a ruthless invader, he had "abetted neither arson nor pillage" and had exhibited no "malignity" toward the South.

Davis even managed to stir up controversy in the South. In 1887, he tackled the prohibitionists, who were at the moment involved in the large task of trying to dry up the state of Texas. The idea of prohibition he regarded as "monstrous," and before this militant skirmish was over, he found himself in a foolish controversy with the Methodist bishop, Charles Betts Galloway, who tearfully denounced the Confederate leader for advocating "the barroom and the destruction of virtue."

To expect Davis to embrace any of the reform movements of his day would have been demanding the impossible. He was a fundamentalist in social matters, as he was in government. He would brook no interference with individual rights, not even where the bottle was concerned. Nor would he countenance such new-fangled notions as woman suffrage. His was a world that did not change. For him only yesterday mattered.

Rarely, indeed, did Davis bother to look toward the present or the future. He spoke occasionally on the subject of the freedman. After all, Jefferson and Joseph Davis, who had experimented with slave self-government in the ante-bellum years and had willingly recognized the emancipation of their Negroes once the war was over, were hardly inclined to be extremists on the race issue. At Fortress Monroe Davis told Craven about what lay ahead for the freed slave in the postwar world:

He saw no reason why they must die out, unless remaining idle. If herded together in idleness and filth, as in the villages established by our military power, the small-pox, licentiousness, and drunkenness would make short work of them. Wherever so herded, they had died off like sheep with the murrain. But remaining on the plantations, as heretofore, and employed for wages, they were a docile and procreative people, altogether differing from the Indians, and not likely to die out like the latter. Their labor was needed; and though they could not multiply so fast in freedom as under their former wholesome restraints, he saw no good argument for their dying out.

The blacks were a docile, affectionate, and religious people, like cats in their fondness for home. The name of freedom had charms for them; but until educated to be self-supporting, it would be a curse. If herded together in military villages and fed on rations gratuitously distributed, rum, dirt, and venereal disease would devour them off the face of the earth in a few years. With peace established, they would return, in ninety-five cases out of the hundred, to their old plantations, and work for their old masters. Freedom was to them an orgie, of which such as had enjoyed it were rapidly sickening. . . . Even during the war, and at penalty of returning to slavery, he had seen many instances—enough to convince him that with freedom assured, or rather its evils to them in their unprepared state better understood—the great majority of the blacks would flock back eagerly.

Although Davis allowed himself to become the apostle of reaction—the pure essence of unreconstructibility—he was not unaware of the fact that while one might *look* backward in time, one could never *move* backward. In their own family life the Davises were not lost in the past. They were cosmopolites rather than provincials. The children were educated in Canada and Europe. There were frequent journeys back and forth across the waters and renewals of friendships far and wide. The eldest daughter married a Yankee from Colorado. Much of Davis' time was spent in New York and New England among Northern friends. The publishers for Jefferson and Varina Davis were in New York; and after her husband's death, Varina spent much of her time in New York City.

The Davises were merely being citizens of the world, as all good Southern plantation families had been in ante-bellum days. Davis never affected the desperate provincialism of the defeated post-bellum South. Indeed, he himself realized that shorn of the superficial differences induced by regional society, economy, and politics, the American people had more in common than they sometimes admitted. "We are now at peace, and I trust will ever remain so," he remarked at a reunion meeting of the Army of Northern Virginia:

We have recently been taught that those whom we had considered enemies, measuring them by standard bearers whose hearts were filled with malignity, that they in our hour of trouble had hearts beating in sympathy with our grief. We have been taught by their generosity, that bounded with quick response to the afflictions of the South, that the vast body of people at the North are our brethren still.

And the heart would be dead to every generous impulse that would try to stimulate in you now a feeling of hostility to those where so large a majority have manifested nothing but brotherly love for you.

In referring therefore to the days of the past and the glorious cause you have served—a cause that was dignified by the honor in which you maintained it—I seek but to revive a memory which should be dear to you and pass on to your children as a memory which teaches the highest lessons of manhood, of truth, and of adherence to duty—duty to your State, duty to your principles, duty to the truth, duty to your buried parents, and duty to your coming children.

So, amid the reviving of memories, his vestigial nationalism reappeared also.

That a man whose business fortunes were an endless series of calamities should hold any views of significance about the economic problems of the postwar South may seem remarkable. Yet sitting in his prison cell in 1865, Davis had pictured to Dr. Craven the South's coming industrial revolution:

In ten years, or perhaps less, the South will have recovered the pecuniary losses of the war. It has had little capital in manufactures. Its capital was in land and negroes. The land remains productive as ever. The negroes remain, but their labor has to be paid for. Before the war, there had been 4,000,000 negroes, average value, $500 each, or total value, two thousand millions of dollars. This was all gone, and the interest upon it, which had been the profits of the negro's labor in excess of his cost for food, clothing, and medicines. Still their labor remains; and with this, and such European labor as will be imported and such Northern labor as must flow South, the profits of the Southern staples will not be long in restoring material prosperity.

The land will not pass to any great extent from its former proprietors. They will lease it for a few years to men with capital, and then resume working it themselves; or sell portions of it with the same object, not materially decreasing their own possessions. When the country is quiet and the profits of the crop come to be known, there will be a rush southward from the sterile New England regions and from Europe, only equalled by that to California on the discovery of gold. Men will not stay in the mountains of Vermont and New Hampshire cultivating little farms of from fifty to a hundred acres, only yielding them some few hundreds a year profit for incessant toil, when the rich lands of the South, under skies as warm and blue as those of Italy, and with an atmosphere as exhilarating as that of France, are thrown open at from a dollar and a half to three dollars per acre. The water-power of the South will be brought into use by this new immigration, and manufactures will spring up in all directions, giving abundant employment to all classes. The happy agricultural state of the South will become a tradition; and with New England wealth, New England's grasping avarice and evil passions will be brought along.

But Davis' surest ground was not speculation, whether about his own future or that of the country. He was more at home when he assayed the past. When he discoursed of the rights of men and states, he was using a language he knew full well from the experience of decades in politics. And in the sphere of political science he proved himself to be the advocate par excellence of the rapidly retreating forces of antifederalism.

In the closing paragraphs of his *Rise and Fall* he condemned the "assumption of the sovereignty of the government of the United States as the corner-stone of our political edifice." This he deemed a revolution, indeed. "Unalienable rights are unknown to this war-begotten theory," he complained. "The day has come in which mankind behold this government founding its highest claims . . . upon deeds done in utter violation of those rights which belonged to its own citizens in every state, North and South."

Then he defined at last the Lost Cause. "When the cause was

lost, what cause was it? Not that of the South only, but the cause of constitutional government, of the supremacy of law, of the natural rights of man." No wonder he could never repent him of secession:

In asserting the right of secession, it has not been my wish to incite to its exercise: I recognize the fact that the war showed it to be impracticable, but this did not prove it to be wrong; and, now that it may not be again attempted, and that the Union may promote the general welfare, it is needful that the truth, the whole truth, should be known, so that crimination and recrimination may for ever cease, and then, on the basis of fraternity and faithful regard for the rights of the States, there may be written on the arch of the Union *Esto perpetua.*

No twentieth-century state-righter has been able to word the gospel of antifederalism more effectively than he. No twentieth-century state-righter ever had more practice at it than he did. No one else has ever had as great an opportunity to implement its preachments.

In November 1889, Davis left Beauvoir for Brierfield, where he came down with acute bronchitis, complicated by his recurring malaria. He was rushed to New Orleans, announcing on arrival that he still had "some things that I have to do in this world." On the morning of December 6, the doctors thought him better. He, however, had now decided otherwise. "I want to tell you that I am not afraid to die," he said firmly to Varina. At seven in the evening, he was offered his medicine. "Pray excuse me. I cannot take it," he murmured; and in three more hours he was dead. The man of will had yielded a little.

Davis was dead, and so, at last, was his Confederacy. All that remained of either was a "memory which should be dear." By the time of his death the high ranks of the Confederates had indeed become thin. Only Wade Hampton, James Longstreet, and Joseph Johnston remained. But already another South had been born—a South that would remember, of course; but it would move forward into the future. Yank and Reb would soon be fighting side by side in Cuba. Presently the industrialization of the South would make another New England of it, perhaps. Davis himself realized all this. Speaking informally to a crowd at Mississippi City in 1888, the eighty-year-old man had at last realized that he was not talking to the tired Confederates with whom he had been consorting for two decades.

The faces I see before me are those of young men; had I not known this I would not have appeared before you, men in whose hands the destinies of our Southland lie. For love of her I break my silence, to speak to you a few words of respectful admonition! The past is dead; let it bury its dead, its hopes, and its aspirations; before you lies the future—a future full of golden promise, a future of expanding national glory, before which all the world shall stand amazed. Let me beseech you to lay aside rancour, all bitter sectional feelings, and to take your places in the ranks of those who will bring about a consummation devoutly to be wished—a reunited country.

No longer did he argue as to whether the New South, the new nation, would be good or bad. They would exist, and whatever came would, he hoped, happen to a Union strong enough to last forever. The Union had never forgiven Davis; he would not let it. But finally he had forgiven the Union. As for the South, Old or New, it was still "our Southland." But the southward flight from Appomattox had ended.

ACKNOWLEDGMENTS

BIBLIOGRAPHY

INDEX

Acknowledgments

The authors are beholden to many persons, books, and libraries for assistance in putting together this book. The bibliography that follows will refer to specific books and manuscripts from which material and ideas were drawn. Here we wish to acknowledge assistance over and above the call of duty or friendship to a host of persons who made easier the task of research and writing or read and criticized the final manuscript. For whatever is good about this book they are largely responsible; for whatever is bad the authors hasten to assume the blame.

The Rev. Roberts Bailey, Grace Church, Gainesville, Georgia
Lynnie Boone, Atlanta, Georgia
Mary Breckinridge, Wendover, Kentucky
Charlotte Capers, Department of Archives and History, Jackson, Mississippi
G. Glenn Clift, Kentucky Historical Society, Frankfort, Kentucky
Courtenay Clingan, Jackson, Mississippi
Herbert Drennon, Mississippi State University
Henry J. Dubester, Library of Congress, Washington, D.C.
Marshall W. Fishwick, Washington and Lee University, Lexington, Virginia
Mary Fontaine, Clarksdale, Mississippi
Sidney Forman, Archivist and Historian, U. S. Military Academy, West Point, New York
Mary L. Garland, Richmond, Virginia
Victor Gondos, Jr., The National Archives, Washington, D.C.
Gilbert Govan, University of Chattanooga, Chattanooga, Tennessee
The Rev. Edward M. Gregory, St. Mark's Church, Richmond, Virginia
Willie D. Halsell, Mississippi State University Library
William B. Hamilton, Duke University, Durham, North Carolina
Albert J. Hanna, Rollins College, Winter Park, Florida
Sadie Galloway Jones, St. Paul's Church, Lynchburg, Virginia

Mary Breckinridge Kirkland, New York City
Warren Kuehl, Mississippi State University
Elizabeth LaBoone, University of Georgia Libraries, Athens, Georgia
Abbott Martin, University of the South, Sewanee, Tennessee
Sylvan Meyer, *Daily Times,* Gainesville, Georgia
Glover Moore, Mississippi State University
Viola Packwood, Freehold Public Library, Freehold, New Jersey
Margarete Peebles, Mississippi State University Library
Paul Ramsey, Princeton University, Princeton, New Jersey
Nellie Mae Rice, Washington and Lee University, Lexington, Virginia
Mattie Russell, Curator of Manuscripts, Duke University Library, Durham, North Carolina
James A. Servies, College of William and Mary, Williamsburg, Virginia
Ralph J. Shoemaker, *The Courier-Journal,* Louisville, Kentucky
Flora B. Walthall, Jackson, Mississippi
W. C. Washburn, Washington and Lee University, Lexington, Virginia
Eudora Welty, Jackson, Mississippi
William W. White, Mississippi State University

A considerable degree of "institutional" indebtedness is hereby acknowledged to the New York Public Library, the New-York Historical Society, the Library of Congress, the National Archives, the Princeton University Library, the Duke University Library, the College of William and Mary Library, the Mississippi State University Library (and those libraries that co-operated with it in making interlibrary loans), and the Mississippi State Department of Archives and History.

In the end, the authors wish to thank those who presided at the typewriters, Marjorie Burger and Ann Chenney, not only for the battles fought with the writers' longhand but also for seeing that the completed manuscript reached the printer in acceptable form.

Bibliography

GENERAL

Alvord, John W., *Letters from the South Relating to the Freedmen* (Washington, 1870).

Andrews, Sidney, *The South Since the War* (New York, 1866).

Ashe, Samuel A., "The Assassination of President Lincoln," *Tyler's Quarterly Historical and Genealogical Magazine,* X (1929), 270-273.

Avary, Myrta Lockett, *Dixie After the War, with an Introduction by General Clement A. Evans* (Boston, 1937).

Badeau, Adam, *Grant in Peace: A Personal Memoir* (Hartford, 1887).

Barnard, Harry, *Rutherford B. Hayes and IIis America* (Indianapolis, 1954).

Barnhart, John D., ed., "Reconstruction on the Lower Mississippi," *Mississippi Valley Historical Review,* XXI (1934-35), 387-396.

Barrett, John G., *Sherman's March Through the Carolinas* (Chapel Hill, 1956).

Beale, Howard K., *The Critical Year; a Study of Andrew Johnson and Reconstruction* (New York, 1930) ; ———, "On Rewriting Reconstruction History," *American Historical Review,* XLV (1940), 807-827.

Bentley, George R., *A History of the Freedmen's Bureau* (Philadelphia, 1955).

Blaine, James G., *Twenty Years in Congress* (Norwich, 1884-86), 2 vols.

Bone, Fanny Z. Lovell, "Louisiana in the Disputed Election of 1876," *Louisiana Historical Quarterly,* XV (1910), 93-116, 234-267.

Bowers, Claude G., *The Tragic Era; the Revolution After Lincoln* (Cambridge, 1929).

Bradford, Gamaliel, *Confederate Portraits* (Boston, 1914).

Buck, Paul H., "The Reconciliation of North and South," Harvard

University, Graduate School of Arts and Sciences, *Summaries of Theses, 1935* (Cambridge, 1937), 139-144; ———, *The Road to Reunion, 1865-1900* (Boston, 1937).

Buck, Solon J., *The Agrarian Crusade* (New Haven, 1921) ; ———, *The Granger Movement* (Cambridge, 1913).

Burgess, John W., *Reconstruction and the Constitution, 1866-1876* (New York, 1902).

Butler, Benjamin F., *Butler's Book* (Boston, 1892).

Cable, George W., *The Silent South* (New York, 1885).

Callender, E. B., *Thaddeus Stevens* (Boston, 1882).

Campbell, Sir George, *White and Black: The Outcome of a Visit to the United States* (New York, 1879).

Carpenter, Jesse T., *The South as a Conscious Minority* (New York, 1930).

Chamberlain, H. R., *The Farmers' Alliance* (New York, 1891).

Chesnut, Mary B., *A Diary from Dixie* (New York, 1905).

Clayton, Powell, *The Aftermath of the Civil War in Arkansas* (New York, 1915).

Cole, Arthur Charles, *The Whig Party in the South* (Washington, 1913).

Coleman, Charles H., *The Election of 1868; the Democratic Effort to Regain Control* (New York, 1933).

Cook, Walter Henry, "Secret Political Societies in the South During the Period of Reconstruction," *Southern Magazine*, III (1869), No. 1, 3-5, 42-43; No. 2, 14-17.

Conkling, A. R., *Life and Letters of Roscoe Conkling* (New York, 1889).

Coulter, E. Merton, *Civil War and Readjustment in Kentucky* (Chapel Hill, 1926) ; ———, *The South During Reconstruction* (Baton Rouge, 1947).

Davis, Susan L., *Authentic History of Ku Klux Klan* (New York, 1924).

Davis, William Watson, *The Civil War and Reconstruction in Florida* (New York, 1913).

Delavigne, J. C., "The Troubles in the South," *Southern Magazine*, IX (1875), 513-519.

Dewitt, David M., *The Impeachment and Trial of Andrew Johnson* (New York, 1903).

Dorris, Jonathan T., *Pardon and Amnesty under Lincoln and Johnson* (Chapel Hill, 1953) ; ———, "Pardoning the Leaders of the Con-federacy," *Mississippi Valley Historical Review*, XV (1928-29), 3-21.

Douglass, Harlan Paul, *Christian Reconstruction in the South* (Boston, 1910).

DuBois, W. E. Burghardt, *Black Reconstruction; an Essay Toward a History of the Part which Black Folk Played in the Attempt to Reconstruct Democracy in America, 1860-1880* (New York, 1935).

DuBose, John W., *Alabama's Tragic Decade, 1865-1874* (Birmingham, 1940).

Dunning, William A., *Reconstruction, Political and Economic 1865-1877* (New York, 1907).

Eckenrode, Hamilton J., *The Political History of Virginia during the Reconstruction* (Baltimore, 1904) ; ———, *Rutherford B. Hayes: Statesman of Reunion* (New York, 1930).

Ficklin, John Rose, *History of Reconstruction in Louisiana* (Baltimore, 1910).

Fleming, Walter L., *Documentary History of Reconstruction* (Cleveland, 1906-07), 2 vols.; ———, *Documents Relating to Reconstruction* (Morgantown, W. Va., 1904).

Flick, Alexander Clarence, *Samuel Jones Tilden; a Study in Political Sagacity* (New York, 1939).

Fuess, Claude Moore, *Carl Schurz* (New York, 1932).

Gipson, Lawrence H., "The Collapse of the Confederacy," *Mississippi Valley Historical Review*, IV (1917-18), 437-58.

Goodrich, F. E., *The Life and Public Services of Grover Cleveland* (Boston, 1884).

Gordon, John B., *Reminiscences of the Civil War* (New York, 1903).

Grant, Ulysses S., *Personal Memoirs* (New York, 1885), 2 vols.

Hamilton, J. G. de Roulhac, *Reconstruction in North Carolina* (Raleigh, 1906).

Hamilton, Peter J., *The Reconstruction Period* (Philadelphia, 1905).

Hanna, Alfred J., ed., "The Confederate Baggage and Treasure Train Ends Its Flight in Florida; a Diary of Tench Francis Tilghman," *Florida Historical Society Quarterly*, XVII (1939), 159-180; ———, *Flight into Oblivion* (Richmond, 1938).

Hendrick, Burton J., *Statesmen of the Lost Cause; Jefferson Davis and His Cabinet* (Boston, 1939).

Henry, Robert S., *The Story of the Confederacy* (New York, 1931) ; ———, *The Story of Reconstruction* (Indianapolis and New York, 1938).

Herbert, Hilary A., *Why the Solid South? Or, Reconstruction and Its Results* (Baltimore, 1890).

Hesseltine, William B., *Confederate Leaders in the New South* (Baton Rouge, 1950) ; ———, "Economic Factors in the Abandonment of Reconstruction," *Mississippi Valley Historical Review*, XXII (1935-36), 191-210; ———, *Ulysses S. Grant, Politician* (New York, 1935).

Hicks, John D., *The Populist Revolt; a History of the Farmers' Alliance and the People's Party* (Minneapolis, 1931).

Horn, Stanley F., *Invisible Empire: The Story of the Ku Klux Klan 1866-1871* (Boston, 1939).

House, Albert V., Jr., "Northern Congressional Democrats as Defenders of the South During Reconstruction," *Journal of Southern History*, VI (1940), 46-71.

Johnson, Robert U., and Buell, Clarence C., *Battles and Leaders of the Civil War* (New York, 1884-87), 4 vols.

Johnson, Roy H., "The Baptist Response to the Rebirth of Nationalism, 1865-1900," *Crozer Quarterly*, X (1933), 429-442.

Jones, James S., *Life of Andrew Johnson* (Greenville, Tenn., 1901).

Josephson, Matthew, *The Politicos, 1865-1896* (New York, 1938).

Kennaway, John H., *On Sherman's Track: The South After the War* (London, 1867).

Kimball, Ralph, "The Lincoln Conspirators and Their Fate," *Wyoming State Bar Association Proceedings . . . for the Years 1930 . . . 1934* (Cheyenne, 1935), 77-81.

King, Edward, *The Great South* (Hartford, 1875).

Lestage, H. Oscar, Jr., "The White League in Louisiana and Its Participation in Reconstruction Riots," *Louisiana Historical Quarterly*, XVIII (1935), 617-695.

Lester, John C., and Wilson, D. L., *The Ku Klux Klan* (New York, 1884).

Lewis, Lloyd, *Sherman, Fighting Prophet* (New York, 1932).

Loewenberg, Bert James, "Efforts of the South to Encourage Immigration, 1865-1900," *South Atlantic Quarterly*, XXXIII (1935), 363-385.

Lonn, Ella, *Reconstruction in Louisiana After 1868* (New York, 1918).

Lynch, Dennis T., *Life of Grover Cleveland* (New York, 1932).

Lynch, John R., *The Facts of Reconstruction* (New York, 1915).

McClendon, R. Earl, "Status of the Ex-Confederate States as Seen in the Readmission of the United States Senators," *American Historical Review*, XLI (1935-36), 703-709.

McElroy, Robert, *Grover Cleveland: The Man and the Statesman* (New York, 1923).

McGinty, Garnie W., *Louisiana Redeemed: The Overthrow of Carpetbag Rule, 1876-1880* (New Orleans, 1941).

McKelvey, Blake, "Penal Slavery and Southern Reconstruction," *Journal of Negro History*, XX (1936), 153-179.

Mallory, Stephen R., "Last Days of the Confederate Government," *McClure's Magazine*, XVI (1900-01), 99-107, 239-248.

Mendenhall, Marjorie Stratford, "Southern Women of a 'Lost Generation,'" *South Atlantic Quarterly*, XXXIII (1935), 334-353.

Merrill, Horace S., *Bourbon Leader: Grover Cleveland and the Democratic Party* (Boston, 1957).

Milton, George Fort, *The Age of Hate; Andrew Johnson and the Radicals* (New York, 1930).

Morgan, W. Scott, *History of the Wheel and Alliance* (New York, 1891).

The Negro in the United States, 1790-1915 (Washington, 1918).

Nevins, Allan, *Grover Cleveland: A Study in Courage* (New York, 1932); ———, *Letters of Grover Cleveland, 1850-1908* (Boston, 1933).

Nichols, Roy F., "A Great Party Which Might Have Been Born in Philadelphia," *Pennsylvania Magazine of History*, LVII (1933), 359-374.

Nixon, Raymond B., *Henry W. Grady—Spokesman of the New South* (New York, 1943).

Nordhoff, Charles, *The Cotton States in the Spring and Summer of 1875* (New York, 1875).

Otkin, Charles H., *The Ills of the South; Or, Relating Causes Hostile to the General Prosperity of the Southern People* (New York, 1894).

Owsley, Frank L., *King Cotton Diplomacy* (Chicago, 1931).

Parker, George F., *Recollections of Grover Cleveland* (New York, 1909).

Patton, James W., *Unionism and Reconstruction in Tennessee, 1860-1869* (Chapel Hill, 1934).

Peck, Harry T., *Twenty Years of the Republic* (New York, 1926).

Pierce, Edward L., *Memoir and Letters of Charles Sumner* (Boston, 1877-93), 4 vols; ———, *Charles Sumner* (Boston, 1893).

Pierce, S., *The Freedmen's Bureau* (Iowa City, 1904).

Pollard, Edward A., *The Lost Cause; a New Southern History of the War of the Confederates* (New York, 1867); ———, *The Lost Cause Regained* (New York, 1868).

Pryor, Sara Agnes, *My Day: Reminiscences of a Long Life* (New York, 1909).

Ramsdell, Charles W., *Reconstruction in Texas* (New York, 1910).

Randall, James G., *The Civil War and Reconstruction* (Boston and New York, 1937); ———, "John Sherman and Reconstruction," *Mississippi Valley Historical Review*, XIX (1932-33), 382-393.

Reagan, John H., *Memoirs* (Washington, 1905).

Reid, Whitelaw, *After the War—a Southern Tour* (Cincinnati, 1866).

Ross, Edmund G., *History of the Impeachment of Andrew Johnson* (Sante Fe, 1896).

Rubin, Louis D., Jr., and Kilpatrick, James Jackson, *The Lasting South* (Chicago, 1957).

Russ, William A., Jr., "Disfranchisement in Virginia under Radical Reconstruction," *Tyler's Quarterly Historical and Genealogical Magazine,* XVII (1935), 25-41; ———, "Radical Disfranchisement in Georgia, 1867-71," *Georgia Historical Quarterly,* XIX (1935), 175-209; ———, "Disfranchisement in Louisiana, 1862-1870," *Louisiana Historical Quarterly,* XVIII (1935), 557-580; ———, "The Negro and White Disfranchisement During the Radical Reconstruction," *Journal of Negro History,* XIX (1935), 171-192; ———, "Radical Disfranchisement in Mississippi," *Mississippi Law Journal,* VII (1935), 365-377; ———, "Radical Disfranchisement in North Carolina, 1867-1868," *North Carolina Historical Review,* XI (1934), 271-283; ———, "Radical Disfranchisement in South Carolina (1867-1868)," *Susquehanna University Studies,* I (1939), 148-160; ———, "Radical Disfranchisement in Texas, 1867-70," *Southwestern Historical Quarterly,* XXXVIII (1935), 40-52; ———, "Registration and Disfranchisement under Radical Reconstruction," *Mississippi Valley Historical Review,* XXI (1933-34), 163-180; ———, "Was There Danger of a Second Civil War during Reconstruction?" *Mississippi Valley Historical Review,* XXV (1937-38), 39-58.

Schurz, Carl, *Reminiscences of Carl Schurz* (New York, 1907-08), 3 vols.

Sherman, General William T., *Memoirs* (New York, 1875).

Shugg, Roger W., *The Origins of Class Struggle in Louisiana* (Baton Rouge, 1939).

Simkins, Francis B., *A History of the South* (New York, 1953); ———, "New Viewpoints of Southern Reconstruction," *Journal of Southern History,* V (1939), 49-61.

Singletary, Otis A., *Negro Militia and Reconstruction* (Austin, 1957).

Smith, Theodore C., *The Life and Letters of James Abram Garfield* (New Haven, 1925), 2 vols.

Somers, Robert, *The Southern States Since the War* (London, 1871).

Squires, William H. T., *Unleashed at Long Last; Reconstruction in Virginia, April 9, 1865-January 26, 1870* (Portsmouth, Va., 1939).

Staples, Thomas S., *Reconstruction in Arkansas, 1862-1874* (New York, 1923).

Stearns, Charles, *The Black Man of the South and the Rebels* (New York, 1872).

Sterling, Ada, ed., *A Belle of the Fifties: Memoirs of Mrs. Clay of Alabama* (New York, 1904).

Storey, Moorfield, *Charles Sumner* (New York, 1900).

Stryker, Lloyd P., *Andrew Johnson: A Study in Courage* (New York, 1929).

Swint, Henry L., *The Northern Teachers in the South 1862-1870* (Nashville, 1941).

Taylor, Alrutheus A., *The Negro in the Reconstruction of Virginia* (Washington, 1926).

Taylor, Richard, *Destruction and Reconstruction: Personal Experiences of the Late War* (New York, 1879).

Tebeau, Charlton Watson, "The Planter in the Lower South, 1865-1880," *University of Iowa Abstracts in History,* II (1927-34), 137-147; ———, "Some Aspects of Planter-Freedmen Relations, 1865-1880," *Journal of Negro History,* XXI (1937), 130-150.

Testimony Taken by the Joint Select Committee to Inquire into the Condition of Affairs in the Late Insurrectionary States (Washington, 1872), 13 vols.

Thomas, David Y., *Arkansas in War and Reconstruction, 1861-1874* (Little Rock, 1926).

Thompson, Holland, *The New South* (New Haven, 1921).

Trowbridge, John T., *A Picture of the Desolated States and the Work of Restoration, 1865-1868* (Hartford, 1868).

Wade, John D., "What the South Figured: 1865-1914," *Southern Review,* III (1937), 360-367.

Wallace, John, *Carpetbag Rule in Florida* (Jacksonville, 1888).

Walmsley, James Elliott, "The Last Meeting of the Confederate Cabinet," *Mississippi Valley Historical Review,* VI (1919-20), 336-349.

Watterson, Henry, "The Hayes-Tilden Contest for the Presidency," *Century Magazine,* LXXXVI (1913), 3-20; ———, *Marse Henry: An Autobiography* (New York, 1919), 2 vols.

Wesley, Charles H., *The Collapse of the Confederacy* (Washington, 1937).

Williams, Charles R., ed., *Diary and Letters of Rutherford Birchard Hayes* (Columbus, Ohio, 1926), 5 vols.; ———, *Life of Rutherford Birchard Hayes* (Boston, 1914), 2 vols.

Williams, T. Harry, "An Analysis of Some Reconstruction Attitudes," *Journal of Southern History,* XII (1946), 469-486.

Winston, Robert W., *Andrew Johnson: Plebeian and Patriot* (New York, 1928).

Woodburn, James A., *Life of Thaddeus Stevens* (Indianapolis, 1913).

Woodward, Comer Vann, *Origins of the New South, 1877-1913* (Baton Rouge, 1951); ———, *Reunion and Reaction: The Compromise of 1877 and the End of Reconstruction* (Boston, 1951).

ROBERT E. LEE

Adams, Charles F., *Lee's Centennial: An Address* (Chicago, 1948).

Blakely, Paul L., "Lee the Educator," *America*, XL (1929), 360-361.

Bond, Christiana, "Recollections of General Robert E. Lee," *South Atlantic Quarterly*, XXIV (1925), 333-348.

Boyd, William K., "Robert E. Lee," *South Atlantic Quarterly*, XXXIV (1935), 211-219.

Bradford, Gamaliel, "A Hero's Conscience: A Study of Robert E. Lee," *Atlantic*, CVI (1910), 730-739; ———, "Lee After the War," *South Atlantic Quarterly*, X (1911), 301-313; ———, *Lee the American* (Boston, 1912); ———, "The Social and Domestic Life of Robert E. Lee," *South Atlantic Quarterly*, X (1911), 103-118; ———, "The Spiritual Life of Robert E. Lee," *Atlantic*, CVIII (1911), 501-512.

Brooks, William E., *Lee of Virginia, a Biography* (Indianapolis, 1932).

Colby, Elbridge, "Introducing a New Lee," *Military Engineer*, XXVII (1935), 123-124.

Dabney, Virginius, "The Original of Lee's Last Order," *Journal of American History*, XX (1926), 160-174.

Davis, Burke, *Gray Fox: Robert E. Lee and the Civil War* (New York, 1956).

Emery, Russell Guy, *Robert E. Lee* (New York, 1951).

Ewing, Robert, "Gen. Robert E. Lee's Inspiration to the Industrial Rehabilitation of the South, Exemplified in the Development of Southern Iron Interests," *Tennessee Historical Magazine*, IX (1926), 215-230.

Fishwick, Marshall, *General Lee's Photographer* (Chapel Hill, 1954).

Fishwick, Marshall William, and Hollis, William M., eds., *Preliminary Checklist of Writings About R. E. Lee* (Charlottesville, 1951).

Fitzhugh, Mrs. William H., and Lee, Mrs. R. E., "Funeral of Mrs. G. W. P. Custis and Death of General R. E. Lee, Described in Contemporary Letters," *Virginia Magazine of History*, XXXV (1927), 22-26.

Frank, Glenn, "Being Dead He Yet Speaks—Robert E. Lee," *Virginia Journal of Education*, XXV (1931), 211-213.

Freeman, Douglas Southall, *Robert E. Lee* (New York, 1934-35), 4 vols.; ———, *Lee's Lieutenants: A Study in Command* (New York, 1942-44), 3 vols.

Fuller, John Frederick Charles, *Grant & Lee, a Study in Personality and Generalship* (London, 1933).

Gaines, Francis Pendleton, *Lee: The Background of a Great Decision, August, 1865: An Address to the Officers and Directors of the Robert E. Lee Memorial Foundation, Lee Chapel, October 12, 1934* (Lexington, 1934).

Grant, Ulysses Simpson, "Lee at Appomattox," *Pennsylvania Magazine of History*, LXXV (1951).

Hendrick, Burton J., *The Lees of Virginia; Biography of a Family* (New York, 1937).

Hobeika, John E., *Lee, the Soul of Honor; an Appreciation by an Orientalist with Additional Facts* (Boston, 1932).

Horn, Stanley F., *Robert E. Lee Reader* (Indianapolis, 1949).

Jenkins, C. W., "Robert E. Lee—an Example of Leadership," *Military Engineer*, XXII (1930), 32-38.

Jervey, Byrd Pendleton, "Derwent in Powhatan County and General Robert E. Lee's Sojourn There in the Summer of 1865," *Virginia Magazine of History*, LVIII (1950), 184-197.

Johnstone, W. J., *Robert E. Lee the Christian* (New York, 1933).

Jones, J. William, *Personal Reminiscences, Anecdotes and Letters of General Robert E. Lee* (New York, 1874).

Lee, Fitzhugh, *General Lee* (New York, 1894).

Lee, George Taylor, "Reminiscences of General Robert E. Lee, 1865-68," *South Atlantic Quarterly*, XXVI (1927), 236-251.

Lee, Robert E., Jr., *Recollections and Letters of General Robert E. Lee* (New York, 1905).

McCabe, James D., Jr., *Life and Campaigns of General Robert E. Lee* (New York, 1866).

McNeel, John A., "About General Lee and Amnesty," *Confederate Veteran*, XVIII (1910), 513-515.

Marsh, C. S., "General Lee and a School of Commerce," *Journal of Political Economics*, XXXIV (1925), 657-659.

Marshall, Charles, "The Surrender of General Lee," *Confederate Veteran*, XXXII (1924), 298-300.

Maurice, Sir Frederick, *Robert E. Lee the Soldier* (Boston, 1925).

Meredith, Roy, *The Face of Robert E. Lee in Life and in Legend* (New York, 1947).

Miers, Earl Schenck, *Robert E. Lee: A Great Life in Brief* (New York, 1956).

Nelson, James Poyntz, "Reminiscences of General Robert E. Lee as President of Washington College, now Washington and Lee University," *Virginia Journal of Education,* XVIII (1924-25), 189-192.

Pollard, E. A., *Robert E. Lee . . . With a Record of . . . His Companions in Arms* (New York, 1871).

Preston, Walter Creigh, *Lee, West Point and Lexington* (Yellow Springs, Ohio, 1934).

Report of the Joint Committee on Reconstruction, at the First Session of the Thirty-Ninth Congress (Washington, 1866).

Riley, Franklin L., *General Robert E. Lee After Appomattox* (New York, 1922).

Smyth, Clifford, *Robert E. Lee, Who Brought the South Back to the Union* (New York and London, 1931).

Still, S. A., "Lee at Appomattox," *Methodist Quarterly Review,* LXIX (1920), 317-332.

Taylor, Walter H., *General Lee: His Campaigns in Virginia, 1861-1865, with Personal Reminiscences* (Norfolk, 1906).

Weaver, Richard M., "Lee the Philosopher," *Georgia Review,* II (1948), 297-303.

White, Henry A., *Robert E. Lee and the Southern Confederacy* (New York, 1897).

Winston, Robert W., *Robert E. Lee; a Biography* (New York, 1934).

Young, James C., *Marse Robert, Knight of the Confederacy* (New York, 1929).

MATTHEW FONTAINE MAURY

Beehler, W. H., "Origin and Work of the Division of Marine Meteorology, Hydrographic Office," *Proceedings, U.S. Naval Institute,* XIX (1893), 267-281.

Brock, R. A., "Matthew Fontaine Maury—Philosopher of the Seas," *Virginia and Virginians* (Richmond and Toledo, 1888), I, 268-270.

Brown, Ralph Minthorne, "Commander Matthew Fontaine Maury," *Southern Literary Messenger,* VII (1840), 147-148.

Caldwell, Andrew J., "Matthew Fontaine Maury," *Tennessee Historical Magazine,* 2d ser., I (1931), 276-278.

Caskie, Jacquelin A., *Life and Letters of Matthew Fontaine Maury* (Richmond, 1928).

Chandler, A. B., "Matthew Fontaine Maury," *Southern Historical Society Papers,* n.s., VI (1923), 223-228.

Corbin, D. F. M., *A Life of Matthew Fontaine Maury, U.S.N., and C.S.N.* (London, 1888).

Coxe, Lewis, "Matthew Fontaine Maury," *U.S. Naval Institute Proceedings,* LI (1925), 1193-1196.

Dill, Jacob S., "American Scientist Who Charted the Oceans—Pathfinder of the Seas," *Journal of American History,* IV (1910), 319-339.

Dorsey, Sarah A., *Recollections of Henry W. Allen* (New York, 1866).

Edwards, John N., *Shelby and His Men or the War in the West* (Cincinnati, 1867).

Edwards, Mary V., ed., *John N. Edwards: Biography, Memoirs, Reminiscences and Recollections* (Kansas City, Mo., 1889).

Gwin, William McKendree, "Memories of the History of the United States, Mexico and California," MS., Division of Manuscripts, Library of Congress.

Hanna, Alfred J., "The Role of Matthew Fontaine Maury in the Mexican Empire," an address before the annual meeting of the Virginia Historical Society, January 17, 1947, MS., Library of the Embassy of the United States, Mexico, D. F.

Harmon, George D., "Confederate Migrations to Mexico," *Hispanic American Historical Review,* XVII (1937), 459-487.

Hellweg, J. F., "The Pathfinder of the Seas," *U.S. Naval Institute Proceedings,* LIX (1933), 93-96.

Hill, Lawrence F., "The Confederate Exodus to Latin America," *Southwestern Historical Quarterly,* XXXIX (1935-36), 100-134.

In Memoriam, Matthew Fontaine Maury (Lexington, 1873).

Lewis, Charles L., *Matthew Fontaine Maury, the Pathfinder of the Seas* (Annapolis, 1927) ; ———, "Matthew Fontaine Maury," *Confederate Veteran,* XXXIII (1925), 296-301; ———, "Maury and the 'Messenger,' " *Southern Literary Messenger,* I (1939), 165-171.

Luis, Blaiso José, *Maximilian, Emperor of Mexico, Memoirs of His Private Secretary* (New Haven, 1934).

"Matthew Fontaine Maury," *Confederate Veteran,* XXVI (1918), 54-56.

"Matthew Fontaine Maury," *Leisure Hour,* XV (1866), 679.

Maury, Matthew F., *Address of Com. M. F. Maury, Before the Fair of the Agricultural and Mechanical Society of Memphis, Tenn., Delivered at the Fair Grounds October 17, 1871* (Memphis, 1871) ; ———, "Address to the National Agricultural Association, St. Louis, Mo., May 29, 1872," MS., Library of Congress; ———, "Addresses to the Memphis Convention of Southern and Western States, November 12, 1845," *Southern Literary Messenger,* XI (1845), 577-602; ———, "Direct Foreign Trade with the South,"

DeBow's Commercial Review, XII (1851), 126, 381; ————, *Elementary, Practical, and Theoretical Treatise on Navigation* (Philadelphia, 1845); ————, *First Lessons in Geography* (New York, 1868); ————, *Founding and Development of the United States Hydrographic Office* (Washington, 1887); ————, "Letter from Commodore M. F. Maury, Virginia Military Institute, Lexington, Virginia, Nov. 17, 1869, to Thomas P. Atkinson, M.D., Danville, Virginia," Norfolk and Great Western Railroad Company, *Proceedings, Third Annual Meeting of Stockholders*, Dec. 2, 1869 (Richmond, 1870), 24-29; ————, *Manual of Geography, a Complete Treatise on Mathematical, Physical, and Political Geography* (New York, 1870); ————, *Physical Geography* (New York and Baltimore, 1873); ————, *Physical Geography for Schools and General Readers* (London, 1864); ————, *Physical Geography of the Sea* (New York, 1855); ————, *Physical Survey of Virginia* (Richmond, 1868); ————, "A Scheme for Rebuilding Southern Commerce: Direct Trade with the South, By an Officer of the U.S. Navy," *Southern Literary Messenger*, VI (1839), 3-12; ————, "Science and the Bible: Educational Ideals of the South," MS., Library of Congress; ————, *Steam Lanes Across the Atlantic* (Washington, 1872).

Maury, Robert L., *A Brief Sketch of the Work of Matthew Fontaine Maury During the War, 1861-1865* (Richmond, 1915).

Mitchell, S. A., "Matthew Fontaine Maury," *Science,* n.s., LXXIII (1931), 632-634.

Noll, A. H., *General Kirby-Smith* (Sewanee, Tenn., 1907).

Nunn, W. C., *Escape from Reconstruction* (Fort Worth, 1956).

Rippy, J. Fred, "Mexican Projects of the Confederates," *Southwestern Historical Quarterly*, XXII (1918).

Rister, Carl Coke, "Carlota, a Confederate Colony in Mexico," *Journal of Southern History*, XI (1945), 33-50.

Smith, C. Alphonso, "Matthew Fontaine Maury," *Southern Literary Studies* (Chapel Hill, 1927), 168-181.

Terrell, Alexander W., *From Texas to Mexico and the Court of Maximilian in 1865* (Dallas, 1933).

Wayland, John W., *The Pathfinder of the Seas; the Life of Matthew Fontaine Maury* (Richmond, 1930).

Wickman, Julia P., "Matthew Fontaine Maury, Pathfinder of the Seas," *Huguenot Society of South Carolina Transactions*, XXXVI (1931), 35-59.

Wilson, Beckles, *John Slidell and the Confederates in Paris, 1862-1865* (New York, 1932).

JOHN C. BRECKINRIDGE

Breckinridge, John C., *Address of Hon. John C. Breckinridge, Vice President of the United States, Preceding the Removal of the Senate from the Old to the New Chamber* (Washington, 1859).

Campbell, John A., *Recollections of the Evacuation of Richmond* (Baltimore, 1880) ; ———, *Reminiscences and Documents Relating to the Civil War During the Year 1865* (Baltimore, 1887).

Clay, Cassius M., *Cassius Marcellus Clay, Life and Memoirs, Writings and Speeches* (Cincinnati, 1886).

Coulter, E. Merton, *The Civil War and Readjustment in Kentucky* (Chapel Hill, 1926).

Dawes, H. L., "Two Vice-Presidents," *Century*, LVII (1895), 463-465.

Dickison, Mary Elizabeth, *Dickison and His Men* (Louisville, 1890).

Dowd, Clement, *Life of Zebulon B. Vance* (Charlotte, 1897).

Duke, Basil W., *History of Morgan's Cavalry* (Cincinnati, 1867) ; ———, *Reminiscences of General Basil W. Duke* (Garden City, 1911).

Farnum, George R., "John Cabell Breckinridge, Lawyer, Statesman and Soldier of the Confederacy," *American Bar Association Journal*, XXIX (1943), 270-271.

Hanna, Alfred J., "Escape of John Cabell Breckinridge as Revealed in His Diary," *Kentucky State Historical Society Register*, XXXVII (1939), 323-333; ———, *Flight into Oblivion* (Richmond, 1938).

Johnson, E. Polk, *A History of Kentucky and Kentuckians* (Chicago, 1912).

Johnston, William Preston, *The Life of Albert Sidney Johnston* (New York, 1878).

Kirwan, Albert D., ed., *Johnny Green of the Orphan Brigade* (Louisville, 1956).

Maltby, Mary Breckinridge, *Mary Cyrene Breckinridge* (New York [?], 1910).

Moore, Frank, ed., *Rebellion Record* (New York, 1862), 10 vols.

Mosby, John S., *Memoirs* (Boston, 1917).

Packard, Joseph, "Ordnance Matters at the Close," *Confederate Veteran*, XVI (1908), 227-229.

Parker, William H., *Recollections of a Naval Officer* (New York, 1883).

Patrick, Rembert W., *Jefferson Davis and His Cabinet* (Baton Rouge, 1944).

Ranck, George W., *History of Lexington, Kentucky* (Cincinnati, 1872).

Reagan, John H., *Memoirs* (New York, 1906).

Sherman, William T., *Memoirs* (New York, 1875), 2 vols.

Speeches and Proceedings Upon the Announcement of the Death of Hon. Jno. C. Breckinridge in the Senate and House of Representatives of Kentucky (Frankfort, 1876).

Stillwell, Lucille, *Born to Be a Statesman: John Cabell Breckinridge* (Caldwell, Idaho, 1936).

Swallow, W. H., "Retreat of the Confederate Government from Richmond to the Gulf," *Magazine of American History*, XV (1896), 596-608.

Thompson, Edwin Porter, *History of the First Kentucky Brigade* (Cincinnati, 1868).

Townsend, William H., *Lincoln and His Wife's Home Town* (Indianapolis, 1929).

Wise, John S., *The End of an Era* (Boston, 1900).

Wood, John Taylor, "Escape of the Confederate Secretary of War," *Century Magazine*, XLVII (1893), 110-123.

Young, J. Russell, *Around the World with General Grant* (New York, 1879), 2 vols.

Young, L. D., *Reminiscences of a Soldier of the Orphan Brigade* (Louisville, 1917).

NATHAN BEDFORD FORREST

Bradley, Mary Forrest, "Lieutenant General Nathan Bedford Forrest," *Southern Magazine*, III (1869), 15-16, 42.

Capers, Gerald W., *The Biography of a River Town: Memphis, Its Heroic Age* (Chapel Hill, 1939).

Coulter, E. Merton, *William G. Brownlow* (Chapel Hill, 1937).

Davidson, Donald, *The Tennessee: The New River* (New York, 1948).

Dinkins, James, "The Last Campaign of Forrest's Cavalry," *Confederate Veteran*, XXXV (1927), 136-139, 177-179.

Drake, Edwin L., ed., *The Annals of the Army of Tennessee* (Nashville, 1878).

Eckenrode, Hamilton J., *Life of Nathan Forrest* (Richmond, 1918).

Fertig, James W., *The Secession and Reconstruction of Tennessee* (Chicago, 1898).

French, Samuel G., *Two Wars: An Autobiography* (Nashville, 1901).

Gailor, T. F., "General Forrest," *Sewanee Review*, IX (1901), 1-12.

Greer, Allen J., "Forrest: Natural Fighting Leader of Fighting Men," *Cavalry Journal*, XLVI (1937), 329-332.

Hearn, Lafcadio, *Occidental Gleanings* (New York, 1925), 2 vols.

Henry, Robert S., *As They Saw Forrest; Some Recollections and Comments of Contemporaries* (Jackson, Tenn., 1956) ; ————, *"First With the Most" Forrest* (New York, 1944).

Johnson, Adam R., *The Partisan Rangers of the Confederate States Army* (Louisville, 1904).

Jordan, Thomas J., and Pryor, J. P., *The Campaigns of Lieutenant General N. B. Forrest and of Forrest's Cavalry* (New Orleans and New York, 1868).

Lyon, Adelia C., *Reminiscences of the Civil War* (San Jose, Calif., 1907).

Lytle, Andrew Nelson, *Bedford Forrest and His Critter Company* (New York, 1931).

McIlwaine, Shields, *Memphis, Down in Dixie* (New York, 1948).

Mathes, J. Harvey, *Bedford Forrest* (New York, 1902).

Reports of the Committee on the Conduct of the War: Fort Pillow Massacre, 38th Congress, 1st Session, House of Representatives Report, No. 65 (Washington, 1864).

Ridley, Bromfield L., *Battles and Sketches of the Army of Tennessee* (Mexico, Mo., 1906).

Seitz, Don, *Braxton Bragg, General of the Confederacy* (New York, 1923).

Shay, J. A., "The Downfall of the Radicals in Tennessee," *East Tennessee Historical Society Publishers,* V (1933), 105-125.

Sheppard, Eric William, *Bedford Forrest, the Confederacy's Greatest Cavalryman* (New York, 1930).

Taylor, Alrutheus A., *The Negro in Tennessee, 1865-1880* (Washington, 1941).

"War Memories—Margaret Ketcham Ward," *Report of the Committee of the Senate Upon the Relations Between Labor and Capital* (Washington, 1885).

Watkins, Sam R., *"Co. Aytch," Maury Grays, First Tennessee Regiment* (Chattanooga, 1900).

Wilson, Maj. Gen. James H., *Under the Old Flag* (New York, 1912).

Witherspoon, William, *Reminiscences of a Scout, Spy and Soldier of Forrest's Cavalry* (Jackson, 1906).

Wolseley, Field Marshal Viscount, "Lieutenant-General N. B. Forrest," *Southern Historical Society Papers,* XX (1892), 325-335.

Wyeth, John A., *Life of General N. B. Forrest* (New York, 1899).

Young, J. P., *The Seventh Tennessee Cavalry (Confederate) : A History* (Nashville, 1930).

ALEXANDER H. STEPHENS

Abele, Rudolph von, *Alexander H. Stephens: A Biography* (New York, 1946).

Acceptance and Unveiling of the Statue of Alexander Hamilton Stephens (Washington, 1929).

Andrews, Eliza F., *The Wartime Journal of a Georgia Girl* (New York, 1908).

Avary, Myrta L., ed., *Recollections of Alexander H. Stephens; His Diary Kept When a Prisoner at Fort Warren, Boston Harbor, 1865, Giving Incidents and Reflections of His Prison Life and Some Letters and Reminiscences* (New York, 1910).

Avery, Isaac W., *History of Georgia* (New York, 1881); ———, *In Memory, the Last Sickness, Death, and Funeral Obsequies of Alexander H. Stephens* (Atlanta, 1883).

Bass, James Horace, "The Attack upon the Confederate Administration in Georgia in the Spring of 1864," *Georgia Historical Quarterly*, XVIII (1934), 228-247.

Beck, Nemias Bramlette, "Alexander H. Stephens, Orator," *University of Wisconsin Summaries of Doctoral Dissertations*, III (1938), 275-277.

Boykin, Samuel, *A Memorial Volume of the Honorable Howell Cobb of Georgia* (Philadelphia, 1870).

Cleveland, Henry, *Alexander H. Stephens; in Public and Private* (Philadelphia, 1866).

Felton, Rebecca, *My Memories of Georgia Politics* (Atlanta, 1911).

Fielder, Herbert, *Life, Times and Speeches of Joseph E. Brown* (Springfield, Mass., 1883).

Flippin, Percy S., *Herschel V. Johnson, State Rights Unionist* (Richmond, 1931).

Ford, Henry Jones, *The Cleveland Era* (New Haven, 1919).

Grice, Warren, *The Georgia Bench and Bar* (Macon, 1931).

Hill, Benjamin H., Jr., *Senator Benjamin H. Hill of Georgia; His Life, Speeches and Writings* (Atlanta, 1893).

Hill, Louise B., *Joseph E. Brown and the Confederacy* (Chapel Hill, 1939).

Howard, Annie Hornady, and Smith, Florine Harden, "Intimate Glimpses into the Life of Alexander Hamilton Stephens," *Georgia Historical Quarterly*, XVI (1932), 38-46.

Johnston, Herschel V., "Autobiography," *American Historical Review*, XXX (1924-25), 311-336.

Johnston, Richard M., *Autobiography* (Washington, 1890).

Johnston, Richard M., and Browne, William H., *Life of Alexander H. Stephens* (Philadelphia, 1878).

Kirkland, Edward Chase, *Peacemakers of 1864* (New York, 1927).

Knight, Lucian Lamar, *Alexander H. Stephens, the Sage of Liberty Hall* (Athens, Ga., 1930) ; ———, *Georgia and Georgians* (Chicago, 1917), 6 vols.

Miller, Stephen F., *The Bench and Bar of Georgia* (Philadelphia, 1858).

Pearce, Haywood J., *Benjamin H. Hill: Secession and Reconstruction* (Chicago, 1928).

Pendleton, Louis, *Alexander H. Stephens* (Philadelphia, 1908).

Phillips, Ulrich B., ed., *The Correspondence of Robert Toombs, Alexander H. Stephens, and Howell Cobb, Annual Report of the American Historical Association for the Year 1911* (Washington, 1913) ; ———, "Georgia and State Rights," *American Historical Association Annual Report, 1901* (Washington, 1902), Vol. 2; ———, *The Life of Robert Toombs* (New York, 1913).

Rabun, James Z., "Alexander H. Stephens and Jefferson Davis," *American Historical Review,* LVIII (1953), 290-321.

Richardson, Eudora Ramsay, *Little Aleck; a Life of Alexander H. Stephens, the Fighting Vice-President of the Confederacy* (Indianapolis, 1932).

Stephens, Alexander H., *Compendium of History of the United States* (New York and Columbia, S.C., 1872) ; ———, *Comprehensive and Popular History of the United States* (Baltimore, 1882) ; ———, *A Constitutional View of the Late War Between the States* (Philadelphia, 1868-70), 2 vols.; ———, *The Reviewers Review* (New York, 1872).

Stovall, Pleasant A., *Robert Toombs, Statesman, Speaker, Soldier, Sage . . .* (New York, 1892).

Thompson, C. Mildred, *Reconstruction in Georgia, Economic, Social, Political, 1865-1872* (New York, 1915).

Trent, William P., *Southern Statesmen of the Old Regime* (New York, 1897), 197-253.

Waddell, James D., *A Biographical Sketch of Linton Stephens* (Atlanta, 1877).

Williams, Jack K., "Three Georgians on Sectional Reconciliation," *Emory University Quarterly,* VII (1951), 217-236.

Woodward, C. Vann, *Tom Watson, Agrarian Rebel* (New York, 1938).

Woolley, Edwin C., *The Reconstruction of Georgia* (New York, 1901).

L. Q. C. LAMAR

Andrews, Garnett, *Reminiscences of an Old Georgia Lawyer* (Atlanta, 1870).

Brough, Charles H., "The Clinton Riot," *Publications of the Mississippi Historical Society,* VI (1902), 53-63.

Callahan, James M., *The Diplomatic History of the Southern Confederacy* (Baltimore, 1901).

Carson, Hampton L., *History of the Supreme Court* (Philadelphia, 1902), 2 vols.

Cate, Wirt Armistead, "Lamar and the Frontier Hypothesis," *Journal of Southern History,* I (1935), 497-501; ———, *Lucius Q. C. Lamar* (Chapel Hill, 1935).

Chamberlain, Hope S., *Old Days in Chapel Hill* (Chapel Hill, 1926).

Connelly, William, ed., *The Writings of John James Ingalls* (Kansas City, Mo., 1902).

Duren, W. A., *Charles Betts Galloway* (Emory, Ga., 1932).

Fitzgerald, Oscar P., *Judge Longstreet: A Life Sketch* (Nashville, 1891).

Garner, James W., *Reconstruction in Mississippi* (New York, 1901); ———, "The Senatorial Career of J. Z. George," *Publications of the Mississippi Historical Society,* VII (1903), 245-262.

Gordon, John B., *Reminiscences of the Civil War* (New York, 1903).

Hamilton, J. G. de Roulhac, "Lamar of Mississippi," *Virginia Quarterly Review,* VIII (1932), 77-89.

Haworth, Paul L., *The Hayes-Tilden Election* (Indianapolis, 1927).

Hoar, George F., *Autobiography of Seventy Years* (New York, 1903), 2 vols.

Johnston, Frank, "Suffrage and Reconstruction in Mississippi," *Publications of the Mississippi Historical Society,* VI (1902), 141-244.

Judson, Harry Pratt, "American Politics: A Study of Four Careers," *The Review of Reviews,* VII (1893), 159-172.

Kendel, Julia, "Reconstruction in Lafayette County," *Publications of the Mississippi Historical Society,* XIII (1913), 223-264.

Lamar, Clarinda P., *The Life of Joseph Rucker Lamar* (New York, 1926).

Lamar, Mirabeau Buonaparte, *Papers,* ed. by C. A. Gulic and Katherine Elliott (Austin, 1922), 6 vols.

Lamar, W. H., "Thomas Lamar of the Province of Maryland," *Southern History Association Publications,* I (1897), 203-210.

Leftwich, George J., "Reconstruction in Monroe County," *Publications of the Mississippi Historical Society,* IX (1906), 53-84.

Lowry, Robert, and McCardle, W. H., *A History of Mississippi* (Jackson, 1891).

McNeilly, J. S., "Climax and Collapse of Reconstruction in Mississippi," *Publications of the Mississippi Historical Society,* XII (1912), 283-474; ———, "The Enforcement Act of 1871 and the Ku Klux Klan in Mississippi," *Publications of the Mississippi Historical Society,* IX (1906), 109-171; ———, "War and Reconstruction in Mississippi, 1863-1890," *Publications of the Mississippi Historical Society,* Centenary Series, II (1918), 165-536.

Mayes, Edward, *Genealogical Notes on a Branch of the Family of Mayes and on the Related Families* (Jackson, 1928) ; ———, *Lucius Q. C. Lamar: His Life, Times, and Speeches* (Nashville, 1896).

Montgomery, Frank, *Reminiscences of a Mississippian in Peace and War* (Cincinnati, 1901).

Rowland, Dunbar, *History of Mississippi* (Jackson, 1925), 2 vols.; ———, "The Rise and Fall of Negro Rule in Mississippi," *Publications of the Mississippi Historical Society,* II (1899), 189-200.

Smedes, Susan Dabney, *Memorials of a Southern Planter* (Baltimore, 1888).

Waddell, John N., *Memorials of Academic Life* (Richmond, 1891).

Wade, John Donald, *Augustus Baldwin Longstreet: A Study of the Development of Culture in the South* (New York, 1924).

Warren, Henry W., *Reminiscences of a Mississippi Carpetbagger* (Worcester, 1914).

Wells, James M., *The Chisholm Massacre* (Washington, 1878).

Wharton, Vernon L., *The Negro in Mississippi, 1865-1890* (Chapel Hill, 1947).

Woods, Thomas H., "A Sketch of the Mississippi Secession Convention of 1861," *Publications of the Mississippi Historical Society,* VI (1902), 91-104.

JOSEPH E. JOHNSTON

Buford, M. M., "Surrender of Johnston's Army," *Confederate Veteran,* XXVIII (1920), 170-172.

Eliot, E., *West Point in the Confederacy* (New York, 1941).

Fremantle, Sir Arthur James Lyon, *Three Months in the Southern States: April-June, 1863* (New York, 1864).

Govan, Gilbert E., and Livingood, James W., *A Different Valor: The Story of Gen. Joseph E. Johnston, C.S.A.* (Indianapolis, 1956).

Harvie, E. J., "General Joseph E. Johnston," *Confederate Veteran,* XVIII (1910), 521-523.

Hendrick, Burton J., *Statesmen of the Lost Cause* (Boston, 1939).

Horn, Stanley F., *The Army of Tennessee* (Indianapolis, 1941).

Hughes, Robert M., *General Johnston* (New York, 1897); ———, "Joseph Eggleston Johnston, Soldier and Man," *William and Mary Quarterly,* XIII (1933), 63-84.

James, Alfred P., "General Joseph Eggleston Johnston, Storm Center of the Confederate Army," *Mississippi Valley Historical Review,* XIV (1927-28), 342-359.

Johnson, Bradley T., *A Memoir of the Life and Public Service of Joseph E. Johnston* (Baltimore, 1891).

Johnston, Joseph E., *Narrative of Military Operations Directed During the Late War Between the States* (New York, 1874).

Jones, J. B., *A Rebel War Clerk's Diary* (Philadelphia, 1866), 2 vols.

Myers, William S., *A Study in Personality, Gen. George Brinton McClellan* (New York, 1934).

Noll, Arthur H., ed., *Doctor Quintard, Chaplain C.S.A. and Second Bishop of Tennessee. Being His Story of the War (1861-1865)* (Sewanee, 1905).

Parks, J. H., *General Edmund Kirby Smith, C.S.A.* (Baton Rouge, 1954).

Pollard, E. A., *Lee and His Lieutenants* (New York, 1867).

Porter, A. T., *In Memoriam. Gen. Joseph E. Johnston* (Charleston, 1891).

Taylor, Richard, *Destruction and Reconstruction* (New York, 1879).

WADE HAMPTON

Allen, Walter, *Governor Chamberlain's Administration* (New York, 1908).

Ball, William W., *The State That Forgot: South Carolina's Surrender to Democracy* (Indianapolis, 1932).

Cauthen, Charles E., ed., *Family Letters of the Three Wade Hamptons, 1782-1901* (Columbia, S.C., 1953).

Cooke, John Esten, *Wearing of the Gray* (New York, 1867).

Daly, Louise Porter, *Alexander Cheves Haskell: The Portrait of a Man* (Norwood, Mass., 1934).

DeForest, John William, *A Union Officer in the Reconstruction* (New Haven, 1948).

Gibbes, James G., ed., *Who Burnt Columbia?* (Newberry, S.C., 1902).

Hampton, Wade, *Address on the Life and Character of Gen. Robert E. Lee, Delivered on the 12th of October, 1871, before the Society of Confederate Soldiers and Sailors in Maryland* (Baltimore, 1871); ———, "Brigandage on Our Railroads," *North American Review,*

CLIX (1894), 665-668; ———, *Address on the Life and Character of Gen. Robert E. Lee* (Baltimore, 1871) ; ———, "Lesson of the Recent Strikes," *North American Review,* CLIX (1894), 188-195; ———, "The Race Problem; What to Do with the Negro," *Arena,* V (1890), 132-138.

Hanson, Joseph Mills, "Wade Hampton," *Cavalry Journal,* XLIII (1934), 30-37.

Hennig, Helen Kohn, ed., *Columbia, Capital City of South Carolina* (Columbia, S.C., 1936).

Higginson, Thomas W., *Army Life in a Black Regiment* (Boston, 1870).

Hollis, John P., *The Early Period of Reconstruction in South Carolina* (Baltimore, 1905).

Jarrell, Hampton M., *Wade Hampton and the Negro: The Road Not Taken* (Columbia, S.C., 1950).

Knight, Edgar W., "Reconstruction and Education in South Carolina," *South Atlantic Quarterly,* XVIII (1919), 350-364.

Mabry, William Alexander, "Ben Tillman Disfranchised the Negro," *South Atlantic Quarterly,* XXXVII (1938), 170-183.

McCabe, James D., *The Life and Public Services of Horatio Seymour, Together with a Complete and Authentic Life of Francis P. Blair, Jr.* (New York, 1868).

McClellan, H. B., *The Life, Character and Campaigns of Major-Gen. J. E. B. Stuart* (Richmond, 1880).

McClure, Alexander Kelly, *Colonel Alexander K. McClure's Recollections of Half a Century* (Salem, Mass., 1902).

Pike, James S., *The Prostrate State. South Carolina Under Negro Government* (New York, 1935).

Post, Louis F., "A 'Carpetbagger' in South Carolina," *Journal of Negro History,* X (1925), 10-79.

The Recent Election in South Carolina: The Testimony Taken by the Select Committee, House Misc. Doc., No. 41, 44th Congress, 2nd Session (Washington, 1877).

Reynolds, John S., *Reconstruction in South Carolina* (Columbia, S.C., 1905).

Rhodes, James Fort, "Who Burned Columbia?" *Historical Essays* (New York, 1910), 301-313.

Rice, John A., *I Came Out of the Eighteenth Century* (New York, 1942).

Russ, William A., Jr., "Radical Disfranchisement in South Carolina," *Susquehanna University Studies,* I (1939), 148-159.

Schaper, William, "Sectionalism and Representation in South Carolina," American Historical Association, *Annual Report, 1900,* I, 237-463.

Selby, John A., *Memorabilia and Anecdotal Reminiscences of Columbia, South Carolina, and Incidents Connected Therewith* (Columbia, S.C., 1905).

Sheppard, William Arthur, *Red Shirts Remembered: Southern Brigadiers of the Reconstruction Period* (Atlanta, 1940); ————, *Some Reasons Why Red Shirts Remembered* (Greer, S.C., 1940).

Sherman, William Tecumseh, *Memoirs of General W. T. Sherman* (New York, 1875), 2 vols.

Simkins, Francis B., "The Election of 1876 in South Carolina," *South Atlantic Quarterly*, XXI (1922), 225-240, 335-351; ————, "The Ku Klux Klan in South Carolina, 1868-1871," *Journal of Negro History*, XII (1927), 606-647; ————, *Pitchfork Ben Tillman* (Baton Rouge, 1944); ————, "Race Legislation in South Carolina Since 1865," *South Atlantic Quarterly*, XX (1921), 61-71, 165-177; ————, *The Tillman Movement in South Carolina* (Durham, 1926).

Simkins, Francis B., and Woody, Robert H., *South Carolina during Reconstruction* (Chapel Hill, 1932).

Taylor, Alrutheus Ambush, *The Negro in South Carolina During the Reconstruction* (Washington, 1924).

Thomason, John W., *Jeb Stuart* (New York, 1930).

Thompson, Henry T., *Ousting the Carpetbagger from South Carolina* (Columbia, S.C., 1927).

Tillman, B. R., *The Struggle of 1876, Being the Story of the Red Shirt Movement* (Anderson, S.C., 1909).

Vest, S. G., "A Senator of Two Republics," *Saturday Evening Post*, February 20, 1904, 8-9.

Wallace, David D., *The History of South Carolina* (New York, 1934), 3 vols.; ————, "The Question of the Withdrawal of the Democratic Presidential Electors in South Carolina in 1876," *Journal of Southern History*, VIII (1942), 374-385; ————, *South Carolina: A Short History* (Chapel Hill, 1951).

Webster, Laura J., *The Operation of the Freedmen's Bureau in South Carolina* (Northampton, Mass., 1916).

Wellman, Manly Wade, *Giant in Gray: A Biography of Wade Hampton of South Carolina* (New York, 1949).

Wells, Edward L., *Hampton and His Cavalry in '64* (Richmond, 1899); ————, *Hampton and Reconstruction* (Columbia, S.C., 1907).

Williams, Alfred B., *Hampton and His Red Shirts, South Carolina's Deliverance in 1876* (Charleston, 1935).

Woody, Robert H., "The Labor and Immigration Problem of South Carolina during Reconstruction," *Mississippi Valley Historical Re-*

view, XVIII (1931-32), 195-212; ————, "The South Carolina Election of 1870," *North Carolina Historical Review,* VIII (1931), 168-186.

JAMES LONGSTREET

Avery, I. W., *History of the State of Georgia from 1850 to 1881* (New York, 1881).

Bradford, Gamaliel, *Confederate Portraits* (Boston, 1914).

Caskey, Willie M., *Secession and Restoration of Louisiana* (Baton Rouge, 1938).

Cooper, Walter G., *The Story of Georgia* (New York, 1938), 4 vols.

Eckenrode, Hamilton J., and Conrad, Bryan, *James Longstreet: Lee's War Horse* (Chapel Hill, 1936).

Felton, Rebecca Latimer, *My Memoirs of Georgia Politics* (Atlanta, 1911).

Freeman, Douglas S., *Lee's Lieutenants: A Study in Command* (New York, 1942-44), 3 vols.

Landry, Stuart O., *The Battle of Liberty Place: The Overthrow of Carpet-Bag Rule in New Orleans, September 14, 1874* (New Orleans, 1955).

Longstreet, Helen D., *Lee and Longstreet at High Tide* (Gainesville, Ga., 1905).

Longstreet, James, *From Manassas to Appomattox* (Philadelphia, 1896).

Lonn, Ella, *Reconstruction in Louisiana After 1868* (Baltimore, 1924).

Louisiana State Museum, *Carpet-Bag Misrule in Louisiana; the Tragedy of the Reconstruction Era Following the War Between the States . . .* (New Orleans, 1938).

Mayes, Edward, *Genealogy of the Family of Longstreet* (Jackson, Miss., 1893).

Sanger, Donald B., *General James Longstreet and the Civil War* (Chicago, 1937).

Sanger, Donald B., and Hay, Thomas R., *James Longstreet* (Baton Rouge, 1952).

Sorrel, G. Moxley, *Recollections of a Confederate Staff Officer* (New York, 1905).

Swinton, William, *Campaigns of the Army of the Potomac* (New York, 1866).

Thompson, C. Mildred, *Reconstruction in Georgia* (New York, 1915).

Wade, John Donald, *Augustus Baldwin Longstreet: A Study in the Development of Culture in the South* (New York, 1924).

Warmoth, Henry C., *War, Politics and Reconstruction: Stormy Days in Louisiana* (New York, 1930).

JEFFERSON DAVIS

Alfriend, Frank H., *The Life of Jefferson Davis* (Cincinnati, 1868).

Ashe, Samuel A., "How President Davis Became Free," *Confederate Veteran,* XXXVI (1928), 411-412.

Bailey, Oscar L., "Jefferson Davis, a Citizen of Mississippi," *Southern Magazine,* II (1868), 16-17, 45.

Bell, Mrs. Bennett D., "Jefferson Davis, Secretary of War in the Cabinet of Franklin Pierce," *Confederate Veteran,* XXXII (1924), 90-91.

Blackford, Charles M., *The Trials and Trial of Jefferson Davis* (Lynchburg, Va., 1901).

Bledsoe, Albert Taylor, *Is Davis a Traitor; or, Was Secession a Constitutional Right Previous to the War of 1861?* (Baltimore, 1879).

Bradford, Gamaliel, "Lee and Davis," *Atlantic,* CVII (1911), 62-72.

Broyles, Nash R., "A Historic Bail-Bond," *Report of the 47th Annual Session of the Georgia Bar Association . . . May 29-30-31, 1930* (Macon, 1930), 257-260.

Burr, Frank A., "Jefferson Davis, the Ex-Confederate President, at Home," *Tyler's Quarterly Historical and Genealogical Magazine,* XXXII (1951), 163-180.

Cox, Virginia Lee, "In Prison, and Ye Visited Me," *Confederate Veteran,* XXXII, (1924), 212-214.

Craven, John J., *Prison Life of Jefferson Davis* (New York, 1866).

Dana, Richard Henry, "The Reasons for not Prosecuting Jefferson Davis," *Massachusetts Historical Society Proceedings,* LXIV (1932), 201-209.

Daniel, John W., ed., *Life and Reminiscences of Jefferson Davis by Distinguished Men of His Time* (Baltimore, 1890).

Davis, Anthony C., "A Jefferson Davis Document," *Journal of American History,* V (1911), 599-600.

Davis, Jefferson, *The Rise and Fall of the Confederate Government* (New York, 1881), 2 vols.

Davis, Varina H., *Jefferson Davis, Ex-President of the Confederate States of America: A Memoir by His Wife* (New York, 1890), 2 vols.

Dodd, William E., *Jefferson Davis* (Philadelphia, 1907).

Eckenrode, Hamilton J., *Jefferson Davis: President of the South* (New York, 1923).

Fleming, Walter L., "The Religious Life of Jefferson Davis," *Methodist Quarterly Review,* LIX (1910), 325-342.

Galloway, Charles B., "Jefferson Davis: His Place in History," *Methodist Quarterly Review,* LIX (1910), 744-772; ———, "Jefferson

Davis: A Judicial Estimate," *Confederate Veteran*, XXXIII (1925), 210-217.

Goins, Craddock, "The Queen of the Confederacy," *Americana*, XXXIII (1939), 141-150.

Gordon, Armistead, *Jefferson Davis* (New York, 1918).

Greene, Charles L., *The Capture of Jefferson Davis and What I Know of It; Paper Read Before the Ohio Commander of the Loyal Legion, October 4th, 1911* (n.p., 1910).

Harrison, Francis Burton, *Aris Sonis Focisque: Being a Memoir of an American Family, the Harrisons* (New York, 1910).

Hart, W. O., "When Jefferson Davis Was Freed," *Confederate Veteran*, XXXI (1913), 208-209.

Hay, Thomas Robson, "Jefferson Davis Once More," *South Atlantic Quarterly*, XXIII (1925), 362-376; ———, "Davis, Bragg, and Johnston in the Atlanta Campaign," *Georgia Historical Quarterly*, VIII (1924), 38-48; ———, "The Davis-Hood-Johnston Controversy of 1864," *Mississippi Valley Historical Review*, XI (1924-25), 54-84.

Houston, Mollie H., "The Misrepresentation of Jefferson Davis in History and Fiction," *Confederate Veteran*, XXVI (1918), 289-291; ———, "President Davis and General Johnston," *Confederate Veteran*, XXVII (1919), 216-218, 256-258, 302-304.

James, Alfred Procter, "Jefferson Davis and His Generals: A Study in the Breakdown of Unity of Command in the Confederacy," *University of Chicago Abstracts of Theses*, Humanistic Series, III (1927), 191-198.

Jennings, Arthur H., "Jefferson Davis's Pre-War Statemanship," *Current History*, XXV (1939), 210-213.

Jones, J. William, *The Davis Memorial Volume* (Richmond, 1890).

Jordan, Donaldson, and Pratt, Edwin J., *Europe and the American Civil War* (Boston, 1931).

McElroy, Robert, *Jefferson Davis: The Unreal and the Real* (New York, 1937), 2 vols.

McNeilly, James H., "Jefferson Davis," *Confederate Veteran*, XXX (1922), 58-59.

Miller, J. J., "Jefferson Davis," *Southern Magazine*, III (1869), 24-26, 48.

Nichols, Roy F., "The United States *vs.* Jefferson Davis, 1865-1869," *American Historical Review*, XXXI (1926), 266-284.

O'Connor, Mary D., *Life and Letters of M. P. O'Connor* (New York, 1893).

Patrick, Rembert W., *Jefferson Davis and His Cabinet* (Baton Rouge, 1944).

Pollard, Edward A., *Life of Jefferson Davis, with a Secret History of the Southern Confederacy* (Philadelphia, 1869).

Richards, Olive, "A Mississippi Heroine, Varina Howell Davis," *Southern Magazine*, II (1868), 11-12.

Richardson, Ralph E., "The Speaking and Speeches of Jefferson Davis," *Northwestern University, Summaries of Doctoral Dissertations*, XVIII (1951), 157-161.

Ross, Ishbel, *First Lady of the South: The Life of Mrs. Jefferson Davis* (New York, 1958).

Rowland, Dunbar, ed., *Jefferson Davis Constitutionalist: His Letters, Papers and Speeches* (Jackson, Miss., 1923), 10 vols.

Rowland, Eron, *Varina Howell, Wife of Jefferson Davis* (New York, 1931), 2 vols.

Schaff, Morris, *Jefferson Davis, His Life and Personality* (Boston, 1922).

Schmitt, William A., *The Last Days of the Lost Cause: The Capture, Imprisonment, and Trial of President Jefferson Davis* (Clarksdale, Miss., 1949).

Shaw, Arthur M., ed., "Mrs. Jefferson Davis at Fortress Monroe, Virginia," *Journal of Southern History*, XVI (1951), 73-76.

Strode, Hudson, *Jefferson Davis, American Patriot* (New York, 1955).

Tate, Allen, *Jefferson Davis, His Rise and Fall* (New York, 1929).

Trent, William P., *Southern Statesmen of the Old Regime* (New York, 1897), 257-293.

Van Deusen, Glyndon G., *Horace Greeley, Nineteenth-Century Crusader* (Philadelphia, 1953).

Watterson, Henry, *Marse Henry: An Autobiography* (New York, 1919), 2 vols.

West, Decca Lamar, "Jefferson Davis, Officer in United States Army, 1828-1835; and in War with Mexico, 1846," *Confederate Veteran*, XXXII (1924), 211-212.

Wheeler, Joseph, "Effort to Rescue Jefferson Davis," *Century Magazine*, LVI (1898), 85-91.

Wilson, J. H., and Steadman, W. P., "Pursuit and Capture of Jefferson Davis," *Century Magazine*, XXXIX (1890), 586-594.

Winston, Robert W., *High Stakes and Hair Trigger: The Life of Jefferson Davis* (New York, 1930).

Young, L., "Historical Petition on Imprisonment of Davis," *Magazine of American History*, XXVII (1892), 61.

Index